# John Stuart Mill's Platonic Heritage

# John Stuart Mill's Platonic Heritage

## *Happiness through Character*

### Antis Loizides

LEXINGTON BOOKS
*Lanham • Boulder • New York • Toronto • Plymouth, UK*

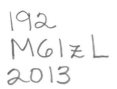
Published by Lexington Books
A wholly owned subsidiary of The Rowman & Littlefield Publishing Group, Inc.
4501 Forbes Boulevard, Suite 200, Lanham, Maryland 20706
www.rowman.com

10 Thornbury Road, Plymouth PL6 7PP, United Kingdom

British Library Cataloguing in Publication Information Available

**Library of Congress Cataloging-in-Publication Data**
Library of Congress Cataloging-in-Publication Data Available

ISBN 978-0-7391-7393-0 (cloth : alk. paper) -- ISBN 978-0-7391-7394-7 (electronic)

♾™ The paper used in this publication meets the minimum requirements of American
National Standard for Information Sciences—Permanence of Paper for Printed Library
Materials, ANSI/NISO Z39.48-1992.

Printed in the United States of America

*To Georgios Varouxakis,*
*philos kai daskalos*

# CONTENTS

Abbreviations    ix
Preface    xvii
Acknowledgments    xxi
Introduction    xxiii

*Part I: Classical Reception in Nineteenth-Century Britain*

**Chapter One: Reform Through Classics**    3
Contesting the Place of Classics    3
Athenian Institutions and Reform    5
Concluding Remarks    13
Notes    15

**Chapter Two: Plato in Pre-Victorian Britain**    21
Rediscovering Plato    21
A Neoplatonist Born Out of Due Season    24
Socrates in Early-Nineteenth Century    27
Socrates, Plato and the Utilitarians    30
Concluding Remarks    33
Notes    37

**Chapter Three: James Mill on Plato**    43
Radicalizing Plato    44
James Mill's 'Platonism'    50
Concluding Remarks    55
Notes    56

*Part II: John Stuart Mill's Appropriation of Plato*

**Chapter Four: Educative Past**    65
Reforming Educational Practice    66
Reforming Social Institutions    69
Reforming Political Practice    71
Concluding Remarks    76
Notes    78

**Chapter Five: Reading Plato**    85
Mill's First Reading: Defining Plato's Creed    85
Mill's Second Reading: Grote's *Plato*    91
Concluding Remarks    98
Notes    99

**Chapter Six: On Plato's Method**                                    105
   Mill's Intellectual Development and Plato                      105
   Mill's Dialectical Method                                     110
   Concluding Remarks                                            117
   Notes                                                         118

## *Part III: John Stuart Mill's Platonic Heritage*

**Chapter Seven: The Art of Life**                                    125
   Reason and Action                                             125
   Mill and the Art of Life                                      130
   An Education for the Art of Life                              140
   Concluding Remarks                                            144
   Notes                                                         146

**Chapter Eight: Character, Ethology and Virtue**                     153
   Defining Character                                            153
   Means and Ends of Character Formation                         161
   Concluding Remarks                                            170
   Notes                                                         171

**Chapter Nine: Eudaimonia and Utility**                              177
   Utility or Eudaimonia?                                        178
   Direction, Pleasures and Lives                               183
   Concluding Remarks                                            197
   Notes                                                         201

Conclusion                                                            207
Bibliography                                                          213
Index                                                                 243

# ABBREVIATIONS

The following abbreviations of John Stuart Mill's writings are arranged by volume from:

Robson, J.M. et al., eds. (1963-91) *The Collected Works of John Stuart Mill*, 33 vols. (Toronto; London: University of Toronto Press; Routledge and Kegan Paul).

**Volume I** (1981): *Autobiography and Literary Essays*

| | |
|---|---|
| A | (1873) *Autobiography*, I.4-290 (also I.608-624). |
| PL | (1824) 'Periodical Literature: *Edinburgh Review*', I.293-325. |
| OG | (1832) 'On Genius', I.329-39. |
| TPV | (1833) 'Thoughts on Poetry and its Varieties', I.343-65. |
| WJR [1] | (1833) 'Writings of Junius Redivivus, I', I.369-77. |
| WJR [2] | (1833) 'Writings of Junius Redivivus, II' , I.381-90. |
| TP | (1835) 'Tennyson's Poems', I.397-418. |
| ATCC | (1837) 'Aphorisms: Thoughts in the Cloister and the Crowd', I.421-9. |
| WLP | (1838) 'Ware's Letters from Palmyra', I.433-61. |
| WAV | (1838) 'Writings of Alfred de Vigny', I.467-501. |
| MLAR | (1843) 'Macaulay's Lays of Ancient Rome', I.525-32. |
| LEED | (1844) 'Letter to the Editor of the *Edinburgh Review*, on James Mill', I.535-8. |
| FOM | (1833) 'A Few Observations on Mr. Mill', I.589-95. |

**Volumes II & III** (1965)

| | |
|---|---|
| *PPE* | (1848) *Principles of Political Economy with Some Applications to Social Philosophy* |

**Volume IV** (1967): *Essays on Economics and Society I*

| | |
|---|---|
| PCCD | (1826) 'Paper Currency and Commercial Distress', IV.73-123. |
| CCP | (1833) 'Corporation and Church Property', IV.195-222. |
| MPE | (1834) 'Miss Martineau's Summary of Political Economy', IV.225-8. |
| DPE | (1836) 'Definition of Political Economy', IV.309-39. |
| CL | (1845) 'The Claims of Labour', IV.365-89. |

**Volume V** (1967): *Essays on Economics and Society II*

| | |
|---|---|
| SMWC | (1850) 'The Savings of the Middle and Working Classes', V.407-29. |
| NPE | (1851) 'Newman's Political Economy', V.441-57. |
| TLC | (1869) 'Thornton on Labour and its Claims', V.633-68. |
| COS | (1879) 'Chapters on Socialism', V.705-53. |

**Volume VI** (1982): *Essays on England, Ireland and the Empire*

| | |
|---|---|
| BHBE | (1824) 'Brodie's History of the British Empire', VI.3-58. |
| WI | (1828) 'Intercourse between the United States and the British Colonies in the West Indies', VI.123-147. |
| NN | (1834) 'Notes on the Newspapers', VI.151-280. |
| FE | (1837) 'Fonblanque's England', VI.351-80. |
| PM | (1837) 'Parties and the Ministry', VI.383-404. |

**Volume VII & VIII** (1974)

| | |
|---|---|
| *SOL* | (1843) *A System of Logic Ratiocinative and Inductive; Being a Connected View of the Principles of Evidence and the Methods of Scientific Investigation* |

**Volume IX** (1982)

| | |
|---|---|
| *EHP* | (1869) *An Examination of Sir William Hamilton's Philosophy and of the Principal Philosophical Questions Discussed in his Writings* |

**Volume X** (1969): *Essays on Ethics, Religion and Society*

| | |
|---|---|
| RBP | (1833) 'Remarks on Bentham's Philosophy', X.5-18. |
| BHMS | (1833) 'Blakely's History of Moral Science', X.21-9. |
| SD | (1835) 'Sedgwick's Discourse', X.33-74. |
| B | (1838) 'Bentham', X.77-115. |
| C | (1840) 'Coleridge', X.119-63. |
| WMP | (1852) 'Whewell on Moral Philosophy', X.167-201. |
| *U* | (1861) *Utilitarianism*, X.205-259. |
| *ACP* | (1865) *Auguste Comte and Positivism*, X.263-368. |
| N | (1874) 'Nature', X.373-402. |
| UR | (1874) 'Utility of Religion', X.403-28. |
| T | (1874) 'Theism', X.429-89. |

DD          (1859) Preface to *Dissertations and Discussions*, X.493-4.
OB          (1832) 'Obituary of Bentham', X.497-8.


**Volume XI** (1978): *Essays on Philosophy and the Classics*

Pr          (1834) 'The Protagoras', XI.39-61.
Ph          (1834) 'The Phaedrus', XI.62-96.
Go          (1834) 'The Gorgias', XI.97-150.
AS          (1835) 'The Apology of Socrates', XI.151-74.
Ch          (c1828) 'The Charmides', XI.175-86.
Eu          (c1828) 'The Euthyphron', XI.187-96.
La          (c1828) 'The Laches', XI.197-209.
Ly          (c1828) 'The Lysis', XI.210-21.
Pa          (c1828) 'The Parmenides', XI.222-38.
TPP         (1840) 'Two Publications on Plato', XI.241-3.
BBTV        (1842, 1843) 'Bailey on Berkeley's Theory of Vision', XI.247-69.
GH [I]      (1846) 'Grote's History of Greece, I', XI.273-305.
GH [II]     (1853) 'Grote's History of Greece, II', XI.309-37.
BP          (1859) 'Bain's Psychology', XI.341-73.
GP          (1866) 'Grote's Plato', XI.377-440.
GA          (1873) 'Grote's Aristotle', XI.475-510.


**Volume XVIII** (1977): *Essays on Politics and Society I*

UAPT        (1832) 'Use and Abuse of Political Terms', XVIII.3-13.
RR          (1835) 'Rationale of Representation', XVIII.17-46.
TDA [I]     (1835) 'De Tocqueville on Democracy in America, I', XVIII.49-90.
SSA         (1836) 'State of Society in America', XVIII.93-115.
Civ         (1836) 'Civilization', XVIII.119-47.
TDA [II]    (1840) 'De Tocqueville on Democracy in America, II', XVIII.155-204.
*OL*        (1859) *On Liberty*, XVIII.215-310.


**Volume XIX** (1977): *Essays on Politics and Society II*

TPR         (1861) 'Thoughts on Parliamentary Reform', XIX.313-39.
RWR         (1859) 'Recent Writers on Reform', XIX.343-70.
*CPG*       (1861) *Considerations on Representative Government*, XIX.373-577.
Cen         (1862) 'Centralisation', XIX.581-613.
TS          (1837) 'Taylor's Statesman', XIX.617-47 (with G. Grote).

**Volume XX** (1985): *Essays on French History and Historians*

| | |
|---|---|
| SLN | (1828) 'Scott's Life of Napoleon', XX.55-110. |
| AFR | (1833) 'Alison's History of the French Revolution', XX.113-22. |
| CFR | (1837) 'Carlyle's French Revolution', XX.133-66. |
| AC | (1837) 'Armand Carrel', XX.169-215. |
| MHF | (1844) 'Michelet's History of France', XX.219-55. |
| GE | (1845) 'Guizot's Essays and Lectures on History', XX.259-94. |
| GL | (1836) 'Guizot's Lectures on European Civilization', XX.367-93. |

**Volume XXI** (1984): *Essays on Equality, Law, and Education*

| | |
|---|---|
| FB | (1853) 'Remarks on Fitzroy's Bill', XXI.103-8. |
| FWNI | (1859) 'A Few Words on Non-Intervention', XXI.111-24. |
| AJ | (1863) 'Austin on Jurisprudence', XXI.167-205. |
| IA | (1867) 'Inaugural Address Delivered to the University of St. Andrews', XXI.217-57. |
| *SOW* | (1869) *The Subjection of Women*, XXI.261-340. |

**Volume XXII** (1986): *Newspaper Writings I*

| | |
|---|---|
| TWN | (03/01/1823) 'The Word "Nature"', XXII.8-9. |
| ONI | (17/10/1823) 'Old and New Institutions', XXII.72-4. |
| EG | (09/11/1823) 'Effects of Gambling', XXII.77-9. |
| SA [1] | (09/01/1831) 'Spirit of the Age, I', XXII.227-35. |
| SA [2] | (23/01/1831) 'Spirit of the Age, II', XXII.238-45. |
| SA [3] | (06/02/1831) 'Spirit of the Age, III, part 1', XXII.252-7. |
| | (13/03/1831) 'Spirit of the Age, III, part 2', XXII.278-82. |
| HPD | (20/03/1831) 'Herschel's Preliminary Discourse', 284-7. |
| SA [4] | (03/04/1831) 'Spirit of the Age, IV', XXII.289-95. |
| SA [5] | (15/05/1831) 'Spirit of the Age, V, part 1', XXII.304-7; |
| | (29/05/1831) 'Spirit of the Age, V, part 2', XXII.312-6. |

**Volume XXIII** (1986): *Newspaper Writings II*

| | |
|---|---|
| PQF | (04/09/1831) 'The Peerage Question in France', XXIII.341-5. |
| IC | (22/01/1832) 'The Irish Character', XXIII.397-8. |
| TBA | (19/02/1832) 'Todd's Book of Analysis', XXIII.411-6. |
| SOS [I] | (25/03/1832) 'Smart's Outline of Sematology, I', XXIII.425-7. |
| SOS [II] | (01/04/1832) 'Smart's Outline of Sematology, II', XXIII.429-35. |
| DJB | (10/06/1832) 'Death of Jeremy Bentham', XXIII.467-73. |

## Volume XXIV (1986): *Newspaper Writings III*

| | |
|---|---|
| WD | (06/01/1835) 'The Word "Destructive"', XXIV.760-3. |
| GAEI | (23/10/1835) 'Grant's Arithmetic For Young Children', XXIV.785-7. |
| ACJ | (10/02/1846) 'The Acquittal of Captain Johnstone', XXIV, 865-6. |
| GG [1] | (04/04/1846) 'Grote's History of Greece [1]', XXIV.867-75. |
| CoI [2] | (07/10/1846) 'The Condition of Ireland [2]', XXIV.885-8. |
| CoI [11] | (26/10/1846) 'The Condition of Ireland [11]', XXIV.913-6. |
| CoI [20] | (19/11/1846) 'The Condition of Ireland [20]', XXIV.955-8. |
| CoI [25] | (02/12/1846) 'The Condition of Ireland [25]', XXIV.972-5. |
| GG [2] | (05/06/1847) 'Grote's History of Greece [2]', XXIV.1084-8. |

## Volume XXV (1986): *Newspaper Writings IV*

| | |
|---|---|
| BHS | (02/09/1848) 'Bain on Science and Health', XXV.1118-20. |
| GG [3] | (03/03/1849) 'Grote's History of Greece [3]', XXV.1121-8. |
| GG [4] | (10/03/1849) 'Grote's History of Greece [4]', XXV.1128-34. |
| GG [5] | (16/03/1850) 'Grote's History of Greece [5]', XXV.1157-64. |
| RPRB | (29/04/1865) 'Romilly's Public Responsibility and the Ballot', XXV.1212-7. |

## Volume XXVI (1988): *Journals and Debating Speeches I*

| | |
|---|---|
| TL | (1820-21) 'Traite de Logique', XXVI.145-190. |
| LNL | (1820-21) 'Lecture Notes on Logic', XXVI.191-253. |
| sUK | (1823) 'The Utility of Knowledge', XXVI.257-61. |
| sPR [1] | (1824) 'Parliamentary Reform [1]', XXVI.261-71. |
| sPR [2] | (1824) 'Parliamentary Reform [2]', XXVI.271-85. |
| sPp | (1825) 'Population' (Proaemium and Speech), XXVI.286-96. |
| sPRT | (1825) 'Population: Reply to Thirlwall', XXVI.296-307. |
| sCo | (1825) 'Cooperation' (Speeches and Notes), XXVI.308-26. |
| sIA | (1825) 'Influence of the Aristocracy', XXVI.326-35. |
| sU [1] | (1826) 'The Universities [1]', XXVI.348-54. |
| sU [2] | (1826) 'The Universities [2]', XXVI.354-8. |
| sBC [1] | (1826) 'The British Constitution [1]', XXVI.358-71. |
| sBC [2] | (1826) 'The British Constitution [2]', XXVI.371-85. |
| sUH | (1827) 'The Use of History', XXVI.392-7. |
| sCM | (1827) 'The Coalition Ministry', XXVI.397-408. |
| sPSL | (1827) 'The Present State of Literature', XXVI.409-17. |
| sPrf | (1828) 'Perfectibility', XXVI.428-33. |
| sWB | (1829) 'Wordsworth and Byron', XXVI.434-42. |
| sMo | (1829) 'Montesquieu', XXVI.443-53. |

**Volume XXVII** (1988): *Journals and Debating Speeches II*

DE            (08 January 1854—15 April 1854) Diary, XXVII.641-68.


**Volume XXVIII** (1988): *Public and Parliamentary Speeches I*

sWE [4]       (08/07/1865) 'The Westminster Election of 1865 [4]', XXVIII.31-
              40.
sAWF          (20/05/1867) 'Admission of Women to Franchise', XXVIII.151-
              62.


**Volume XXXI** (1989): *Miscellaneous Writings*

APHM          (1869) Editorial notes on James Mill's *Analysis of the Phenomena
              of the Human Mind*, XXXI.95-253.

James Mill's manuscripts:

CPB           *Commonplace Books*, 5 vols.

              Volumes 1-4 are located at the London Library. They are also
              available at www.intellectualhistory.net/mill/. Volume 5 is
              located at the British Library of Political and Economic Science
              (London School of Economics and Political Science).

              Passages from James Mill's *Commonplace Books* are cited in the
              following form: volume, folio number and folio side (e.g.,
              CPB:I.1v).


The following abbreviations of works from ancient Greek and Roman writers are
arranged by author's name and work (followed by the edition used for the Greek
text):

*EE*          Aristotle, *Eudemian Ethics*.
              Susemihl, F., ed. (1884) *Eudemian Ethics* (Leipzig: Teubner).

*EN*          Aristotle, *Nicomachean Ethics*.
              Bywater, J., ed. (1894) *Ethica Nicomachea* (Oxford: Clarendon
              Press).

*Pol*         Aristotle, *Politics*.
              Ross, W.D., ed. (1957) *Politica* (Oxford: Clarendon Press).

| *Rhet* | Aristotle, *Rhetoric.* |
| | Ross, W.D., ed. (1959) *Ars Rhetorica* (Oxford: Clarendon Press). |

| *Top* | Aristotle, *Topics.* |
| | Ross, W.D., ed. (1958) *Topica et Sophistici Elenchi* (Oxford: Clarendon Press). |

| *DL* | Cicero, *De Legibus.* |
| | Plinval, G., ed. (1959) *M. Tullius Cicero; De Legibus* (Paris: Belles Lettres). |

| *AT* | Demosthenes, *Against Timocrates.* |
| | Butcher, S.H.; Rennie, W., eds. (1907) *Demosthenis Orationes* (Oxonii: Typographeo Clarendoniano). |

| *LOEP* | Diogenis Laertius, *Lives of Eminent Philosophers.* |
| | Hicks, R.D., ed.; trans. (1925) *Lives of Eminent Philosophers* (Cambridge: Harvard University Press, 1972). |

| *IA* | Isocrates, *Archidamus.* |
| | Norlin, G., ed. (1928) *Isocrates,* 3 vols. (London: W. Heinemann). |

| *AN* | Isocrates, *To Nicocles* |
| | Norlin, G., ed. (1928) *Isocrates,* 3 vols. (London: W. Heinemann). |

| *HoR* | Titus Livius (Livy), *Ab Urbe Condita.* |
| | Foster, B., ed. (1919) *The History of Rome,* bks. 1-2 (London: W. Heinemann). |

| *PL* | Plutarch, *Parallel Lives.* |
| | Perrin B. (1914) *Plutarch's Lives,* 10 vols. (London: W. Heinemann). |

The following abbreviations of Plato's dialogues are arranged in alphabetical order:

| *Alc I* | *Alcibiades I* |
| *Apol* | *Apology* |
| *Char* | *Charmides* |
| *Crat* | *Cratylus* |
| *Ethm* | *Euthedemus* |

| | |
|---|---|
| *Gor* | *Gorgias* |
| *GrH* | *Greater Hippias* |
| *L* | *Laws* |
| *Mx* | *Menexenus* |
| *Mn* | *Meno* |
| *Phdr* | *Phaedrus* |
| *Phl* | *Philebus* |
| *Prot* | *Protagoras* |
| *Rep* | *Republic* |
| *Sym* | *Symposium* |
| *Tht* | *Theaetetus* |
| *Tm* | *Timaeus* |

The edition used for the Greek text of Plato's dialogues is:

Burnet, J., ed. (1903) *Platonis Opera* (Oxford: Oxford University Press).

The edition used for the English translations of Plato's dialogues, unless specified otherwise, is:

Hamilton, E.; Cairns, H., eds. (1961) *The Collected Dialogues of Plato, including the Letters* (Princeton: Princeton University Press).

# PREFACE

This book is a revised PhD thesis (defended in 2011) which was completed at Queen Mary, University of London. Though all chapters have been reworked, some quite extensively, while others less so, the argument remains the same: a better understanding of Mill's background in ancient Greek thought and his reading(s) of Plato's dialogues leads to innovative interpretations of his moral and political thought. Here, I explore various connections of Mill's thought to ancient Greek philosophy primarily in relation to his conception of happiness.

In part one of the book, the first chapter explores how the classics and ancient Greek history came to command considerable time and energy in public deliberation in nineteenth-century Britain. Mill's writings on ancient Greek history and philosophy were directly associated with public debates on educational, social and political reform. Rarely do students of Mill take a hard look at how ancient Greece was involved in public debates in nineteenth-century Britain, which often leads them to ignore important aspects of his arguments and his rhetoric. Though historians of classical studies may not find much that is new in this chapter, discussing the major themes that appeared in the nineteenth-century interest in ancient Greece provides the necessary background for an appraisal of Mill's own involvement with the past. In similar spirit, chapter two sets out to examine the reception of Plato's dialogues in Britain between the time of James Mill's reviews of Thomas Taylor's English edition of Plato's works (1804) and the time of the publication of John Stuart Mill's translations of four Platonic dialogues (1834-5). Historians of classical studies have discussed the rediscovery of Plato in Victorian Britain, as a result of George Grote's and Benjamin Jowett's works. However, early-nineteenth-century Platonic scholarship, the period during which the younger Mill first studied Plato, has remained largely in the dark. A survey of the different readings of Plato, including that of Samuel Taylor Coleridge, facilitates the discussion on the originality of the two Mills. Chapter three pays close attention to James Mill's intellectual engagement with Plato. First, the chapter investigates the elder Mill's direct commentary on Plato to find out what might have been taught to John Stuart Mill: the focus on Plato's dialectical method rather than his transcendentalism was no ordinary choice in early-nineteenth-century Britain. Next, this chapter examines how the elder Mill's view of Plato as a radical reformer seeking to define a model of social happiness made its way into James Mill's own arguments on social and political reform. Third, this chapter investigates James Mill's indirect engagement with Plato's dialogues in order to sketch how he appropriated Platonic ideas in his arguments on education, utility and pleasure. I argue that the elder Mill was not a blind adherent to Jeremy Bentham's doctrines; he was the first to infuse 'Platonic' ideas (e.g., the importance of rational agency; qualities of pleasure; higher and lower grades of existence) into the Benthamite conception of happiness. Though many have called into question the widely diffused caricature of him as Bentham's mouthpiece, a closer study of James Mill's engagement with Plato's works, shows that he was as much concerned with 'broadening' certain aspects of Bentham's theory as his son.

In part two, chapter four examines three key areas of John Stuart Mill's works in which his 'intoxication' with Greece manifested itself: educational, social and political reform. First, this chapter studies Mill's response to the question of the usefulness of classics in education. A preliminary result of this examination consists in highlighting Mill's view of the importance of classical studies in imparting critical habits to individuals—as Mill complained, up to then the classics were often used to emphasise tradition, not progress. Second, Mill's insistence on instilling critical habits to individuals led to a similar emphasis regarding the need to create those social conditions (i.e., a social setting of individual liberty) in which individuals can engage in a process of trial and error and learn discursively. Finally, the full picture of Mill's call for the formation of critical habits in individuals is completed by his argument concerning the need for citizens to be competent in identifying those specialists who will serve the interests of all. To this effect, according to Mill, Socratic citizens, inquisitive and discursive, are as much required in a representative government as Platonic rulers, social-interest-oriented specialists who—reluctantly—take up the responsibility to lead. Chapter five explores the younger Mill's overall engagement with the Platonic corpus. Mill re-read and wrote about Plato both before and after he published (or prepared first drafts of) his most important writings on ethical, social and political thought. This study fills a gap in the critical attention to Mill's preoccupation with Plato; it also assists in assessing the extent of his originality. First, this chapter follows Mill's short introductions to his translations of Plato's *Protagoras*, *Phaedrus* and *Gorgias* in 1834-5. Mill's reading of Plato differed slightly from his father's, though still situated within the Radical interpretational framework (i.e., in which the focus is on Plato's method) sketched in part one. In this way, this chapter shows that the younger Mill's Plato was not a utilitarian. However, translational novelties introduced by John Mill bring out other aspects of his early education, such as the connection of theory to practice. Second, this chapter turns to a discussion of Mill's 1866 review of George Grote's eagerly anticipated *Plato, and the Other Companions of Sokrates* (1865). Though Mill's review was quite favorable, a comparison with Grote's other reviewers shows how Mill exhibited his ability to test and accept or reject some of Grote's claims. In chapter six, I take a closer look at the connection between John Stuart Mill's reading of Plato and some important aspects of his methodology in moral and political subjects. In the first part of the chapter, I explore the ways in which Plato's dialogues directly played a part in John Mill's intellectual development. To this effect, the chapter discusses John Mill's view of the worth of Plato's dialectical method. It seems that in the younger Mill's reading—as in the elder Mill's—Plato is transformed to a radical philosopher: his main character, Socrates, is at once a model seeker of 'truth' and critic of 'popular phraseology'. Moreover, the chapter turns to John Mill's 'crisis in [his] mental history'. It is frequently argued that a 'dejected' John Mill turned to the translation of Plato to find inspiration. Thus, commentators argue, John Mill was led to a 'Coleridgean' reading of Plato, which later informed his critique of the theory of his utilitarian predecessors. In the second part, I discuss the connection between John Stuart Mill's 'Philosophy of Error', which had much to do with identifying erroneous reasoning in moral and political discussions, to Plato's dialectics, Jeremy Bentham and James Mill. I focus on two particular examples of John Mill's application of Plato's method: 'nature' and 'justice'.

Part three takes on one particular aspect of Mill's reading of Plato: its relation to his notion of happiness. Chapter seven initiates this inquiry by examining Mill's 'Art of Life'. Recent scholarship re-evaluates Mill's discussion of an 'Art of Life' and highlights its centrality to his notion of happiness. However, though its importance has been correctly insisted upon in late years, the direct connection of Mill's 'Art of Life' to the Socratic tradition of the 'Art of Living' has been entirely ignored. The discussion shows that not only did Mill's idea that life can be the subject-matter of a craft resemble ancient Greek ethical thought but also the structure and inner-workings of Mill's 'Art of Life' seem to have been directly appropriated from Plato's *Gorgias*. Making use of Plato's *Gorgias* and Mill's writings on Plato brings to the fore the exact relation of the constituent parts of Mill's 'Art of Life' (morality, expediency, aesthetics) with one another and highlights another aspect of this 'Art' which has been overlooked: a particularly 'Greek' use of the concept of '*to kalon*' (*the beautiful, fine* or *noble*) in his discussion of aesthetics. Lastly, this chapter turns to Mill's ideas on what kind of training is requisite to the successful practice of the 'Art of Life' and once again, his high estimation of the classics takes the centre stage. Chapter eight expands upon the last discussion on education and focuses on Mill's theory regarding character formation. As this chapter argues, two primary concerns guided Mill's probing into character formation: the need for self-development and the need for those social institutions which would allow it. This chapter also studies another of Mill's allusions to ancient Greek thought that have gone largely unnoticed: that his use of 'character' drew on the ancient Greek sense of *éthos*. Consequently, it seems that when Mill was writing about character, he was writing with an evaluative sense in mind: the formation of virtuous character—the 'self-fashioned' practitioner of the 'Art of Life'. Moreover, it seems that Plato's dialogues played an active part in the shaping of Mill's argument for the importance of both intellectual and emotional cultivation in self-development and self-government. Finally, chapter nine employs the findings of the previous chapters to make an important claim about Mill's utilitarianism. It is argued here that his reading of Plato led Mill to a distinctively eudaimonistic conception of happiness. To this effect, I proceed to examine how both utility and eudaimonia came to be introduced in his theory. However, many revisionist interpretations of Mill's utilitarian theory suggest that his use of eudaimonistic features put his notion of utility at odds with that of Jeremy Bentham. These interpretations sacrifice the pervasive role of pleasure in Mill's theory—which kept him within the utilitarian tradition—for the sake of consistency. Though I share the revisionists' belief that Mill had a consistent conception of happiness, I argue that pleasure retained a pervasive role in it. In order to prove this claim, I distinguish between additive and directive conceptions of happiness, of which both pleasure and reason remain essential components—what differs is how pleasure and reason are integrated in the two conceptions. Thus, taking together Mill's reading of Plato, his 'Art of Life' and his science of character formation (Ethology) leads me to argue for identifying a directive notion of happiness in his works: that the 'good life' consists in rational agency rather than 'swelling an aggregate' of particular goods and, what is more, that rational agency provides the direction which results in the usefulness of particular goods. This analysis shows that Mill transformed—rather than rejected—the 'narrow' hedonistic foundation of the utilitarian theory he inherited. In his 'broader' conception of utility, moral, prudential and aesthetic ends are harmoniously incorporated into a kind of living, in which pleasure inevitably follows.

# ACKNOWLEDGMENTS

I am grateful to the Cyprus Research Promotion Foundation and the Framework Programme for Research, Technological Development and Innovation, 'Young Researchers of Cyprus' (co-funded by the Republic of Cyprus and the European Regional Development Fund), for a research grant which allowed me to complete my PhD thesis and to work on publications afterward, including this book. I am also grateful to Palgrave Macmillan for the kind permission to reproduce parts of a work which appeared in K.N. Demetriou; A. Loizides, eds. (2013) *John Stuart Mill: A British Socrates* (Basingstoke: Palgrave Macmillan).

As all students of John Stuart Mill's works, I am especially indebted to the late John M. Robson and his collaborators for their game-changing edition of Mill's writings. I owe a similar debt to the late Robert A. Fenn for his laborious endeavour to transcribe James Mill's *Commonplace Books* and marginalia and to identify James Mill's numerous (anonymous) articles. I will forever be in debt to Kris Grint for kindly forwarding to me Fenn's transcriptions.

I extend my appreciation to the staff of the Somerville College Library, Oxford; the London Library, the British Library; the University College London Library; the British Library of Political and Economic Science; the Senate House Library, the Library of Queen Mary, University of London and the Library of the University of Cyprus for their willingness to facilitate my research and answer any question pertaining to their collections. I would also like to thank the staff and faculty of the School of History of Queen Mary, University of London and of the Department of Social and Political Sciences of the University of Cyprus.

Special thanks go to my family and friends—in particular Demetris Lazarou and Anastasia Yiangou—for their unwavering support. Furthermore, I would like to thank Fred Rosen, Stuart Jones, Thomas Dixon and Richard Bourke for their encouragement and advice. I am sure that without their searching questions my interpretation of Mill would have been severely lacking in many respects. I am also indebted to Gregory Molivas for helpful comments on an earlier draft of chapter seven. Similarly, I would also like to thank the anonymous reviewers who read my work and helped me clarify various aspects of my arguments.

I also take this opportunity to thank Kyriakos Demetriou. This is long overdue. His meticulous studies of Plato's 'legend' and of George Grote's reading of Plato have been shining examples of how work in classical reception should be carried out. Kyriakos Demetriou is responsible for stirring my interests in the history of political thought and political theory. What is most important, he has been selflessly offering his support and advice ever since I was a first-year undergraduate student at the University of Cyprus. I owe him much more than I can ever repay.

I would also like to express my deepest gratitude to Georgios Varouxakis, to whom this book is dedicated. He was there for me in every step and misstep along the 'long and winding road' of my doctoral dissertation, which was completed under his supervision. He has done more than he can possibly know in shaping me both as a student of Mill and as a person. His diligence, fair-mindedness and extensive knowledge of Mill's life and works as well as his generosity, affability and kindness have been a model for me to emulate. Without his optimism, enthusiasm and encouragement, what humbly began as a collection of random ideas on Mill would have never end up as a book. I can never thank him enough.

Last but foremost, I wish to thank my dear wife Marina Soteriou, who has put up with me talking about the Mills almost incessantly, at all hours of the day and, at times, night, for the past five years. Her unconditional love and support has given me the strength to carry on working on John Stuart Mill. For more than fourteen years now, Marina has been the 'wind'—and what a fine and fair wind she is—to my 'sails'. If Aristophanes was really on to something in Plato's *Symposium*, then I have indeed found my 'other half'. Hopefully, I complete her, as she completes me.

Nicosia, June 2012
A.L.

# INTRODUCTION

In his *Autobiography* (1873),[1] John Stuart Mill acknowledged his debt to Plato's dialectics and exhibited his fascination with ancient Greece. Though there have been attempts to examine Mill's thought in the light of the influence of antiquity, much more needs to be done. For example, the renewed focus on Mill's views on democracy and its relation to liberalism constitutes only part of the picture of his intellectual debts to Athens in general and to Plato in particular.[2] Thus, although it is recognized that Plato influenced Mill, questions such as how this happened, to what extent and with regard to which aspects of Mill's thought are still open. What is more, Plato's influence on Mill's conception of happiness—in his attempt to broaden the utilitarian theory of life by infusing it with eudaimonistic features—remains an understudied aspect of Mill's thought.

However, Mill's debt to Plato is obscured by many factors. First, though admittedly an eclectic,[3] Mill mentioned Plato's influence nowhere in relation to happiness. Moreover, Mill called himself a utilitarian—thus a student of Jeremy Bentham and James Mill—but still likened his notion of happiness to that of Thomas Carlyle—which was explicitly directed against what Carlyle dubbed the 'mechanical school' of Bentham. To this day, scholars have a hard time making these claims consistent, which is exactly what this book tries to do by way of Plato's dialogues. Second, Platonism today is frequently associated with Idealism. It is well known that Mill criticized those who held that some knowledge can be reached by intuition (i.e., with no recourse to sense-experience). Thus, Plato, usually thought as the 'Father of Idealism', seems an unlikely source of influence on Mill who argued that *all* knowledge derives from experience. Third, Mill's special note of his debt to Plato's dialectics has misled scholars to assume that there is no need to search for influence elsewhere (i.e., beyond the 'proper' method of pursuing 'truth'). Fourth, it is quite difficult to make a case for specific ancient Greek influences in Greece-fixated Victorian Britain. If Mill was led to Hellenic ideals because it was common practice, it could be said that this indicates indirect influence from the 'spirit of the age', rather than direct influence from Plato. What makes it more difficult to substantiate such a case is that, unlike some of his peers engrossed with Greece (e.g., Thomas de Quincey), Mill never tried 'to prove himself by displaying his qualities as a Grecian'.[4] Thus, in order to suggest influence where Mill did not admit any, one needs to discuss in detail the circumstances and his habits of, and reasons for, referring to ancient Greeks, where he did.

The book sets off by an examination of the historiography on ancient Greece and Platonic scholarship in nineteenth-century Britain—that is, a study in reception. Classical-reception studies try to outline the various appropriations of antiquity in later times, asserting that '[t]exts mean differently in different situations'.[5] But if the interpretation of a text requires agreement by a majority of competent judges,[6] then this agreement draws as much attention to the receiving society as to the text itself. When the focus is on the receiving society (i.e., Victorian Britain) rather than the ancient texts themselves, students of Mill's works can attend to some perplexing aspects of his own work on the ancients—it being very much related to contemporary debates. What is more, by establishing what was original or peculiar in Mill's reading of the ancients, one can identify areas of his works where he was not simply indirectly influenced by 'the spirit of the age'. However, it is important to keep in mind that the general preoccupation with the ancients during this time provided Mill with an environment which sanctioned rather than rejected (e.g., as irrelevant or as outdated) the expression of Greek ideas; and this environment was thus as much an integral part of their development as it was of their expression.

Moving to the second and third obscuring factors, Mill developed certain 'sympathies' during his ancient Greek studies under the supervision of his father; these, as the younger Mill claimed, were 'always on the contrary side' to the sympathies of conservative writers such as William Mitford or intuitionists such as William Whewell.[7] Thus, given the fact that John Mill was no armchair philosopher, the Athenian example became a valuable practical experiment that corroborated as well as suggested many ideas in reference to educational, social and political reform. Similarly, the focus of the two Mills on Plato's dialectics, rather than his 'poetic fancies', set their Plato apart from all the other 'Platos' in the early nineteenth century. It was also a reading of Plato's dialogues which had educational, social and political implications for their respective notions of happiness. For example, it seems that the elder Mill held a conception of utility with strong Platonic echoes, which was rather underplayed in his best known writings. But James and John Mill's Platonizing has not been subjected to much scrutiny—neither has the possibility that their reading of Plato may shed light on the extent of James Mill's influence on John's later views. For this reason, by means of their shared admiration of Plato, the intellectual connection between father and son becomes a recurrent theme of this book.

Revisiting John Mill's education shows that important aspects of his later writings which display differences from his utilitarian precursors and which are attributed to Romantic influences were closely related to his reading of ancient

Greek texts: e.g., dialectics and the aesthetic appreciation of virtue. More importantly, this book argues that unless one reads Mill through Plato, no interpretation of his complex utilitarian theory can fully accommodate—without tension—Mill's discussions of an 'Art of Life', of character formation as the cultivation of virtue, but also higher pleasures as part of noble lives. Thus, I argue a prevalent trend in Mill scholarship, which takes the influence of the 'Germano-Coleridgian school' on Mill's 'enlargement project' to be all-embracing, needs qualification. Still, unlike the factors mentioned earlier, this aspect of the neglect of other influences on Mill's intellectual development has much to do with Mill's own obsessive concern with 'half truths' and 'many-sidedness'—ideas he claimed to have found in S.T. Coleridge and J.W. Goethe.[8]

Mill himself confessed that he was 'apt to get enthusiastic about those who do great things for progress & are immensely ahead of everybody else in their age'. Often this 'enthusiasm' led him to argue strongly in favor of something, as with Athens or classical studies, when he thought 'there [was] a growing reaction to the opposite extreme, producing a danger on that side which being the side most in harmony with modern tendencies [had] the best chance of being ultimately the stronger'.[9] He also acknowledged that some of his writings give 'too strong an impression of the writer's sympathy with the reaction of the nineteenth century against the eighteenth'.[10] Though he qualified his claims regarding his Romantic influences, Mill did argue that it was imperative to be aware of the 'great danger' of

> overlooking what is; since clever & intelligent men hardly ever err from [...] [seeing what is not real], but no powers of mind are any protection against the evils arising from imperfect and partial views of what is real; since not errors but half truths are the bane of human improvement, it seems to follow that the proper mode of philosophizing & discussing for a person who pursues the good of mankind & not the gratification of his own vanity, should be the direct opposite of the *philosophie critique* of the last century.[11]

Mill thus admitted that he felt a special obligation to preach 'the meaning & necessity of a catholic spirit in philosophy'.[12] Unless Mill emphasised his connection with Romanticism, he would not have been true to his 'special obligation' in the pursuit of the 'the good of mankind & not the gratification of his own vanity'. However, Mill's emphasis diverts one's attention away from a latent function of his Romantic influences; the Romantics seem to have revitalised now forgotten and overseen aspects of James Mill's works: e.g., the role of intellectual elites in social improvement and stability via education; the importance of cultivating emotion; and, the necessity of a proper method of reaching (and preserving a vivid impression of) 'truth'.[13]

# NOTES

1. For bibliographical details for works by John Stuart Mill, see *infra*, pp. ix-xiv.

2. E.g., Urbinati, 2002; Devigne, 2006.

3. J.S. Mill to G. D'Eichthal, 07/11/1829, XII.42; *A*:I.156.

4. See further, Goldhill, 2002:178ff.

5. Martindale, 2006:4. See also, Martindale, 1993:18-23; Machor and Goldstein, 2001.

6. As Behan McCullagh notes (1991:303-4), this agreement may be reached by taking into account the text's language as well as the author's biographical, literary and historical contexts. See further, Hardwick and Stray, 2008.

7. *A*:I.15; J.S. Mill to G. Grote, 22/04/1866, XVI.1160.

8. *A*:I.171.

9. J.S. Mill to H. Taylor, 17/03/1849, XIV.17-8; J.S. Mill to H. Spencer, 09/02/1867, XVI.1237; J.S. Mill to G. D'Eichthal, 07/11/1829, XII.42.

10. DD:X.494. See also, *A*:I.227.

11. J.S Mill to G. D'Eichthal, 07/11/1829, XII.42.

12. J.S. Mill to J. Sterling, 04/10/1839, XIII.411. To this effect, writing about Coleridge rather than Bentham gave him the 'opportunity of shewing what this' spirit was. See also, *SOL*:VII.cxii.

13. See further, Loizides, 2012.

# PART ONE

## Classical Reception in
## Nineteenth-Century Britain

# CHAPTER ONE

## REFORM THROUGH CLASSICS

> The truth is that priests and people alike, while
> taking their nominal creed from the New
> Testament, take their real creed from Homer. Not
> Christ, but Achilles is their ideal.[1]

Classical studies and ancient Greece came to a prominent place in nineteenth-century British educational and constitutional debates. The debate on the place of classical studies in education held a small but significant place in an overall reconsideration of educational practice. At the same time, contemporary political rivalries on constitutional reform in Britian also animated the examination of ancient history, leading eventually to a noticeable paradigm-change in the reception of Athens between mid-eighteenth-century and mid-nineteenth-century histories of ancient Greece.

## CONTESTING THE PLACE OF CLASSICS

Nineteenth-century Britain witnessed an unparalleled growth of preoccupation with education primarily because of its connection to the concurrent social and political restlessness. As education was considered to have the ability to change drastically the social situation of the poor, it became a major part of the 'general movement towards a higher standard of life'.[2] Thus, the pressure to consider the future of the lower classes led both government officials and private individuals, from early in the century, to exhibit an interest in 'free' education.[3]

By the mid-1800s, governmental schemes addressed many practical problems of education; education itself increasingly acquired scientific status.[4] The political discussions concerning the place of classics became heated, as Elizabeth Potter has recently showed, due to the connection of Hellenic values to ideas about leadership, the role of the elite, the role of education and the franchise. Moreover, maintaining their status as the standard for suitability for administrative positions, educational qualifications offered new opportunities by facilitating the sharing of common values with members of the political elite.[5] In this way, unlike questions about state-education and its content (e.g., secular or religious), which primarily concerned the lower ranks of the society, the question regarding the place of classics in education concerned the middle and higher ranks. For this reason, one of the most important criticisms of classical education was that it 'served to enforce and maintain' class division.[6]

For the critics of classical studies not only did the teaching of 'dead languages', while ignoring pressing educational needs (e.g., science, modern literature), fail to serve the interests of students, it also failed to serve social interests.[7] Indeed, for many years classical studies were of great usefulness, they argued, leading people 'to think, to reason and to judge for themselves', by infusing doubt in scholastic logic and metaphysical theology. This was a result of the evolution of printing and the mass availability of ancient texts in the original Greek or Latin, which made the mediation of cleric-teachers (who enjoyed exclusive access to manuscripts) unnecessary.[8] But after four hundred years of a vital role in education, for many, classical studies themselves had been reduced to scholasticism. What was more important, knowledge was not to be found solely in ancient texts anymore.[9]

In the wake of the industrial revolution, Greek and Latin were thus considered to be at least outmoded, as scientific discoveries and technological advances displaced them from their position of dominance. For this reason, the time and effort being spent to the teaching of Latin and Greek was considered by many critics to be a waste, first, because the time and attention classics received did not bestow any substantial benefit; second, what students did gain from such studies was insignificant compared to the benefits a more scientifically oriented education could confer—knowing many different words about a thing, they argued, did not give knowledge of the thing itself.[10]

As a result, already by the late eighteenth century, some argued that the educational system did not suit those 'gentlemen [...] designed to fill the principal stations of *active life*', it being 'adapted to the *learned professions*'. Accordingly, classical studies were thought to lead to a passive life, in a society that rewarded energy, industry and self-made individuals. Classics, critics argued, were only useful for those professions which required the study of ancient texts.[11] At the same time, scientific and technical training was increasingly manifesting its usefulness, even though there were advances made in the improvement of classical instruction.[12] Likewise, by the end of the century, a 'new' science of politics shook the 'old' history off its classical foundation: '[t]o turn history away from the past to the present is in fact to give it the interest of an experimental study' and, as J.R. Seeley further added, 'past history is a dogmatist, furnishing for every doubt ready-made and hackneyed determinations. Present history is a Socrates, knowing nothing, but guiding others to knowledge by suggestive interrogations'.[13]

Thus, like many other issues in this period 'the onus of proof was on the status quo. Did it elevate? Did it improve?'[14] Rather predictably, proponents of classics responded that in a society fixated with commercial growth not only did classics cease to be a fitting basis of commercial education they ceased to be a fitting basis for all kinds of education. Thus, utility, they added, ceased to consist in training reason and cultivating taste, i.e., pursuing knowledge for itself; utility meant knowledge 'marketable and convertible into cash'.[15] In consequence, the 'pound, shilling, and pence utility' of the time and the requirements for administrative positions led to a very limiting idea of education as an aggregate of information rather than a 'species of mental gymnastics'.[16] Though a 'good Robinson Crusoe' was a safe education, John Grote—brother of the eminent historian of Greece—argued, 'the independent activity of thought' and the 'point of intellectual sympathy among men over a considerable surface of the world' pointed to the higher usefulness of classics.[17]

Throughout the nineteenth century, classicists affirmed the place of classical studies as a key part of humanism in education, by being a source of valuable experience and, concurrently, of cultivation of form and style.[18] But even if they did not always agree on whether Latin or Greek ought to dominate the curriculum, proponents of classics did agree that ancient texts 'involve[d] profound and extensive wisdom'.[19] Still, for some time scholars resisted the growing ascendancy of Greek studies over Latin studies—some reminisced the time when Latin and the model of Rome dominated 'the literary and intellectual culture of men's minds'. Thus, scholars such as William Whewell argued that a renewed focus on Greek studies was an act of estrangement with both the traditional and modern trends of scholarship—he did not wish to 'let the assumed progress of literary taste in the present day break off the tradition of literary sympathy with past generations'.[20] But this renewed focus was a likely development given that supporters of classical studies had for long idealized the ancient Greeks. What is more important, champions of the classics agreed that the past was the source from where 'all the intellect of civilized Europe breathes their spirit and takes their form'.[21] Thus, for them, the classics provided 'a bond of mental union' between generations and nations and formed a common ground in the development of thought and understanding throughout Europe—a bond which expanded beyond the bounds of the Athenaeum Club.[22]

## ATHENIAN INSTITUTIONS AND REFORM

Preoccupation with Greece during this period was evident in activities other than scholarship; it grew considerably toward the end of the nineteenth century.[23] From an interest in architecture, travel and topography in eighteenth-century Britain, as Richard Jenkyns has argued, the next century saw the rise of ancient

Greece as *Helen*, the idea of beauty itself, 'a shimmering fantasy on the far horizon' and 'the supreme example of a non-Christian society that had reached the highest degree of human civilization'.[24] However, the history of Greek historiography indicates that the transition to the above view was neither smooth nor sudden.[25] It was the outcome of a long and, as Timothy Webb puts it, 'complex and continuous process of redefinition'.[26] Turning to antiquity for instruction and ultimately legitimisation for instantly recognizable political positions on current affairs was perhaps most evident in late-eighteenth-century historiography, since such historical works were carried out with a particular reading of history under the 'threat' of constitutional reform that the French revolution and British radicals had created; but it was a trend that persisted well into the next century.

## Athens and the Virtues of a Balanced Constitution

By the mid-eighteenth century, conservative writers increasingly commented on the example of the rise and fall of Athens. The lesson which ought to be learned from this example was that only a mixed constitution secured both person and property.

Edward Montagu was one of the many to argue that 'the British constitution, as settled at the revolution, [was] demonstrably far preferable to, and better formed for duration, than any of the most celebrated Republicks of antiquity'. Montagu argued that the history of Athens taught that 'luxury', 'effeminacy' and 'corruption' posed a true danger to the superior British constitution. Changing it would only 'serve the ends of faction', precipitating the fall of Britain 'from her present height to the abject state of Athens', which was caused by a form of government that allowed demagogues to manipulate popular temper.[27]

Montagu's was not an isolated opinion. Temple Stanyan had already argued that the examples of Sparta and Athens formed two extremes of government, failing to balance power with liberty; these examples fell short of serving 'the ends of government' in such a secure and stable manner that a mixed constitution could; for Stanyan, the British constitution was much better adapted to those ends, nearing perfection.[28] Similarly, Oliver Goldsmith provided detailed descriptions of incidents in the life of historic figures, whose actions focused on the search for a balanced constitution, checking both sides of government—a constitution that guaranteed peace and tranquility.[29]

Thus, it was not strange that writers such as William Drummond found monuments 'of virtue and prudence [...] in the ruins of antiquity'. As William Young added, Athenian history provided many points of interest to the British reader: for example, 'their ardent love of liberty, and high pretensions to command occasionally drooping in subserviency' and 'the hasty increase of wealth and of marine power from sources of trade, and thereon trade introducing a spirit of dissipation and self-interest to dissolve the strength and prosperity it gave birth to'.[30] Though Drummond and Young did not share the same view of

Athens, they did agree on one main point: the 'mixed' British constitution singularly protected civic liberty and promoted civic prosperity.[31]

Critics of democracy argued that allowing the majority to take rule, like in Athens, would open up both internal and external policy to caprice, which would ultimately lead to the ruin of Britain. Athens had shown that institutions established by the anti-aristocratic majority threatened 'person and property' (e.g., ostracism, taxation)—though mostly the 'rich and noble' would be considered to be the oppressed in Athenian 'democratical despotism'. Likewise, the ignorant Athenian majority, critics argued, being manipulated by demagogues and corrupted by Sophists, led Athens to become a tyrannical empire in search of funds to satisfy their licentiousness. Thus, even for eighteenth-century Radicals, Athens was considered too faction-ridden to be of any use in the debate for reform.[32]

John Gillies and William Mitford reinforced the above negative picture of Athens. For example, Gillies believed that whatever balance between liberty and government which Cleisthenes' constitutional reforms had achieved, Aristides, with 'much secret reluctance' managed to destroy. Once Aristides' democratic innovations were enlarged (allowing the lower classes to 'make further invasions to the prerogatives of their superiors'), the course that 'finally terminated in the ruin of Athens and of Greece' was set.[33] By the time of Ephialtes' reforms, Gillies added, 'invidious measures' being 'most obnoxious to the rich and noble' had reduced Solon's 'wise institutions [...] to an empty form'; Athens itself was reduced to 'a wild and capricious democracy' that could be 'successfully swayed, at will', by anyone who could gain the trust of the popular assembly, by appealing to their vanity and greed, and gratifying 'their taste for pleasure without expense'.[34]

Gillies drew a grim image of Pericles' motives and the condition of the 'rich and noble' under democratic rule; in a place with such strong anti-aristocratic sentiments, there was no security for them and their property. Thus, if this had been the experience of the democratic institutions of Athens, Gillies argued indirectly, then Britain ought to know better than be swayed by home-grown demagogues in attempting a constitutional reconstruction. Whatever prosperity Athens had enjoyed, and Gillies admitted that Athens had progressed greatly because of its liberty and imperial success, was soon counteracted by licentiousness (caused by sudden wealth) and moral decadence (caused by the teaching of the Sophists, who were encouraged to travel to Athens by Pericles). Thus, the instability of democratic institutions highlighted, he maintained, the 'incurable evils inherent in every form of Republican policy'.[35]

Eventhough Gillies's history was never particularly read at home, that of Mitford spread widely a similar depiction of Athens. But, as Kyriakos Demetriou points out, Mitford was a more dangerous critic, being more willing than Gillies 'to distort facts or to give vent to conjectures simply to prove his political convictions'. But despite his anti-democratic prejudices, Mitford did not appeal to some form of authoritarian government and he defended the 'balanced' British constitution.[36] For example, at the very beginning of his treatment of Athenian

politics, Mitford noted that Athenian government had become 'A TYRANNY IN
THE HANDS OF THE PEOPLE' already from the time of Solon. Under such a
form of government, Mitford maintained, Athenians could not have enjoyed 'the
glorious security provided by English law' as 'life and property were rendered
insecure' beyond anything imaginable to be possible under any form of
government.[37] Athens, he argued, was a volcano that on 'the outside bore an
appearance so fair and flourishing', but on the inside 'tumult and destruction
were preparing'; thus, justifiably, he added, 'men of rank and property desired a
change'.[38]

## A 'Fickle People': Demagogy, Ostracism and Sophistry

Conservatives were so much convinced that the condemnation of democratic
Athens established the superiority of their political position that they forced their
opponents to refute their assertions. While at first Radicals were reluctant to
defend Athens, Mitford's provocative historical account invited discredit, since
some parts must have indeed 'astonished even conservative readers'.[39]

Still, Mitford was essentially preaching to the choir. Many shared the belief
that the 'imperfect' Athenian constitution was justly censured by advocates of
monarchy. In the mid-1820s, Thomas Babington Macaulay tried to 'reduce [this]
overpraised writer to his proper level', being a 'vehement admirer of tyranny and
oligarchy' with 'a perfect hatred' of democracy, and whose biases appeared
'thoroughly conspicuous and undisguised'.[40] However, this being as it may,
Mitford 'was the first writer of any note who found out that Grecian history was a
living thing with a practical bearing'.[41] What is more, '[s]o complete had been
[Mitford's] condemnation of the character of [Athens] and so widespread was the
acceptance of his views', Frank Turner has noted, 'that he had in effect also
established the grounds on which the reputation of Athens would have to be
restored'.[42]

Demagogy was one main ground on which the battle for the vindication of
Athens was fought, even though the word itself is rarely found in Thucydides.[43]
Critics argued that the principle of equality in Athens failed to prevent the
emergence of factions, but it also encouraged jealousies and discontents; these, in
turn, were exploited by demagogues. Thus, the 'great assembly of the Athenian
people', uneducated for the affairs of the state, Drummond argued, submitted
itself 'to the capricious government" of those envious and malicious
demagogues,[44] who watched 'every turn of temper in that variable people' and
'took care to adapt to every circumstance [...] offered to their own ambitious
views' to gain dominance in the state, preserving 'a perpetual spirit of faction'.[45]
Thus, in these histories, individuals such as Cleon and Hyperbolus were depicted
as highly intelligent and manipulative, enjoying the 'true' power in Athens: being
able to appeal to the 'whim[s] of a thoughtless multitude', which was 'frantic
with the wild joy of recovered power, and not less mad with jealousy of superior
men'.[46]

Edward Bulwer-Lytton's *Athens: Its Rise and Fall* (1837) was the first extensive history that challenged that of Mitford.[47] Since it appeared soon after the 1832 Reform Bill, its importance was evident: the appropriation of Athens as a model for radical democracy had made its way through to historical discourse. Even if Bulwer did not try to defend the demagogues, the recently published manuscripts of his history show that he was one of the first to put into question Thucydides' impartiality regarding the depiction of Cleon, 'the able demagogue', who belonged to the party which Thucydides opposed.[48] George Grote afforded sufficient evidence to confirm Bulwer's suspicion: 'Thucydides is reserved and even indulgent towards the errors and vices of other statesmen, harsh only towards those of his accuser'.[49] But Grote's novelty consisted in arguing that demagogues, Cleon in particular, were essentially 'opposition speakers', serving, not undermining, the interests of democracy by protecting the people against the oligarchic aspirations of the nobles.[50] On the other hand, Connop Thirlwall pointed out that the manipulations of demagogues were not an invariable trait of democracy. To this effect, Thirlwall argued that Mitford had failed to acknowledge that other forms of government shared the same flaws which traditionally were attributed to Athenian democracy. Thirlwall believed that the usual view of demagogues was exaggerated in respect to their character, the power they had exerted and their popularity.[51]

Another 'battlefield' for the vindication of Athens was the institution of ostracism. The fear of a single individual acquiring illegitimate authority, Montagu had argued, led the 'unsteady' Athenians to extreme suspicion; they imprisoned and banished the 'best and ablest citizens', while the demagogues prospered.[52] Those who did not have 'the ear of the people', as Young put it,[53] had to be particularly careful. But also anyone, Gillies had claimed, who 'seemed capable of disturbing the equality of republican government'—even 'without the proof or allegation of any positive crime'.[54] Unlike monarchical forms of government which secured submission 'from the lower orders of mankind', Drummond noted, Athens did not protect the 'just gradation [...] of hereditary rank'.[55] The institution of ostracism was thus abused in order to prevent people of 'great abilities and superior character' from gaining any kind of power; by this 'peculiar' way the assembly chose to guard 'against the overbearing influence of individuals'—a necessary way to 'bring men to a just level'.[56] Ostracism, Mitford concluded, though 'less invidious', was still an effective way to eliminate political adversaries; neither integrity nor modesty warranted sufficient protection against such an attack.[57]

However, as Drummond noted, advocates of democracy retorted that 'according to its original intention', ostracism was 'one of the wisest institutions ever adopted by ancient nations'.[58] Indeed, almost half a century later, Bulwer would still argue that the circumstances of ancient commonwealths had made clear 'the (almost) necessity' of ostracism for the protection of the constitution; since this was a time when liberty was 'tender and insecure'. But if ostracism was proof of excessive power for the people of Athens, Bulwer added, then 'the popular party in Athens seems to have been much more moderate and less unprincipled even in its excesses than its antagonists'.[59]

Likewise, Grote argued that ostracism was 'a salutary and protective institution'. Its purpose was to 'uphold democracy [...] against all attempts to subvert it'.[60] Moreover, ostracism allowed, Grote maintained, other democratic institutions to mature, without itself being as harmful (i.e., without harming either the property or the name of those who were banished) or as arbitrary as similar 'preventive measures' of oligarchs or dictators.[61] Ostracism was necessary because when the power of Athenian nobles was substantially limited by the people, the nobles 'had yet to learn the lesson of respect for any constitution'. Ostracism, Grote added, allowed the co-existence 'of freedom and self-imposed restraint' and combined respect of, and obedience to, the constitution with 'the habit of open speech, of action subject only to definite legal control'.[62] Thus, from being represented as a dangerous weapon in the hands of the 'democratical despotism', in Mitford's work, ostracism, in Grote's history, was seen as fostering a sense of 'constitutional morality', similarly found in the 'aristocracy' of England as well as the 'democracy' of the United States.[63]

Concurrently, Grote's history was the first systematic work to challenge also the traditional portrayal of the Sophists,[64] who, by teaching 'immoral' and 'sceptical' doctrines in frequent visits to Athens, were singled out as a main cause of the 'moral decay' of the Athenian populace. As Gillies wrote in the late eighteenth century, the Sophists 'supplied the springs with which Epicurus watered his gardens; and their captious logic furnished the arguments by which Pyrrho attempted to justify his scepticism'. The implications of this statement were obvious to Gillies's contemporaries; not only did the tenets of the Sophists undermine 'ancient and popular superstitions' but also they 'boldly' defied the rich tradition of 'useful maxims of conduct' and 'salutary discoveries of reason' which restrained 'the intemperance, injustice, and violence, of individuals and communities'.[65] The way the Sophists caused this degradation was by taking 'either side of any question; political or moral', since their 'glory' was 'to make the worse appear the better cause'.[66]

Samuel Taylor Coleridge's *The Friend* (1818) similarly criticized the 'immorality' of these 'wisdom-mongers'. However, Coleridge was one of the first in Britian that pointed out the lack of a 'common character', the possession of many talents and extensive knowledge by the Sophists—all evident in Plato's and Aristotle's works. Still, Coleridge's verdict was a harsh one: 'from the immoral nature of [their] objects and the baseness of [their] motives', Gorgias and sophists alike, 'will ever be cited as [...] instance[s] of prostituted genius'— these, Coleridge noted, not their sophisms, made them sophists.[67] Moreover, Coleridge argued that the sophists separated ethics from religion, and thus the principle of expediency, 'which properly belonged to one and the lower part of morality, was made to be the whole'—he extended these remarks to apply to the school of Bentham.[68]

It took many years to combat this view of the Sophists. Thus, even if Bulwer did suggest that the doctrines of the Sophists were not 'wholly pernicious', he still noted that the 'sect of the Sophists' was the 'most dangerous of all ancient sects': for the sake of the 'babble of gaudy sophists', 'the young generation of the wellborn' deserted the 'ancient and manly forms of education' and abandoned 'the moral discipline and hardy habits of the gymnasia'.[69] Though less suspicious than Bulwer, Thirlwall argued that these 'pretenders to wisdom' agreed to provide all those who 'regarded the pursuit of fame, wealth, and power as the great business of life [...] with the means of acquiring that ascendancy over the minds of men, which is readily yielded to superior wisdom and virtue, by the simple force of words'. Neither 'truth' nor 'right', he added, was a suitable subject for the education of statesmen; the art of persuasion led to the highest rewards—Athens afforded many prospects for the Athenian youth to test their skill in Sophistic techniques.[70]

On the other hand, Grote's history presented a meticulous argument against the 'usual representation' of the Sophists. Like John Stuart Mill and George Henry Lewes before him, Grote attempted to set the record straight: they 'were men of similar calling and pursuits, partly speculative, partly professional; but they differed widely from each other, both in method and doctrine'; they were neither a sect nor a school of men.[71] Thus, Grote argued that not only was the hostile view of the Sophists found in Plato's dialogues unfairly accentuated; but also that Plato was ill-disposed against the Sophists because they were paid to teach. More importantly, Plato criticized them because they taught in accordance with tradition and common morality, not against it. Scholars prior to Grote were inclined to highlight the Sophists' break with tradition, not Plato's.[72]

## Through the Looking-Glass: Bulwer, Thirlwall, Grote

Mitford's reading of Athenian history had long called for a sustained refutation. For example, James Mill had put young John on his 'guard against [...] [Mitford's] Tory prejudices [...], his perversions of facts for the whitewashing of despots, and blackening of popular institutions'.[73] But not only was ancient Greece relevant to British politics, modern Greece had also recently received a lot of attention, and aid, in their war for independence from Ottoman rule.[74] Thus, it is no coincidence that at the time when Bulwer published his history, Thirlwall and Grote were in the process of writing their own histories of Greece; still, the polemical nature of these histories revealed the underlying biases on either side.

Bulwer, a frequenter of Bentham's circle,[75] consciously attempted to abstain from pressing ancient history 'into the service of heated political partisan[ism]', being aware of the political uses of history. But frequently alluding to and commenting on British history and contemporary affairs, he failed to refrain from such practice. Thus, his reviewers, in some cases defending Mitford, showed how Bulwer remained within the tradition of that kind of historiography he censured, i.e., employing the past for 'fugitive interests and party politics'.[76]

Like Macaulay before him, Bulwer severely criticized Mitford's lack of familiarity with social aspects of Athenian history and insufficient 'acquaintance with human nature generally'.[77] Also, Bulwer often alluded to Mitford's repeated distortion of facts about Athenian history, where tyrants were cast under a positive light.[78] As Bulwer inimitably noted, there were moments when he thought difficult to choose between Mitford's stupidity and his dishonesty.[79]

For Bulwer, the history of Athens included 'in itself the history of the human mind'; whereas that of Sparta contributed 'no single addition' to the world's 'intellectual stores'.[80] But Bulwer revealed his 'philosophic discrimination', a reviewer argued, by describing Spartans more or less as 'courageous brute[s]'.[81] Moreover, for his critics, Bulwer's wording in such passages 'was pregnant with meaning at the present crisis', since he would not hesitate to write that the constitutional reforms which Athens experienced showed that while 'popular change [...] irritates the party that loses power, it cannot content the party that gains', the latter being enabled to demand further concessions.[82] Since Bulwer believed that '[a]ncient times are not then so opposite to the present',[83] his critics criticized his pretentions of impartiality. By being as suspicious as the Athenians of the conduct of 'superior' men, either in virtue or in genius, and by rejecting the 'best sources of strength', some argued that Bulwer wasted his literary talents writing a history which was as much partisan as Mitford's.[84]

Thirlwall's and Grote's accounts differed in many ways from earlier histories. First, both showed that paying no attention to European (German) scholarship constituted a serious limitation, if not defect, of earlier histories and, thus, marked a significant departure from the existent modes of historiography. Second, theirs were histories of considerable scholarly merit (both because of their method and their scope), in which the 'facts' mentioned in ancient sources were often used to criticize the inferences of the ancient writers themselves, rather than reiterate the original findings and biases.[85]

When the first volumes of his history appeared, Thirlwall noted that he wished to avoid treating Greek history as a 'vehicle' for expressing his own opinions on modern political questions. He insisted that Athenian politics were very different from modern politics. Though his predecessors did recognize this difference, Thirlwall was the first to maintain a sense of impartiality, viewing historical events from varying perspectives. In an attempt at a sober analysis of the history of Athens, Thirlwall argued that criticizing Athenian democracy bore no effect on modern political arguments.[86] In 'two-faceted propositions', Demetriou observes, Thirlwall drew a conclusion (critical or justificatory) and then qualified it. For example, Socrates' trial was argued to be an instance of the spirit of intolerance that prevailed in Athens, but Thirlwall then also argued that, given Socrates' peculiar ideas, it was surprising that Socrates was not prosecuted earlier.[87] Similarly, Thirlwall argued that poor Athenians were much more cultivated and informed about state affairs than the majority of the middle classes of his day; but he added that they had managed to alienate, consciously and short-sightedly, the nobles, by making them feel they shared no interests with the rest of the society.[88]

It was George Grote's path-breaking work which opened the way to viewing the Athenian democratic attempts in the historical perspective of their time.[89] As George Gooch noted, it was rather with ease that Grote managed to 'make his readers feel the reality of the problems which the statesmen and thinkers of

Greece attempted to solve'.[90] Still, commenced 'in part with a polemical intention, to destroy Mitford's legacy and vindicate [Grote's] favourite city', Grote's work cannot be read without having his radical and utilitarian background in mind.[91]

However, Grote's was no small achievement: he had managed to undermine the Tory view of Athens despite the great amount of ancient sources that had been used to sustain such a reading. Grote's liberal utilitarian outlook, unlike Thirlwall's pretensions of neutrality, Terence Irwin notes, forced him to substantiate a liberal argument from the same sources, not by perverting and distorting facts but by enabling him to find flaws in contemporary arguments and find evidence in the original sources. Grote showed not that his Tory adversaries had less to work with but that they never really understood what they had to work with in the first place.[92] Still, Grote did not hesitate to argue that Athens had lost its 'liberty, dignity, and security', because when Athenians had the opportunity to prevent their enemies from attacking, their unwillingness to do without the luxuries they came to enjoy (at a time when the danger was not so imminent) did not let them—but this should not be mistaken, he argued, for an invariable law of Democracy.[93]

Thus, in the aftermath of Romanticism, historians reassessed the political institutions of classical Athens and highlighted the presence of emotional and irrational elements in its history, in an effort to do justice to the diverse causes of the rise and fall of Athenian democracy.[94] Still, it formed part of an attempt at 'enabl[ing] England to recapture the cultural brilliance to which Athenian democracy had given birth'; the focus on Athenian institutions gave way to discussions about the character, genius and culture of ancient Athenians.[95] But attempts to direct the consideration of Athenian democracy away from political discourse of the time failed. This focus radically transformed Athens' unpopularity by mid-century and created a myth about Athens that would stipulate social reforms. But even if these reforms were not radical enough for George Grote and his company, they first turned the 'tide' to favor Athens.[96]

## CONCLUDING REMARKS

Both contesting the usefulness of classical education and affirming the relevance of antiquity in constitutional debates evinced a shift from Rome in the eighteenth century to Greece in the nineteenth. As we saw, the classics seemed to provide a forum in which the 'educated elite' could explore, often in a manner which excluded other social classes, public issues of current interest. First, the classics provided a basis for a polemical application, which in the nineteenth century led to a shift of interest from Roman to Greek historiography. Second, as ancient Greece-related works other than histories were increasingly being published, disagreements and challenges in the way of reading ancient sources led to challenges concerning opinions on modern issues. Third, well-known individuals—often associated with specific political parties or schools of thought—invited extensive examinations of their works on Greece with other than scholarly interest, evoking 'criticism and debate over the classical subject [they] had discussed'.[97] Still, in these debates, nineteenth-century Britain preserved the eighteenth-century didactic link between classical studies and public affairs, but also demonstrated the versatility of classical studies and their adaptability to preconceived ideas and cultural needs.[98]

As the Victorians seemed to view Athens as an ideal type of society, rather than an ideal type of government, i.e., 'socially close-knit, culturally active, intellectually outstanding',[99] the turn to ancient Greece reflected 'a widening of horizons'.[100] The search for 'new cultural roots' was connected to the realization that Greek values, ideas and concepts could be alternatives to the Christian tradition and French classicism, which increasingly seemed problematic.[101] Greece became the 'patron saint of vernaculars, the epitome of a particularized virtue as against the universalizing power of Latin and of Rome': the recent appropriation of Roman ideals by the French and by conservatives, Christopher Stray notes, seemed to prevent their revival in Britain. Thus, Greece seemed to provide 'an older, alternative legitimizing source of value',[102] even if the ancient world was already a source of 'prescriptive values and of illustrative moral and political allusions', as Turner has argued. Thus, while people argued about the structure of educational institutions, the tendency to use classical studies as a point of intellectual contact in modern issues invited commentators from various disciplines and convictions, each trying to adapt a version of antiquity to their own, which led to a re-orientation within classical studies themselves.[103]

At the same time, Hellenism seemed to receive a 'new and powerful role [...] in the ideological maintenance of the ruling class': its members 'were linked by much more than occupational relationships; they held a sense of identity from shared religious, cultural and social ideas' as fostered by the educational institutions of their time.[104] Moreover, commerce created a landless aristocracy, who discovered classics in an attempt to transform 'capital into culture' and thus gain social status—Greece especially seemed to offer 'cultural authority'. Thus, during this time, as Simon Goldhill puts it, '"[k]nowing Greek" always means more than an acquaintance with an ancient language'.[105] Overall, as Stray concludes, the *Hellenic* grew to be more suitable to the English character, social structure and the search for recognition; and Athens in particular, Ogilvie argues, 'possessed all those qualities which the age of revolution most admired'.[106]

Though both in Britain and in Europe Romantic Hellenism had its origins in the eighteenth and early-nineteenth century,[107] the primary reason why the 'tyranny of Greece' did not take place earlier, at least in the case of Britain, was due to the feeling—which knowing Latin bestowed—of connection with the recent past. Another—more practical—reason was the easy transition from having knowledge of Latin to acquiring knowledge of modern languages.[108] However, the influence of Latin could not have disappeared completely in the next century; it was as much part of the tradition as it was a 'vehicle of social status'. This was attested, as we saw, by dissenting voices who urged against the increasing dominance of ancient Greek culture.[109]

Thus, despite the intellectual sway which Greece was to exercize later on, at the turn of the nineteenth century, Greece 'had practically no effect on English life'. But by the mid-nineteenth century, the Victorians discovered enough similarities between themselves and Athens to 'tempt [them] into feeling a spiritual kinship'.[110] By late-nineteenth century, ancient Greece became a source of humanism; Victorians traced an 'elastic freedom' in Greek intellect and found 'a living charm' in Greek poetry and art—a 'nostalgia' which was a primarily nineteenth-century phenomenon.[111] The shift in educational focus was an effect, rather than the cause of this phenomenon.[112] It was the 'pervading' and 'quickening' nature of the spirit of Hellenism, Victorians seemed to believe, that allowed its integration with other elements, while maintaining its distinctiveness, and reinforced the feeling that Greece had something to teach.[113]

Thus for all men of culture, the classics remained (in the words of an American contemporary) 'the only oracles which are not decayed'.[114] In such an environment, the 'Greece-intoxicated' John Stuart Mill wrote in good company. Even though the nineteenth century was a period when 'men of letters' had multiple connections to the governing elite,[115] the study of ancient Greece remained an opportune source of practical insights and a forum for modern political criticism, since, only in the second half of the century, as Mill noted, was 'freedom of discussion [...] the conceded point'.[116]

# NOTES

1. H.Spencer to E.Cazelles, 06/12/1896, in Duncan, 1908:400.
2. Woodward, 1962:474; Harrison, 1971:165-9; Simon, 1974:72. See also, Bentham, 1838-43:VIII.395-7.
3. For contemporary takes on parliamentary debates, see Anon., 1838; Pakington, 1856; Baines, 1856; on the education of the poor, see Guthrie, 1847; 1860; Cornwallis, 1851; Bartley, 1871. For an introduction to the rival systems of education, see Midwinter, 1970. For a brief introduction to the history of British education, see Best, 1971:168-90 (see further, Silver, 1965; Silver and Lawson, 1973; Silver and Silver, 1974; Simon, 1974). For some statistical data on nineteenth-century education, see Ellis, 1973; West, 1970, 1971; Kiesling, 1983.
4. Tate, 1857:2-8.
5. Potter, 2005:ch.2; Collini, 1991:32-3 (also, Sullivan, 2009:344-6). See also, Pycroft, 1847:50.
6. Wallace, 1997:21-2.
7. See Clark, 1855:285-6; Hill, 1836:I.18-9, 204, 209-11, 224 (see further, Kennedy, 1837:3, 9-14, 29, 35; Blackie, 1866:2, 1852; Payne, 1866:20; Combe, 1848:13-6). Thus, a single copy of the *Times* could be argued to be more useful than the whole of Thucydides' *History* (for the story, see Anon., 1880:302; Morley, 1908:II.430n1).
8. Morell, 1827:326. See further, Harrison, 1971:163.
9. J. Grote, 1856:78 (for some early responses to this question, see Temple, 1690 and Swift, 1704).

10. Kennedy, 1837:2-3; Combe, 1848:11-3; Payne, 1866:18. See also, Clark, 1855:285. Some did argue that classical studies could lead to commercial success even if only indirectly (Newman, 1859:167-8).

11. Priestley, 1788:xvii. See also, Hodgson, 1866:4.

12. Thomas Arnold's focus on character formation greatly influenced the way classics were taught (Stanley, 1845:I.139). For this reason, the grammar schools became very prestigious and held a vital role in the debate (Best, 1971:172; Simon, 1974:95ff.). Eventually, Oxford and Cambridge reformed their practice (Gilmour, 1993:149), after the suggestions of the 1850 Royal Commissions. For contemporary takes on the history of classical studies, see Whewell, 1850; Stedman, 1887; for recent historical accounts see Stray, 1997, 1998, 1999; Stopper, 1981; Todd, 1999.

13. Seeley, 1870:314, 316 (see further, Shannon, 2004). See further, Collini, Winch and Burrow, 1983:chs.6-7.

14. Harvie and Matthew, 2000:6.

15. Clark, 1855:282-4, 291; J. Grote, 1856:13-4. See also, Ogilvie, 1964:96.

16. Gray, 1836:4-8; see also, J. Grote, 1856:82-3, 83n.

17. J. Grote, 1856:13-4, 86-98.

18. Jebb, 1907:521, 539-40 (see further, Jenkyns, 1980:2).

19. Sewell, 1830:284. However, this was an agreement which often extended to criticism against modern languages (for example see, Stanley, 1845:I.440; Clark, 1855:306-7; J. Grote, 1856:86, 112).

20. Whewell, 1850:I.82-3; Turner, 1986:584. Whewell did join the 'Hellenic bandwagon' eventually, by publishing his translations of a number of Platonic dialogues (1859-61). Also, Whewell's works show that the shift from Latin to Greek was an issue noticed and discussed (see, J. Grote, 1856:81, 85-6. See further, Harris, 1993:247-8), but generally his contribution to the debate on the usefulness of classics is neglected (e.g., Turner, 1981:372, 376, 388).

21. Clark, 1855:306-7.

22. Whewell, 1850:I.10-2; 1838:34. See further, Sullivan, 2009:346; Collini, 1991:19. However, critics still responded that neither the 'cultural ties' to Greece and Rome nor the 'expansion' of the mind of young people sufficed to make classical studies useful (Harris, 1879:198-9). Richards (2009:ch.1) provides a brief account of how the Victorians interacted with the ancient world in some more general ways.

23. See Bowen, 1989:177.

24. Jenkyns, 1980:13-4. See further, Webb, 1982.

25. Jenkyns, 1980:14-5. See also, Peardon, 1933:84-5; Gooch, 1967:289-90. For more detailed discussions of the trends in historiography and the relevance of ancient Greece in nineteenth-century Britain see also, Ogilvie, 1964; Turner, 1981; Roberts, 1994, Demetriou, 1996c, 1999; and Potter, 2005.

26. Webb, 1982:32.

27. Montagu, 1760:375, 90.

28. Stanyan, 1739:II.xx-xxi; I.180.

29. Goldsmith, 1774:I.20, 212. Goldsmith argued that the Spartan constitution guaranteed these ends, while he considered Athenian democracy to be a monarchy in disguise.

30. Drummond, 1794:v; Young, 1804:viii-ix.

31. Drummond, 1794:60-1; Young, 1804:xiii-xiv. See also, Blackstone, 1771:I.154-5 (quoted in Whedbee, 2004:73).

32. Turner, 1981:189-91, 197. Athens' instability may suggest why Sparta was favored over Athens for many years across Europe (see further, Rawson, 1969).

33. Gillies, 1786:I.464-5. See also, Ferguson, 1768:225, 286-7; Robertson, 1768:appx. 1; Murray, 2004a:5-7.

34. Gillies, 1786:I.466-7, 449. See further, Sinclair, 1988.

35. Gillies, 1786:I.468-71, ii.

36. Demetriou, 1999:58. T.B. Macaulay argued that Mitford frequently distorted facts (1824:286-9)—a mistake which Turner argues that Grote did not commit (1981:204-5; see also, Murray, 2004a:9).

37. Mitford added: 'at least before the French Revolution' (1808:II.8-9, 15). See, Turner, 1981:192ff.

38. Mitford, 1808:II.20-1, 24-35. See further, Taylor, 1984.

39. Demetriou, 1999:39 (see also, Redesdale, 1829:xiii). See further, Turner, 1981:208; Whedbee, 2004:77.

40. Macaulay, 1824:286, 289. See also, Grote, 1826:284.

41. Freeman, 1856:143n (quoted in Turner 1981:194; Demetriou, 1999:58).

42. Turner, 1981:204. See also, Roberts, 1994:254.

43. Finley, 2004:164-5,180-4.

44. Drummond, 1794:171-2. Gillies, 1786:I.424 (also, Montagu, 1760:84). Finley, 2004:164-5,180-4.

45. Montagu, 1760:89-101; see also, Stanyan, 1739:I.379-80; Goldsmith, 1774:I.321; Gillies, 1786:I.643ff.

46. Mitford, 1808:II.303, 512.

47. See also, Murray, 2004a; Demetriou, 1999:47-51.

48. Bulwer-Lytton, 2004:583, 584n (see further, Murray, 2004a:10, 17; 2004b:529); see also, Grote, 1875:VI.414.

49. Grote, 1875:VI.481.

50. Grote, 1875:VI.133, 483-4; VIII.43. See further, Chambers, 1996:16-7; Demetriou, 1999:100-7.

51. Thirlwall, 1845-52:III.459n3; 1835-47:IV.215-7. See also, Demetriou, 1999:53. Grote considered Thirlwall's view of Cleon to be in accordance with tradition (1875:VI.414n2; see further, Whedbee, 2004).

52. Montagu, 1760:84-5.

53. Young, 1804:76.

54. Gillies, 1786:I.302,465.

55. Drummond, 1794:173.

56. Mitford, 1808:I.423; II.303.

57. *Ibid.* I.524, 559, 562, 590; II.303.

58. Drummond, 1794:175. See also, Young, 1804:88n, 91, 143.

59. Bulwer-Lytton, 1837:294-305, 424, 434.

60. Grote, 1875:III.145-6. Grote argued that ostracism was even safer than Solon's earlier measures, since Solon would assume that the 'fierce party-feud' had already led them to be armed and ready to engage, while the institution of ostracism would call for the mediation of the public much earlier.

61. *Ibid.* IV.150-2.

62. *Ibid.* IV.153-4. See further, Kagan, 1961; Forsdyke, 2005:ch.4.

63. Grote, 1875:III.154.

64. For a summary of the 'traditional' interpretation of the Sophists, see Whedbee, 2008:607-13.

65. Gillies, 1786:I.476.

66. Mitford, 1808:III.95.

67. Coleridge, 1854:II.398-400.
68. *Ibid.* pp. 403-4, 405, 407; III.401-5; 1818-9:I.172-3.
69. Bulwer-Lytton, 1837:460, 467; 2004:561.
70. Thirlwall, 1845-52:III.312-33. See further, Whedbee, 2008:618. Once again, Grote (1875:VII.37n) did not consider Thirlwall's view radical enough.
71. Grote, 1875:VII.37n; VIII.355. See also, J.S. Mill, Pr:XI.39-61; Lewes, 1845:102-21.
72. Karen Whedbee (2008:614), trying to qualify Grote's originality, fails to take notice of this aspect of Grote's contribution. As far as the sceptic nature of many of their teachings was concerned, as Demetriou argues, Grote showed that it was a sign of the times, rather than a cause of it (Grote, 1875:VIII.356-8, 366ff; Demetriou, 1999:222).
73. J.S. Mill, *A*:I.15.
74. Goldhill, 2002:183-4 (see also, Webb, 1982:29-30). See also, Rosen, 1992:104-11; Wallace, 1997:178-208.
75. See further, Mitchell, 2003:chs.9-10.
76. Bulwer-Lytton, 1837:xii (see also, pp. 63, 145, 398n, 416, 485n, 491).
77. Bulwer-Lytton, 1837:206n. See also, Macaulay, 1824. Bulwer provided numerous examples to illustrate Mitford's weak historical analysis (e.g., 1837:206n, 207n, 211n, 215n, 216n, 294-5, 347n, 404n, 434).
78. Bulwer-Lytton, 1837:207n, 231n, 232n.
79. *Ibid.* p. 234n.
80. *Ibid.* pp. 467, 195.
81. Anon., 1837a:211. For positive reception, see Donne, 1837; Anon., 1837c; 1837d.
82. Bulwer-Lytton, 1837:200, 394, 420; Anon., 1837b:348. See also, Sandford, 1837:161-2.
83. Bulwer-Lytton, 1837:295.
84. Sandford, 1837:151, 166-7, 176-7; Anon., 1837b:351. Alison (1837:44) was astonished to find out that someone had actually defended 'the most dangerous form of government, and the most fatal enemy of that freedom which it professes to support'.
85. See further, Demetriou, 1999:chs.2-3.
86. Thirlwall, 1845-52:I.464, 466-9. See further, Turner, 1981:211; Demetriou, 1999:54-5.
87. Thirlwall, 1835-47:IV.273; Demetriou, 1999:55.
88. As Thirlwall noted the institutions of Athens was 'a school of practical knowledge', of eloquence and wit (Thirlwall, 1835-47:IV.214, 218-9).
89. Lane, 2001:23-4.
90. Gooch, 1967:292-7.
91. Demetriou, 1999:125; Jenkyns, 1980:14. Grote's confidence in the people and the leaders of Athens, as Chambers (1996:16) notes, 'carried him beyond where modern historians often stop'.
92. Irwin, 1998:426-31.
93. Grote, 1875:XI.279-80; Turner, 1981:231-4.
94. Hansen, 1992:25; Demetriou, 1999:71.
95. Saxonhouse, 1993:488. Potter, 2005:74.
96. Turner, 1981:210, 234; Hansen, 1992:8-9, 11. See also, Robinson, 2004:4. Eventually, the American example replaced the Athenian as a model of democracy (Potter, 2005:68-74. See further, Crook, 1965)
97. Turner, 1982:4-5; 1989:62-4. See, J. Grote, 1856:112.
98. Breisach, 1994:249-50; Gilmour, 1993:43.
99. Potter, 2005:73.
100. Ogilvie, 1964:77-8; see also, Turner, 1981:2-5, 9-10.
101. Turner, 1981:2. See also, Dowling, 1994:xiii-iv.

102. Stray, 1998:18,15. See also, Nelson, 2004:ch.3.
103 Turner, 1981:1-14. See also, Ogilvie, 1964:90.
104 Bowen, 1989:163; Goldhill, 2002:193-4. See further, Ogilvie, 1964:92-3.
105. Stray, 1998:22; Goldhill, 2002:190.
106. Stray, 1998:26-9; Ogilvie, 1964:77, 80-1, 106-7.
107. See further, Webb, 1982; Wallace, 1997; Butler, 1935, Güthenke, 2008.
108. Stanier, 1941:103.
109. See further, Turner, 1986; Sachs, 2009.
110. Stray, 1998:16. Ogilvie, 1964:82-5, 97-9, 106-8. See further, Dowling, 1994:chs. 2-3; Wallace, 1997:13.
111 Jebb, 1907:521-7, 539-42, 555-7, 563-8. See further, Stray, 1998; Cartledge, 2001:ix. Evangelista, 2009:9. However, Güthenke (2008:19) argues that 'models of nostalgia or common idealism or "tyranny"' of Greece over Europe do not do justice to the complexity of the appropriation of ancient Greece trends which developed in the nineteenth century. Concurrently, 'Hellenic ideals' would be invoked, as Jose Harris (1993:247) notes, to legitimize as well as dignify diverse activities and institutions, such as boarding-schools, civic architecture, homosexual relationships, organized charity, mystical religion, and women's rights. Still, as Turner has argued (1981:32), Hellenism could not have broken all 'bounds' of 'conventional taste and polite morality'.
112. Ogilvie, 1964:86.
113. Jebb, 1907:571.
114. Thoreau, 1854:112 (in Sullivan, 2009:130).
115. Heyck, 1982:36.
116. J.S. Mill, *A*:I.89. See further, Demetriou, 1999:33; Gooch, 1967:289; Stopper, 1981:275-6.

# CHAPTER TWO

## PLATO IN PRE-VICTORIAN BRITAIN

The study of philosophy—in contrast to that of history—excited little interest in Britain prior to the second half of the nineteenth century.[1] As a result, scholars highlight a 'general neglect' of Plato, until the mid-Victorian period in Britain. Originating in the late seventeenth century, prior to which the Cambridge Platonists (or 'more truly Plotinists')[2] still studied Plato, this neglect was terminated by the exertions of George Grote and Benjamin Jowett.[3] Although early-nineteenth-century Platonic scholarship has not attracted much critical attention, an outline of what preoccupation with Plato entailed in this period is all that can be attempted here. To this effect, this chapter examines the period from Thomas Taylor's 1804 English edition of the Platonic corpus, which prompted James Mill to criticism, twice, to the mid-1830s publication of the younger Mill's translations of Plato. Setting about with a brief discussion on Platonic scholarship at the turn of the nineteenth century, the chapter proceeds to consider Taylor's reading of Plato and its immediate reception. Then, a concise overview of the various characteristics of Plato and Socrates, in connection to contemporary concerns, is followed by a consideration of some early utilitarian responses. A brief analysis of Samuel Taylor Coleridge's complex portrait of Plato serves as a way of summing up the main findings of this chapter.

## REDISCOVERING PLATO

As we saw, classicists translated ancient texts because they considered the lessons contained in them too important to ignore—even if ancient languages gradually fell into disfavor. Thus, as the classical influences in the work of eminent thinkers of the Scottish Enlightenment attest,[4] during the time when Britain was fully engaged in the debate on the usefulness of classical studies, ancient Greeks, particularly Plato, still found a way into modern discourse. By the mid-1830s, university professors had increasingly incorporated Plato into their lectures.[5]

It is generally argued that Plato's popularity in Victorian Britain owed to the 'protean character' of his works. Plato's dialogues were, at once, very inspiring to poets and artists, who sought something transcendental, and appealing to individuals with diverse political convictions; the same seemed to apply to both religious sceptics and their rivals.[6] Though there was indeed 'something for everyone in Plato',[7] he eventually assumed his 'proper' place as the 'father of Idealism' in late-Victorian Britain.[8] And though it cannot be denied that Plato did not exert any great influence during the eighteenth century, counting 'for less in this age than in previous or succeeding phases of British culture', the Victorian turn to Plato was not as sudden as is usually suggested.[9]

Platonic commentary had indeed 'never developed into a coherent academic engagement' in the eighteenth century. However, though 'a relatively barren period' for work on Plato, editions, translations and studies of Plato's dialogues did appear in pre-Victorian Britain, especially in Scotland.[10] In the 1763 English edition of Plato's *Republic*, Henry Spens noted the need to transform the current 'spirit of inquiry into ancient learning'; but the 'sublime philosophy' of classics, regarding virtue and the conduct of life, was becoming increasingly inaccessible to young readers, while many other areas of culture and learning expanded on ancient modes of thought. Likewise, Ebenezer Macfait complained that '[t]he taste of this present age' did 'not seem to be great for books of ancient learning'.[11] Translations of ancient texts would allow interested readers 'in this inquisitive age' to see for themselves the 'merit of the renowned Sages of antiquity'—Plato was the 'sage' who engaged in the 'arduous task' of uncovering the falsity of the opinions of 'wicked flatterers and impostors' and inquired into, examined and ascertained the proper regard of the powers of each of 'the passions and affections of the human heart'.[12] For these scholars of the Scottish Enlightenment, Plato was a celebrated moralist, 'justly intitled to uncommon applause', by giving moral subjects 'the firmer hold of our hearts' and by combining the qualities of philosophic and poetic genius.[13]

Already by the mid-eighteenth century it was recognized that '[t]here is scarce any author whose fame has been so variable as Plato's'; a philosopher with the 'most copious and exuberant imagination' and most qualified for the 'successful pursuit of philosophical studies'.[14] This was a view of Plato's importance that was rapidly spreading throughout the British Isles.[15] This gradually made Plato more relevant to the re-examination of religion, morality and society. Scottish philosophers had already begun to move toward a philosophical method based on observation, experience and introspection and which defined mental principles analyzing all facets of human interaction.

Ebenezer Macfait's succinct summary of Plato's dialectic method showed why this was so:

> the mind [...] by help of the dialectic art assumes certain hypothesis [sic], not as principles, but as suppositions only, until by these helps and steps it ascends to some general principle; and having obtained this general principle, descends gradually from thence, by close and necessary connection, to particular cases.[16]

It was a matter of time for Plato's method to be rediscovered and applied in politics by a Scotsman, James Mill.

A primary reason for the lack of interest in the study of Plato's works in Britain up to that time was their being available mostly only in Latin or Greek editions and associated with the metaphysical speculations of the Cambridge Platonists, who introduced Plato in Britain in the seventeenth century. The Cambridge Platonists saw themselves—to some extent—as part of the continental Neoplatonic tradition,[17] blending their discussions on contemporary religious and philosophical subjects with the philosophy of Plato and the Neoplatonists. But by coloring the interpretation of Plato with Neoplatonic overtones, they severely hindered a wider appeal. Thus, as it was often believed that Plato wrote '*designedly*, above comprehension', he needed first to be 'demystified'.[18]

Though in the second half of the eighteenth century a process of demystifying Plato did begin, the amateurism of most intellectual forays into Plato's dialogues—more evident in reviews—persisted well into the nineteenth century.[19] The purported practical turn of mind of the British led John Stuart Blackie to point out that '[b]etween Plato and the English nation there is in fact a gulf which cannot be passed'.[20] Even in 1865, scholars 'feared' that '[t]here is nothing good [...] in English on this subject'.[21] But the 'bad quality' of views on Plato did not mean that Plato was out of sight 'for a century or more' or that there were 'almost two centuries of general neglect'.[22]

In the first half of the nineteenth century, Frank Turner has argued, Plato was not yet seen as 'the philosopher for an age of improvement, progress and utility'.[23] In due time, many debates developed out of the different attitudes toward either to his doctrines, the chronology of his works or the growing discussion whether Plato was a sceptical or dogmatic philosopher. Moreover, his 'discovery and rediscovery' in the second half of the nineteenth century was indeed due to the influence of 'a number of prominent individuals'.[24] Thus, direct or indirect discussions in books, reviews, articles, encyclopedic entries and even poems on Socrates and Plato regularly appeared, keeping Plato in sight, but it was not until George Grote's and Benjamin Jowett's contributions that any systematic work on Plato was carried out; and their respective analyses formed two prominent interpretations. By the end of the century, Plato's increasing eminence was reflected both in classical scholarship and university teaching.[25]

# A NEOPLATONIST BORN OUT OF DUE SEASON

In 1804, Thomas Taylor published the first complete English edition of the works of Plato. He considered his efforts to be a great service to Platonic studies, by treading 'in paths which have been untrodden for upwards of a thousand years' and thought himself the only one who possessed the 'piercing eyes' required for the mystical journey into Plato's mind,[26] using the Platonists of Alexandria as guides.[27] He thus viewed the Platonic philosophy as an exposition of the mystical and transcendental 'divine natures'. He tried to introduce to the English-reading public Plato's 'hidden manner', which had not allowed the 'occult and venerable splendour' of Plato's philosophy to be valued by the 'superficial readers' of the past. In his attempt 'to shift the emphasis from the customary moral or political reading of Plato to [Plato's] spiritual doctrine',[28] he drew attention to Plato both through criticism and inspiration.[29]

Taylor argued that Plato stood above all other philosophers regarding the first principle of things, the supreme cause, the 'highest God'. His analysis was a symptom of his conviction that Platonists had not superadded a theology not already present in Plato.[30] Plato developed his most important doctrines, Taylor argued, in the attempt to understand the nature of the 'Deity', the principle of all things and the primary causes of wholes. He found in Plato a tripartite 'superessential' One (prior to and beyond being, power and energy), which had influenced the Christian conception of Trinity.[31] His 'divine Plato' defined the soul as 'an apostate from deity', in a fallen condition, exiled from light.[32] Thus, Taylor did read Plato in a way that had been forgotten for many years; for him, Plato's philosophy encompassed, in a religious fashion, the truth of being.[33]

According to Taylor, Plato's theology transcended, as well as originated, that of the Christians. He used the familiar Christian imagery to describe Plato's theology, but argued for the superiority of that of Plato. His comments on Plato's doctrine of ideas, the constitution of the soul and the doctrine of reminiscence, followed the same pattern. He concluded that Plato's philosophy was most 'friendly to true piety, pure morality, solid learning and sound government'.[34] According to Taylor, Plato advanced his doctrines on the nature of the 'great world' and the 'microcosm man', by following, for example, a 'divinely inspired energy' or symbolically stating the 'ineffable idioms' of their nature.[35]

However, Taylor added, Plato's 'master science' was the dialectical method—the only method which could ascend to the Good itself.[36] Though Plato's method brought into 'consummate perfection' the '*definitive* and *divisive*, *the demonstrative* and *analytic*' powers, according to Taylor,[37] it was not a mere method of reasoning or of logic. Being neither simply demonstrative nor exclusively 'conversant with opinion', Plato's method dealt with 'nobler' pursuits. Taylor argued that dialectics put into effect a three-step move from things grounded in matter to abstract ideas accessible only by reason: the first step 'is an ascent from sensibles to the first intelligibles; a second is an ascent through things demonstrated and subdemonstrated, to undemonstrated and immediate propositions; and a third proceeds from hypothesis to unhypothetical principles'.[38] This view of Plato's method, Taylor noted, would appear novel especially to 'those who have been nursed as it were in the bosom of matter, the pupils of experiment, the darlings of sense'; being incapable of understanding the true nature of things—one that can only be captured by the 'spontaneous, unperverted, self-luminous conceptions of the soul'.[39] Thus, Taylor conceived Plato's dialectical method as intuitive, not grounded in experience, one that was most capable of transcending the individual into the ineffable.

William Axon's short biography of Taylor showed that mostly ridicule and mockery surrounded the efforts of Thomas Taylor 'the Platonist' (also dubbed 'Plato Taylor')—not least due to his admission of being a 'philosophic polytheist'.[40] This estimate is confirmed by a brief consideration of the reviews of Taylor's *Plato*.[41] Though all critics more or less argued against what they saw as Taylor's Neoplatonic absurdities, no one, except James Mill, criticized the Neoplatonic reading of Plato's method. Likewise, even to the harshest reviewer, Taylor's interpretation of Plato's ideas on providence and fate seemed appropriate.[42]

Almost all reviewers agreed: Taylor's endeavor was as much awaited as disappointing. While all reviewers were sympathetic to Taylor's effort, given the breadth of the scope and minute expositions through the commentaries of later Platonists, almost all were in accord in that it would be better if this arduous task had been reserved for a better scholar. His translation, his notes as well as his introduction to Plato failed to satisfy all but one of his reviewers, who considered Taylor's edition 'a safe book of reference for the English reader'.[43]

What seems to have struck his critics most, even beyond the style, lack of accuracy and lack of sense of the translation, was Taylor's unquestioning approval of Neoplatonic readings of Plato.[44] They argued that the Neoplatonists were 'fanatics professing themselves [Plato's] disciples, who wished to find in him what he never professed to possess—complete information upon every question'. Taylor was thus as much condemnable as they for 'twisting and turning' Plato's meaning.[45] Instead of illuminating Plato's doctrines with new light, his critics argued, Taylor bended and sometimes forced Plato's words to agree with the interpretations and assumptions of later Platonists.[46] Taylor's rendering of Plato's doctrines, a reviewer noted, fell within the strain of 'unintelligible mysticism' and 'incoherent reveries of Plotinus, Proclus and Jacob Behnmen'.[47] Taylor's 'violent attachment to Pagan mythology in general and that of the Platonists in particular' was 'insulting and offensive'[48] and covered Plato with 'a veil of impenetrable obscurity'.[49] This overwhelming negative reception of Taylor's reading shows at the same time that the eighteenth-century reception of Plato was not dominated by 'mystical' readings. Likewise, all reviewers censured Taylor's criticisms of experimental science—one critic strayed from his subject at hand and attempted a defence of experimental science as a legitimate source of knowledge.[50]

Concurringly, the reviewers had also argued against Taylor for the superiority of Christian faith and morality, in accord with the traditional commentary on Plato. More specifically, the *Critical Review* writer demolished

Taylor's arguments regarding Plato's doctrines of abstract ideas or reminiscence. He argued that, even though Plato's mind was obviously 'great and cultivated', Plato did not escape the disadvantages to which all 'pagan writers' were exposed. Thus, it was surprising, given Plato's fanciful and erroneous reasoning, the critic argued, that Plato's ethics and theology managed to 'so far outstrip' other pagan writers. Still, Plato's imperfections, including the use of metaphoric language or 'trifling subtleties' that hindered the discovery of truth instead of illustrating it, the critic added, were not enough to damage Plato's eminence.[51] However, this was not a shared opinion. The *Imperial Review* critic noted that Xenophon, Plato and Aristotle had given to the world the 'noblest gift'; they produced works that taught how to form a just estimate of things and instructed readers accurately of their duties—their writings had led individuals 'in a word, to the very threshold of Christianity', by illustrating with such vividness that people 'sadly mistake their interest whenever they prefer the body to the mind, or pleasure to virtue'.[52] Thus, the estimate of Plato varied according to what was conceived to be the connection between Plato and Christianity.

Moreover, unlike other reviewers, the *Critical Review* writer was critical of Plato's philosophy and thought that Socrates deserved more praise than Plato, as the latter's ideas on 'subjects of the first importance to the happiness of man' were not as unexceptionable as those of Socrates. Thus he argued that Plato's *Republic* was not 'a polity perfect in all its parts', being founded on 'horrid' principles—ones that even the disciples of the 'philosophic infidelity' could not approve in full: exposure of infants, abolition of the rites of marriage and the destruction of parental and filial affection. The reviewer further noted that '[i]f a superstructure, founded on such a basis, be 'the greatest effort of the human mind', we thank God for that inferior degree of intellect, which is alike incapable of admiring or recommending it.'[53] The 'venerable Socrates', on the other hand, during the last moments of his life had managed to impress everyone's 'mind with a just sense of the dignity of virtue, and the peace and serenity which conscious innocence affords', by becoming 'a martyr to good order and good government, dying, as he did, to maintain the one, and support the other'.[54]

Despite Taylor's immodest proclamations, his reviewers argued that he had 'read Plato *without ability* to understand him'.[55] What was more important to them, not only did Taylor seem to adhere to Plato's 'pagan' beliefs, but also he argued that Plato's system originated and surpassed the Christian tradition. In all subjects of Platonic philosophy that the 'half-witted Taylor' had tried to examine, his reviewers agreed that he had made himself unable to be understood.[56] This 'most industrious' scholar was not the most useful one, being 'convert to the platonic systems of physics, metaphysics and theology'—subjects that in the early nineteenth century appeared to have 'the farthest distance from truth and reality', especially since 'the labours of Bacon, Locke and Newton'.[57] Thus, his attempt to 'exhibit' Plato 'in popular form' failed: not only had Taylor turned Plato's elegant Greek into 'unintelligible gibberish' in English, his efforts to do justice to the complexity of Plato's ideas were 'if possible, still more insufferable', causing them to ask themselves how anyone 'not absolutely insane could pen such nonsense'.[58]

## SOCRATES IN EARLY-NINETEENTH CENTURY

In the early nineteenth century, the main previously existing obstacles to Plato's popularity almost at once ceased to be present: first, there was a growing interest in ancient Greece; second, Plato's dialogues, especially his depiction of the Sophists and his criticism of Athenian democracy, were increasingly getting 'caught up in the cultural battles of the age'; third, the sweeping criticism of Neoplatonic readings by Taylor's critics exhibited the need to demystify Plato.[59] All these had set the ground for the subsequent re-evaluation of Plato's thought.

In the first place, when both John Gillies's and William Mitford's histories appeared, Socrates' trial and death were used to add to the stock of arguments against the 'unjust rigour' of Athenian institutions. Socrates, Gillies noted, was an innocent man whose 'illustrious merit' disgraced 'the vices and follies of his contemporaries'—it was surprising, Gillies commented, that someone who 'never disguised his contempt for the capricious levity, injustice, and cruelty of the multitude' survived so long in Athenian democracy.[60] The Athenian state of affairs, in which the people were 'seduced by eloquence, intimidated by authority, and corrupted by every species of undue influence' Gillies argued, foretold the outcome of Socrates' trial. However, Gillies also pointed toward the influence of Aristophanes' *Clouds* as a cause of Socrates' conviction, though the first would persist much longer than the second cause.[61]

Moreover, Gillies's treatment of Plato was similarly directed against democratic Athens. Had Plato administered his abilities properly, Gillies maintained, his age and nation would have had greatly benefited.[62] Though Plato wandered away from Socrates' firm ground in observation and experience, his pursuits still involved bringing both the natural and moral world together with the 'wise government of a self-existent unchangeable cause'. According to Gillies, Plato studied the various aspects of human nature to create a system of ethics which promoted both the independence and security of the present state and the happiness and perfection of a future state of existence.[63] Thus, Gillies found a strong religious outlook in Plato: God's providence had united the summit of pleasure and pain and directed people away from material pursuits toward intellectual pursuits, true happiness and virtue.[64]

Similarly, the divine origin of Socrates' inquiry into, and teaching of, 'the duty of man to man' were subjects that Mitford considered to be hazardous 'under the jealous tyranny of democracy'.[65] Thus, he shared Gillies's opinion concerning Socrates' conviction.[66] Socrates, primarily a public figure, Mitford added, appeared 'wherever he could find most company'. Unlike the Sophists, the brilliant and eloquent Socrates communicated his opinions by means of conversation, proposing a question and, via an interrogatory argument, leading his interlocutors to the 'just conclusion'. Socrates denied the advantages of his instructive, and amusing, conversations to nobody, Mitford further argued, as he accepted invitations to 'private entertainments' but not to private or paid instruction.[67]

Many shared Mitford's view. It was commonly accepted that Socrates believed in the virtue of being good and not merely appearing so. For many, this seemed to explain how the Sophists, with their 'wretched philosophy', 'ostentation, and absurdities', made the Athenians arrogant and afforded them with no 'foundation of real knowledge'.[68] The Sophists, men of 'shewy acquirements' and 'slender qualifications', simply 'taught the art of maintaining any set of principles or opinions, that might be dictated by inclination, passion or caprice'.[69] Mitford saw in Socrates a man without political ambitions but with a strong sense of civic duty; and others agreed that by choosing not to escape an unjust punishment, Socrates, in *Crito*, had set the foundation of the concept of civil obedience.[70] As we saw in chapter one, the above depiction of the Sophists and of Athenian Democracy persisted well into the nineteenth century in Britain. Conveniently, neither Mitford nor Gillies saw Socrates' actions as part of the democratic institutions of his time; but James Jackson recognized their relation to the political stability and progress of Athens.[71]

In the second place, many pointed out that while other philosophers had been preoccupied with philosophical issues unrelated to the 'business of human life',[72] Socrates made human happiness the object of his contemplation and thus became the 'inventor of morality'.[73] For Mitford, Socrates was deeply influenced by Anaxagoras' description of God and divine providence, seeking to examine one's social duties, as part of one's duty to God. God's nature, the creation of the world and 'the laws of the heavenly bodies' were more important, more useful and more accessible to more people than philosophy up until Socrates' time. Still, Mitford presented Socrates as having had a Christian-like conception of God, even though he shared the superstitions of his 'heathen religion'.[74] Similarly, Joseph Priestley noted that Socrates 'devoted himself' to 'promoting virtue in others'. Once more the test of this moral purity was his 'magnanimous' attitude during and after his trial and conviction.[75] Thus, more frequent among Plato's readers came up a 'pious' portrait of Socrates.

Jackson agreed with Mitford that there were features in the ideas Plato's Socrates expounded that resembled Christianity: the belief in the providence of God and a future state of rewards and punishments.[76] On the other hand, Priestley found no evidence of Socrates' belief in a future state or rewards and punishments, but attributed such beliefs to Plato's philosophical speculations (rather than firm religious beliefs).[77] However, Priestley, like Mitford, did recognize a divine origin in Socrates' *daimonion*, something that Jackson was reluctant to admit.[78] However, it is important to note that if one wished to see Socrates undistorted by Plato's religious mysticism, Xenophon's, not Plato's, works were considered to be the best source.[79] Furthermore, Socrates was not without faults, these writers maintained; though they accepted that his faults were related to the time he lived.[80] Thus, they argued that neither Socrates' original, rational and sublime thoughts on the nature of divinity nor Plato's genius could have escaped the 'idolatrous nature' of their time.[81] Still, Socrates justly held the 'first rank amongst heathen philosophers', Jackson argued, because of his superior genius and purity of life as well as 'the utility and practical tendency of which he taught'.[82]

The pattern that emerges is that Plato's dialogues were read only in the attempt to draw comparisons between Socrates, Plato and Christianity as well as to criticize Athens. These comparisons gave rise, as contemporary writers noticed, to two different views of Socrates: first, a 'party among the moderns' thought Socrates' morality all that was necessary (making the duty as defined from revelation unnecessary).[83] The second group were those who had heavily criticized Socrates in response to the 'exaggerated encomiums' of sceptics.[84] Some classicists, in contrast, resisted making comparison between Socratic and Christian ethics, as they believed it created a rather false portrait of Socrates.[85] However, such protests were insufficient to stop Plato's works from primarily being read as if 'the knowledge of the one true and living God, and the glimmering belief of future dispensations, had broken out in a feeble ray over the darkness of the world' in Plato's dialogues.[86]

However, as time neared Victoria's reign, when the Philosophic Radicals were widening their popular appeal, the inquisitive nature of Plato's dialogues came to the fore. In an article on Socrates, a young writer began his discussion by calling the nineteenth century a 'doubting age'—what the past tried to discover and establish as truths, the present endeavoured 'to overturn'.[87] Thus, Henry Matthews alluded to an age of transition, wary of authority, standing in contrast to the 'natural' ages of the past.[88] Even if some of the works of 'philosophical doubters' were overly sceptical (e.g., some still claimed the earth was at the center of the universe), Matthews argued, 'the love of novelty', if limited only to experimental sciences, could not be of service 'to the cause of truth'.[89]

The usual representation of Socrates was considered by Matthews to be similarly 'a crime against human nature, amounting almost to sacrilege'. Matthews attempted to illustrate Socrates' time by its original sources.[90] But, despite his intentions, he failed to add anything new to the discussion concerning Socrates' character. Socrates was still appreciated as pointing to a Christian-like God, even though he could not refrain from embracing many of the religious practices of his time. Likewise, Socrates acted up to his civic duties when it was necessary but also stood firm against both the 'barbaric oligarchy' of the Thirty Tyrants and the 'capricious', 'despotic', 'many-headed monster' called Athenian democracy.[91] Matthews also argued that Socrates' depiction in the *Clouds* was 'distorted and caricatured to serve the purpose of the satirist'. However, he did defend Socrates' seeming approval of same-sex relationships by arguing that it was a different kind of love—even if the habits of the time suggested otherwise.[92] Portrayals of Socrates, such as Priestley's and Jackson's or even Mitford's, were still defended well into the 1830s.

Similarly, Plato was thought to have come 'nearer to the doctrines of revelation than any other of the heathen philosophers that came after him, even than Socrates himself'.[93] For example J.P. Potter's books echoed Jackson's and

Priestley's arguments, pointing to a more pious, deeply religious Socrates—a pre-Christian yet Christian saint.[94] Likewise, the popular lectures on Plato by William Sewell in late-1830s Oxford did not do anything to change this view. As Martin Clarke noted, Sewell's lectures on Plato's *Republic* viewed this work 'as a kind of prophecy of the Catholic church', to such an extent that 'his class did not know whether he was lecturing on St Paul's Epistles or Plato's dialogues'.[95] But while Jackson and Priestley were preoccupied with examining the parallels between ancient Athens and Christianity, it was Jackson's comments on Socrates' method and the stability of Athens that would anticipate some of John Stuart Mill's and George Grote's arguments. James Mill's pupils argued that viewing Plato as merely an obscure heathen philosopher, whose ethics and theology resembled the doctrines of revelation and Christian morality, failed to do justice to the force of the inquisitive nature of his dialogues and thus failed to extract any benefit.

## SOCRATES, PLATO AND THE UTILITARIANS

As the above suggest, Socrates had indeed assumed a heroic stature in the nineteenth century, as he was considered 'the Jesus Christ of Greece'.[96] As we saw earlier, Socrates' beliefs, his devotion to virtue and duty, his commitment to 'saving' his contemporaries by making them see their 'wrong ways', his disregard for personal gain and security as well as his death, were used to illustrate similarities in many ways to Jesus. But, as mentioned in passing, there was a different reading, one that appropriated Socrates' habit of *questioning* convention. As Richard Jenkyns notes, Socrates, 'a devout, even superstitious man', blended the characteristics of personal commitment and of a natural inclination to question established ideas; to sceptics, contemplating Socrates' life provided 'religious emotion without the religion', i.e., the 'stubborn lumps of dogma and the unyielding claims of revelation' with which Christianity clogged 'the flow of sentiment'.[97] For them, Socrates, as portrayed by Plato, was silenced because of his radical opinions.

    The 'radical' interpretation of Plato is usually attributed to James Mill's influence to both John Stuart Mill and George Grote, as subsequent chapters discuss in more detail. The first break from the traditional rendering of Plato and Socrates as pre-Christian saints, other than James Mill's reviews, appeared in an 1822 article titled 'The Republic of Plato'.[98] This overlooked article took note of the general neglect regarding Plato's works, and the negative reception of Plato's *Republic*, as it was 'thrown aside as mere chimera and reverie'. Even though Plato's *Republic* 'was addressed to a people of manners and circumstances so widely different', the writer argued, Plato's intentions deserved to be defended. Plato, it was claimed, was one of the few 'political writer[s]' who 'has kept his eye steadily fixed' on the greatest happiness of the society, identifying the obstacles which stood in its way and devising 'all the means in his powers for their removal'.[99]

Thus, very early in this article, Plato's work was cast under a very different light: Plato was no longer an obscure metaphysician or a proto-Christian. He was a great political writer who strove for the cause of the greatest happiness; a 'visionary' with 'exceptionable proposals', greatly different even from modern writers, who made 'no scruple of throwing aside' the 'happiness of the community' for the 'convenience of the governing aristocracy' when the two clashed. Furthermore, Plato's *Republic* was very important, because it illustrated 'the moral effects of a vicious government'; and, Plato was instructive even when some of his proposals were false.[100] Thus, though critical of the mainstream interpretations, this reading of Plato was different from the less well-known tradition of Plato as a sceptic which ran through the eighteenth century.

In addition, the writer argued that Plato examined the 'earliest impressions made upon' the minds of the citizens and attempted to filter ideas based on the possibility of negative impressions, while encouraging ideas that created positive ones. Plato's 'first and foremost of all securities' of just governance was education.[101] Proper education ensured the happiness of all classes; but if that was not possible, the writer added, 'to ensure the happiness of the whole [...] that of any particular part must be surrendered without reserve'. General happiness was to be achieved by associating one's own well-being with that of his/her fellow citizens. This system of education endowed citizens with the necessary virtues of social cooperation and was supplemented by Plato's 'remarkable regulations' in order to increase 'corporate and patriotic affections'.[102] Thus, the *Republic* was not based on 'horrid' principles; Plato employed all the means available to him in order to increase social happiness and social cooperation—an argument which would be made by James Mill as well.[103]

Many features of this article point to James Mill's influence, since during this time, his 'Government', originally published in 1820, had become the holy scripture of Radical politics. Thus, the writer referred to the greatest happiness of the community, argued against the 'convenience of the governing aristocracy' and compared Plato with Helvetius. Perhaps more importantly, the anonymous writer drew attention to the importance of Plato's insights on the moral influence that government has over its citizens and the cohesion of the polis. Moreover, like James Mill, and unlike Jeremy Bentham,[104] the writer argued for the instructiveness of Plato's ideas. However, unlike James Mill, the writer did not refer to either the identification of interest between rulers and ruled or the inquisitive nature of Plato's dialogues.

Also, around this time, George Grote wrote the brief essay 'The Character of Socrates', which was never published during Grote's life. Kyriakos Demetriou argues that there is not much evidence regarding James Mill's influence on this piece, because Grote did not draw particular attention to Socrates' inquisitive nature.[105] However, a brief analysis of the specific references to dialectics in the two 'utilitarian' pieces suggests that Grote was closer to James Mill's ideas than previously recognized. Grote argued that Socrates' attitude toward both physical and moral subjects was 'purely negative and elenctic, so as to refute the dogmatist and expose the insufficiency of his proofs without substituting any more certain conclusions'.[106] On the contrary, the anonymous writer—being closer than Grote to Macfait's view of Plato's method—argued that, in 'moral subjects', Plato's dialectical method had the 'power of investigation and analysis, accompanied with the capacity of stating and illustrating its results in conversation', which enabled 'a man to penetrate by means of his intellect, extricated from the disturbing influence of sensation, into the essence and reality of things' by unfolding the 'ratiocinative powers'—it was, thus, 'the leading purpose of all instruction'.[107]

While both accounts differed from Thomas Taylor's view of Plato's dialectics, the focus on the inquisitive and elenctic nature of the Platonic dialogues, advocated by the elder Mill two decades earlier, appeared primarily in Grote, while the educational value of Plato's dialectics—exercising one's 'ratiocinative powers'—was also highlighted in the *New Monthly* article.[108] Similarly, as we will see later on, in his own discussion of Plato's method, John Stuart Mill drew attention to the dialectic method's 'twofold obligation, to be able to maintain our opinions against the criticism of opponents and refute theirs, and never to use a term in serious discourse without a precise meaning'.[109] Two things stand out: first, in the radical view of Plato, the dialectic method can take anyone to the heart of arguments but not to the 'ineffable'; second, what was more important, to be able to engage in a dialectic exercise, 'τοῦ διδόναι καὶ δέχεσται λόγον', on any subject, required suitable social conditions, since not knowing in advance what the conclusion would be ran the risk of reaching a conclusion that would not be favorable to the religious and/or political status quo.[110]

Though Grote was not the only one to separate 'Socrates from the guise of a Christian saint, positive and doctrinaire' or call 'attention to the fact that the image of Socrates had been formed exclusively from the writings of his more enthusiastic pupils',[111] his novelty consisted in the concurrent favorable reception of Socrates' worth and the explanation for the negative reception of Socrates by his own contemporaries, including the Sophists (who were also favorably received by Grote): '[t]he Athenian public could only have known him as an expert sophist: to his disciples alone could he have appeared as wholesome or improving instructor'. Socrates, when dealing with the Sophists was 'altogether polemical and aggressive', seeking 'purely and simply to wound and disarm an antagonist'. Thus, 'the sympathies of an indifferent bystander, in a controversy so managed, are more likely to have been on the side of the defender than on that of the aggressor'.[112]

Grote's essay, however brief, marked a significant departure from previous analyses, since the Athenian democracy was defended against Socrates' failure to consider 'popular intervention' as a 'check upon' government. Grote attributed Socrates' unpopularity, first, to 'the special provocation of the eminent literati'; second, to 'the dislike of the general mass'; third, to Socrates being 'destitute of all those circumstances which dispose men to recognise pretension and to acquiesce in superiority' (i.e., 'poor and of no family distinction'); and, finally, Grote pointed to Socrates' professed opinions which were 'avowedly hostile to several essential parts of the democratical constitution' and 'did not harmonise either with oligarchical or democratical persons'.[113] Socrates was a Radical.

## CONCLUDING REMARKS

This final section explores how the often-noted diversity of readings of Plato in Victorian Britain can be traced back to the earlier 'period of neglect' of Platonic scholarship. By means of a concise discussion of Coleridge's complex portrait of Plato, 'the first of his spiritual ancestors',[114] this concluding section discusses the images of the prophetic, the sceptic and the idealist Plato, summarizing at the same time the above discussions.[115] Each portrait corresponds to a different contemporary controversial issue, as Frank Turner shows, which developed primarily in the search for a 'counterbalance to individualistic liberalism', highlighting both Plato's relevance and Coleridge's diversity of interests— Coleridge, more than anyone else, 'had a foot in more than one camp'.[116] However, the discussion of how Coleridge's Platonizing moral and political philosophy, 'revived and purified from impure mixtures',[117] shaped his ideas regarding the function of religion, education and government cannot not be discussed here.[118]

### The Prophetic Plato

Frank Turner discusses first a group of Victorian writers who appropriated Platonic philosophy in order to uphold 'vestiges of Christian or transcendental doctrines in the wake of utilitarian morality, positivist epistemology, and scientific naturalism'. As we saw, various writers had already employed Plato in the struggle against 'sensualists, materialists and sceptics'—those 'modern Sophists'. For them, Plato, a renowned non-Christian philosopher, had 'revealed' the existence of 'divine natures', i.e., those transcendental elements which substantiated as well as provided meaning and purpose to the material world.[119]

The move from Plato to Christianity was an easy one to make. Many had argued that Christian theology could be traced back to Plato—even though some resisted pointing to extensive anticipations, they would still, like writers in the late nineteenth century, criticize 'mystical' interpretations of Plato's doctrines, in support of a reading that was more in tune with Christianity. Like their late-century counterparts, they believed Plato offered an intuitive kind of knowledge, one that transcended 'logical or discursively reasoned' arguments, and they linked Plato's idea of the Good to a certain extent with the all-present God. As Turner shows, at no point did they consider Plato's philosophy to be identical with Christianity, maintaining a belief 'in the unique character of Christianity'.[120]

Having closely studied both Christian theology and the theology of Plato, Coleridge found profound religious ideas in 'Platonists' and 'Plotinists' alike and incorporated them into his discussions on the nature of philosophy, religion and

God.[121] Like many of his contemporaries, Coleridge suggested that Plato was a 'genuine prophet and anticipator' of Christianity. According to Coleridge, Plato, 'the wild-minded Disciple of Socrates', had correctly unified power, intelligence and benevolence, asserting their existence 'in God in an infinite Degree'. Like others that espoused a prophetic view of Plato, he noted that Christians had 'learned their Trinity in Unity' from Plato.[122] Thus, he shared Taylor's belief that Platonists and Plotinists taught that 'all things are God, and eternally indigent of God' and God to be 'the Good' itself, 'the only One, the purely and absolutely One'.[123]

Only the disciples of Plato's philosophy, Coleridge argued, could apprehend the notion of a Supreme Reason as the creator of the world—the Λόγος of the evangelists. Thus, to the materialist philosophy of Epicurus the idea of a 'causative thought' appeared contradictory—no substance could be created 'out of shadow'. But for a Platonist the idea that reason is causative was 'necessarily pre-supposed in every other truth', even if this was dressed 'in the garb of Nonsense'—the 'dear, gorgeous nonsense' that Coleridge loved.[124] Plato had managed to unite the 'speculative physiology' of Pythagorean philosophy with the moral philosophy of Socrates,[125] which Coleridge considered to be the nearest one to Christianity, as it was contrasted to that of Hartley and Locke.[126]

## The Sceptic Plato

As we saw, the usual representations of Plato highlighted both the importance and the novelty of the view that James Mill initiated and George Grote, most effectively, brought forward to the British public. Platonic scholarship had been so much associated with a specific 'cast of mind and philosophical proclivity' that when George Grote's book on Plato appeared in 1865 all, except John Mill, rushed to point to a paradox.[127] Thus, cast in the tradition of James Mill, both John Stuart Mill and George Grote sought to detach Plato's method from Plato's conclusions and argued both for its value in philosophical inquiry and for the general social and political preconditions necessary to foster such an inquiry.

Unlike writers that espoused a prophetic interpretation of Plato, writers that found a sceptical strain in Plato's thought were not restrained by any religious assumption. Thus, they were at liberty to employ Plato's method to criticize Plato's own doctrines, including the ones appropriated by religious advocates. Similarly, as Frank Turner illustrates,[128] agreement on the value of Plato's method did not lead to agreement about other aspects of Plato's dialogues. For example, Coleridge championed Plato's method, just like John Mill and Grote would do later in the century, but this did not necessarily mean that Coleridge shared their social or political vision—though, in the case of Mill this was much more complex.[129]

Coleridge believed that the Socratic method, an instance of 'decided genius and true science', was the 'progressive transition' or 'principle of progression' which appears 'in that just proportion, that union and interpenetration, of the universal and the particular'.[130] Plato's method was for Coleridge 'a distinct science, the offspring of philosophy'; the 'common end' that formed the 'larger and more valuable portion' of Plato's dialogues; one that completed and stood over the specific purpose of each dialogue: 'to establish the sources, to evolve the principles, and exemplify the art of method'. Coleridge, like James Mill, viewed Plato's method as the link 'by which philosophy becomes scientific and the sciences philosophical'.[131] Plato's dialectics, Coleridge argued, was that science of method which allowed 'secure and ever-progressive, though never-ending, investigation of truth and reality'.[132]

Moreover, Coleridge even argued that had Francis Bacon read Plato's original works unprejudiced, without confusing him with the 'absurdities and phantasms of his misinterpreters', he would have recognized that they were both chasing 'truth' from opposite ends.[133] Plato's purpose was 'not so much to establish any particular truth' but to remove obstacles in the pursuit of truth. Thus, Platonism was not an impediment to science. Coleridge believed that Plato allowed room for speculation on the question of how to reach scientific ends whether 'we must set out from principles or ascend towards them'.[134]

Coleridge's inquisitive Plato (though not his prophetic Plato) resembled the Plato of the two Mills. Many years after James Mill's reviews on Taylor's *Plato*, Coleridge commented that Plato's dialogues were 'preparatory' or 'logical exercises for the mind', and that '[l]ittle that is positive is advanced in them'. Like the two Mills, Coleridge argued that Plato's method aimed to educate the intellect, 'by awakening the principle and method of self-development'; not by cramming information, but by creating the circumstances that would 'gradually excite the germinal power that craves no knowledge but what it can take up into itself, what it can appropriate, and re-produce in fruits of its own'.[135]

In his lectures on the history of philosophy (1818-9), Coleridge noted another way to read Plato's dialogues: the Platonic dialogues did not 'convey the peculiar opinions of Plato'.[136] For Coleridge, Plato's dialogues offered nothing concrete or systematic in reference to Plato's ideas—a view shared by James Mill. But Coleridge added that Plato's *unwritten* doctrines drew out the 'true' Plato—the 'esoteric' dimension of Plato's thought. The logical part of the dialogues—the best intellectual discipline 'till the time of Lord Bacon'— 'scientifically' studied the truth of established beliefs. The 'propaedeutic' part of Plato's dialogues, thus, highlighted the insufficiency of all current modes of thought. Coleridge was convinced that the Platonic dialogues were the means to identify those individuals that were ready for Plato's 'true' doctrines.[137]

## The Idealist Plato

Frank Turner has pointed to a link between the social and religious reconstruction that took place throughout nineteenth-century Britain with the appropriation of Plato, not as a prophet or a sceptic, but as the philosopher that provided an 'idealist surrogate for Christian social and political values'. Commercialism and self-interest were combated with Plato's ethics of self-sacrifice and duty to a higher social good. Late in the century, Kantian and Hegelian philosophy was infused in Platonic commentary to highlight and contest at once the inevitable shortcomings of an ancient philosopher, yet believed to provide indispensable wisdom in relation to modern British affairs. Plato's cast of mind seemed to allow late-Victorian British thinkers to place 'the divine above the human; the spiritual above the material, the one above the many, the mind before the body'. Thus, this group of writers, Turner argues, ignored or read metaphorically those parts of Plato's dialogues that did not serve the above aims. With 'unconscious self-deception', they believed Plato to adhere to the ideal of social unity and common purpose, devising various means to protect and strengthen the moral fabric of society, unifying the individual and the state in a 'single moral purpose'.[138]

Many argue that Coleridge was the founder of nineteenth-century British idealism.[139] But Coleridge did not strictly follow the traditional distinction between idealism and empiricism.[140] As he famously said, Aristotelians and Platonists 'are two classes of men, beside which it is next to impossible to conceive a third'.[141] Since both Mill and Coleridge branded themselves Platonists,[142] it is imperative to discuss the chasm that divides empiricism and idealism. Coleridge did so by looking into why Plato did not name Aristotle as his successor at the Academy.

Coleridge argued that there were irreconcilable differences between Plato's and Aristotle's philosophies. Aristotle's frame of mind could have never allowed him to see 'what Plato meant by an idea'.[143] An Idea, Coleridge added, is 'neither a sensation nor a perception'; 'neither individual (that is, a sensible intuition) nor general (that is, a conception)'; it 'neither refers to outward facts, nor yet is abstracted from the forms of perception contained in the understanding'. It is 'an educt of the imagination actuated by the pure reason, to which there neither is nor can be an adequate correspondent in the world of the senses'. It is a mysterious power, 'living, seminal, formative, and exempt from time'.[144]

Plato became Coleridge's ally in arguing that the thinking power itself and the power of will, rather than the senses, were the active powers that allowed the moral and intellectual being (the 'supersensual' nature of individuals) to come into contact with one's 'sensual' or corporeal nature and confirm one's intuitions. For Coleridge, Plato conceived the mind as a power that could discover the principles of truth, questioning its findings through the senses, whereas Aristotle began from the mind as an empty receiver. For Coleridge, Plato's idealism blended with his dialectical method.[145]

Thus, Plato tried to prepare the minds of his disciples for something which, Coleridge added, that of Aristotle was not capable to accept: 'propositions involving in themselves a contradiction in terms, are nevertheless true; and which, therefore, must belong to a higher logic—that of ideas'. They were contradictory only in Aristotelian logic, the instrument of understanding—the faculty of 'thinking and forming of judgments' about what one passively receives; reason is the 'power by which we become possessed of principles'. In works other than pure science, Coleridge added, 'definitions of necessity' do not precede reason, but follow it.[146]

However, Paul Shorey called the above reading of Plato's 'Reason', the 'Coleridgian poison' disseminated by Benjamin Jowett. For Plato, Shorey argued, logical contradictions called for one to define one's terms more carefully, not 'appeal to the higher logic'.[147] Similarly, remaining within the sceptic tradition of Platonic interpretation, John Stuart Mill believed that Plato's inconclusiveness in many dialogues illustrated that Plato's 'dogmatic conclusions' in other dialogues were more likely to be 'poetic fancies', whereas for Coleridge, Plato's inconclusiveness was a demonstration of 'the inadequacy of the discursive understanding' and 'the need for something beyond it'— something 'eternal amid the temporal and passing phenomena of the world of time and space'.[148]

Plato defined the common ground between reason and experience 'in a supersensual essence', Coleridge argued, 'which being at once the ideal of the reason and the cause of the material world, is the pre-establisher of the harmony in and between both'. Thus, he concluded, Plato made religion 'the ultimate aim of philosophy'.[149] Religion had primacy over all other aspects of culture, being 'the root and trunk of the knowledge' of civilized man, Coleridge maintained, giving 'unity and the circulating sap of life to all other sciences'. It gave unity to society, through the Clerisy, whose aim would be to produce and reproduce, preserve, continue and perfect 'the necessary sources and conditions of national civilization'. Education would be the key to this unity, as Coleridge believed that '[t]he perfect frame of a man is the perfect frame of a state', referring to the unity of a person's reason, understanding and will.[150]

Plato was indeed the 'sunny mist' or 'luminous gloom'[151] which drew people from various directions. For those who read Plato through the 'pseudo-mystics', 'Phantasts' and Plotinists (who joined 'Theurgy with philosophy' and reduced the latter 'into magic and mere mysticism'),[152] he was a prophet, a 'consummate genius' who 're-asserted the idea of a God, the maker of the World'. For the students of Locke and Hartley, Plato was a seeker of truth, equipped with a scientific method capable of breaking through prejudices and prevailing beliefs— for them, most of Plato's dialogues were 'smoke and flash from the witch's caldron of a disturbed imagination'.[153] Precisely for this reason, Plato's dialogues appealed to 'Shelley and his friends'. In their works, Plato 'once more became an inspiration and a passion' in the nineteenth century,[154] identifying the transcendent, eternal and unifying Reason as Plato's most important gift to mankind.

# NOTES

1. Stopper, 1981:277-81.
2. Coleridge, 1854:V.266ff.

3. Evans, 1943:107; Turner, 1981:374; Glucker, 1987:150; Rogers, 1994:181, Demetriou, 1999:157.

4. See Vivenza, 2001; Garrett, 2004.

5. Clarke, 1959:71-2, 79.

6. Jenkyns, 1980:229, 236, 234, 245. See also, Turner, 1981:283; Blackburn, 2006:chs. 11-13.

7. Jenkyns, 1980:239; Burnham, 1977:209; Vigus, 2009:ch. 1. See further, Demetriou, 1999:chs. 5-6.

8. Turner, 1981:369; Demetriou, 1999:160. See also Blackie, 1857:2, 5-6, 14.

9. Evans, 1943:107; Rogers, 1994:181.

10. Demetriou, 1999:15; Vigus, 2009:13-4; Evans, 1943:107.

11. Spens, 1763:xl, xxxviii. Macfait, 1760:3.

12. Spens, 1763:xxxv; Geddes, 1748:73, 96.

13. Spens, 1763:xxxiv; Duff, 1767:96, 104-5, 112. See further, Demetriou, 1999:ch. 5.

14. Macfait, 1760:3; Duff, 1767:104.

15. See further, Marback, 1995. See also, for example, Floyer Sydenham's (1759) well-received introduction to Plato; still, his attempt at a complete translation of Plato was considered unnecessary (Anon., 1759:I.421-2). Sydenham eventually abandoned the task of such an edition due to lack of funds.

16. Macfait, 1760:206-7. For an excellent recent discussion on Plato's method see, Benson, 2006.

17. Geddes, 1748:140. See also, Macfait, 1760:68, 74.

18. Anon, 1759:I.422. See further, Rogers, 1994:181-3.

19. Some Victorian critics, such as Mark Pattison, consciously tried to 'break with what they regarded as the amateurish (though often brilliant) reviewing that had prevailed in the age of Macaulay and before' (Jones, 2007:56-7). See also, Demetriou, 1999:157.

20. Blackie, 1857:5-6 quoted in Turner, 1981:369; Demetriou, 1999:160.

21. B. Jowett to J.S. Blackie, 22/03/1865, in Turner, 1981:371n4.

22. Glucker, 1987:150; Turner, 1981:374. See also, Jenkyns, 1980:228; Prince, 1996:166; Rogers, 1994:181-5.

23. Turner, 1981:384-5

24. Glucker, 1987:150. See also, Demetriou, 1999:185-6.

25. Turner, 1981:370-5. See further, Demetriou, 1999:chs. 5-6.

26. Taylor, 1804:I.iv.

27. Taylor (1793:v) wrote with 'an eye to the commentaries of the latter Platonists' and drew mainly on Proclus, but also Plotinus, Porphyry, Iamblichus, Damascius and, to a lesser extent, on Ficino's Latin translation (whose Christianized Neoplatonism, Taylor rejected; see further, Webb, 1982:181ff). They were 'truly', he noted, the 'links of the golden chain of deity' (going back to Plato), freeing 'all that is sublime, all that is mystic in the doctrines of Plato [...] from its obscurity and unfold[ing] into the most pleasing and admirable light' (1804:lxxxviii). The 'Socratic, aporetic element in Plato for which these philosophers and theologians had no use' was entirely abolished (Tigerstedt 1974:7).

28. Taylor, 1804:lxxxvi.See also, Webb, 1982:181. The Platonic corpus was called, in one occasion, 'the SCRIPTURES of the ancient Heathen world' (Clark, 1806:189).

29. For example, Taylor's 'Proclus-ian' view always inspired Coleridge. The focus on Plato's transcendental elements suited the reactionary mood of the Romantic poets who sought something other than Aristotle's 'down to earth' philosophy (see further Evans, 1940; Raine, 1968:107-8; 1969:3, 8; Jenkyns, 1980:228-9; Webb, 1982:23).

30. Taylor, 1804:I.v-xxxvii. See, for example, Taylor's discussion of Plato's *Parmenides* on how Plato's theology 'most truly' revealed the 'ineffable exemption' from all things and the incomprehensible 'transcendency' of the highest God, being a 'scientific' account of the doctrine that God is all things.

31. Taylor, 1804:I.xxiv-xxv; xxxv. See further, Hedley, 2000:18-40; Vigus, 2009:16-9.

32. Taylor, 1804:I.lxiii.

33. *Ibid.* p. iv.

34. *Ibid.* pp. xxxv, lxxxvi.

35. *Ibid.* pp. lxxii, xxxv.

36. *Ibid.* p. lxix.

37. Taylor, 1797a:332.

38. Taylor, 1804:I.lxx.

39. *Ibid.* pp. lxxix, lxxxiii.

40. Axon, 1890:1, 7; Mouldon, 1901-4:V.291; Anon., 1794:248; Rigg, 1898:468. See also, Taylor, 1790.

41. Taylor was not well-received as a Greek scholar in general (e.g., Wood, 1802). See also, Raine, 1969:19.

42. Anon., 1804b:I.130. For James Mill's review, see *infra*, chapter three.

43. Anon., 1804a:544.

44. Anon., 1804a:338-46; Anon., 1804b: parts II and III; Anon., 1804c:322-6; Anon., 1806:579-91. Floyer Sydenham's translations were highly praised by these critics.

45. Anon., 1804b:IV.139.

46. Anon., 1804a:338.

47. Anon., 1804c:323, 325.

48. Anon., 1806:578-9.

49. Anon., 1804c:323.

50. Anon., 1804b:I.131-2; Anon., 1804a:347; Anon., 1804c:323-4. Similarly, Charles Crawford (1773:xvii) had argued that the 'latter Platonicians' raised 'a superstructure that [was] altogether grotesque and uncouth' to Plato's already 'flimsey foundation for science'.

51. Anon., 1804b:I.129-30, 122; II.286.

52. Anon., 1804c:326.

53. Anon., 1804b:II.276-7.

54. *Ibid.* pp. 286, 283. Thus, the reviewer adhered to the common view concerning Socrates' relation to the Athenian Democracy (see also, *ibid.* III.9).

55. *Ibid.* III.8

56. Anon., 1804c:322. See also, H. Walpole to M. Baroness Holland, 26/11/1789, in Cunningham, 1866:IX.237 (see also, Webb, 1982:182; Raine, 1969:27).

57. Anon., 1804a:347.

58. Anon., 1804c:323-4; Anon., 1806:578-9. See also, Taylor, 1797b:519.

59. These 'obstacles' are mentioned in Rogers, 1994:181-3.

60. Gillies, 1809:III.127, 129.

61. *Ibid.* p. 131. See also, Mitchell:1820:I.cxxxix-cxliv, cl.

62. Gillies, 1809:III.502.

63. *Ibid.* pp. 522, 507-12. At the bottom of Plato's doctrine of ideas and ethical theory, Gillies argued, lay a system of theogony and cosmogony.

64. *Ibid.* pp. 516, 518.

65. Mitford, 1838:IV.128.

66. *Ibid*. IV.131-5. Unlike Gillies, Mitford did not believe that Aristophanes played a part in Socrates' death (Gillies, 1809:III.128; see also, Jackson, 1802:306-7). Mitchell, in his detailed discussion of this aspect of Socratic commentary, argued that Plato's and Aristophanes' accounts of Socrates were not so different (1820:cxxx. See also, Anon., 1821a:433-4).

67. Mitford, 1838:IV.127-8.

68. Priestley, 1803:16.

69. Matthews, 1821:557-8.

70. Mitford, 1838:IV.130; Jackson, 1802:312.

71. Jackson, 1802:316, 321-3.

72. Jackson, 1802:308-39. See also, Priestley, 1803:11-3.

73. Matthews, 1821:559.

74. Mitford, 1838:IV.127, 129.

75. Priestley, 1803:1-3.

76. Jackson, 1802:329 (see also, Ireland, 1809:235, 241, 321, 325).

77. Priestley, 1803:21-6.

78. *Ibid*. p. 30; Jackson, 1802:334.

79. Potter, 1831:10, 10n. See also, Priestley, 1804:121ff. It seems that this was an attitude toward Socrates which can be traced back to Shaftesbury (Jaffro, 2008:257).

80. Potter, 1831:331-3. See also, Priestley, 1803:5. Throughout the eighteenth century, this interpretation offered an alternative to prominent Neoplatonic readings (to which the English translations of A. Dacier's French edition of Plato and Ficino's Latin edition gave credence. See further, Tigerstdt, 1974:45).

81. Priestley, 1803:6; 1804:135. For this reason, Priestley engaged in a thorough comparison between Jesus and Socrates, discussing differences of character, method, purpose, content and target of their teachings, aiming to justify the known maxim that 'the life and death of Socrates carry the marks of a sage, the life and death of Jesus proclaim a God' (Priestley, 1803:33-48; 1804:149-53. See also, Morgan, 1795).

82. Jackson, 1802:301.

83. Potter, 1831:ii-iii.John Potter specified as modern sceptics (and 'sceptic-makers') those who advocated a system of utility.

84. Jackson, 1802:304.

85. Mitchell, 1820:I.cxxviii.

86. Anon., 1821b:77. See also, Priestley, 1804.

87. Matthews, 1821:555 (See also, Redding, 1860:I.191).

88. Matthews views echoed those of the Saint-Simonians; according to John Mill such ideas were common in Europe from early in the century (*A*:I.171-4; SA[1]:XXII.230-4).

89. Matthews, 1821:555.

90. *Ibid*. pp. 556-7.

91. *Ibid*. pp. 560-2.

92. *Ibid*. p. 565-7.

93. Priestley, 1804:147.

94. Potter, 1831:10, 13-14 (see further, Potter, 1845).

95. Clarke, 1959:101-2. See also, Sewell, 1841.

96. Symonds, 1897:42 in Jenkyns, 1980:229. See also George Adams's tragedy on Socrates' death (1746). The wisdom and virtue of Socrates, T.B. Macaulay noted, provided an 'incomparable and inestimable' 'example of benevolence, patience, and self-possession', even when his reasoning did not (Trevelyan, 1907:65).

97. Jenkyns, 1980:230. See further, Levi, 1956; Turner, 1981:265; Sullivan, 2009:154.
98. This was a subject initially deemed 'too uninteresting' (Redding, 1860:I.313).
99. Anon, 1822:I.512.
100. *Ibid.* See especially the third part of this article, in which also the writer in passing compares Plato's originality on social influences with the theory of Helvetius.
101. Anon, 1822:I.513-7; II.69-70. The 'noble lie' and the lack of property for the ruling class were some other securities.
102. Anon, 1822:II.70-3. Patriotic sentiments created 'an entire community of pleasure and pain' without 'becoming at all separated and individualized'. T.B. Macaulay (Trevelyan, 1907:58) made a similar note of Plato's 'Patriotism'; at the same time, he did justice to Plato's originality concerning women, unlike the anonymous writer.
103. Anon, 1822:III.153-4, See further, chapter three. Interestingly, according to the author, Plato was more democratic than Hobbes, since Plato's exclusion of the majority from power was based on the 'universal doctrine, that no man is to exercise more than one calling', whereas Hobbes' exclusion was 'founded upon radical mistrust of their soundness and capability' (Anon, 1822:III.156n).
104. See further, Bentham, 1983b:135, 137. As John Mill noted (B:X.90), Bentham's views on Plato and Socrates were put in terms 'distressing to his greatest admirers'.
105. Demetriou, 1996a:37.
106. Grote, c1825-6:45.
107. Anon., 1822:III.154.
108. See also, Grote, c1825-6:44, 46.
109. J.S. Mill, GP:XI.411.
110. See chapters four and six.
111. Demetriou, 1996a:43.
112. Grote, c1825-6:44-6. Grote, like others as we saw, believed that though Aristophanes caricatured Socrates, he 'must have suited his picture to the preconceptions of the mass of spectators' (*Ibid.* p. 45). Macaulay also sketched a similar portrait of Socrates' 'annoying' habits (Trevelyan, 1907:59)
113. Grote, c1825-6:46-7. For an alternative view of Socrates' fate, see Malkin, 1829:91.
114. Pater, 1866:111. See also, Ogilvie, 1964:81.
115. For more details on the 'many-sided and contradictory' Plato (Ogilvie 1964:122), see Turner, 1981:ch. 8; Demetriou, 1999:chs. 5-6; Lane, 2001:ch. 2. As there are many studies that examine in detail Plato's influence on the Romantic poets, I do not attempt a similar discussion here (e.g., Evans, 1940; Notopoulos, 1949; Burnham, 1977:ch. 2; Jenkyns, 1980:ch. 10; Sotelo, 2006:part I).
116. Turner, 1981:374-5.
117. Coleridge, 1854:III.342. See Gregory (2003:ch. 3) for a more detailed discussion of the relation of Coleridge's 'anachronistic conformation of ancient philosophy to contemporary controversial needs' (Gregory, 2003:118, 92-3).
118. James Vigus (2009) offers so far the best discussion on Coleridge's Platonism.
119. See also, Turner, 1981:374-6, 380.
120. *Ibid.* pp. 376-9, 381-3. See further, Demetriou, 1999:150-1.
121. S.T. Coleridge to W. Sotheby, 26/08/1802 (in 1895b:I.406); Hedley, 2000:33-40. See further, Hunt, 1976.
122. Coleridge, 1795:208-9. See also, Hedley, 2000:36-7; Turner, 1981:382-3.

123. Coleridge was not one of those who hastened to dismiss Taylor's works, which formed part of his 'darling Studies', as meaningless (1895a:50, 17; 1854:III.322-3; S.T. Coleridge to J. Thelwall, 19/11/1796, in 1895b:I.181).

124. Coleridge, 1795:208-9; 1854:I.479; II.422; S.T. Coleridge to J. Thelwall, 31/12/1796, in 1895b:I.211.

125. Coleridge, 1818-9:I.216-7; 1854:VI.276. See also, Turner, 1981:382.

126. Coleridge, 1854:IV.22-2; 1895a:259-60 (See further, Haven, 1959). For John Muirhead (1930:115) the theological extension of Coleridge's metaphysics was 'what is most mediaeval, and perhaps repulsive, in English Platonism'.

127. Turner, 1981:385.

128. *Ibid.* pp. 383-414.

129. See further, Irwin, 1998; Giorgini, 2009.

130. Coleridge, 1854:II.416-7.

131. *Ibid.* pp. 429, 422. See also, Schleiermacher, 1833.

132. Coleridge, 1854:II.446. See further, Perkins, 1997.

133. Coleridge, 1854:II.425n, 445; VI.88n. However, Bacon did note the originality of Plato's method (1645:122-3, something which James Mill did made a note of in his copy of Bacon's book).

134. Coleridge, 1854:II.429-30, 419. Pamela Edwards (2004:142) discusses how Coleridge saw 'Platonism as a superior ground for natural science rather than an impediment to it'.

135. Coleridge, 1854:VI.276 (*Table Talk*, 08/05/1824), 302 (*Table Talk*, 30/04/1830); II.429-30.

136. Coleridge, 1818-9:I.110-241; Coburn, 1934:434.

137. Coleridge, 1818-9:I.182-3, 186, 189-94. See further, Edwards, 2004:142-3; Vigus, 2009:ch. 5.

138. Turner, 1981:417-20.

139. Muirhead, 1931:125, 413; Turner, 1981:419, 427. See, Haven, 1959; Hunt, 1976; Vigus, 2009.

140. Turner, 1981:374-5, 414-46. Edwards, 2004:142.

141. Coleridge, 1854:VI.336 (*Table Talk*, 02/07/1830).

142. E.g., J.S. Mill, *A*:I.24-5; Coleridge, 1854:III.342.

143. Coleridge, 1818-9:I.218-21; 1854:VI.336 (*Table Talk*, 02/07/1830).

144. Coleridge, 1854:I.484; III.213n. See further, Vigus, 2009:47-8.

145. Coleridge, 1818-9:I.228-9, 232. See further, Haven, 1959.

146. Coleridge, 1854:VI.302 (*Table Talk*, 30/04/1830); II.164n. See also, Turk, 1988:70.

147. Shorey, 1938:224-5. See further, Vigus, 2009:104ff.

148. Cunliffe, 1994:209; Notopoulos, 1949:17, 213. See also, J.S. Mill, *A*:I.25.

149. Coleridge, 1854:II.422.

150. *Ibid.* VI.53-5, 57-9; I.457. See further, Perry, 2002:130; Kitson, 2002:167.

151. Coleridge, 1895a:31.

152. Coleridge, 1854:VI.129-30, 347 (*Table Talk*, 24/09/1830). Coleridge (1854:V.267) noted at some point that there were 'echoes', not anticipations of the Christian faith in Plato and he resisted comparing Jesus and Socrates (VI.498, *Table Talk*, 03/01/1834; see also, 1818-9:I.197); see further, Vigus. 2009:118.

153. Coleridge, 1854:VI.302 (*Table Talk*, 30/04/1830), 347 (24/09/1830); I.475.

154. Jenkyns, 1980:228; Vigus, 2009:16. See further, Raine, 1968 and 1969; Webb, 1993; Wheeler, 1999.

# CHAPTER THREE

## JAMES MILL ON PLATO

It is no secret that James Mill admired Plato. All those who knew him were aware of how he felt most indebted to Plato 'for his own mental culture', as his eldest son put it. For such 'a keen student of Plato', Plato's dialectics did not remain the only trace of influence; he recommended Plato's works to young students as much for their ability to sharpen the intellect as for their 'moral impressions'.[1] Thus, George Grote, three decades after James Mill's death, pointed to the elder Mill as 'the one who stood least remote from the lofty Platonic ideal of Dialectic'.[2] Similarly, John Black, editor of *The Morning Chronicle*, had heard James Mill 'speak with great warmth of the impression which the writings of Plato made on his youth', leading him to 'regulate his conduct strictly according to an elevated ethical standard'.[3]

James Mill's Scottish education played a great part in the formation of his lifelong philosophical interests.[4] His lasting engagement with Plato thus began at Edinburgh; while a revival of Plato was underway throughout the British Isles.[5] In this Scottish center of Enlightenment, Mill combined a Presbyterian training with the 'inspiration of the Greeks', according to his biographer, and acquired 'the destructive weapons of criticism from the scientific spirit of the age'. He also developed a strong background in logic and 'mental philosophy', commenced his studies in historical and social philosophy and acquired 'a dead set at Plato'. He must have raised some eyebrows at the university library, when as a second-year divinity student he added Plato to an already unusual reading list.[6]

His early study of Plato, his reputation as a Greek scholar (which led to his being offered the Greek chair at the University of Glasgow in 1818), his son's education as well as the copious citations of ancient Greeks in his *Commonplace*

43

*Books* have been used to point out his high regard for ancient Greek thought and suggest possible influences in his works.[7] Such suggestions highlight the need to explore the elder Mill's atypical take of Plato's dialogues and draw out those 'platonic' ideas, if any, which seem to inform his political and ethical thought. First, I discuss Mill's view of Plato's dialogues as it appeared in his two reviews of Thomas Taylor's *The Works of Plato* (1804) as well as in later writings. Then, I turn to consider how the elder Mill appropriated ideas found in Plato's dialogues; his attitudes toward education and utility are thus also briefly discussed. Though the first part of this chapter supplies new material on Mill's more or less known place in the history of British Platonic scholarship, the second part brings out the rarely discussed platonic proclivities in his writings. However peculiar a Platonist James Mill may have been, this chapter suggests a break from the traditional position that views Bentham as 'the spiritual father of Mill' and James Mill as the blind adherent to, and propagandist of, Bentham's principles.[8]

# RADICALIZING PLATO

## Plato: A Sceptic, Not a Dreamer

As we saw, James Mill agreed with the general estimation of 'Plato Taylor', which was discussed in the previous chapter. However, this agreement ended in Mill's discussion on Plato's method; not only did he argue for a different kind of usefulness of Plato's dialogues, but also his Plato developed into a completely different philosopher.[9]

Like other reviewers, James Mill took issue with Taylor's translation. The translator's task, as Mill perceived it, is to proceed in accordance with the merits of the language of translation and not the original; translated texts ought to preserve the true nature, spirit and tendencies of the original text in eloquent English—supplemented with explanations and instructions.[10] Taylor's translations had failed on all counts. Taylor also failed to transfer the simple pleasure of reading Plato's 'charming and elegant' dialogues, by choosing 'literary exactness' for the few who did not need the translation over intelligible English for the numerous readers who did. More importantly, Taylor's translational failings, most evident in translations of Plato's abstract discussions, caused interpretational problems by misrepresenting key arguments.[11] There are great things to be learned from antiquity, Mill argued, if ancient texts are read properly, but Taylor's shortcomings diminished much of Plato's overall utility.

However, James Mill argued that Taylor's edition was inadequate primarily because Taylor failed to distinguish between Plato and Neoplatonism. Mill refused to accept that Plato held the 'mysterious and visionary speculations of the latter Platonists' more strongly than other critics.[12] Accordingly he argued Taylor had 'not elucidated, but covered [Plato] over with impenetrable darkness'. Plato, the 'truly philosophic friend of Socrates', had nothing to do with his 'diadohoi' (his successors); Mill expected the 'striking difference' between Plato's and their speculations to be 'distinctly pointed out'.[13]

According to James Mill, a good translation of Plato's dialogues, 'an eminent part of the precious remains of ancient literature', would give access to sources of 'improvement and pleasure'. Moreover, Plato's ingenious and eloquent dialogues—philosophy could not be better pursued than in a dialogic form—were most appropriate for 'sharpening' the 'ingenuity of youth' and 'engendering' 'the love of science and of virtue':[14] there was nothing 'more calculated to sharpen the faculties; to render acute in discerning, and ingenious in exposing fallacies; to engender a love for mental exercise; and to elevate with the ambition of mental excellence'. What is more important, Mill highlighted Plato's dialectics 'as a method of scientific inquiry as well as a practical instrument of education and inspiration' concurrently with Friedrich Schleiermacher.[15]

In Plato's dialogues, James Mill argued, though both sides of a question are investigated, nothing positive is ever affirmed, except when 'what concerned virtue' was the subject at hand. Thus, *epochê* did not constitute Plato's aim; rather, he aimed 'to refute the tenets and expose the ignorance of some of those sophists who travelled about Greece'. Mill argued that due to Plato's metaphorical language and metaphysical reasoning commentators mistook Plato's 'rapid and hasty conjectures' and 'hypotheses' for his 'fixed and deliberate opinions', even when they did recognize that Plato wrote 'in a manner between jest and earnest'.[16]

Like his father, the younger Mill did find 'proof' that Plato, 'always in his poetics', wrote in jest, rather than earnest, which he considered to justify his belief that Plato had no dogma. John Mill pointed to *Phaedrus* (265c-d), in which Socrates says that all the discussion up to a certain point was a mere 'play' or 'sport'; and to *Philebus* (28c), in which Socrates calls the previous discussion as 'playful' (παίζειν).[17] These passages led the younger Mill to remark that 'Plato's poetics' were always written in playful manner ('[ἐ]ν παιδιᾷ' in the first case; 'in joke' in the second). On both occasions, the dialogue proceeds immediately to classification and dialectical analysis of the concepts at hand. Thus, both Mills, where Plato's language was not written in '*jeux d'esprit*', found insightful 'hypotheses'.[18]

Though he was 'steeped in Platonism' at Edinburgh University,[19] James Mill's interpretation of Plato was influenced by Cicero. Mill cited Cicero as 'authority [...] sufficient to confirm [his] opinion respecting the writings of Plato': for Cicero, Socrates never asserted an opinion himself but always strove to reveal the limitations of popular beliefs, primarily diffused by the Sophists. Mill, as many others, accepted that Socrates 'was said to have brought philosophy down from heaven to earth', as metaphysics did not seem to contribute as much to 'advancement in life' as the discovery of the rules and motives of good conduct. Mill seemed to believe that it was only through Plato's method that the rules and motives of good conduct could be discovered: Plato's dialectics deconstructed traditional modes of thinking, and allowed philosophical (or scientific) inquiries by supposing nothing in advance. Because of this method, not only was committing Plato to any particular doctrine unjustifiable, but also it was untrue to Plato's reasoning and intent.[20] When Plato conceived that 'seeing the one in the many' and 'the many in the one' as the business of philosophy, Mill argued in 1835, he merely referred to the operation of classing as many objects as possible under one head.[21]

Though Plato could affirm some opinions more than others, Mill argued, these could not form doctrines by themselves; in the attempt to enlist Plato's authority to their writings, the 'Alexandrian worthies' 'dreamed' the Platonic dogmas—Plato's ideas were often 'misrepresented, for the benefit of jug[gernaut]'.[22] Mill thus considered himself justified in thinking that Plato, 'even in the most serious dialogues', developed his expository arguments 'only for a momentary or particular purpose' and 'by no means as fixed and deliberate opinions'. By following Cicero, Mill viewed Plato wholly as an inquisitive philosopher, who defined the ideal method of deliberating upon matters of practical importance.[23]

Some commentators are reluctant to attribute to James Mill a 'ciceronian' reading of Plato; however, such an interpretation would account for Mill's choice to ignore the ancient distinction between inquisitive and expository dialogues.[24] Moreover, given that Cicero's works served as the basis of the teaching of moral philosophy '[f]rom the sixteenth century onwards', it would not have been so strange for Mill to go back to Cicero's authority.[25] James Mill's 'ciceronian' reading of Plato may have been corroborated, if not influenced, by Michel de Montaigne's *Essais* (1580). There is evidence that James Mill read the essay 'Apologie de Raimond de Sebonde', in which Montaigne rejected the mystic and idealist Plato for the sceptic.[26] Mill's rejection of Plato's metaphysical doctrines as merely arguments of 'momentary purpose' seems to echo Montaigne: '*Je ne me persuade pas aysement qu' Epicurus, Platon et Pythagoras nous ayent donné pour argent contant leurs Atomes, leurs Idées et leurs Nombres. Ils estoient trop sages pour establir leurs articles de foy de chose si incertaine et si debatable*'.[27] Similarly, a few pages earlier, Montaigne had noted that some

> *ont estimé Plato dogmatiste; les autres, dubitateur; les autres, en certaines choses l'un, et en certaines choses l'autre. Le conducteur de ses dialogismes, Socrates, va tousjours demandant et esmouvant la dispute, jamais l'arrestant, jamais satisfaisant, et dict n'avoir autre science que la science de s'opposer.*[28]

Thus, Mill was as undisturbed as Montaigne, by Plato's ability 'to defend contrary opinions with equal effectiveness'. According to Montaigne, Plato loved that mode of philosophizing and purposely adopted it '*pour loger plus decemment en diverses bouches la diversité et variation de ses propres fantasies*'.[29]

Despite the many differences between the two reviews and the great changes in his personal life, Mill's view of Plato did not change; neither did the nucleus of his critique to Taylor. But Mill's style and focus did change; irony and ridicule became his primary weapons of criticism and classical studies at the universities were added as an enemy—little did prosody form habits of 'looking into frivolous things' or do justice to the 'superlatively good things' found in ancient texts. Still, with regard to Plato's value, while Mill was evidently employing Benthamite language, his references to the principles of reform and utility in the 'twenty-four angry pages' (as Kathleen Raine has put it) of his 1809 review remained within the outline of his 1804 review.[30] '[C]learly an able scholar', Frank Evans notes, the *Edinburgh Review* critic (unaware that the reviewer was James Mill), 'had certainly not gone very far in Plato', expressing typical eighteenth-century views.[31] But there was nothing typical in Mill's discussion of Plato's attempt to 'expose some of the false impressions which are most apt to prevail in the minds of men, and to lead to the most dangerous consequences'— what James Mill and Jeremy Bentham called 'political fallacies' was similar in purpose. Thus, Mill was one of the initiators of that, as Richard Jenkyns has noted, 'critical spirit of Socratic questioning' which appeared in the search for 'a more rational, more democratic, and more secular' Britain.[32]

## The Philosopher and the Radical

I have already discussed in previous chapters how the standpoint from which modern critics read ancient texts was most likely to influence what they found important in them rather than vice versa. Thus, John Glucker argues that Mill, because of his contact with Bentham, ascribed to Plato 'Benthamite' features, while Kyriakos Demetriou, following Robert Fenn, notes that the elder Mill 'tried to make Plato into a utilitarian'.[33] These claims were connected to Fenn's remark that Mill 'was in the habit of pillaging classics for support for radical arguments'.[34] Thus, the elder Mill is criticized of having done the same thing that he, and many others, accused the Neoplatonists of having done: bending Plato's words to match their convictions.

But did James Mill 'pillage' Plato to support radical arguments? First, as we saw, the elder Mill believed ancient texts to be an invaluable source of wisdom. Second, he did not confine himself to finding Plato's dialogues to be consistent or inconsistent according to a particular dogma. Hence, he could select from Plato's works those 'hypotheses' or 'philosophical conjectures' of momentary purpose (which he considered most ingenious or philosophically illustrative) and employ them in arguments of an equally fleeting purpose. And so he did. Plato was one of the authorities that confirmed Mill's views on education and liberty of the press; also, a quotation from Plato's *Republic* strategically surfaces to clarify his position on the expansion of the franchise. Likewise, he utilized passages from Plato's *Republic* in his attempt to answer the Whig critics of his article 'Government'. His CPBs abound with various quotations from Plato, ready-to-use references as per his projects demanded. Thus, it seems that Plato's authority was indeed employed in support of James Mill's radicalism.

However, I want to suggest that the relationship ran deeper. Mill's belief in the power of education regarding character formation is well known.[35] In 1812, writing about the poor and their education, amid the controversy over the monitorial educational systems, James Mill noted that the character of individuals depends much upon the circumstances created by the government; a position that he would often repeat more or less unaltered, always strategically concise, in his arguments on educational reform

> Where the government is good, the people are virtuous: Where the government is bad, the people are vitious [sic]: The qualities of the people may always be taken as a criterion, and that an exact one, of the practical operation of the political system.[36]

Plato appeared first in Mill's list of authorities that shared this maxim.

James Mill examined social and political influences on character formation in more detail in his famous essay 'Education'. But, there, Plato's name is not invoked. Mill named the government's ability to shape the character of its citizens, through its various institutions and practices, 'Political Education'. Character depended on 'the direction given to the desires and passions of men'; a direction that is determined, he maintained, by associating 'admirable qualities' in individuals (e.g., 'great intelligence, perfect self-command, and over-ruling benevolence'), not wicked ones (e.g., 'flattery, back-biting, treachery'), with the 'grand objects of desire'.[37] However, Mill did not employ Plato's authority to support this radical (however indirect) claim for reform in the ways people think and act about education, even though he had located an 'admirable dissertation' by Plato on how '*Morals and Intellect of the People* [are] *always what the Government makes them*' and was confident that Plato had proved that society and government were '*the grand instruments of education*'.[38]

Furthermore, just as government has power to do 'good' through education, Mill argued, it has also power to do 'evil'. Thus, in order for political education not to create 'habits of servility and toleration of arbitrary power', it needs to be 'joined to another inestimable blessing': the liberty of the press.[39] The press was awarded the role of a 'high and constant observer' in checking whether the conduct of those who rule and the institutions of the government in general did not betray the people's trust to pursue the common good, by pursuing their own alone.[40] This important 'security' was discussed in another *Encyclopaedia Britannica* article. Once again, though Plato's name does not come up there, Mill's notes are replete with quotes and references to Plato. Uncensored press, Mill seemed to argue, had the Socratic function to help people develop the ability to form their own estimate of things; freedom of discussion 'is the only security which the people can have for the prevalence of truth'. Hindering the diffusion of opinions that are not favorable to authority established 'the doctrine "that justice is what interests the stronger"', as 'truth is not left to the support of her own evidence' through an unbiased and thorough examination of the evidence on both sides of any matter.[41] However, Mill once again did not use any of Plato's 'admirable' passages he collected to support his argument that uncensored discussion—done properly—protects the common interest, by pursuing truth (as it is never wrong to bring bad qualities or actions 'to light') and by checking that the government acts not for the gratification of individual pleasures but for the good of the whole community.[42]

Plato's authority was invoked in Mill's essay 'Ballot'. There, Mill paraphrased the well-known maxim, found in Plato's *Republic*, 'δεῖ[ν], ὅταν τῳ ἤδη βίος ᾖ, ἀρετὴ ἀσκεῖν', as '[a] man has peculiar advantages for attaining the highest excellence of his nature, when he is above the necessity of labouring for the means of subsistence'.[43] With this piece of ancient advice, Mill argued for the need that 'government should be placed in the hands of the Αριστοι'; not only those who were truly excellent, the best (the Greek sense of Βέλτιστοι), but those who could also afford the time needed to focus solely on their duties to govern, i.e., 'the Αριστοι and Βελτιστοι'.[44] Only they, he maintained, had the opportunity to cultivate these excellences, and create the conditions to diffuse them to all.[45] However, though Mill's Platonism 'was a contributing factor to his elitism',[46] Fenn tries to explain, Mill's call to 'the Rich' should not be taken as evidence of 'a growing conservatism'; it was a way to force the governing elite to attend to the needs of a majority (through an extended franchise) that could not pursue politics themselves (though they were still able to find the fittest to do so on their behalf).[47] Not only did this secure good government, it provided also a proof of the fitness of those who governed (serving the common good). Thus, Mill indeed discovered 'a healthy democratic side to Greek thought'.[48]

The above show that James Mill appropriated many Platonic ideas, while at the same time he rejected Plato's undemocratic conclusions. But this appropriation does not show that Mill was unconscious, as Fenn says, of the contradiction.[49] Rather, it demonstrates his selective reading of Plato.[50] James Mill considered Plato a very important ally in his call for reform; an ally who argued also for a specialized government, designed to pursue the happiness of all, not just one class—through educational, political and economic reform.[51]

In his *Fragment on Mackintosh* (1835), Mill employed various authorities to defend the position advanced in his 'Government', against James Mackintosh's (as well as T.B. Macaulay's) critique. He did not expand much on the criticisms of his method, but focused mainly on the arguments about the best way of achieving identity of interests since all that interested him was 'to shew, by what means good legislation can be effected'.[52] Mill first noted that good government is defined by the pursuit of the happiness of all the citizens. Then, he argued that the pursuit of one's own happiness was a 'universal principle of human action'. Thus, Mill concluded, the best security for a good government was to identify, through 'any contrivance', the interest of the rulers with that of the ruled.[53] Plato's *Republic*, Mill noted, was 'in many of its parts, a masterly development' of this principle.[54]

Plato's guardians, Mill argued, were intelligent, capable and cared for the interests of the community; in Plato, care was found in the things one loved. Thus, according to Mill's interpretation of Plato, good government was secured when one's own interests as well as others' were promoted through the 'same events'. Then people pursue both 'with the same constancy' and become happy or unhappy in the same ways. Different interests posed a danger: things that make one group happy may make another unhappy. If the same things produce pleasure and the same things produce pain, to the greatest number, no faction between various groups can threaten the state. The greater the unity, Mill wrote through Plato, the better the state is governed: unless there is such a unity, the rulers become wolves, not guardians.[55]

Thus, it not being possible for him to think of the 'divine principle of representation', Mill argued, Plato had 'bent the whole force of his penetrating mind' to find other means to effect this unity.[56] In a similar manner, Mill tried to find the best means to secure good government and good legislation, by identifying the interests of the law-makers with those of the community (i.e., by the election of 'real representatives'). He did not try to explain 'the immense variety of political facts' (passions, habits, opinions and prejudices discovered by experience); though he did believe that any complete account of human nature should be able to explain such facts. Like Plato's Socrates in *Republic*, James Mill thought that a number of little changes would in time lead to a substantial reform of any state of affairs, including personal, but above all social.[57]

## JAMES MILL'S 'PLATONISM'

At no stage in his life did Mill attribute a dogmatic side to Plato; he insisted that the emergence of a dogmatic Plato was a creation of later commentators. Thus, it is important to bear in mind that James Mill was often led to exaggeration regarding the 'sagacious mind of Plato'.[58] Still, many of the elder Mill's writings display his indebtedness to Plato's method, especially his *Analysis of the Phenomena of the Human Mind* (1829).[59] If it is the adoption of Plato's method, not the subscription to his 'dogmatical conclusions', which awards the 'title of Platonist', as John Stuart Mill claimed, then the elder Mill was surely a Platonist. Concurrently, James Mill's unshaken reverence for Plato casts doubt over the pervasive nature of Bentham's influence.[60]

In many articles, e.g., 'Government' or 'Liberty of the Press', Mill did not employ Plato's authority in support of ideas he thought widely accepted.[61] But as Plato's dialogues showed to Mill, people accepted qualities or things to be praiseworthy, when they thought themselves included in the praise.[62] Thus, a quote here or there from an accredited philosopher led people who did not agree with Mill's conclusions, to feel more comfortable with his premises.[63] But once his premises were accepted, Mill believed that his conclusion would be undeniable.

It is impossible to do justice to James Mill's thought or his intellectual debts to the ancients in any depth here. But it is important that at least a brief discussion of both be attempted, as John Stuart Mill's notion of happiness developed dialectically out of (for some, against) this background. James Mill considered turning to 'ancestral wisdom' justifiable, so long as it was true to 'the principles of human nature'.[64] In this vein, this section examines James Mill's attitudes toward theory and practice, the principle of utility and the relation between pleasure and modes of lives which constituted key aspects of his utilitarian theory.

## Theory and Practice: Theorizing on Education

From very early in his career to the very end, James Mill thought and wrote on the connection between theory and practice.[65] John Stuart Mill clearly recorded his father's indignation at the popular belief that theory was 'at variance with practice'.[66] The proper meaning of theory, the elder Mill protested, is *'viewing or observing, and correctly recording the matters observed'*,[67] both in the attempt to account for a natural phenomenon and, especially, to guide conduct.[68]

Theory is 'the right ordering of the instances of the past' (i.e., the results of experience) and the subtraction of 'just inferences' from them, Mill argued, for 'the guidance of the future'; it is 'systematized experience'. In contrast, practice, not guided by theory, he added, is '[r]andom imitation' (i.e., the generalization of individual cases with a 'rude glance', a rash or even accidental 'inference from one particular case for the guidance of another'), 'empiricism', 'mere mechanism; and had as well be done by inanimate matter'—arguments which drew on Plato's *Gorgias*.[69] Excluding theory from practical affairs confounded empiricism with experience and allowed ignorance 'to grope its way in the dark'; the statesman, 'vulgarly called' the 'practical man', James Mill added, 'throws [theory] away with both his hands; and kicks at it with both his feet', and thus fails to act 'upon a plan' with forethought and foresight.[70] While the 'speculator' brakes down generalizations with exactness, the practical man mistakes 'forms for substances, formalities for essentials; concomitants for principals' and sacrifices 'ends to means'—the latter is governed by the senses, the former by reason: '[i]t is not by *seeing* much that a man gets much experience, but by profiting by what he sees'.[71]

Where the 'practical man' follows 'an established routine', Mill noted, the philosopher establishes the routine: 'Practical men, as such, look only at one part, and that a small part of the subject; speculative men, as such, at the whole', observing exactly the facts and perfectly collecting them.[72] Science, he maintained, 'is the foundation of art, and art is built on science', good practice can have no other foundation than 'sound theory'. Theory supplies the whole of knowledge of a subject into the order and form that good practical rules can be easily drawn from: 'To recommend the separation of practice from theory is, therefore, simply, to recommend bad practice'.[73] But unless 'the elemental grounds' and reasons of a case are considered, Mill believed, it is bad theory, as particular truths are 'the only real truths'. The role of philosophy lies in the discovery of those truths which make 'mistaken practice [...] no longer possible'.[74]

Mill's attitude toward education exhibits his demand for a comprehensive theory, in order to achieve good practice. Action, he argued, is determined by trains of ideas that have either direct or indirect influence; neither 'bodily' nor 'mental' actions (e.g., a change in one's mental state), usually regarded as voluntary, can be without a motive: 'i.e., the association of an idea of pleasure or of exemption from pain with the act or the mental modification'.[75] Thus, as Fenn has showed, Mill's theory of association was deterministic to a great extent.[76]

Moreover, action, Mill added, can be either coherent or incoherent. It is coherent when it follows some 'grand suggesting and selecting' principle; it is incoherent, when it follows varied principles and ends. In connection, the choice of ends is important, he argued, as they create either stability or 'a state of perpetual fluctuation'. Both coherence and stability depend on the habitual association to ideas of 'great purposes of life'.[77]

But also these 'great purposes of life' connected education with the pursuit of happiness. As Mill argued, if a person achieves 'the greatest command over his ideas' and forms strong and numerous associations to the 'grand sources of felicity', then education has 'performed its most perfect work; and thus the individual becomes, to the greatest degree, the source of utility to others, and happiness to himself.'[78] But, first, proper education needs to 'make certain feelings or thoughts take place instead of others', by working on a person's mental successions. Proper associations and sequences of ideas, he added, make all the difference 'between the extreme of madness and of wickedness, and the greatest attainable heights of wisdom and virtue'. Second, education needed to create those associations that are most conducive to intelligence, temperance, justice and generosity, as these were considered to contribute to happiness.[79] Moreover, if strong associations are not produced for intelligence, temperance, justice and generosity, according to Mill, the latter will lose much of their 'useful tendency' and 'lessen the quantity of Virtue, and thence of Felicity, in the world'. Thus, '[t]he business of a good education' is to associate the 'grand purposes' of life with the appropriate pleasures, since, for Mill, education has the power to produce those feelings, thoughts and actions that enable a person to pursue happiness and be a vehicle of the happiness of others: 'Let no man ever despair of the efficacy of instruction; it is all-powerful'.[80]

Personal happiness depends upon intelligence (knowledge and calculation), Mill argued, and the ability to control one's appetites and desires in effecting the choices that have been approved through deliberation. The happiness of others is promoted through justice and generosity.[81] However, neither personal nor social happiness, Mill maintained, can be achieved in bad physical conditions. Health, sufficient nourishment and non-exhaustive labor are necessary to reach the physical state which allows individuals to become 'instruments' of happiness; without such appropriate conditions, individuals would not be able to develop their nature to its full capacity.[82] Thus, a theory of education, that would ensure good practice, needed to be supported by a theory of government.

Without entering into a full comparison between James Mill's views on theory and practice or education and Plato's dialogues, some connections do need to be mentioned. First, like in Plato, James Mill sought to define the 'truth' of some matter, irrespective of whether the whole world thought it to be false, and illustrate the need to create an environment of free inquiry.[83] Second, like in

Plato, Mill believed true education went a long way in achieving both good government and a good state.[84] Third, the elder Mill repeated the Platonic Socrates' belief that there are no 'useless studies' or sciences, and thus, good education is invaluable for good practice.[85] Lastly, there are traces of intellectualism that appear both in Plato's dialogues and the elder Mill's comments on education.[86]

Similarly, Terence Ball (1982) has already discussed the platonic traces of Mill's argument on penology and the correlation between education, labour (i.e., social function) and punishment. In general, law and education were considered to be remedies to the social problems troubling the 'lower orders'.[87] Thus, punishment looked to the future; the best corrective was education and habituation in loving labor. Drawing on Plato, these features highlighted the role of the socio-political environment in character formation.[88]

## Utility, Pleasure and Rational Existence

John Stuart Mill is usually credited for widening the scope of Benthamite utilitarianism, by introducing quality as well as quantity in the consideration of pleasures. However, those who study James Mill suggest that he would not have objected to this introduction—particularly in light of his portrait in J.S. Mill's *Autobiography*. This section is confined to a brief discussion of James Mill's works to bring out ideas traditionally considered proof of the son's dissent from the Benthamite conception of happiness.

Isaac Newton's 'true mode of philosophising', James Mill noted, applied in ethical discourse, requires the conformity of 'all moral phenomena of human life' to one principle: 'man pursues happiness [...] and flies from misery, in other words seeks pleasure, and avoids pain'. This fact, Mill argued, was 'completely sufficient to account for all moral phenomena', which can be classified and analysed down to this principle, 'in the most satisfactory manner'. It is the only principle that depends both on reason and experience. If there is any doubt about the efficacy of one's reason, Mill maintained, experience provides sufficient guidance.[89] Mill considered himself to be 'in good company' advancing this thesis.[90]

For Mill, the principle of utility was 'founded by Plato', 'the philosopher of the most brilliant imagination' and it appeared clearly in three platonic dialogues: *Protagoras*, *Meno* and *Republic*, where the relation of knowledge and calculation to individual excellence was examined, showing those mental qualities—properly used—which can lead to happiness.[91]

In Plato's *Protagoras*, both interlocutors agreed that pleasures (and pains) need to be weighed and compared against their short-term and long-term consequences, including attributes such as intensity and quantity. However, such a calculation was not enough, both the sophist and the philosopher agreed, as a person needs knowledge, or correct opinion about the consequences of any given choice; that was the *art* of measurement—combining calculation with knowledge. People will never knowingly choose the lesser instead of the greater benefit (or pleasure), and thus, proper conduct in life depended on possessing this art.[92] Thus, it is not strange that Mill 'always tended to assimilate the pursuit of pleasure to the pursuit of virtue', as virtue had much to do with this process of calculation.[93]

As we already saw, the elder Mill singled out the famous passage of Plato's *Republic* in which the happiness of all, not just one class, is made the main political end.[94] In *Republic* also, Mill found the principle of utility in passages where calculation and reason appeared as the most important functions of the soul and highlighted the passage in which Socrates notes that whatever people consider excellent, beautiful or right, they do so in relation to the specific function or use to which they believe it is subservient.[95]

Robert Fenn was one of the first to notice that James Mill's view of the ends of life takes Platonic overtones, while at the same time Plato 'is made into an honorary utilitarian'.[96] Like Plato's *Protagoras*, James Mill argued that there are two kinds of ends: either secondary ends ('good only as contributing to the attainment of something which is good') or ultimate ends. The role of knowledge in achieving this 'measurement' has already been mentioned; but Mill, more importantly, believed that education allows individuals to rise 'higher in the scale of rational existence'.[97] This was related to having proper and strong associations, i.e., both the knowledge and the character to go after the 'great purposes of life'.[98]

There are things that promote the welfare of the body, Mill argued, and things that promote the welfare of the mind. 'It is well-known', he noted, 'how small is the value of all the merely corporeal pleasures, when taken nakedly by themselves, and without the addition of anything mental'. Moreover, he argued that 'only the lowest of our species' are under the influence of bodily pleasures, stripped off the mental ones: 'the purely mental pleasures, those which begin and end in the existence of pleasurable thoughts, hold a high rank among the enjoyments of our nature', and their causes 'we denominate useful'.[99]

It is the property of knowledge, wrote Mill, 'to elevate and refine our nature'; it enables 'man to find satisfaction in his own bosom', and, what is more important, 'not only to produce a taste for intellectual delights, but to destroy the keen relish for gratification purely sensual'.[100] The pleasures of taste, intellectual exertion and virtue 'acquire when duly cultivated, a power of controlling the solicitations of appetite, and are esteemed a more valuable constituent of happiness than all that sense can immediately bestow'. Similarly, it seems that early in his career, Mill believed taste to be 'intimately connected' with morality, providing the transition from bodily to mental pleasures.[101] James Mill's greater and lesser purposes in life were defined in reference to the 'power' of the intellectual nature to control the appetitive nature of man, by pursuing what one 'deliberately approves'.[102]

Thus, the elder Mill pointed to an elevated and refined human nature, in which pleasures originated in one's intellectual pursuits as the way to happiness. Some things, Mill maintained, such as forms of art, have 'the power of calling up such a train of interesting associations as constitute some of the highest of the pleasures of imagination'.[103] This seems in line with his notes in the CPBs, in which the elder Mill discusses whether 'certain kinds of pleasure' 'should have our esteem' or whether '[t]here is [...] a gradation in pleasures'—but the discussion there affords no clear answer, as Mill was aware that such a consideration required 'taking a different ground' pertaining to their origin. He did seem to hold that some kinds of pleasures are nobler, which comes to corroborate an earlier claim that some pleasures have intrinsic, rather than relative value, i.e., the ones of modes of life 'higher in the scale of rational existence',[104] in which the principle of utility keeps one's duties in the 'proper order' and leads them to pursue the higher rather than the lower good.[105] He was reluctant to concede any further ground, other than arguing that, though pleasure is a sensation ('[a] man knows it, by feeling it') which one would prefer prolonged, it is its origin or cause that matters the most.[106]

## CONCLUDING REMARKS

As we saw, James Mill seemed to believe greatly in the educational value of Plato's dialogues. As he developed his utilitarian interests, he found in Plato utilitarian motifs; and thus started to value the affirmative, not just the inquisitive, aspects of Plato's dialogues. There seems to be something more to this change of focus, than simply a shift of philosophical interest.[107] This chapter examined two key aspects of Mill's thought in which Mill's utilitarian and Platonic concerns dialectically interacted, as both James and John considered themselves justified in taking Plato to be on the side of Progress rather than the side of Permanence.

William Thomas argues that James Mill drew from two different traditions: the Utilitarian (or Hobbesian) and the Platonic (or Classical). The former informed his position on the franchise and the checks upon governments; the latter, on the relation of education to the right to vote. Not only did Mill overrate 'the popular appetite for instruction', Thomas argues, but also he appealed to the upper classes as an 'ideal of a ruling class of virtuous and enlightened men', trying to convince them that it was in their best interest to educate 'their inferiors'. Thomas identifies this strain of thought as paternalistic and points out the tension between paternalistic and utilitarian claims. However, Wendell Carr seems right to respond that Mill's utilitarian (e.g., reform) and his Platonic (e.g., paternalism) concerns were 'two sides of the same coin'.[108]

James Mill sought to define a comprehensive theory in order to secure good practice: his theory of life informed his theory of education, which in turn informed his theory of government, and so forth. He argued that identity of interests would be better reached by an improved representative system and extension of the franchise. A good government makes the necessary social, political and educational changes—which shape the intellectual and moral character of individuals—in order to make the vote informed and, thus, effective.

I have argued that James Mill's reading of Plato was not influenced solely by his radicalism. He read Plato prior to his contact with Bentham and brought something of Plato along with him. So, it is important to keep in mind that James Mill did not just exploit Plato to support radical arguments. He learnt from Plato. His manuscripts are an index to these lessons, not a proof of 'pillaging'.

Almost twenty years after James Mill's death, John, at one point making note of the fall into oblivion of his father's name, remarked: 'What is now wanted is the creed of Epicurus warmed by the additional element of an enthusiastic love for the general good'.[109] The utilitarian and the Platonist James Mill had both qualities. He seemed to believe that in a good social and political environment individuals would not only achieve happiness, they would also rise 'higher in the scale of rational existence'—the higher the level, the higher the regard for the social good. Thus, James Mill's Platonizing radicalism called the best and the virtuous to become politically engaged, to be part of those who make, not follow, the routine; even if only to avoid '*[t]he greatest of all punishments—that of being governed by the bad*'; these, and other, ideas resurfaced in his son's work.[110]

## NOTES

1. J.S. Mill, *A*:I.24-5, 24nC; Stephen, 1950:II.3. See also, Ball, 1982:223-4; 1992b.
2. Grote, 1873:283. James Mill was, as Grote put it, 'competent alike to examine others, or to be examined by them' ('τοῦ διδόναι καὶ δέχεσται λόγον'). See further, Bain, 1882a:459; H. Grote, 1873:23; Thomas, 1979:97; J.S. Mill, APHM:XXXI.100.
3. Quoted in Bain, 1882a:456. See also, J.S. Mill, *A*:I.48-9.
4. J. Mill to M. Napier (10/07/1821, in Napier, 1879:27; Bain, 1882a:16). Also, Fenn, 1987:7.
5. Some argue for an even earlier Greek influence on James Mill, originating in his school days at Montrose academy (Cumming, 1962; Pappé, 1979:297).
6. Bain, 1882a:14-5, 18-9; Burston, 1973:38-9; Fenn, 1987:5 (see further, Haakonsen, 1985; Fenn, 1987:ch. 1).
7. Bain, 1882a:166-7, 464-5; Benn, 1906:293; Burston, 1969:1 and 1973:38.
8. Bentham, 1838-43:X.498; Halévy, 1929:266. See also, Ball, 1995:163; Ripoli, 1998:105-6. James Mill had himself to blame for this caricature (Bain, 1882a:137; Robson, 1964:249). However, later in life, James Mill said that he was not someone 'who took anybody for a master' (J. Mill, 1835a:124. See also, J.S. Mill, *A*:I.213; LEED:I.538).
9. Turner (1981) ignores James Mill's role in the revival of nineteenth-century Platonic scholarship. See further, Demetriou, 1996b; 1998; 1999; Burnyeat, 1998; 2001a; 2001b; 2001c.
10. J. Mill, 1804:I.450; 1809a:191. Demetriou (1999:179-80) traces in James Mill's discussion of the 'proper approach' to Plato 'an almost disciplinary guideline' to George Grote.
11. J. Mill, 1804:II.578-80, 587. A brief comparison with Benjamin Jowett demonstrates James Mill's skills in translation (J. Mill, 1804:II.582; Jowett, 1892:IV.241, 194, 196-7). See futher, Burnyeat, 2001c:110.
12. J. Mill, 1804:I.454; 1809a:192.
13. J. Mill, 1809a:190, 197 and 1804:I.451, II.580.

14. J. Mill, 1804:I.449-50 and 1809a:188-9, 199. J. Mill wrote several dialogues (e.g., 1835c; 1836b; 1836c).
15. J. Mill, 1809a:199 (also, 1804:I.449); Pappé, 1979:299. See also, Lamm, 2000:216-7.
16. J. Mill, 1809a:199-200 and 1804:I.453. Though James Mill here seems to hold the traditional view of the Sophists, an early entry note in his CPBs reads that 'these ordinary philosophers' (1804:I.451) 'intended to teach [Athenians] to speak what was proper, and act what was just; to associate on equal terms with their compatriots; to have no desire for shameful things, and a great desire for honourable' (CPB:V.54v). In reference to Plato's seriousness, for example, T. Taylor (1793:247) also commented that Plato managed 'to jest seriously, and sport in earnest' (see further, Brant, 1998:71).
17. These appear at the end flyleaf of J.S. Mill's copy of I.Bekker's edition of Plato (1826:I.153-4; V.479).
18. J. Mill, 1809a:200. See Loizides, 2012.
19. Burnham, 1977:198.
20. J. Mill, 1804:I.451-4; 1809a:191, 199-200. Also, Burnyeat, 2001c:105; 2001a:2.
21. J. Mill, 1835a:25.
22. J. Mill, marginalia: Cudworth, 1743:I.19
23. J. Mill, 1804:I.453; 1809a:194; 1835a:25. See also, Degraff, 1940:151; Annas, 1992:62.
24. Demetriou, 1999:177; Glucker, 1996:399. Besides the traditional division between inquisitive and expository, Plato's dialogues were classified into tetralogies (Laertius, *LOEP*:III.49-50. See further, Chroust, 1965:34-46; Tarrant, 1993:16-30). Following Cicero, Mill could choose to adhere to either classification; since not only was Cicero closer to Plato than the later Platonists historically speaking, but also he had direct access to the Academy (Field, 1924:134; Marshall, 1976:254). The sceptical view of Plato's doctrines was already known to Laertius (*LOEP*:III.51; see further, Woodruff, 1986).
25. Vivenza, 2001:42; Stewart, 1991:288-9. Contra Burnyeat, 2001c:105; 2001a:2.
26. J. Mill, CPB:III.204r. See also. Kellermann, 1956:315-6; Hartle, 2003:174; O'Brien, 2005:67. Mill (CPB:IV.131r) also cites Montaigne's 'De l'institution des enfants', which Kellermann (1956:316) calls 'a great Platonic essay'.
27. Montaigne, 1739:III.201.
28. *Ibid.* p. 193.
29. Kellermann, 1956:315. Montaigne, 1739:III.194. There may be an echo of Montaigne's Plato in J.S. Mill's view of Plato's metaphysics as 'poetic fancies' (*A*:I.25. On Montaigne's *fantasie* and *fancy*, see O'Brien, 2005:54).
30. J. Mill, 1809a:188-9 (see also, Glucker, 1996:397). Raine, 1969:20.
31. Evans, 1940:1071-2. Still, James Mill (1804:I.454 and 1809a:192) did claim that modern languages could not capture the gracefulness of the dialogic form and that Plato was both instructive and entertaining—indeed typical eighteenth-century claims (Brant, 1998:71).
32. J. Mill, 1809a:199; Burnyeat, 2001a:20-1; Jenkyns, 1980:233. Also, Sullivan, 2009:38. See further, chapter six. Mill (1804:I.454) compared Plato to Jesus, both being used as authorities to justify complex doctrines. Unlike his contemporaries, he made the comparison only to strike blows against the Christian and the Neoplatonic traditions—revealing concurrently his own growing discontent with the Church.
33. Glucker, 1996:40; Demetriou, 1999:178. See further, Fenn, 1987:51, 51n78 and 1972:II.330.
34. Fenn, 1987:136 (see also, Fenn's editorial note at the beginning of Mill's CPB:V).

35. See Burston (1973) and Fenn (1987) on the pivotal role of education in James Mill's political thought. Burston (1973:ch. 3) discusses Mill's practical engagement with education.

36. J. Mill, 1812d:321. See also, 1813a; 1813b, 1813c; 1825:VII.J. Mill (CPB:II.22v) collected a number of quotes from various ancient writers about social influences; with regard to Plato, James Mill noted passages from *Tht*:172d-3b; *GrH*:184a; *Alc I*:134b; *L*:705e, 708d; *Gor*:515bc.

37. J. Mill, 1825:VII.46. It is quite interesting how on this issue James Mill (CPB:II.30-1) blended a reference to Plato (*Rep*:361a) in an argument extracted from Bentham (1838-43:IX.78-92).

38. J. Mill, CPB:I.163r; II.22v (*Gor*:513c-5e); III.36v (*Rep*:492a); V.62 (*Prot*:323a-4e, 326d, 327b). See also, CPB:II.22v (*Alc I*:134b; *L*:705e). Also note the references to Cicero on Plato (CPB:II.16r, 22v).

39. J. Mill, 1813a:212. Discussion and controversy, Mill (1815:175) noted, improve all sciences.

40. J. Mill, 1825:III.10, 25-9. See also, Burston, 1969:34-5.

41. J. Mill, 1825:III.29-30. CPB:I.100v (Plato, *L*:714c), 167v (*Rep*:496c-e). See also, 1826b:9, 1836b:564.

42. Mill quoted from Plato's *Gorgias* (480b-d at CPB:I.15r; 521d-2a at CPB:I.15v). Unsurprisingly, he mostly used the *Apology* with regard to uncensored discussion (21a, 33c, 39c-d at CPB:I.8r, 14r, 97v; III.142v, 210v). He further pointed out that it is in the interest of a bad government to persuade their subjects that philosophy is a bad thing (CPB:I.167v on *Rep*:496c-e). He also pointed to *Theaetetus* (150e at CPB:III.98v) to illustrate that it is also in their interest to 'blind' their subjects into considering 'impostures and images' to be 'of more importance than the truth'. He takes Socrates in *Meno* (81d-e at CPB:III.98r) to say that disputing the claims of established things to be perfect as they are, makes people energetic and inquiring, instead of idle and indolent (also, *Tht*:172c-d at CPB:I.138r for the importance of freedom to individual energy and virtue). Plato's *Charmides* (166d at CPB:III.140r) is quoted on the importance of the discovery of truth for the common good; Mill points to Plato's *Republic* (496c-e at CPB:I.167v) regarding the importance of not being afraid to speak the truth publicly.

43. J. Mill, 1830:37; Plato, *Rep*:407a. Jowett's (1892:III.94) translation was 'as soon as a man has a livelihood he should practise virtue'. Mill's use of 'excellence' was closer to the ancient Greek notion of ἀρετὴ.

44. J. Mill, 1830:38. Mill mentioned Plato's 'inventions' that secured the city against misrule: a strict course of education and no possession of property for those who governed, as well as their being dependent on the city for their basic needs (*Rep*:415a-7b): 'Only two securities as against the governors', Mill noted, 'have ever been invented—one that they shall have no property—another that they shall have none but a dependent, and easily revocable power' (CPB:I.166r).

45. Mill referred not to the aristocratic, but to the middle rank, that 'intelligent and virtuous rank' which had direct conduct with the lower rank and could influence them (1825:I.31-2; VII:43-6. Also, CPB:I.119r-121r; 1826a:V.536-7. Thomas, 1979:103-4).

46. Fenn, 1987:93; Demetriou, 1999:178.

47. Fenn, 1987:136-7. As James Mill noted, '[t]he grand difference between the people, those abused as ignorant by the aristocrates; and the aristocratical multitude itself—both are equally ignorant, but the aristocrates fancy they have knowledge' (CPB:III.144v on Plato, *Apol*:21d). Ball (2004) argues that the experience of being 'forced to support himself by tutoring the sons and daughters of several noble families' early in his career,

created James Mill's 'hatred for hereditary aristocracy'. See also, Bain, 1882a:74; Capaldi, 2004:2.
48. Fenn, 1987:136-7.
49. Fenn, 1987:136. Mill was familiar with the 'remarkable testimonies' which illustrated the 'aristocratic feelings' of Athens (Plato, *Gor*:512c at CPB:V.120r; see also, 1825:V.8-9).
50. Thus, rather than Mill himself becoming more of an authoritarian (Thomas, 1979:138), which seems to misread the combination of 'radical and democratic government with intellectual elitism' by the utilitarians (Rosen, 1981:62), James Mill seems to have made Plato less of an authoritarian—a rendering of Plato's thought which was no more selective than the Victorian 'selective portrayal of Greece' (Turner, 1981:34-6, 61-2).
51. See also, J. Mill, CPB:I.52r on Plato, *Rep*:420b.
52. J. Mill 1835a:291. Thus, he focused on 'the more general laws of [human] nature, rather than the exceptions', since he did not seek 'to explain the immense variety of political facts at all' (*ibid.* pp. 279-84, 293).
53. J. Mill, 1825:I.17-20 and 1835a:279-84.
54. J. Mill, 1835a:285-91. Mill quotes Plato's *Republic* on two other occasions, 416a (CPB:I.166r which also appears in Bekker, 1826:VI.449), 462a-e (CPB:I.166v which also appears in Bekker, 1826:VI.527-8). Also marked in J.S. Mill's copy of Bekker (1826:VI.443) is 412c-d.
55. J. Mill, 1835a:285-8. Since justice is what creates the unity of interest (Plato, *Rep*:351c-d at CPB:I.165r), James Mill noted that justice can make the state happy (*Rep*:462b at CPB:I.166v).
56. J. Mill, 1835a:289. For Mill, Plato's methods 'has been the subject of much ignorant ridicule', but 'it will not be easy to find another combination of means better adapted' to so important an end that renders 'it expedient to employ the most extraordinary means for its attainment' (*ibid.* p. 290). According to Mill, Plato 'describes beautifully' what is required to create this unity of interests. He identified this as an 'admirable passage' to be used 'for quotation on any occasion, when the necessity of this community of interests is to be displayed' (*Rep*:462b at CPB:I.166v). See also the many other passages at CPB:I.165-7, where Mill, around 1825, gathered material on reform.
57. J. Mill, 1835a:291-4 and 1836c:231-2; Plato, *Rep*:473b (CPB:I.167r).
58. J. Mill cited Ralph Cudworth (the leading Cambridge Platonist) to argue that the 'false' impression that Plato believed that ideas exist outside the human mind originated with Aristotle (1878:I.256).
59. See further, J. Mill, 1878:I.237n76, 271, 248-9; II.2n1 (also I.272-3n79; II.93n23).
60. J.S. Mill, *A*:I.25. See also, Ball, 1995:164.
61. For example, Mill located, but did not use, many passages in Plato's dialogues which related to the 'intellectual and moral endowments', qualities or knowledge, that judges, lawgivers and all men in power need to possess: CPB:I.54v (*Crat*:389a); II.22v (*L*:708d); III.140r (*Gor*:521d-2e), 140v (*Alc I*:119b), 144v (*Apol*:21d); V.132r (*Rep*:429c). See also, J. Mill, 1825:I.32; II.36; 1836a:294.
62. This insight was drawn from Plato, *Mx*:235d (CPB:III.100v); *Gor*:513c (CPB:I.15v).
63. For example, Mill (1811:421) notes that those who are not willing to be persuaded by his own arguments, do not have to, as he can supply the arguments from authorities for which they have the highest regard.
64. J. Mill, CPB:I.171V.
65. One of James Mill's earliest articles (1802) and the last (1836c) explored this connection.

66. J.S. Mill, *A*:I.34-5.
67. J. Mill, 1878:II.402-3. To the mind of James Mill, his son noted, 'the bearings of speculative philosophy on the practical interests of the human race were ever present' (J.S. Mill, APHM:XXXI.288).
68. J. Mill, 1836c:227.
69. J. Mill, CPB:I.106v, 107r, 112r-3v; Plato, *Gor*:463b at CPB:I.112v.See J. Mill, CPB:I.163r for a translation on the relation between virtue, knowledge and order (*Gor*:506c-8b). Though William Thomas was right to point to the use of 'empirical' as meaning 'haphazard' or 'unsystematic' by both Mills, he missed the connection to Plato's *Gorgias* (Thomas, 1979:118).
70. J. Mill, CPB:I.107r; V.125; 1825:II.25. Also, 1815:193; 1836c:232-3.
71. J. Mill, CPB:I.108. J.S. Mill's copy of Bekker highlighted a similar passage in Plato, *Phdr*:275b (at Bekker, 1826:I.187).
72. J. Mill, CPB:I.109r, 108v; 1825:VII.34. Good science, he (1836b:556, 561-2) added, combines all those true and important propositions which 'embrace' (in a 'comprehensive and commanding view') the whole subject, in the most suitable way for the end pursed.
73. J. Mill, 1802:1-2 and 1825:VII.5.
74. J. Mill, CPB:I.112v, 114v; 1815:184; 1836c:231-2; Fenn, 1987:58-9, 97-9, 128.
75. J.S. Mill, APHM:XXXI.250.
76. Fenn, 1987:50.
77. J. Mill, 1878:II.371-2, 376-7.
78. J. Mill, 1878:II.379; 1825:VII.3. Also, Fenn, 1987:50.
79. J. Mill, 1825:VII.9, 12, 22.
80. J. Mill, 1878:II.300, 259; 1825:VII.3, 9; 1813b:111.
81. J. Mill, 1825:VII.14-6. Also, J. Mill, 1878:II.293.
82. J. Mill, 1825:VII.29-30. Also, J. Mill, 1826a:V.541 (see further, Woodcock, 1980:477-8).
83. J. Mill, 1836b:569-70; Plato, *Gor*:466a-73e (CPB:III.110r); *Rep*:506a-e (CPB:III.147v); *Apol*:21a, 33c, 39c-d (CPB:I.8r, 14r, 97v; III.142v, 210v).
84. Plato, *Rep*:416a-d (CPB:I.166r), 492a (CPB:III.36v); *Prot*:327d (CPB:V.62r).
85. Plato, *Rep*:527d-e (CPB:III.36v). Also, J. Mill, 1836b:563.
86. Plato, *Prot*:357d. Also, J. Mill, CPB:I.107v, 114V.
87. J. Mill, 1813b:113, 101; 1812d:337-8; 1825:I.4, II.21-2. See further, Plato, *Rep*:421c; *L*:631e-2a.
88. Ball, 1995:168, 227-8. See also, Plato, *Prot*:323b-4b (CPB:I.139r; also marked in Bekker, 1826:I.288; see also J. Mill's marginalia on Montaigne, 1739:III.19). Also, Woodcock, 1980:493; Thomas, 1979:109.
89. J. Mill, 1815:195-7. Experience affords guidance through 'popular or moral sanctions' and 'political, including legal, sanctions' (the first by society, the second by government). Mill made special mention that he is merely '*exhibiting* opinions, *advocating* none'. See also, J. Mill, 1825:I.4
90. J. Mill, 1835a:279.
91. J. Mill, CPB:V.49r, 107; I.52r. Plato, *Prot*:351b-9b; *Mn*:88a-d. See also, J. Mill, 1825:VII.3.
92. Plato, *Prot*:353d-4d, 356b, 357d. Also, J. Mill, 1825:VII.15.
93. See further, J. Mill, 1835a:160 (cf. J.S. Mill *U*:X.205). William Thomas, as in the case of 'theory vs. practice' and penology, ignores the connection between James Mill and Plato: he explains James Mill's notion of virtue solely in regard to Mill's Puritanism (1979:100 and 1985:26-7).

94. Plato, *Rep*:420b (CPB:I.52r).

95. Plato, *Rep*:426de (Bekker, 1826:VI.467), 601d-3a, 604d (Bekker, 1826:VII.195ff; J. Mill, 1835a:264).

96. Fenn, 1987:51, 51n78 and 1972:II.330.

97. Plato, *Prot*:354b-c; J. Mill, 1835a:310; 1812f:652. J.S. Mill also referred to such a 'scale of existence' (TPR:XIX.323-4). The elder Mill (1835a:279) thought that it was obvious whose ends were served when people preferred 'the lower to the higher good'.

98. J. Mill, 1878:II.376-7.

99. J. Mill, 1836b:557-8. In J.S. Mill's copy of Bekker is noted that the foundation of political economy was 'correctly laid' in Plato (*Rep*:369c-72c at Bekker, 1826:VI.359ff). See also, J. Mill, 1826a:IV.11; Thomas, 1979:103.

100. J. Mill, 1812f:652. This was a refinement that the middle rank possessed (J. Mill, 1825:I.31-2).

101. J. Mill, 1878:II.366; 1805b:387 (also, Fenn, 1987:176).

102. J. Mill, 1825:VII.15. Thus, Fenn (1987:51) wonders if Mill had not entirely 'transcended hedonism by a Platonizing form of utilitarianism'.

103. J. Mill, 1836a:287. Also, 1836b:557-8; 1878:II.250ff. See also, J.S. Mill, APHM:XXXI.225-6.

104. J. Mill, CPB:IV.4r; 1805b:388. See further, Burston, 1969:8 and 1973:99-100.

105. J. Mill, 1835a:270. Also, Thomas, 1979:102-3; 1985:43.

106. J. Mill, 1878:II.184, 186-8. Ripoli (1998:116) goes as far as to claim that, as a disciple of Bentham, Mill could not have noted his ignorance on what happiness consists in, and yet he did (J. Mill, 1825:VII.17).

107. See Demetriou, 1999:178.

108. Thomas, 1971:737-8 (also, Thomas, 1969 and 1979:137, 141; Woodcock, 1980); Carr, 1972:320 (also, Carr, 1971).

109. J.S. Mill, DE:12/01/1854:XXVII.642; 08/04/1854:XXVII.666.

110. Plato, *Rep*:347a-c (J. Mill, CPB:I.165r). See also, J.S. Mill, *CRG*:XIX.384, 398.

# PART TWO

## JOHN STUART MILL'S

## APPROPRIATION OF PLATO

# CHAPTER FOUR

## EDUCATIVE PAST

John Stuart Mill considered the relevance of ancient Greek history to modern English history to be undeniable.[1] However, his commentary upon ancient literature was primarily indirect. He discussed the past, for the most part, in essays on the present or in reviews on both the past and the present. However, such erratic treatment has created the impression that Mill's 'didactic comparisons' of past and present were random.[2] Reconstructing Mill's views from works of different subjects, objects and genres reveals a unifying theme: that 'mankind owe a debt' to the people and institutions of Athens 'such as they owe to no other assemblage of men'.[3] Though not completely uncritical of the socio-political structure of ancient Greek city-states,[4] Mill seemed to have learned his father's lesson well: no better reply could be given to 'the calumniators of liberty' than the attainments of Athens.[5]

This chapter expands on how John Mill's reading of the history of ancient Greece, and particularly that of Athens, informed three major currents that ran through his major works: educational, social and political reform. He retained the same high opinion regarding the worth of classical studies throughout his life—a constancy that some analyses of his intellectual development underestimate. Although scholars agree on the role of ancient Greece in some of his works, the emphasis is frequently on influence rather than reception. But these are communicating vessels. Just like with George Grote,[6] attempting to label Mill's mode of analysis as if he sought to establish 'bare facts' free from ideology or as if he substituted one ideology for another fails to do him justice—even if he did habitually study the past with one eye on the present.

# REFORMING EDUCATIONAL PRACTICE

During the most heated period of the debate on classical studies,[7] Mill's 'Inaugural Address Delivered to the University of St. Andrews' (1867) reiterated the need to reform educational practice. As we saw, proponents of classical education argued that classics created 'a bond of mental union' between generations and nations throughout Europe.[8] But Mill was aware that the non-classical education of most radicals prevented them from appreciating views and opinions that presupposed familiarity with styles, expressions and thoughts from the 'literary branch of knowledge'.[9] Consequently, he was one of the few individuals who could use his access to that 'bond of mental union' to propagate radical ideas.

Mill's method of combining 'half-truths' brought together life-long convictions about the usefulness of classics (which he shared with many individuals, including conservatives), with similarly enduring beliefs about 'conservative' universities with obsolete teaching methods, which suited an 'agenda' of permanence rather than progression (a common conviction among radicals). The 'great outburst of speculative thought' and freedom of the ancient Greeks (the 'most remarkable people who have yet existed'), Mill argued, was best suited to offer a course of education which brought 'us somewhat nearer to the perfection of our nature' and kept up or even raised 'the level of improvement which has been attained'.[10]

Instruction, Mill maintained, is carried out via either 'the system of cram' or 'the system of cultivating mental power'. In this recurring pair of opposites in his work, the first referred to 'stuffing' a person's memory with other people's results; students were considered to possess 'nothing but a memory'. In contrast, the second enabled students to reach conclusions by their 'own observation, experience and reflection'; exercising and strengthening their intellect. Thus, cram, Mill argued, begins from abstractions and 'trust[s]to Providence' that the student will find meaning in the particulars; mental cultivation begins from an accurate knowledge of particulars and then proceeds to generalizations.[11]

Accordingly, for Mill, the system of 'cram' suited the intentions and served the ends of the 'ancient universities'; that these were places 'where the sons of English gentlemen are steeped in the foulest mire of Toryism', hardly anything more than 'ecclesiastical establishments', made it impossible to follow a mode of instruction that requires questioning every established opinion.[12] As a result, whatever dexterity of intellect 'cram' achieves, he added, is found in the application of certain technical rules. Cram leaves no room for discovery, no room for improvement of any science—neither command over nor apprehension of principles can be achieved. Thus, cramming, he maintained, leads people to act and think 'not upon knowledge of the thing, but upon a hearsay of it'—not reason but routine. In contrast, whatever opinion has been accepted on trust, the method of mental cultivation provides the means to rediscover its reasons or to remake it if needed. Thus, it encourages activity, whereas cram promotes a kind of passivity, which, for Mill, perpetuated the prejudices of common morality.[13]

The history of Greece and the way it was studied at the 'two great "seats of learning"' offered a counter example to prevalent educational practices; it informed Mill's critique about a lack of studies 'calculated to strengthen [the students'] intellects or render them capable of thinking for themselves'. Since classical studies, as all other studies, were deprived of any such usefulness, students were never 'called upon to exercise their judgment either upon the matter or manner of a work'—both were taught as 'catechism'—; thus, keeping their intellect and opinions 'stationary'. Consequently, Mill was not surprised that Plato's or Aristotle's texts, for example, which promote the exercise of one's own judgment, were either unheard of or taught without deriving 'one particle of advantage from them'.[14]

Keeping 'the masses' from becoming wiser, Mill noted, is 'one of the worst qualities of an aristocratic government'; education is rendered an instrument 'not to emancipate the mind but to hold it in perpetual bondage, not to expand it but to keep it for ever shackled and debased'. Cram and rote keep the intellect in atrophy; there is no self-reliance, but only reliance on guidance by others and custom.[15] Thus, the 'poisonous' instructiveness of Greek history and culture, Mill argued, threatened state authority and permanence equally; this virus to the prevailing 'Tory prejudices' found its 'English antidote' in Mitford's *History*.[16]

Whereas ancient Greek education consisted in 'a series of exercises' that encouraged thinking and created an 'active and vigorous' mind, enabled to 'go forth and know', Mill argued, modern education 'grind[ed] down other men's ideas to a convenient size, and administer[ed] them in the form of *cram*'. Thus, unlike the moderns, the ancients had 'the aid of suitable culture'. First, they were forced to find out many things on their own; second, activity itself was directly associated with all their notions of excellence. There was both an opportunity for learning by doing, and a need for tolerance to allow it: their education formed great individuals, 'not mere knowledge-boxes'.[17]

Furthermore, wisdom in antiquity, according to Mill, 'was less the fruit of speculative study, than of intercourse with the world, practice in business, and the long habit of deliberating on public affairs': '*cram* was of no use'. Nurtured in dialectics, individuals depended on their 'genuine *power*' and were encouraged to form 'an intellect fitted to seek truth for itself and to find it'. Such an education, Mill added, did not teach settled doctrines; rather it prepared 'the mind for learning from its own consciousness and observation'. Thus, modern society had mistaken its priorities, rewarding memory at the expense of all other intellectual functions; more crucially, it stigmatized independent thinking. This was a theme most markedly developed in Mill's *On Liberty* (1859).[18]

Thus, Mill's input to the debate on the usefulness of classics revolved around the axis of 'reason vs. routine'. It seems that he would not have questioned Robert Ogilvie's remark that Greek poems being 'learnt by heart' were 'absorbed into the personality of the student', but to him rote-learning hindered such absorption: 'Modern education is all *cram*—Latin cram, mathematical cram, literary cram, political cram, theological cram, moral cram. The world already knows everything, and has only to tell it to its children, who, on their part, have only to hear, and lay it to rote (not to heart)'.[19] Mill's insistence that classical education cultivates and expands the human mind was not original; but his insistence that the classics, if studied properly, undermine routine, custom and tradition, was. He agreed with the proponents of classics (and of liberal education) that the university was not a place to teach the 'business of the world'—classical studies ought to maintain their current place in the curriculum. But he also argued that the university was not a place to make disciples, and, thus, classical studies ought not to promulgate common morality, but cultivate critical habits.[20]

The classics, Mill argued, were an invaluable source for intellectual, moral and aesthetic cultivation. Hence, instead of wasting time on prosody, classics needed to be studied 'far more really and deeply'.[21] Being able in life after school 'to read the great works of ancient literature with ease' was important to Mill: he argued that no modern ethical or philosophical work could at once *teach* 'both by precept and example' the mode of investigating truth and *inspire* 'the search after truth and for applying it to its highest uses'. Hence, ancient literature was a 'fountain' in which 'the sense of beauty, the admiration of exalted personal excellence, and the most varied powers of thought, are all nourished and called into action, each in the highest degree, and not separately but simultaneously'.[22]

Likewise, though Latin and Greek could facilitate the teaching of modern languages, Mill argued, the utility of being able to read the classics in the original was manifold.[23] Not only did the value of Latin or Greek consist in saving one from 'mistak[ing] words for things' (turning the argument of the advocates of scientific education on its head);[24] but also it consisted in their artistic perfection (which had a great emotional impact on the reader)[25] and their service to 'logical and metaphysical analysis' (due to the complexity and symmetry of their grammar).[26] What is more, Mill argued, without being able to think in an ancient language and receive the understanding for those times directly from the 'fountain head' itself, people remain with 'intellects only half expanded'.[27] All these were lessons well-taught by James Mill.

However, Mill was charged with being too favorable to classics. He replied that he had stated his case so strongly because he considered modern tendencies to side with scientific education, with the danger of completely overshadowing classical instruction.[28] A combination of literary with scientific subjects, he maintained, infused the 'perfection' both of expression and of thinking. But what was more important, such perfection required institutions of 'free speculation'; institutions that made 'capable and cultivated human beings'; institutions that aimed to qualify individuals 'for at least keeping up, and if possible for raising, the level of improvement which has been attained'. The English universities, Mill argued, were not such institutions.[29]

At the beginning of his rectorial address, Mill noted that '[e]ducation makes a man a more intelligent shoemaker, if that be his occupation, but not by teaching him how to make shoes: it does so by the mental exercise it gives, and the habits it impresses'. Thus, an education of rote failed to make 'capable and sensible men', trained to believe on evidence acquired through personal enquiry—as Plato's Socrates argued in *Gorgias*, a craftsman needs to have a rational grasp of his craft otherwise it is just routine.[30] But a 'suitable culture' may foster such critical habits. These ideas, extensively discussed in *On Liberty*, are not usually traced back to Mill's reading of ancient Greek history and Plato in particular.

## REFORMING SOCIAL PRACTICE

John Stuart Mill's most lengthy discussion of 'the aid[s] of suitable culture', which made possible the 'great outburst of speculative thought' of the Athenians, occurred in his reviews of Grote's *History of Greece* (1846-56). According to Mill, ancient Greece was as much the medium 'of the good to after-generations' as was the intellectual and moral eminence which made Athens 'the centre of good to Greece'. As much as Grote, he regarded this superiority to be 'wholly the fruit of Athenian institutions', which afforded Athenians with 'boundless publicity and freedom of speech'.[31] These ideas remained constant in his major works as part of the worth of Greek history as a lesson in social and political education. However, as Elizabeth Potter has argued, his reviews, rather than his major works, contained a more nuanced view of Athens.[32]

Like his contemporaries, the younger Mill found in Greek history 'lessons applicable to other times and circumstances than those of Greece'.[33] Grote's history gave Mill the opportunity to lay special emphasis on how Athenian democracy, given its time and circumstances, surpassed all other ancient city-states in practical good government.[34] As 'a government of unlimited publicity, and freedom of censure and discussion', the Athenian institutions were most 'favourable to progress'; of all the aids of 'suitable culture' which allowed Athens to prosper, Mill seemed to believe, these contributed most to the creation of the social conditions which fostered 'the splendid development of individual intellect'. As the Grote reviews, *On Liberty* and *Considerations on Representative Government* suggest, this was a lesson that Mill really wanted his peers to learn.[35]

Mill thus argued that Athens 'had the liberty of the bema, of the dicastery, the portico, the palestra, and the stage; altogether a full equivalent for the liberty of the press'. The Athenians could come into contact with 'every sort of question, public and private, discussed by the ablest men of the time'—exemplars in 'earnestness of purpose and fulness of preparation belonging to actual business, deliberative or judicial'. The 'daily workings of Athenian institutions', Mill concluded, constituted a course of political education, habituating Athenians in the 'love of fair play', and 'hearing both sides of a case'.[36] These, Mill added, made 'every individual in the multitude identify his feelings and interests with those of the state, and regard its freedom and greatness as the first and principal of his own personal concerns'.[37]

Unlike British society, Mill argued, that of Athens did not look 'jealously and distrustfully on original people' or impose 'its common level of opinion, feeling, and conduct, on all its individual members'; rather, Athens encouraged 'the wonderful display of genius'. Thus, in comparison with such a temper of mind, Mill did not wonder why modern times were so mediocre: 'genius, in such a soil, is either fatally stunted in its growth, or if its native strength forbids this, it usually retires into itself, and dies without a sign'. Originality requires suitable social conditions in order to grow and carry every one along with it above the 'common notions of the time'—conditions which had made Athens illustrious.[38]

Furthermore, in Athens, Mill claimed, authority did not supersede reason, it guided and appealed to reason through 'long-sighted policy, and keen and sagacious observation of life and human nature'. However, to enable individuals to free themselves from unfit guidance and authority certain means of reaching 'truth' become essential; i.e., the ability to form and maintain private judgments—the source of improvement and 'the ultimate refuge, the last and only resource of humanity'.[39] But when discussion becomes 'the mere rehearsal of a lesson got by rote', Mill added, thinking for one's self falls 'into disuse'; authority no more guides or appeals to reason and private judgment is silenced indirectly. Thus, in a social setting of blind attachment to tradition, in which no established opinion can be questioned, discussion loses its ability to discover and preserve a vivid conception of 'truth' as well as to weaken error.[40]

Thus, for neither John nor James Mill was there any question about the importance of liberty in Athens; its people 'dared and suffered all things rather than desert the liberty of Greece'—they thought '*liberty their country*'.[41] However, the younger Mill's comments on ancient liberty seem contradictory. In his 'Grote's History', he appeared convinced by Grote: Pericles' funeral oration 'wholly conflicts [...] with what we are so often told about the entire sacrifice, in the ancient republics, of the liberty of the individual to an imaginary good of the state'. But four years earlier, in 'Guizot's Essays', Mill noted that ancient liberty 'was compatible with [...] [the] subjection of every individual to the state'.[42]

According to Guizot, ancient liberty referred to a particular form of political organization; it did not affirm the 'individual freedom of action', 'the private freedom of each citizen'. Such a conception, Mill noted, was compatible with 'a more active interference of the ruling powers with private conduct', than that of 'the most despotic governments' as well. On the contrary, the spirit of modern liberty asserted individual independence, 'freedom of action, with as little interference as is compatible with the necessities of society'—the only authority was one's own conscience. More importantly, the moderns' self-will, 'moderated and limited by the demands of civilized life', was correctly attributed by Guizot, according to Mill, to other influences than those of Greece or Rome.[43]

In Mill's reading of Guizot, the ancient duty of citizenship, i.e., the 'sacrifice of *each* to *all*', repudiated the moderns' 'spirit' of liberty, since 'the imaginary being, the *civitas*, the πόλις, demanded the annihilation of every individuality'.[44] However, in 'Grote's History', Mill argued that the 'Funeral Oration' showed that the public interest was 'held of paramount obligation' only in things that concerned it; public opinion did not interfere in private matters. Thus, Athenian society, for Mill and Grote, was liberal and tolerant. Mill even seemed to reverse Guizot's conclusions in noting that in 'the ethical practice of the moderns [...] no one is required by opinion to pay any regard to the public, except by conducting his own private concerns in conformity to its expectations'.[45]

To a certain extent, as Eugenio Biagini has argued, the inconsistency between Mill's claims can be explained by his historical relativism.[46] Mill defined the 'abnegation of self-will' observed in ancient city-states as a 'mixture of Spartan and stoical impassibility', justified by the ever-present danger of war. Athens, having acquired imperial power, became a rare exception in enjoying the tranquillity of feeling secure from outside threats. For a brief period of time there was no need to 'sacrifice' each to all—it was 'a social period in many respects similar to [Mill's] own'. Thus, during that time, not only did the Athenians' notion of liberty become blended with their conceptions of excellence, activity and religion; it became associated with relatively independent spheres of public and private action.[47]

In his brief mention of the 'ancient vs. modern liberty' debate, Mill did not attempt to respond to Benjamin Constant's (1819) well-known objections regarding the resemblance of Athenian liberty to the modern—though one would expect him so, being familiar with Constant's work.[48] Constant made a note of the Athenians' 'excessive love of individual independence' and peculiar circumstances, but, he argued, they were not so ahead of their age: not only was Athens a place that in order for some to be free, others needed to be slaves, its political (e.g., ostracism) and religious (e.g., Socrates' conviction) institutions allowed little doubt about the *polis'* 'complete authority' over its members.[49] While Mill was silent on ostracism (which Constant, and Grote, considered a necessary protective mechanism), he recognized that religion was a public matter of vital importance in antiquity (over which the *polis* had complete authority), which rendered individual liberty nominal rather than real. But when it was about 'the right of human reason to explore for itself', he *unqualifiedly* praised the Athenian legacy, often excessively. Still, the debate on 'ancient vs. modern' liberty concerned a different issue: individual liberty rather than religious liberty or liberty of thought and discussion, which Mill did not address.[50]

However, the discrepancy demonstrates the strategic aspects of his writing. A 'more complex, nuanced view of Athens' did emerge in his reviews rather than in his major works; but it seems that in his major works Mill qualified his claims on Athenian history to avoid diverting attention from his claims on more pressing social and political issues. It seems that Mill tried to avoid engaging in too many fronts; especially when he was more interested in that aspect of the Athenians' civic life that Constant ignored: their 'lively interest and energetic participation in public affairs' rather than their (as Stephen Holmes puts it) 'collective involvement in punishing, banishing, and putting fellow citizens to death'.[51]

## REFORMING POLITICAL PRACTICE

Benjamin Constant saw the danger 'that, absorbed in the enjoyment of our private independence, and in the pursuit of our particular interests, we should surrender our right to share in political power too easily'. Similarly, Mill argued that it was possible to excite 'lively interest and energetic participation in public affairs' (when the public interest '[is] held of paramount obligation in all things which [concern] it'), without public opinion interfering with 'that part of the conduct of individuals which concerned only themselves'; but, as we saw, for Mill, 'in the ethical practice of the moderns, this is exactly reversed'.[52] The question was how to avoid such reversal, without sacrificing participation.

As noted at the beginning, the chapter's focus is on reception—i.e., what Mill perceived the key functions of Athenian educational, social and political institutions to have been and *how* this perception was developed and integrated in his call for educational, social and political reform. The appropriation of Athens in his writings on representative government is perhaps the most studied aspect of his political thought as far as his Greek influences are concerned. For this reason, here only a cursory discussion will be attempted in relation to Athens.

It is well known that a nation's economic, social and political circumstances provided Mill with a 'social laboratory'. Such 'practical experiments', though not duplicable, could test his psychological assertions and inform his moral and political theory.[53] For example, Athens and France afforded insights that were integrated in arguments about change in England's and Ireland's conditions. But Athens' experiment belonged to the distant past. Though on no occasion could all facts be acquired, familiarity with Athenian circumstances was in addition inevitably mediated, which forced Mill to constantly rebuke the traditional representations of Athens so that the Athenian experience could be integrated in his argument on constitutional reform.[54] He was aware of the obvious limitations of such an appropriation (e.g., slavery, the position of women, Athenian imperialism and the aristocratic tendencies of Athenian society),[55] but because of Grote's efforts, whose history filled much of the lacunae regarding Athenian institutions, Athens could and did test the grounds of his ideas about politics.[56]

In practical politics, Mill argued, representative government provides the most suited institutions for the *organization* of the existing moral, intellectual and active qualities in the people, both collectively and individually, and the *improvement* of those qualities. That Mill argued that the difference between these functions (the organization of existing qualities and the improvement of these qualities) is a difference in *kind*, not in degree, illustrated his concern that no matter how well one of those two functions worked, unless the other worked as well, no set of political institutions could pass the test of good government.[57] According to Mill, the Athenian example showed the way to this dual function of government: institutions which aimed to protect and preserve the present well-being, but also to educate the uninstructed and improve their political competence by using the existent political competence of the instructed few.[58]

The importance that Mill bestowed on this 'difference in kind' has not received much attention in discussions either of Mill's Platonizing in general or of his argument concerning representative government. For example, Peter Burnham completely ignores this aspect in his analysis of Mill's Platonism.[59] On the other hand, though Dennis Thompson's analysis of Mill's *Representative Government* expands on this duality, he does not discuss it as a distinction involving kinds.[60] Discussions of Mill's ancient Greek influences lay emphasis on a different part of the distinction, reducing the difference to one of degree rather than kind. Frank Turner, Joseph Hamburger and recently Robert Devigne have stressed the elitist side of the distinction in their study of Mill; Nadia Urbinati and, to a lesser degree, Dana Villa have focused on the participatory side; while, more recently, Giovanni Giorgini has also argued for the existence of 'two Mills' in John Mill.[61]

Without entering into the details of his discussion regarding the election mechanisms of representative government, Mill seemed to be mostly concerned with combining the extended participation of popular government with the efficiency of expert bureaucratic government. This combined the selection, monitoring and control of those who govern by those whose benefit the governing body ought to pursue, with making the parliament a place in which all the opinions present in the society regarding the common interest (properly conceived or not) were represented. But Mill was especially concerned with the opinions of the educated elite. He argued that in parliament, popular views, often pervaded by class interests, would have to stand their ground against the views of the educated minority; parliament became a place for combating ideas, in which its members had to prove, restrain within the bounds of reason as well as justice and maintain a vivid conception of what they believed.[62]

Mill seemed to believe that remarkable individuals have much influence on progress. As we saw, he considered the Athenian educational and social institutions to facilitate 'individual greatness' (which, according to Mill, was then 'abundant'). But Athens, Mill noted, was an extreme example of how the mixture of 'ordinary accidents' and individual character proved so 'vitally important', to 'the fortunes of mankind'. Mill sought to establish educational, social and political conditions that reduced chance and allowed, if not cultivated, individual greatness. In no way, Mill added, can we 'foresee the advent of great men'; all that science can do, is 'trace through past history the general causes which had brought mankind into that preliminary state, which when the right sort of great man appeared, rendered them accessible to his influence'.[63]

Athens' 'right sort' of circumstances had much to do with Athens reaching a 'natural state' of society.[64] Political power and moral influence were assigned to the fittest individuals to manage state interests; Athenians were competent to discern who 'possessed the greatest personal qualifications for administrating the affairs of the state'. Thus, the distinguished few were trusted 'to think and judge rightly and usefully' for all. But in transitional societies, those who could bestow such influence—being in conflict—did not enjoy such trust. Athens had overcome a state of 'perpetual flux' owing to the political and moral authority of 'eminent men'. Historians of Mitford's stamp had distorted this view of Athenian history, a view which corroborated Mill's Socratic and Platonic claims—the need for a coexistence of a 'socialized version of Socratic dialectics' which brought 'intellects into stimulating collision', a society in which both sides were heard, enabling an active body of citizens to distinguish the fittest, i.e., the most *skilled* or enlightened, to govern.[65]

According to Mill, Athenian institutions kept able men in public sight, giving them the opportunity to engage in the public business actively as well as to make their opinion heard. The number of supporters did not guarantee the prevalence of any opinion in Athenian politics, as talent was not ignored. Thus, Mill argued, some individuals, despite being a minority, ought to win a seat in parliament when they are reasonably expected to be good advisers, even if sometimes such expectations are disappointed. For example, in Athens, Nicias, Theramenes and Alcibiades, who, despite being 'known to sympathize more with oligarchy than with democracy', had exerted more influence than Cleon and Hyperbolus, who were considered to be attached to the people.[66]

But some 'tension' within Mill's encomium may be felt: Athens' democratic institutions were praised as the work of a 'succession of eminent men' and yet 'men of rank and fortune' remained a 'dark' power which led to Athens' ruin.[67] However, an odd mixture of Saint-Simonism and James Mill's Scottish background informed Mill's argument that for 'the peculiar and excellent organization of her own democracy, Athens was indebted to a succession of eminent men'.[68] Solon's personal excellence, Mill maintained, and the excellence of his legislation were 'the principal source of the deep-rooted respect for the laws' and the *eunomia* for which Athens was renowned. As much as Solon, men such as Cleisthenes, Aristides, Ephialtes and others were praised for guarding 'the workings of Athenian institutions against the dangers to which they were most liable'. Each had a share, Mill and Grote argued, in moulding the Athenians' mind and making them capable for their heritage of freedom—though Pericles received the most praise.[69] Irrespective of social origins, these individuals were praised for their intellectual and moral excellence as well as their benefiting influence.

Not many other prominent Athenian politicians were so praised by Mill; especially when their social origins made them a constant source of danger, not a stabilising influence and source of improvement. The 'richest and most highborn men' in the state, 'the chiefs of aristocracy', Nicias and Alcibiades, Mill considered to be the worst advisers of the Athenian public—a public which after all proved to have 'too easy and good-natured a confidence', rather than the 'democratic irritability and suspicion' they were usually accused of. Mill, following Grote, noted that 'men of rank and fortune' were a dark and 'active power' in the Athenian state that led to its ruin, mainly when there were no 'opposition speakers' to balance their influence—the latent function of Athenian demagogy, as we saw.[70]

Moreover, according to Mill, that '[t]he conduct of affairs' in Athens 'was habitually in the hands of the rich and great, who had by far the largest share of personal influence'[71] was a fact that pervaded all governments, ancient and modern: not only do wealthy individuals have more means to acquire influence and cultivation, they are aided by the suspicion people have of their 'equals in fortune and condition'. What popular institutions can do, if the leisured class is to have political influence, Mill argued, is to force the 'rich and great' develop their social and human feelings so as to diminish the distance between themselves and their poorer fellow citizens, and consider their interests as well, but not as shepherds do for sheep.[72] In contrast to the talent-deficient Nicias, who maintained his influence by being 'equal and conciliating' toward the poorer citizens and by keeping the social and religious decorum,[73] Pericles was a great politician because he was a member both of the leisured and the learned class— 'all those [...] who were above their age, either in positive knowledge or in freedom from superstition'. Thus, being a member of the leisured class was not enough for Mill. He would later tone down its importance; the importance of a learned class would be ever so present in his thought.[74]

Statesmanship, Mill argued, needs to be practiced as an art; but as Plato's *Gorgias* had taught him, an art whose principles are not in sight degenerates into routine. As we already saw, Mill dealt extensively with how routine, rote and tradition create passivity. He believed that when vitality is lost, it takes efficiency soon with it.[75] In the modern *agora*,[76] he maintained, frequency decided influence. He believed that the 'decay of individual energy' had carried the public 'in the predicament of an indolent man', who [could] not bring himself to apply his mind vigorously to his own affairs'. Athenians heard, at least, both sides of a question to choose the best. But as 'the influence of superior minds over the multitude' weakens, Mill noted, so does the 'efficacy of public opinion as a restraining power'; people are swayed by non-rational arguments.[77] In Athens, a 'function of antagonism' allowed conflicting influences to dialectically keep 'one another alive and efficient', though not to the extent required by democracy.[78]

Mill's was an argument for the improvement of the many; utilizing the expertise of the few could not become the foundation of Progress, without establishing institutions to benefit the uninstructed. Wide participation and skilled government were equally important; each without the other was insufficient for the preservation of the ideally best constitution. Thus, Mill applauded eminent individuals as much as those 'who were willing to so be led'. Not only did improvement depend on the presence of enlightened opinion, but also on people having some part in the administration—local and national. Universal suffrage provided the latter aspect of participation; though that was greatly important, local civic duties needed to be added to it. Such a constitution would both be inclusive and create the requirements for active citizenship. The Athenian institutions, he pointed out, provided such opportunities. Like Aristotle, Mill seemed to believe that people become citizens through participation, and through participation they became politically educated.[79]

In this way, first, universal suffrage, Mill maintained, created a bond of trust between citizens. By electing someone or being themselves elected, people are, in effect, in a position of power over others. Trusted with the vote, individuals become morally obligated to take under consideration public interests, not private. Voting ought to 'be performed under the eye and criticism of the public', he concluded, as it formed a public duty. Thus, Mill noted that 'no Athenian voter thought otherwise'; participants felt themselves 'a trustee for all [their] fellow citizens and posterity'. They felt this to such an extent, Mill maintained, that even in the time that they enjoyed greater stability 'freedom might for the time be destroyed by a single unfairly obtained popular vote'—voting was 'a valuable instrument of order' and supported Athens' eunomia (rather than endangered it).[80]

Second, the public needed also greater opportunities 'of sharing personally in the conduct of general affairs of the community'. The public, Mill thought, was required not only to think (often without the responsibilities of action), but to act as well—not only 'passively receiving' the thoughts of other people. Local representative bodies provided opportunities to a larger number of citizens both to engage actively in public affairs and address their local interests. With the help of central authority, individuals would then be accustomed 'to act upon, and feel the value of, principles'; they would be taught 'to compare different modes of action, and learn, by the use of their reason, to distinguish the best.[81] Athenians, by frequently being called to decide for their future, acquired such political education. The choices of the Athenian people might have been either 'right or wrong, wise or foolish', Mill noted, but they were never the choices of 'ἀπαίδευτοι', 'untaught or unexercised people'—whatever wrong choices they made, those seemed to be the best in relation to the options presented to them.[82]

Thus, both a 'succession of eminent men' and the established institutions had fostered a safe environment which allowed Athens to prosper. Not only were Athenian leaders a source of influence, but Athens had developed institutions in which individual excellence was encouraged for mutual benefit.[83] '[B]etter institutions and better doctrines' can 'be elaborated', Mill believed, only by allowing enlarged views and the analytic skills of men of intellect to come together with the experience of practical men—an insight gained as much from Athenian society as from Plato.[84] Athens' political education, laws, institutions and leaders, according to Mill, interworked to ensure that 'every individual in the multitude' could not but 'identify his feelings and interests with those of the state'. Athenian society managed to combine all the elements being considered necessary for stability: a system of education, loyalty to a fixed object and 'a strong and active principle of cohesion among' its citizens—all present in Pericles' (retranslated) funeral oration and in Plato's *Republic*.[85]

## CONCLUDING REMARKS

It is well known that Mill was required to develop his own ideas out of the discussions between him and his father on civilization, government, morality and mental cultivation. On one such occasion, James drew John's attention to the light shed on the people and institution of Athens by Demosthenes. It was one of those occasions, when his father's lesson was too advanced for young John to immediately apprehend.[86] And though his father had given him the tools to remake any idea they discussed, John never remade those insights on Athens.

To the 'Greece-intoxicated' Mill, ancient Greece was a heroic poem—one whose characters, situations and incidents acted with great force on the imagination.[87] Thus, both its history and its literature, could 'call forth the greatest possible quantity of intellectual *power*, and [...] inspire the intensest *love of truth*', inculcating 'the spirit of free inquiry, not of dogmatic imposition' in order to form great minds. For this reason, the classics, Mill maintained, provided 'the sole ennobling feature in the slavish, mechanical thing which the moderns call education', calling forth 'high aspirations' and teaching students to think and act for themselves. Thus, classical studies were important for Mill because '[n]ot what a boy or a girl can repeat by rote, but what they have learnt to love and admire, is what forms their character'.[88] On the contrary, by mere cramming of their teachers' doctrines, students do not develop love for virtue—but only obedience, which affords 'only the abject feelings of a slave'.[89] As Alan Ryan has observed, Mill in effect was reiterating the Socratic dictum that 'the unexamined life is not worth living'.[90] General improvement could only be brought about via individual improvement. Mill was another piece of the puzzle of the humanistic Hellenism of Victorian Britain; like many of his contemporaries he looked to the past to find out 'how to forge a more beautiful world and a better quality of life' in the present.[91]

Elizabeth Potter criticised both Eugenio Biagini and Nadia Urbinati for failing to consider how Mill had integrated Athens in his major works in a way that was slightly at odds with his reviews of Grote's *History*. Does this mean that he could be accused of 'pillaging' Athenian history to support radical arguments, much like his father?[92] It does not seem so. Mill's 'radical' depiction of Athens was in no way 'popular', as neither was Grote's. Athens, in Mill's *Representative Government*, appeared as much to correct popular misconceptions (as in 'Grote's History') as to inform and corroborate his moral and political assertions. He argued that Athenian institutions provided valuable insights regarding 'a well constituted popular government'; but, as frequently, he argued that criticizing Athenian institutions in light of modern advancements was 'simply finding fault with the third century before Christ for not being the eighteenth century after'. For Mill, his contemporaries had as much to learn about Athens as to unlearn.[93]

But Athens always seemed to carry Mill to exaggeration; he blamed for this the usual image of Athens, which was critical of what he considered the best of what Athens had produced. Accordingly, for Mill, the Athenian society was 'immensely ahead' of its age and 'an average Athenian was a far finer specimen of humanity on the whole than an average Englishman'.[94] Mill (and Grote) seemed to believe that Athens exhibited such a 'picture of generous tolerance towards social dissent, and spontaneity of individual taste', that, regardless of constitutional form, no society, in the 'comparative mediocrity of modern times', had managed to display equally well.[95] Had Athens preserved its freedom 'the world would have been now a thousand years further advanced'.[96]

According to Mill, ancient Greek history was 'the most abounding in consequences to us who now live'. '[H]ardly any other authentic history', he added, presented such epic and heroic manifestations of human nature. Greek history offered to students 'a certain largeness of conception', by familiarising them with the 'action of great causes' and 'the great principles by which the progress of man and the condition of society are governed'. But '[t]he general disregard of historical studies in English education' was 'a melancholy topic of reflection' for Mill.[97]

Athenian society showed, Mill maintained, that mental cultivation, social and political stability, in an environment that not only tolerates diversity but encourages it, also encourages individual genius and originality. Mill stressed that its education (which formed great thinkers in the private sphere), its liberty (which fostered diversity in the social sphere), lawfulness and participation (which nurtured mutual concern for the common good in the political sphere), had made Athens great. Not accidently, all were vital to Mill's argument for reform. Similarly, Plato's scientific basis of government and division of labour as much as his dialectical method, aimed at making the governed wise and virtuous; as virtue and wisdom constituted the summit of happiness, the end of such a political design was the happiness of the citizens.[98]

Mill is frequently criticized for making the same mistake, which Mill himself criticized Plato for making: that he gave up his Radical background and the importance of 'socialized version of Socratic dialectics' for individual and social improvement. However, Plato's and Samuel Taylor Coleridge's influence on this aspect of Mill's thought has led scholars to argue that Mill was more conservative that usually admitted. In 1868, a similar claim led Mill to protest to a critic: 'You are misinformed on the subject of my political principles; I am *not*, as you tersely express it, "an out and out Conservative"'.[99] But, both many of Mill's contemporaries and some recent commentators have failed to take into account that Mill was in the habit of combining 'half truths'. As we saw, according to Mill, Plato's government by 'enlightened' individuals was only one half of the truth'; the experience of Athenian Democracy provided the other half—the need for an active body of citizens. On a similar discussion concerning the future of the laborers, Mill noted that they indeed feel 'respect for superiority of intellect and knowledge, and defer much to the opinions, on any subject, of those whom they think well acquainted with it', but also he added that this does not prevent them from judging 'for themselves of the persons who are and are not entitled' to their deference.[100] Thus, keeping the *polis* permanently on the track of improvement, i.e., through the 'function of antagonism', calls for a combination of participation and specialization in its organization.

# NOTES

1. J.S. Mill famously noted: '[t]he battle of Marathon, even as an event in English history, is more important than the battle of Hastings' (GH[I]:XI.273. See also, Mill to H. Taylor Mill, 21/03/1855:XIV.384).
2. Turner, 1981:25.
3. GG[1]:XXIV.868. Likewise, for Mill, Athens was 'the true hero of the epopee of Greek history, the most gifted community of human beings which the world has yet seen' (GG[2]:XXIV.1087).

4. Still, asking for more, J.S. Mill noted, would be to ask what had not even been achieved in a 'more advanced age' (GH[I]:XI.273; GH[II]:XI.313. See also SA[II]:XXIII.257). See also, J. Mill, 1811:428; 1825:I.9.
5. J. Mill, 1811:428. The elder Mill added: '[i]t could not be a very detestable tree which bore such exquisite fruit'. What had created the Athenian cultural excellence, James Mill tried to explain, 'was the free scope allowed to aspiring merit, the certain prospect of reward held out to excellence of every sort, and the absence of all laws tending "to keep people in their places"' (J. Mill, 1805a:906).
6. Irwin, 1998:426-30 (contra Turner, 1981:208).
7. See further, Goldhill, 2002:195-213.
8. Whewell, 1850:I.10-2; 1838:34.
9. Mill to T. Carlyle, 22/12/1833:XII.201.
10. IA:XXI.217; N:X.381; GP:XI.377; GH[I]:XI.273 (cf. J. Mill, 1826a:I.142n2). See also, UR:X.409 (J. Mill, 1813b:111). For J.S. Mill's theory of education, see also Garforth, 1979, 1980; Donner, 2007; Ryan, 2011.
11. GAEI:XXIV.786.
12. WD:XXIV.763; sU[1]:XXVI.348-50; GP:XI.399. James Mill dubbed the ancient universities 'excellent schools of *Priggism*', 'prone to Toryism' and part of the ecclesiastical establishment, whose 'fixed creed and fixed forms' aimed 'to keep the human mind where it is' (CPB:III.33; V.65r; 1835a:31).
13. sU[1]:XXVI.351-2. See also, CFR:XX.161; IA:XXI.218, 222; GAEI:XXIV.787; OL:XVIII.247; OG:I.334; A:I.34-5; Mill to T. Carlyle (22/10/1832:XII.128) and to W. J. Fox (end of 1849:XIV.39).
14. Pr:XI.39; TPP:XI.241; EHP:IX.476; sU[1]:XXVI.351-2. Mill's debating speeches drew much on his father's CPBs (cf. J. Mill, CPB:III.33v;V:215r. See also, Fenn, 1991:50).
15. sPR[2]:XXVI.274; NN:VI.181; CRG:XIX.411, 401 (See also, J. Mill, 1811:428).
16. A:I.14-5 (also, MHF:XX.224); sU[1]:XXVI.352-3; SA[IV]:XXII.292; GG[1]:XXIV.867-8; SD:X.45; GH[I]:XI.275; GH[II]:XI.336.
17. OG:I.334-6. See also, MLAR:I.531.
18. SA[IV]:XXII.294; OG:I.334, 336, 338; PPE:III.943. See also, OL:XVIII.243-4, 251, 262; Garforth, 1979:129.
19. OG:I.337; Ogilvie, 1964:85. For Mill's view on the importance of 'laying [a truth] to rote' rather than 'to heart', see OL:XVIII.249ff (also, A:I.34-5; Mill to T. Carlyle, 22/10/1832:XII.128).
20. Civ:XVIII.139-40; IA:XXI.218; GA:XI.510. For a discussion of the 'struggle for the allegiance of undergraduates' through classical studies, see Preyer, 1982:48-53. See also, Jones, 2007:157-9.
21. IA:XXI.223-5; Civ:XVIII.139, 143; TPP:XI.241; TS:XIX.624-5. See also, J. Mill, 1809a:188-9.
22. IA:XXI.220-1, 228-32; OG:I.338; Civ:XVIII.145; SD:X.43n.
23. IA:XXI.222-4; Pr:XI.39; sU[2]:XXVI.356.
24. IA:XXI.225; SOL:VII.79-80; VIII.760. J. Mill, 1878:I.249. See further, Goldhill, 2002:206.
25. IA:XXI.231; Mill to R.B. Fox, 12/03/1841:XIII.469. TDA[II]:XVIII.195n; A:I.8, 23.
26. IA:XXI.228; SD:X.43n; GAEI:XXIV.786; EHP:IX.477. See also, J. Mill, 1809a:188-9.
27. IA:XXI.226-8 (also, TDA[II]:XVIII.195n; J. Mill, 1809a:189); Pr:XI.53, 60. Ogilvie, 1964:106-8; Turner, 1981:8; Preyer, 1982:62; Goldhill, 2002:203.

28. Mill to H. Spencer, 09/02/1867:XVI.1237. See further, Bain, 1882b:126-8.
29. IA:XXI.219-21, 234, 250; SD:X.34n; Civ:XVIII.139-40. See also CRG, XIX.387ff.
30. IA:XXI.218, 222; OG:I.336. Plato, *Gor*:463b (also, J. Mill, CPB:I.112v); *OL*:XVIII.308 (cf. TDA[II]:XVIII. 170). See further, sU[I]:XXVI.350; J. Mill, 1809a:188-9.
31. GH[II]:XI.324. Also, GG[2]:XXIV.1088; sBC[1]:XXVI.367.
32. Potter, 2005:ch. 3.
33. GG[3]:XXV.1125; GH[II]:XI.309. On philosophical history, see MHF:XX.222-5 (Williams, 1982:14). James Mill (1826a:II.60) also argued that intellectual maturity (J.S. Mill's third stage of historiography) transforms a 'record of the past' into 'guidance of the future' (see also, Thomas, 1979:98).
34. Grote's *History*, Mill argued, provided a 'triumphant vindication' of Athenian democracy (GG[2]:XXIV.1088; GG[5]:XXV.1161). For the elder Mill, Demosthenes had already proved the point: *'The People alone can be entrusted with the guardianship of the laws which protect themselves'* (CPB:I.147r on Demosthenes, *AT*:37).
35. GG[5]:XXV.1161; GG[4]:XXV.1131; GH[II]:XI.320; *OL*:XVIII.ch. 2. The Athenian *eunomia* was also an important factor for the tranquillity and stability which Athens enjoyed (GH[II]:XI.316; SA[IV]:XXII.291-2).
36. See further, *PPE*:III.763. This was an early lesson by James Mill (J.S. Mill to J. Mill, Autumn 1822:XII.13. See also, J. Mill, CPB:I.5v, 9v). William Mitford (1836:VII.282) had argued the opposite regarding discussion in Athens (cf. J. Mill, CPB:II.11r).
37. GH[II]:XI.324-5. Also, *CRG*:XIX.411. James Mill had already insisted upon this aspect of government (1825:VII.45; 1835a:287-9)—something which Alan Ryan (1974:200, 202), in his discussion on John Mill's defence of 'democratic politics', neglects to consider. Robert Devigne ignores the extent of agreement between Mill and Grote—a result of completely disregarding James Mill's influence on both of them (2006:242n5).
38. GH[II]:XI.320-1; GG[4]:XXV.1131. Also, OG:I.336ff; *OL*:XVIII.267ff.
39. SA[II]:XXII.239-40; SA[IV]:XXII.293; SA[III]:XXIII.253.
40. OG:I.337, 330; SA[I]:XXII.233; *OL*:XVIII.247.
41. GH[II]:XI.319. J. Mill, CPB:II.25v quoting Isocrates, *IA*:43 ('πατρίδα μὲν τὴν ἐλευθερίαν νομίσαντες'; Norlin, 1928:I.370-1). James Mill added: 'So say I, liberty is my country'.
42. GH[II]:XI.319; GE:XX.274.
43. GE:XX.274; GL:XX.384 (Mill to J. Blanko White, 21/10/1835:XII.280 and to H.S. Chapman, c. 11/1835:XII.284). Also, *OL*:XVIII.225-6.
44. GH[II]:XI.319; GL:XX.384.
45. GH[II]:XI.319; GG[4]:XXV.1129. See, Williams, 1982:5; Rosen, 2004:191-2.
46. See Biagini, 1996.
47. WAV:I.489; *OL*:XVIII.226; GH[II]:XI.319, 321; GH[I]:XI.274, 303 (Mill to J.M. Kemble, 16/07/1842, CW:XIII.532). See, Williams, 1982:8-9; Biagini, 1996:35-6. Athens presented one of those 'rare combinations of circumstance', Mill argued, as far as the 'progress of mankind' is concerned (*PPE*:II.12, 15-6).
48. See Lachs, 1992.
49. Constant, 1819:313n, 314-6, 321-3.
50. GE:XX.271-4 (Guizot, 1829:III.191ff); GH[II]:XI.319ff. Mill to H. Taylor, 17/03/1849:XIV.17-8.
51. Potter, 2005:133, 129; Constant, 1819:316ff; Holmes, 2009:53 (see also, Jennings, 2009).
52. Constant, 1819:326; GH[II]:XI.319ff.

53. A nation's affairs as a 'practical experiment' was an early acquired notion (sPR[1]:XXVI.268; sUH:XXVI.394. J. Mill, CPB:V.151r on Aristotle, *EN*:1103b2), which was further developed later on (e.g., DPE:IV.327-8).

54. Mill's Athens, as Roberts (1994:247) notes, was 'a slap in the face to the Mitfordian tradition'.

55. sPR[2]:XXVI.283; SSA:XVIII.110; GH[II]:XI.331, 314-5, 321-4.

56. GH[I]:XI.274. Also, SD:X.45.

57. *CRG*:XIX.392. Miller (2010:ch. 9) and Riley (2007) acknowledge this aspect of Mill's synthesis.

58. See further, Thompson, 1976; Biagini, 1996; Urbinati, 2002; Riley, 2007; Miller, 2010:ch. 9.

59. Burnham, 1977:254. Preyer (1982:58) also ignores this aspect.

60. Thompson, 1976:10-1.

61. Turner, 1981:401ff; Hamburger, 1999:ch. 1; Devigne, 2006:93-7; Urbinati, 2002:3-7; Villa, 2001:105; Giorgini, 2009:629.

62. *CRG*:XIX.438-40, 457-60; RWR:XIX.347; PCCD:IV.111-20. Ryan, 1974:ch. 7; Garforth, 1980: chs. 3-4.

63. *OL*:XVIII.265; *SOL*:VIII.938-9, 942. Both Devigne (2006:96-7) and Urbinati (2002:6) seem to underestimate the interdependence of great individuals and social conditions— each leans on a different side of the interaction. Mill considered the appearance of great individuals deciding 'critical moments' favorably to progress, despite unfavorable social conditions, 'happy accidents' (*CRG*:XIX.419, 438).

64. Thus, Mill did not believe that Athens and England 'stood in the same phase of cyclical development', as Thomas Arnold did (Turner, 1981:209-10). See also, Williams, 1982:4.

65. See, Villa, 2001:ch. 2. See also, SA[I]:XXII.230; SA[II]:XXII.238; SA[III]:XXII.252-3; SA[IV]:XXII.291-2; DTA[II]:XVIII.195n (ONI:XXII.73); *PPE*:II.209; GP:XI.436 (see further, Friedman, 1968).

66. GH[II]:XI.334-6; *CRG*:XIX.460. Here, Mill does not seem to argue that diachronically people opt for mediocre leaders, as Potter argues (2005:117-8, 128-9), rather it seems to be part of his argument that Athens was not Mitford's 'democratic dictatorship' after all.

67. Sparshott, 1978a:xxxv.

68. James Mill (1826a:I:154) had argued that 'superior spirits' accelerate the progress of their community and John Mill did after all call his father a 'philosophical historian' (*PPE*:II.321. See further, Thomas, 1979:176-7; Stafford, 1998:24, 37, 52; Kinzer, 2007:65). However, the elder Mill was not a typical follower of the 'Scottish school of philosophical history' (Thomas, 1979:99-100). For a discussion on the two Mills and Scottish historiography, see Burns, 1976 (cf. Vaio, 1996).

69. GH[II]:XI.326; GG[2]:XXIV.1088; GG[5]:XXV.1161.

70. GH[II]:XI.327-8, 331-2 (see also, J. Mill, 1825:V.8-9; CPB:V.120r).

71. GH[II]:XI.331; GG[5]:XXV.1160.

72. RR:XVIII.23, 26. Comparing these interests of the rulers and the ruled as shepherds and sheep (*CRG*:XIX.412; sWE[4]:XXVIII:32; CFR:XX:140) alludes to Plato (*Rep*:343a); the fable Mill used to discuss different class interests in reference to representation (RR:XVIII.44n; sBC[2]:XXVI.375-7) echoes the fables both from Aesop and Voltaire (in J. Mill, CPB:I.52r; II.50v).

73. Nicias, according to Grote, was mediocre 'in intellect, in education, and in oratory' (Grote, 1875:VI.286 quoted in GH[II]:XI.335; GG[3]:XXV.1124).

74. GH[II]:XI.333; PM:VI.402-3; Mill to J. Austin, 13/04/1847:XIII.713. Burns (1957:I.164-5, 175) ignores James Mill's influence, who had already suggested the election of the 'Aristoi and Beltistoi' (J. Mill, 1830:38; 1825:I.31-2. See also, Cicero, *DL*:III.31-2 in CPB:II.22v).

75. RWR:XIX.347; *CRG*:XIX.439-40; *OL*:XVIII.308.

76. For the role of the press and the railway in the mass dissemination of ideas, see TDA[II]:XVIII.165; *CRG*:XIX.378. Finley (1973:36) calls Mill's example a false analogy, but seen in the historical context of the time, public rail transport in 1820s- and 1830s-England was as much groundbreaking for communication as has been the world wide web for the last two decades.

77. Civ:XVIII.134-6, 138; GH[II]:XI.314. See also, Garforth, 1980:15.

78. *CRG*:XIX.439, 458; TPR:XIX.325. See also, GE:XX.268 (contra Urbinati, 2002:48-53).

79. GH[II]:XI.326, 334; GG[3]:XXV.1123; *CRG*:XIX.403-4, 411; TDA[II]:XVIII.169; TPR:XIX.322. Aristotle, *Pol*:1275a22 (in J. Mill, CPB:I.50v), 1276a9-b35, 1278b33ff (Coleman, 2000:I.216). See also, Ryan, 1974:202; Villa, 2001:100. See further, Jones, 2000:292.

80. *CRG*:XIX.488-91; Mill to G. C. Lewis, 20/03/1859:XV.608.

81 *CRG*:XIX.535-7, 545. For an equivalent example in Mill's economic theory, see *PPE*:II.280.

82. Whatever their faults, Mill argued, the Athenians 'abound[ed] in human nature' and yet they were never presented as a 'clown or a boor'; their political education—which included practice, as we just saw—had raised their 'intellectual standard', since those who governed appealed to their reason and did not simply exercise authority (*CRG*:XIX.411; SA[III]:XXII.253; SA[IV]:XXII.293; GH[II]:XI.316-7. See also, J. Mill, 1825:I.9 on the 'brilliant career' that human nature ran in Athens).

83. *CRG*:XIX.431; GG[2]:XXIV.1087-8.

84. C:X.138; *CRG*:XIX.484, 498; TS:XIX.641; GP:XI.436; WJR[1]:I.373. See also Burns, 1957:I.160; Pappé, 1979:306; Thomas, 1979:141; Garforth, 1980:24, 41, 65; Stafford, 1998:41; Irwin, 1998:433-9; Yake, 2006:10-2; Villa, 2001:117; Sotelo, 2006:369-70.

85. GH[II]:XI.325 (Plato, *Rep*:412b-5d); C:X.133-4; *OL*:XVIII.266. See also, Biagini, 1996:37; Irwin, 1998:437-9.

86. *A*:I.10-1, 32-3, 20-7.

87. GH[I]:XI.273; GH[II]:XI.316; GG[4]:XXV.1134. See also, Bain, 1882b:94.

88. Civ:XVIII.144-5; WLP:I.460; OG:I.337.

89. BHMS:X.27, 29. See, *OL*:XVIII.220. See also, Ogilvie, 1964:113-5.

90. Ryan, 1997:xxxv.

91. See Turner, 1981:68.

92. Potter, 2005:129; cf. Devigne 2006:6. Both Potter and Devigne seem to neglect to consider the connection between Mill's early studies and his later conclusions. Mill's argument for reform, as Urbinati (2002) has convincingly argued, drew on his radical reading of Athenian history.

93. SSA:XVIII.110; SA[III]:XXII.257; GH[II]:XI.336; sBC[1]:XXVI.367. James Mill argued similarly about Plato's *Republic* (1835a:289; from material collected around 1825 in CPB:I.165-7). Comparing Athens to England, the Utilitarians 'quickly realized', Ogilvie notes, that only representative government was feasible (1964:107).

94. Mill to H. Taylor, 17/03/1849:XIV.17-8. See also, Williams, 1982:7-8; Yake, 2006:8.

95. Grote, 1875:VI.200-2; GH[II]:XI.320.

96. Mill to H. Taylor Mill, 21/03/1855:XIV.38.

97. GH[I]:XI.273; Civ:XVIII.145; GL:XX.369.

98. These features did seem to make Plato attractive to utilitarianism, as Ogilvie has argued (1964:108-9). However, Mill believed that in pursuing this direction he differed from his utilitarian predecessors (*A*:I.177).

99. This letter (to Horace Horseleech, dated 'Blackheath, Nov. 5th') is not included in Mill's *CW*. It was published in *Fun* (02/01/1869:171). After Harriet's death (03/11/1858) Mill usually spent this time of year in Avignon, which makes it more likely that he composed this letter in 1868, when he was in England.

100. *PPE*:III.765.

# CHAPTER FIVE

## READING PLATO

Mill's translations stand out in the early-nineteenth-century rediscovery of Plato, while his later review 'Grote's Plato' was considered by Paul Shorey to be 'the best available general introduction to the study of Plato'. Mill, he added, rightly claimed the title of Platonist, combining 'severe logic with a passion for reforming the world'.[1] However, the lack of interest in studying the consequences of Mill's preoccupation with Plato runs counter to the wide recognition that Plato held a central role in Mill's intellectual development. In this chapter, I examine John Mill's early and novel attitude toward Plato. I then turn to Mill's review of Grote's *Plato, and the Other Companions of Sokrates* (1865) and Grote's reception. As already mentioned, James Mill, John Stuart Mill and George Grote argued primarily for the Sceptical or Radical Plato, rather than the Prophet or the Idealist Plato. Still, as this chapter attempts to show, the younger Mill's contribution bore the marks of his distinct intellectual make-up.

### MILL'S FIRST READING: DEFINING PLATO'S CREED

As we saw in the previous chapter, John Stuart Mill was very critical of the state of classical studies in England. This criticism applied to the state of Platonic studies as well: 'there are, probably, in this kingdom, not so many as a hundred persons who ever *have* read Plato, and not so many as twenty who ever *do*'.[2] In 1834, Mill tried to transform Plato 'from a dead word [...] into a living and challenging personality', one which could speak to Mill's time.[3] However, Mill did not attempt exact translations: '[i]t would [...] require a Plato, so to translate Plato as to render the ideas intelligible to an English reader'. As Mill noted, with a 'bald and verbose' English style, he traded in Plato's eloquent Greek for 'the very thoughts of Socrates, and his very mode of stating and illustrating those thoughts'.[4] But Plato's chosen literary form, as Mill indicated, posed serious problems; more so when the main speaker was a renowned philosopher with 'decided and known opinions' of his own—Socrates.[5] Trying to 'shew to the reader Plato himself', Mill drew his readers' attention to the absence of a definite doctrine, the 'lofty' moral ideals of Plato and Plato's method.[6] Concurrently, the value of Plato's moral teachings, Mill seemed to assert, was not undermined by shifting the focus from Plato's metaphysics to Plato's dialectics.

At the same time, Mill's short introductions offered one of the first defenses of the Sophists. The Sophists, as we saw, were often compared to the Radicals, in that by standing for 'materialism' and by challenging tradition, they were seen as having had a destructive effect on morals. However, Mill claimed that in the fallacies and 'verbal quibbling' of sophistic teachings 'there by no means appears to have been a greater proportion of doctrines having a pernicious tendency, than has existed in all ages'. More importantly, Mill argued, Plato's dialogues did not justify such negative attitude toward the Sophists. For example, if any view in Plato's *Protagoras* resembled Benthamite calculation in moral matter, it was Socrates', not Protagoras' view.[7]

However, Mill maintained, Plato's *Protagoras* showed that dialectics went 'much beyond the point which they [the Sophists] had attained in moral and political philosophy', without portraying them by way of 'ridicule or obloquy'. Mill may have been addressing those modern Sophists as well, when he noted 'that, on the whole, they left the science of mind and of virtue in an extremely unsatisfactory state'. What was required, Mill argued, was not 'a mere delivery of doctrines from master to student', practiced by the Sophists (and in Mill's time), but a close discussion between two persons in search of truth.[8]

As far as Plato was concerned, Mill, much like his father, criticized the attempts to build a system out of 'detached passages' from Plato's works. According to Mill, Plato's Socrates overthrew 'vague' and popular doctrines without putting others in their place and, quite as often, the use of irony would put into question the seriousness of any idea advanced. Thus, Socrates' worth in Plato's dialogues did not lie in the conclusions he reached (or failed to reach), Mill argued, but in the innovative mode of pursuing truth. In 'Phaedrus', Mill discussed in more detail the service to philosophy that constituted Plato's most important contribution: Plato required in any discussion 'a just and unambiguous definition of the subject-matter', which called for 'a process of [...] decomposition and recomposition, first distinguishing a whole into its kinds or parts, and then looking at those kinds or parts attentively, in such a manner as to extract from them the idea of the whole'. 'This two-fold process of analysis and synthesis' showed that 'when the subject-matter of the discussion [...] [was] the nature and properties of knowledge in the abstract, the opinions of Plato [...] [seemed] never to vary'.[9] Thus, drawing on Schleiermacher, Mill argued that though Socrates professed that he knew nothing, 'he however knew also what knowledge *was*, and how it was to be come at'.[10]

However, father and son did not share the same opinion, first, on the usability of Plato's *Protagoras* as indicative of Plato's creed; and, second, on the effectiveness of any form of intellectualism. In relation to the first difference, Mill argued that it was obvious that Plato's *Protagoras* was 'intended rather as an exercise in the art of investigating truth, than to inculcate any particular set of philosophical opinions', including utilitarianism. Though there was no need to attach to Plato a 'fixed creed' regarding the basis of virtue, Mill claimed, Plato was 'favourable to the opinion that certain qualities of mind are good or evil in themselves, independently of all considerations of pleasure or pain'.[11]

In relation to the second difference, according to Mill, Plato's *Gorgias* tried 'to enforce, by all manner of considerations, the superior dignity and eligibility of a virtuous life'. However, Mill added, Socrates had failed to convince his interlocutors about the intrinsic value of a virtuous life. Though reason can grasp arguments on how to live virtuously, it cannot create the desire for such a life: 'It is impossible', Mill claimed, 'by any arguments, to prove that a life of obedience to duty is preferable, so far as respects the agent himself, to a life of circumspect and cautious selfishness'. This had become an important aspect of Mill's filial dissent; and it played a great part in the development of his moral thought: trying to overcome, as Henry Sidgwick was to put it later, the 'duality of practical reason'.[12]

Mill came to believe 'that the understanding has no inducements which it can bring to the aid of one who has not yet determined whether he will endeavour to live virtuously or no'. But this put into question the educational precepts of Mill's fellow reformers: 'All valid arguments in favour of virtue, presuppose that we already desire virtue, or desire some of its ends and objects'. Thus, according to Mill, knowing one's enlightened interests, though necessary, was not sufficient to induce one to act on them: '[N]o arguments which Plato urges have power to make those love or desire virtue, who do not already: nor is this ever to be effected through the intellect, but through the imagination and the affections'.[13]

Such 'noble' feelings, i.e., the love of virtue, cannot be forced upon a person, Mill argued, but only be transferred by inspiration or sympathy from those who already possess it: individuals that 'we love and reverence' or from 'our ideal' of the life and character of individuals that reflect 'all noble qualities'. In addition, inspiration is found in the work of poets and artists who 'can clothe those feelings in the most beautiful forms, and breathe them into us through our imagination and our sensations'. Plato was a great moral writer, Mill added, by inspiring love for virtue through his 'stern resolution never to swerve from it'— an effect of imagination frequently underestimated by utilitarians. A life of *obedience* to the duty to act for the 'greatest happiness'—even if such a life is argued to be the best life—alluded to coercion. In contrast, a virtuous character suggests no coercion.[14]

Thus, emotional, rather than intellectual, cultivation could provide the *natural* attachment to virtue which Mill had in mind.[15] Still, Francis Sparshott wonders why Mill's 'normally cool tone' transformed to 'an oddly histrionic pathos', in the discussion of the connection between virtue, happiness and the fate of the modern Socrates. Sparshott suggests that Mill felt that 'his own virtue has been unjustly despised and rejected, and whose toil has been without reward',[16] it being a period during which he often brought up the absence of a 'suitable culture' to encourage originality. However, Sparshott ignores Mill's literary engagement with poetry during this time. Mill's 'pathos' may have been an attempt to recapture some of the lost charm of his translation—it being 'ill fitted to convey any idea of the degree in which this dialogue makes the feelings and course of life which it inculcates commend themselves to our inmost nature'.[17]

To recapitulate, Mill's 'Protagoras' argued, first, that the most important feature of the Platonic dialogues was Plato's method; second, that Plato's dialogues did not give reason to cry down the Sophists; third, that Plato's only creed was that there was a deep connection between knowledge and virtue—a connection, of which the Sophists, both ancient and modern, could only grasp a shallow version (in which the principle of expediency was of paramount importance). Thus, whatever other tendencies appeared in Plato's dialogues, Mill argued, Plato's only 'deliberate and serious creed' was 'that whoever had knowledge to see what was good, would certainly do it'; but this reduced morality to 'a branch of intelligence'—knowledge was all that was required for virtue.[18] Furthermore, Mill's 'Gorgias' expanded on this connection: virtue required holistic cultivation, both intellectual and emotional. In this dialogue, Mill argued, Plato attempted to do this at two levels. The first level was what took place between Socrates and his interlocutors. But Socrates failed to convince them, as mere argument was insufficient. It required inspiration to make them see that virtue was preferable to cautious selfishness. Still, Plato pursued this at the second level: between reader and the work itself. Thus, the reader sees both arguments played out in the dialogue; but only Socrates' devotion to virtue and truth, in the face of all dangers, excites the reader's feelings. Though Plato's *Republic* did discuss emotional cultivation (starting from a similar deadlock in the first book), it was perhaps too long to be translated; Socrates' example would have to be enough—perhaps this is the reason why Mill published Plato's *Apology*, unabridged and unannotated, last.

## Mill's Novelty

It remains a question why Mill chose to translate Plato in the late 1820s. He was probably being honest when he said that he had made his translations for his own and his siblings' studies.[19] It is not very likely that he intended to show them to anyone else at this time. If he did so, George Grote would have been the expected recipient—especially since in the second half of the 1820s Mill and his friends gathered at the 'Threddle' (George Grote's house on Threadneedle Street) for their 'social studies', while Grote was preoccupied with his 'Digest of the

Dialogues of Plato' and the history of Greece.[20] However, just like Grote showed no sign of being familiar with Mill's translations so did Mill with Grote's 'digests' which primarily focused on Schleiermacher's introductions to Plato. Mill seems to have been first introduced to Schleiermacher's reading of Plato in 1833—just before the publication of his own translations.[21]

As we saw, Mill stressed that Plato, the 'most gifted of Greek writers', had 'definite views' on the 'theory of the pursuit of truth' (i.e., 'the proper course for inquiry' and 'the spirit in which it should be conducted'). Moreover, Mill argued that Plato, being preoccupied 'with confuting the absurdities of others', lacked what could 'be called, with any assurance, tenets or a philosophy'. This was James Mill's Plato: expanding on various ideas, 'the value of which he was not certain', often in sport or without seriousness—he had after all gone through all the volumes of the *Edinburgh Review* (in which his father's review essay on Plato appeared) just a few years earlier. [22] Thus, John Mill considered his choice to limit the 'dramatic excellencies' of the dialogues justified; in contrast, the 'more important and interesting' argumentative parts were 'very little curtailed'.[23]

In her discussion of Mill's 'Protagoras', Alexandra Lianeri confirms Mill's radical reading of Plato. Discussing Mill's philological exertions, Lianeri argues that Mill remained faithful to the 'Socratic spirit'. Other translators have since defined calculation (in the 'measuring art' section of the dialogue) as *either* the art *or* knowledge of immediate and distant utility. But, by dropping the conjunctive syntax of the original, which rendered the translation '*both* the art (*technê*) *and* knowledge (*epistêmê*)' of utility, they failed to capture Socrates' call for the 'harmonious concordance of word and deed, of thought and practice'.[24]

However, Lianeri further argues that by effacing Socratic irony, Mill failed to capture Socrates' critique of authority. But Mill had already identified the destructive effect of Socratic irony as a means to overthrow 'vague doctrines' and questioned the seriousness of 'the entire discourse'.[25] It is essential to remember that Mill did not try to produce an English edition of his works. Lianeri ignores that Mill's abridgements focused almost exclusively on the parts that exhibited the method of 'decomposition and recomposition', often giving a partial picture of the dialogue and diminishing its 'beauty and power'.[26] That Mill acknowledged that 'the finest specimens of the higher comedy have hardly equalled, and certainly not surpassed' Plato's use of irony and then moved on to the argumentative parts of the dialogue,[27] was a symptom of taking, perhaps mistakenly, irony to be part of its 'dramatic excellencies'. However, Mill aimed to show that Socrates' profession of ignorance and his attempt to bring out the ignorance of others was 'an absolutely necessary' first step 'towards inducing them to acquire knowledge'.[28]

In his translation of Plato's *Protagoras*, Lianeri adds, Mill saw dialectics as 'the collective and critical mode of sifting opinions carried out by free and equal interlocutors, none of whom is in firm possession of knowledge'. Lianeri's discussion on Mill's view of Plato's dialectics makes no effort to move beyond this particular abridged translation, i.e., to the brief discussions in Mill's 'Phaedrus', *On Liberty* and 'Grote's Plato'. Thus, Lianeri takes 'free and equal interlocutors' as the sole alternative to a 'master and student' relation; she also takes it to mean that none of the interlocutors was in 'firm possession of knowledge'. However, Mill believed that the greatest source of friendship is community of purpose and reciprocal superiority, rather than intellectual equality—as he noted in an early letter: '[e]ach of us knows many things which the other knows not, & can do many things which the other values but cannot himself do, or not so well'. By each supplying what the other lacks, Mill argued, two people have more chances to approximate 'truth'.[29]

The 'agonistic debate' in search of 'truth' thus depends on the interlocutors being different and possessing different parts of knowledge, rather than considering any 'firm possession of knowledge' as a presumption of infallibility. However, Mill argued that '[t]o suppose that dialectic training only trains dialecticians, is great ignorance of its power and virtue. Such training is an indispensable education for dogmatic thinkers'. Likewise, Mill was familiar with the 'dialectical contests' of ancient Greeks, in which they did not go after 'truth' but victory—Plato displayed his philosophic and poetic genius, James Mill argued, by defeating other thinkers in their own field of expertise.[30] Thus, Lianeri claims that Mill's view of Plato's dialectics (i.e., the negation of authority and dogmatism that such 'agonistic process of critical persuasion and consent' involves) pointed to the 'inseparability of philosophy and democratic politics'.[31] But Mill's essays on ancient Greek thought suggested a much more complex connection between authority, truth and democratic institutions.

Unlike Lianeri, Karen Whedbee is aware that Mill's translations did not simply form part of 'an abstract academic exercise in philology or in the history of philosophy'. In her discussion of Mill's 'Gorgias', Whedbee argued that Mill's search for a 'usable' Plato 'simultaneously assumed and advanced a specific political and religious agenda'. Mill tried to do this through the rejection of the prevalent readings of Plato. Like Grote's and Macaulay's recent critiques of Mitford, Mill followed the practice of criticizing the conservative ideas that pervaded religious, educational and social institutions by commentary on the classics.[32]

Mill, Whedbee argues, responded to two distinct readings of Plato: Taylor's 'religious mysticism', which carried Plato into metaphysical realms in the attack on 'the materialism of consumer culture and modern science', and Macaulay's 'technocratic materialism'. For Macaulay, Whedbee notes, the contrast between Plato and Bacon 'illuminates the progressive improvement of philosophy through the ages'; Plato encouraged 'readers to strive toward vain and unattainable absolutes', when Bacon 'aimed at less lofty but more easily attained goals' of immediate and practical utility.[33]

Strictly speaking Whedbee's argument is anachronistic (Macaulay's 'Bacon' appeared three and a half years after Mill's 'Gorgias'). But Mill did come across such ideas in debates on the usefulness of classics and in Bentham's works. Unlike Bentham, Macaulay, considered the words of the ancient philosophers 'noble' in aiming to form 'the minds of men to a high degree of wisdom and virtue'—writing from India in 1835, 'deep in Plato', he found Plato's genius to be 'above praise'.[34] But, like Bentham, he thought that ancient philosophers 'filled the world with long words and long beards; and they left it as wicked and as ignorant as they found it'—Bacon's philosophy 'began in observations and ended in arts', whereas Plato's 'began in words and ended in words'.[35]

However, contrary to Taylor and Macaulay, Mill drew his readers' attention to the value of Plato's dialectics in both the search for truth and the attempt to clarify popular ideas of practical importance. He steered the interpretation of Plato toward the radical view, arguing that the 'substance' of Plato's method lay in being 'a well-conducted and unbiased inquiry into the meaning of established terms'. But also Mill argued that Plato, not Bacon, was 'the person who first turned the minds of speculative men, long occupied in verbal disputes, to the discovery of new truth'.[36]

Whedbee was right in arguing that Mill published his translations, particularly the 'Gorgias', to recommend 'a platform for reflecting on the role of virtue in an age of popular commercial culture'.[37] This is corroborated by Mill's claims in 'Protagoras', and other writings of the time, that the modern commercial life would bring to an end 'the tranquil pursuit' of literature.[38] However, Whedbee ignores the connection between this pursuit and self-cultivation and thus overemphasises the comparison between Socrates and Christ—a common view as we saw—claiming that Mill was 'infused with a kind of religious enthusiasm'.[39]

Still, Whedbee does point toward Mill's more pressing concerns. Cultivating the affective capacity of individuals was part of his re-framing of the utilitarian conception of human nature. Mill suggested that inspiration did not point so much to a limitation of reason, but that it was a function for which the faculty of reasoning was not responsible.[40] However, Whedbee lays special emphasis on Mill's view regarding 'the attitude and spirit of dialogic performance', arguing that Plato's 'specific doctrines and arguments are not especially important by themselves' to Mill. Whedbee concludes that Mill saw that the 'moral insight brought about by elenchus is the awareness of human fallibility and the need to resist self-satisfaction'. Thus, Mill's novelty consisted in highlighting that Plato's dialectics teach 'us to challenge the conceit of "half thinkers" who rush to their conclusions without taking the trouble to understand the perspectives of others'.[41] Though Whedbee does see an indirect connection between these dialogues and Mill's major works, in the chapters that follow I argue that some of Plato's 'specific doctrines and arguments' *were* 'especially important by themselves'.

## MILL'S SECOND READING: GROTE'S *PLATO*

Three decades after Mill's translations, George Grote published his *Plato*. Combining detail, accuracy and extended familiarity with ancient sources and the most recent German literature, Grote's book became 'a major literary event' in

English and continental scholarship.[42] But it 'did not win immediate popularity'. Interested readers and scholars seemed to be sceptical of Grote's intentions, since they would view it as a covert campaign for 'philosophical liberalism', but also in several aspects, a misreading of Plato. However, sharing many of Grote's 'prejudices' on the worth of Plato as a philosopher, Mill saw no 'apparent paradox of a radical, democratic, utilitarian author publishing a work on the most spiritual and idealistic of ancient Greek philosophers'; theirs was the Sceptical and Radical Plato.[43]

Grote's reviewers can be distinguished into two groups: those who did not consider his radical-utilitarian credentials to be a problem to his interpretation, and those who did. This dichotomy still persists today.[44] Both Mill and Grote were aware of the dangers of bias; but, as Mill noted, impartiality should not be confused with having no opinion.[45]

Alexander Bain's, George Henry Lewes' and James Richard Thursfield's focus was on the worth of Plato as a Sceptic. To this effect, philosophy, Bain argued, is primarily polemical—the philosopher calls for proof where others believe without it; scepticism, Lewes added, 'is the initial state of all true knowledge'.[46] In the opinion of these reviewers, Grote was nothing like previous classical scholars. In his work, Plato's *negative* dialogues were extolled for their contribution to philosophical progress. Accordingly, for Thursfield, Grote's reading had diminished the value of Plato the philosopher of the conservative party and of the romantic poets and had revealed the worth of the Sceptical Plato.[47] Following Grote, the Socratic method was accepted as 'the initiative of a genuine scientific operation'; Socrates, Bain added, was the 'originator of Inductive Definition'. Moreover, Grote had managed to illustrate the value of Plato's negative dialogues, in which '[t]here is a process of inquiry, of search, not only fruitless, but devious, circuitous, and intentionally protracted'; a process, Bain argued, which cancelled the relation between a teacher and a student, indicating a 'co-partnery in intellectual labour' and admitting no 'shame in the confession of ignorance'. Thus, according to these reviewers, Grote had pointedly argued that Plato's method, inherited from Socrates, illustrated 'that philosophy is a process of investigation'—'a method, not a body of truth', which removes 'false persuasions'.[48]

Moreover, accepting Grote's view on Plato's canon, this group of reviewers argued that Plato had 'passed round from the negative to the affirmative pole of philosophy' in his late years.[49] Plato's early phase owed much to the eminence of dialectics, Thursfield argued, which more than anything else 'familiarizes people with the idea of there being others who disagree with them, and thus it tends indirectly to set up a reaction against the intolerable supremacy of mere custom'—one can see why this review caught Mill's eye.[50] Plato was a Sceptic, Lewes added, it being impossible to fix down his views convincingly. More importantly, Thursfield noted, Plato's contribution to philosophy lay rather in his role of 'a searcher, tester, and impugner than that of an expositor, and dogmatist'. Thus, in an inverted career with that of Plato, Bain wrapped up his review, Grote emerged in his literary endeavor as a champion of the liberty of thought.[51]

However, not all reviewers were impressed by all these aspects of Grote's iconoclastic work. Edward Caird noted that Grote was wanting in imagination, and was neither subtle nor speculative, as 'delicate distinctions and shades of meaning' were 'either obliterated or exaggerated by his strong but heavy pen'—these were similar to comments made privately by Mill in 1833.[52] Likewise, Lewis Campbell noted that Grote's 'cast of mind' was so inherently different from Plato's, that Grote could not appreciate certain aspects of Plato's thought. Similarly to Caird, Campbell argued that Grote's intellectual powers were insufficient for Plato's ideal philosophy—especially when 'clothed in an imaginative form'. For example, Grote's philosophical sympathies afforded no preparation for either the treatment of knowledge in Plato's *Theaetetus* (a point of criticism shared by Mill) nor for appreciating Plato's conception of the Good.[53] Similarly, Benjamin Jowett asked Grote, his 'father Parmenides', to forgive him for differing on Plato's Canon, and on his treatment of the Sophists as well as for approaching Plato's philosophy from 'a point of view which is opposed to his own'.[54]

Even if this group of reviewers did not agree with all aspects of his study, Grote's work was considered to be 'invariably interesting and instructive'.[55] When the philosophical interest was closer to the speculative sympathies of Grote, Caird noted, the reader's mind was 'braced by the atmosphere of intellectual energy' and saw that Plato's process of inquiry was 'at once a stimulus and a discipline'. In the dialectical combats of Plato, Caird added, Grote proved to be the best spectator or judge. But when the philosophical interest did not accord with Grote's speculative sympathies (i.e., in those dialogues where not the negative, but the 'speculative or constructive element predominates'), Grote's performance was unsatisfactory. More importantly, Grote had failed to capture Plato's 'characteristic transfusion of emotion and thought', Caird noted, because of bias and theoretical inflexibility.[56]

Thus, Plato was 'less sceptical and less dogmatical' and contradicted himself 'less violently', Campbell noted, than Grote had supposed—a distortion of Plato which was attributed once again to Grote's intellectual sympathies.[57] Furthermore, Caird argued that Grote's distinction between earlier and later dialogues was too sharp, and did not take under consideration that the answers of Plato's later years still aimed in addressing the issues of his youth—they were the required metaphysical basis to Socrates' morals. Moreover, Grote's arrangement of Plato's dialogues, Campbell added, failed to depict accurately the nature of Plato's method. Though he respected Grote's emphasis on negative dialectics, Campbell argued that Plato's negative search was not completely detached from his positive expositions. Plato's negative dialectics had a positive aim: Socrates revealed the ignorance of his interlocutors to 'awaken in them the desire of knowledge'; Plato was not a mere sceptic but a 'rational inquirer'; his method had a 'silent inward dialectic', 'a deeper movement of the intellect'. Thus, the results of Plato's elenchus were influenced by presupposed positive ideas.[58]

Grote's 'misconceptions' did not mean that he was not amply praised even by his severest critics. He pointed to a side of Plato that needed to be studied more, Campbell argued, which would—and did—lead to the revitalization of Platonic studies in Britain.[59] Grote's original interpretation, Whewell noted, unlocked a 'treasure of new thoughts'.[60] It is illustrative of the extent of Grote's impact on Platonic scholarship, that some complained that

> [s]o much has been done lately to bring out the dialectic and negative elements in the Platonic dialogues that it may not be without use to call attention to this positive and (so to speak) prophetic side of his work, which is now in some danger of being forgotten.[61]

However, Grote's interpretation held its ground, its impact on Plato scholarship still being evident today.[62]

## Mill on Plato Through Grote

Mill undertook the task of preparing for and producing a review of Grote's *Plato* with excitement.[63] Before reading all three volumes, he was already very satisfied.[64] His impression was that Grote said 'exactly those [things] which it was good to say, and which required saying'. Grote's work was important, Mill added, because not many people were 'sufficiently familiar both with Plato and with philosophy, without being full of wrong ideas on the latter, if not on both'.[65] Thus, even if it took longer than desired,[66] Grote had produced an 'inexpugnable' general conception of Plato and an excellent piece of scholarship.[67] Much like his 'digests' of thirty years earlier, Mill discussed Plato's lack of a definite creed; his forceful moral ideals; his original method; and his reception of the Sophists.[68]

Rather expectedly, Mill quickly dissociated Grote and himself from the Neoplatonic systems of 'little intrinsic value'. Grote had convinced Mill that what platonic elements appeared in them owed 'chiefly to the decadence of Plato's own mind'.[69] This was an important difference between the two Mills. James Mill had never accepted any such 'decadence'. Still, father and son agreed that Socrates had set aside the early physical and metaphysical speculations and applied the method of cross-examination to the 'generalities relating to life and conduct'. Moreover, in Plato's dialogues, Mill noted, morals and politics were considered 'an affair of science'.[70] This was the chief value of Plato's dialectics, as we saw. Thus, similarly with Grote's first group of reviewers, Mill distinguished between negative and positive dialogues and pointed to the 'real uncertainty' with regard to Plato's opinions: Plato tried and rejected many beliefs without advancing 'a consistent system of opinions, always adhered to and always coming out victorious'. Though he must have held positive opinions, Mill noted, the bulk of Plato's works exhibited 'mere negation and confutation'.[71]

Any direct evidence from Plato's dialogues, Mill added, must be accompanied with a study of the surrounding circumstances, to justly infer and deduce theories from them.[72] The lack of such attentiveness was the reason for the prevailing wrong views about the Sophists. Similarly, Mill thought that those who rendered Plato the father of Idealism, who argued against the 'materialism' of his contemporaries, had a simplistic view of Plato's thought.[73] This was mirrored in Mill's depiction of Plato's metaphysical doctrine as being the latter's weak point.[74] Plato's strong point was the pursuit of truth (which was connected to his metaphysical speculations) and his dialectical method. True to his father's convictions, Mill viewed Plato's attachment to the pursuit of truth as Plato's only philosophical creed—the rest were cast aside as 'poetic fancies', as Mill put it in his *Autobiography*.[75]

Moreover, it was a natural consequence that Plato would be antagonistic to those who carried and reproduced false opinions—namely the Sophists, but rhetoricians and aspiring politicians as well. According to Mill, Plato sought to define concepts that were considered invaluable to human conduct, such as justice, virtue, good and evil. For this reason, by means of the character of Socrates, Plato often inquired into common opinions and standards, to find the essence and the meaning of the words that were not really understood: false standards of good and evil of the multitude corrupted young men and filled them with 'vulgar ambition'.[76] This indirectly aimed Mill's England, as I discuss in the next chapter.

Mill pointed to two principles in Plato's search for the relevance of truth in a person's life: first, that there was a need for a method for ethics and politics; second, that this method required 'rigorous negative dialectics'. In ethics and politics, Mill commented on Plato, study and training, theory and practice, thought and action provided the necessary knowledge, but individuals needed to form habits of looking at both sides of a question, at what could be said *for* it as well as *against* it, and be able to sift between opinions until every logical and practical objection has been removed. Plato's method offered the only way to 'light the ideas that lie at the bottom' of such concepts as *good* and *evil, just* and *unjust, honourable* and *shameful*, and locate the common attribute of particular instances—since, Mill added, knowing what made an act just or good or virtuous, was a prerequisite for an individual to become just, good or virtuous.[77]

Retaining his early view to Plato's method as a process of 'decomposition and recomposition', Mill argued that its *negative* part sought to find all difficulties of or objections to an opinion—internal or external contradictions with facts or with earlier hypotheses, aiming to discern *apparent* from *real* knowledge. The *positive* part, the search for the common feature of things classed together, exhibited Socrates' and Plato's originality, i.e., the 'bond of union' of particulars, whose original idea Plato conceived as self-existent. Plato's dialectics were an invaluable means to guide one's life according to reason not custom, i.e., an 'art of living': it exposed ignorance, stimulated the pursuit of knowledge and required people neither to take opinions on trust nor maintain belief in 'vague generalities'.[78]

However, Plato's dialectics, Mill concluded, tend to lead philosophers to a 'solitary and despised position', in absence of a culture of freedom of thought: no one can easily accept their 'deep-seated, long familiarised notions' being questioned, or being themselves required to put those 'vague generalities, which serve as the standard of censure or applause in common discourse [...] on the logical rack'. Plato's dialectics elucidated 'truth' as a 'double-question'—defending a true belief from objections but also confuting opposite opinions. But 'the discipline which purges the intellect itself, protecting it from false generalization, inconclusive inference, and simple nonsense, on subjects which it imperfectly knows', was 'absent from all but a few minds'.[79] Unlike eristic, Plato's dialectical method was not antagonistic but a *joint* pursuit of truth, the 'genuine, unbiased, untampered with, conviction of the individual reason, after giving an impartial hearing to every argument that can be thought of',[80] aiming to encourage and stimulate students to exercise their mind and clear their 'thoughts from confusion'—this was precisely what, and how, James Mill had taught young John.[81]

However, the above did not mean, to Mill's mind, that Plato's method was only concerned with the intellectual part of a person's cultivation. The proper definition of popular terms was often 'connected with emotional sentiments and practical impulses and restraints'. For example, if the conduct of individuals was motivated by a conception of justice, being supported by the required sentiments and impulses, then the clarification of what justice is would direct their conduct to proper just actions. This, Mill argued, presupposed an agent to be already disposed to acting justly—i.e., had the feeling and needed only guidance.[82]

According to Mill and Grote, Plato abandoned this insight in his late years. The Dogmatic Plato was a different person from the Socratic Plato by either choosing not to apply this method on his later views, or ignoring its implications. For Mill, Plato's faith in the efficacy of dialectics had diminished. He became convinced that every truth could stumble on some insoluble objection, and that the doctrines with the 'best ethical tendency should be taught, with little or no regard to whether they could be proved true, and even at the risk of their being false'; no longer was knowledge seen to be the product of 'long and varied course of dialectic debate', but came out 'by a sort of instantaneous flash'. From scepticism, Plato had moved 'to the most intolerant affirmative dogmatism'.[83]

However, according to Robert Devigne, Mill saw in Grote's *Plato* the 'reflection of a long-standing problem with empiricism's view of liberty and morality'. By contrasting Mill to Grote, Devigne has argued that Mill embraced a Coleridgean view of Plato's dialectics. Devigne seems right in arguing that Mill did not want to be identified with Grote. However, this may have had more to do with Mill trying to be considered as an independent thinker.[84] Mill accepted Grote's conclusions on the most important debates of the time: the Platonic canon, the Sophists, Socrates' character and the value of dialectics. Though Grote did not discuss the failure of reason to motivate virtue in Plato's *Gorgias*, Mill had pointed to Grote's analysis of the Protagorian *homo mensura* thesis as the *only* 'important point' of disagreement between them, which Mill attributed to the vague use of language in Plato's text. Moreover, Mill did not criticize Grote's empiricism, but the implications his reading of the text had on 'truth'.[85] More importantly, not only does Devigne fail to see that Mill's review remained strictly within the outlines of Grote's book, but also seems unaware that Grote, in turn, had been influenced by Mill's *On Liberty*.[86]

There were undeniable differences between the two men and Mill considered Grote 'more a disciple of [...] [his] father than of anyone else'.[87] But Devigne forgets that the two Mills and Grote argued primarily for the Sceptic Plato. Ignoring the complex relationship between James Mill, John Mill and George Grote regarding Plato weakens Devigne's suggestion that the younger Mill read Plato through Coleridge.[88] James Mill was as original as Schleiermacher, whose insights on Plato's dialectic James Mill had anticipated in Britain.[89] As we saw, Mill's father turned to Cicero because: '[o]pinions such as those of the latter Platonists were justly held unworthy of the serious examination of a sensible man'. The elder Mill considered himself to be a sensible man, and so he had turned to the sceptical academy to find what he thought to be the real Plato. He had still distinguished between Plato's attempts to expose the fallacies and dangers of popular impressions and attempts to advance hypotheses—without establishing 'any system of opinions', but indicating tendencies, the younger Mill added.[90]

However, according to John Mill, Plato was also a 'powerful master of virtue', as he never wavered on 'the transcendent worth of virtue and wisdom' and 'the infinitely superior eligibility of the just life'. Plato was a 'Great Teacher', a philosopher and a poet, Mill added, because he could make his readers feel what he felt: '[o]thers can instruct, but Plato is of those who form great men, by the combination of moral enthusiasm and logical discipline'. Mill was thus still convinced that Plato produced the effects he sought 'by working on the feelings and imagination': the 'picture of the moral hero [...] against the hostility and contempt of the world,' Mill argued, gave Plato's *Gorgias* its 'splendour and power'—showing that 'the disinterested love of virtue is an affair of feeling'. Socrates did not prove that there is no worse evil than injustice; he made the readers feel it 'by the sympathy he calls forth with his own intense feeling of it'. Plato's *Gorgias* was for Mill one of the greatest steps 'ever made in moral culture—the cultivation of a disinterested preference of duty for its own sake, as a higher state than that of sacrificing selfish preferences to a more distant self-interest'.[91]

Notwithstanding Plato's merits, Mill could not find a firm criterion of virtue or excellence. Unlike *Gorgias*, Plato's *Republic* offered some more weighty arguments for the 'excellence and inherent felicity of the just life'; virtue referred to the superiority of reason in the harmonious soul, whereas Plato's *Protagoras* established a hedonistic criterion to virtue. Plato's *Philebus* identified five things that were constituents of the *Good*. The 'grand defect' in these ethical considerations, Mill noted, was Plato's failure to notice 'that the essential part of the virtue of justice is the recognition and observance of the rights of other people': by being grounded in reason, it was defined as the agent's own good. Sparshott justly wondered how Mill could fail to realize the indications that justice did concern the good of others, especially when Mill himself commented on how Plato's *Republic*'s 'perfect commonwealth' was not trying to establish the happiness of one class but the happiness of the whole. But this was not the only thing that did not quite fit here. Mill agreed with Grote that Plato failed to see that social virtues needed to be grounded in the social feelings as well as reason to stimulate care for others but he still named Plato a 'Great Teacher' because of the combination of philosophical method and the excitement of noble feelings.[92]

In addition, according to Mill, when Plato identified virtue and knowledge via the measuring principle, he never showed by what criterion life must be regulated. It required a discriminating faculty to decide when people ought to act virtuously and how, but Plato could only prove that 'the knowledge in question is one of the conditions of virtue, but not that it is virtue itself; something else besides the knowledge of what is right being necessary to induce us to practise it'. Plato would answer, Mill argued, that by knowing that something is good, people desire it. Still, the 'habitually vicious man' could not be convinced. Thus, as Plato advanced in life '[t]he idea of Measure as a good in itself' became 'independent of any end beyond it'—it became 'the One'—; and 'the noble light of philosophy in Plato [...] [went] out in a fog of mystical Pythagoreanism'.[93]

Mill concluded his review by discussing Plato's 'irreparably flawed' political design. As Malcolm Schofield aptly summarizes, Mill drew the image of a 'Scientific Governor' from Plato's *Statesman* rather than his *Republic*. In the former dialogue, the statesman possesses 'philosophic and reasoned knowledge of human affairs'—the science 'of what is best for mankind', whereas in *Republic* the philosopher-king possesses metaphysical knowledge—which could not interest Mill less. Thus, 'the *Statesman* explains what scientific government *is*,' through a view of knowledge as being 'geared to practice'; but, Schofield adds, 'the *Republic* [...] tells us the social and educational arrangements we need if we are to produce people qualified for the job of the government'.[94] By dividing labor, each citizen focused only on the business which s/he had a natural aptitude for. In this way, scientific government managed the interests of the whole community—the unscientific multitude did not have a joint authority on issues of their own interests. Mill noted that '[t]he error of Plato, like most of the errors of profound thinkers, consisted in seeing only one half of the truth'. Plato had focused on scientific rulers to protest at the institutions and customs of his country. Thus, by 'clinging' to one principle—the infallibility of scientific governors—, Plato neglected the Athenians' side of the truth—i.e., that they ought to be involved in the administration of their interests.[95]

## CONCLUDING REMARKS

Around 1828, translating from the new edition of Immanuel Bekker,[96] John Mill, like his father, viewed the suitability of Plato's dialectics for the pursuit of truth as the only thing certain about Plato. Plato's dogmatism was entirely attributed to his successors.[97] John Mill's admiration for Socrates as a freethinker curing the false impressions of his time echoed, to some extent, James Mill. So did the inability to attribute seriousness to his arguments because of Socrates' frequent use of irony. Thus, scholars have pointedly connected Mill's and Grote's interpretations of Plato as an 'open-minded critical philosopher' to James Mill. Their views stemmed from the originality of 'their common teacher', whose role in shaping their views must not be underestimated. Still, as Kyriakos Demetriou puts it, Mill and Grote read Plato 'each in his own fashion and in accordance with his own temperament'.[98]

Mill agreed in the main with Grote—he did mention that he would attempt to reproduce Grote's thoughts in a condensed form.[99] Rather necessarily, Mill abridged some and ignored others of Grote's materials, thinking that in the short space a review allowed there were more important issues to be discussed—e.g., Plato's relation to Socratic dialectics. He was excited at the prospect of discussing so much of Plato in the same space, being offered the long sought occasion to write his own thoughts on Plato.[100] Thus, he devoted himself to this review, hoping the amount of 'time and pains' he had spent on it to be 'well employed', by doing 'justice to the subject'.[101] Doing justice to the subject required seeing both of its sides, and Mill's minor disagreement echoed some aspects that Caird and Campbell had raised, as we saw. Still, Mill observed that in his 'compendious account of all [Plato]' there was not 'anything both important and new in it'; Grote had 'left nothing to do: except that every fresh turning over of the ground makes some of the things that are turned up look new by some new light which falls on them'.[102]

More importantly, very few, according to Mill, would doubt 'that had there been no Socrates, no Plato, and no Aristotle, there would have been no philosophy for the next two thousand years, nor in all probability then'.[103] Whereas Samuel Taylor Coleridge pointed to the *Theaetetus*, *Sophist*, *Statesman* and *Republic* as Plato's most important dialogues, Mill considered *Protagoras*, *Gorgias*, *Phaedrus* and *Republic* to be Plato's masterpieces.[104] These were indeed the dialogues that, had Plato been alive in Mill's time, would force the privileged of the political establishment to regard him in much the same way 'as they regard other freethinkers, socialists, and visionary reformers of the world'.[105]

## NOTES

1. Shorey, 1938:231-2 (also Sparshott, 1978a:xxxiii). Shorey even claimed that Mill was 'perhaps the greatest of nineteenth-century Platonists'.
2. Pr:XI.39-40. Also sU[1]:XXVI.352. As we saw, even when Plato's voice was heard in early-nineteenth century, the emphasis was either on the connection of Plato to Christianity or 'on the ability to construe and compose' (Ogilvie, 1964:101-2. Also, Clarke, 1959:101-2; Sparshott, 1978a:xxi; Turner, 1981:369; Irwin, 1998:441). See further, Demetriou, 1999:ch. 6.
3. Borchardt, 1946:1-2. See also, *A*:I.206-7.
4. AS:XI.152. Mill took his father's strictures on translation seriously (see, J. Mill, 1804:II.578ff). However, John Mill presumed that skipping over the dramatic parts of the dialogues affected neither the thoughts of Plato's Socrates nor his method of stating them.
5. Pr:XI.40. Who speaks for Plato remains a live question in Platonic studies (cf. Press, 2000; Lane, 2001).

6. Mill to T. Carlyle, 02/03/1834:XII.216; Pr:XI.60; Go:XI.97.

7. Pr:XI.43, 61.

8. This was what was needed in order to *inspire* virtue (see, BHMS:X.27-9).

9. Ph:XI.93. Here, John followed his father's view on 'philosophical analysis' (J. Mill, 1826c:13-4. See further, Loizides, 2012).

10. Mill to T. Carlyle, 05/10/1833:XII.181.

11. Pr:XI.40-2, 44, 61 (contra Burnham, 1977:212, 216). As in the case of Athens, Mill's discussions of Plato and Socrates in his reviews of Grote's works and his own translations were more nuanced than in his major works. For example, contrary to what he discusses in 1834, in *Utilitarianism* (*U*:X.205), he argues that Socrates in Plato's *Protagoras*—as James Mill thought—was advancing the theory of utility. This led Grote to write to Mill to correct him that Plato's Socrates in *Protagoras*, unlike utilitarians, argued for 'the happiness of the agent himself', not the happiness of mankind. But for Mill that Socrates defined happiness in terms of pleasure and pain was sufficient to call him a utilitarian (See G. Grote to J.S. Mill, 01/1863, in H. Grote, 1873:257-8 and J.S. Mill to G. Grote, 10/01/1862, XV.764).

12. Go:XI.97, 149. See also, Sidgwick, 1907:508-9.

13. Go:XI.149-50 (also,B:X.91).

14. Go:XI.150; Pr:XI.53; Ch:XI.175n; GP:XI.408. See also, *OL*:XVIII.269; Yake, 2006:14; Donner, 2007:254-5.

15. See, RBP:X.17; SD:X.50.

16. Sparshott, 1978a:xxV. Still, Mill's analysis of the dialogue had severe omissions: Mill failed to see the aesthetic quality present in Callicles' 'superhuman' or to appreciate Socrates' attempt to show that Polus' and Callicles' standards of life were unintelligible to *themselves* (see also, Sparshott, 1978a:xxv; Irwin, 1998:445).

17. Go:XI.150. See further, Burnham, 1977:200, 248; Yake, 2006:2.

18. Pr:XI.61 (also, J. Mill, 1804:I.453).

19. See, Sparshott, 1978a:xviii-xX. James Mill also translated a section of Plato's *Gorgias* (CPB:V.4-6). But as it did not follow the discussion in the dialogue strictly it could not have been of use to the younger Mill. What is more, the excitement of a new edition of Plato may have indeed led the younger Mill to an attempt to render Plato suitable for discussion (cf. Glucker, 1987:169; Sparshott, 1978a:xix). Giorgini (2009:619) argues that Mill translated Plato to popularize him. But Mill's translations were drafted many years before publication.

20. *A*:I.123. See further, Demetriou, 1999:62-3.

21. Mill to T. Carlyle, 05/10/1833:XII.181. See, Schleiermacher, 1833.

22. *A*:I.93-5.

23. Pr:XI.39, 41-2; Ph:XI.62.

24. Lianeri, 2007:167, 180-3. See also, Yake, 2006:10-2.

25. Lianeri, 2007:172; Pr:XI.40-1.

26. Go:XI.150. See further, Sparshott, 1978a:xxv-xxviii.

27. Pr:XI.41-2; Mill to T. Carlyle, 10/05/1833:XII.181.

28. GH[II]:XI.309n-310n; GP:XI.404.

29. Mill to W.B. Adams, 20/10/1832:XII.123-4 (see also, *SOW*:XXI.336); Lianeri, 2007:172. Perhaps Mill was writing with Plato's *Lysis* (which he translated) or Aristotle's view on dialectical reasoning (e.g., *Top*:100b18; see also, GA:XI.505-6) in mind.

30. GP:XI.410; GA:XI.507-8; J. Mill, 1809a:200.

31. Lianeri, 2007:172, 182-3 (Lianeri draws heaving on Urbinati, 2002). Turner (1981:306) and Fitzpatrick (2010:49, 69) also ignored Mill's qualification in their discussion of Mill's use of Plato's dialectics.

32. Whedbee, 2007:20, 25.

33. *Ibid.* pp. 26-8, 37n18.

34. Macaulay, 1837:80; Macaulay to T.F. Ellis, 29/05/1835, in Trevelyan, 1876:I.383. See also, Sullivan, 2009:154ff.

35. Macaulay, 1837:80-1 (also, p. 92); Bentham, 1834:I.39-40.

36. Ph:XI.95-6. As we saw, James Mill highlighted this point in his copy of Bacon's *Novum Organum* (1645:122-3).

37. Whedbee, 2007:38n19, 30. See also, Semmel, 1984:82.

38. Pr:XI.40. Also, Civ:XVIII.124ff ; SD:X.34n, 69; TDA[II]:XVIII.169, 195n.; TS:XIX.620; IA:XXI.253.

39. Whedbee, 2007:31, 38n23.

40. Whedbee, 2007:32. Mill did make the cultivation of the affective faculties the business of reason (via Ethology) in his solution to the problem of 'Philosophical Necessity'.

41. Whedbee, 2007:33.

42. Glucker, 1987:170. Also, Demetriou, 1999:ch. 7.

43. Demetriou, 1996b:255-6 (also, 1999:ch. 9); Turner, 1981:385.

44. See Irwin, 1998:446; Taylor, 1949:vii-viii (also, Sparshott, 1978a:xxxvii-xli).

45. *SOL*:VIII.738; GH[II]:XI.330; GG[I]:XXIV.868. See further, Grote, 1865:II.220n.

46. Bain, 1865:194; Lewes, 1865:173. See further, Demetriou, 1999:257-8.

47. Thursfield, 1865:461-2; Bain, 1865:198. Bain (1865:457), ignoring the two Mills, noted that Grote's take on the negative vein in Plato's dialogues had an 'air of discovery'. Similarly ignoring John Mill's work, Lewes noted that he had anticipated Grote on the Sophists (1865:170; see futher, 1845).

48. Bain, 1865:198-200; Thursfield, 1865:467; Lewes, 1865:174.

49. Bain, 1865:201; also, Thursfield, 1865:464; Lewes, 1865:177.

50. Thursfield, 1865:476-7; Mill to G. Grote, 10/11/1865:XVI.1116.

51. Lewes, 1865:180-3; Thursfield, 1865:467; Bain, 1865:472.

52. Mill to T. Carlyle, 02/08/1833:XII.170; Caird, 1865:353.

53. Campbell, 1866:129-30, 142-3.

54. Jowett, 1892:I.x-xiI.

55. Campbell, 1866:109.

56. Caird, 1865:353-4. See further, Demetriou, 1999:259-60.

57. Campbell, 1866:127, 125.

58. Caird, 1865:356; Campbell, 1866:116-8. Mill seems to have held a similar view (e.g., Ph:XI.93).

59. Campbell, 1866:150-1, 109. See further, Demetriou, 1998.

60. Whewell, 1866:413. Mill praised Whewell's review only for agreeing with Grote on the Sophists (Mill to G. Grote, 22/04/1866:XVI.1160)—Whewell did not agree with Grote on anything else.

61. Westcott, 1866:199 in Turner, 1981:378.

62. Demetriou, 1999:273.

63. Mill to T. Hare, 29/05/1865:XVI.1061; to G. Grote, 26/11/1865:XVI.1021.

64. Mill to G. Grote, 11/03/1865:XVI.1010. Also, Mill to T. Gomperz, 30/04/1865:XVI.1040.

65. Mill to G. Grote, 11/03/1865:XVI.1010 and to J. Chapman, 30/07/1865:XVI.1083-4.

66. Mill was 'very impatient' for Grote's book (Mill to G. Grote, 11/06/1862:XVI.781). He commented on Grote taking a 'length of time' already from 1859 (Mill to A. Bain, 15/10/1859:XV.639-40; 14/11/1859:XV.645). In a letter to Grote, Mill expressed his wish that Grote could prepare his book for publication by the end of 1862 (10/01/1862:XVI.763).

67. Mill to G. Grote, 11/03/1865:XVI.1010; GP:XI.377. Grote's service was double: first, he eased 'the study to those who can read the original', and, second, he made 'the results accessible to those who cannot' (GP:XI.383) by 'showing' Plato himself—as Mill had also tried to do.

68. When asked to show these early translations in 1864, Mill replied that Grote's book would be enough to take someone 'at the pith of Plato' (Mill to A. de Morgan, 17/10/1864:XV.959).

69. GP:XI.378.

70. *Ibid.* pp. 380-2, 385, 390.

71. *Ibid.* pp. 384-5. See also, Burnham, 1977:209-11.

72. GP:XI.386-7.

73. *Ibid.* pp. 387-8. For Mill's treatment of the Sophists, see *ibid.* pp. 387-404 (especially pp. 403-4).

74. *Ibid.* p. 406.

75. *A*:I.25.

76. GP:XI.388, 390, 394, 396, 400, 403.

77. *Ibid.* pp. 382-3, 403-4.

78. *Ibid.* pp. 404-6, 423. See also, J. Mill, 1878:I.271; 1835a:25.

79. GP:XI.409-12, 398-9. Grote (1865:I.ix-xil) also talked about the 'individual reasoning mind' and the role of dissent in society (echoing Mill's *On Liberty*; see further, Demetriou, 2009). See also, Lane, 2001:24-5.

80. GP:XI.423. Also, Burnham, 1977:201.

81. GP:XI.393. Also, Burnham, 1977:198; Thomas, 1979:153.

82. GP:XI.406. Also, Yake, 2006:3.

83. GP:XI.412-3, 415, 431.

84. Devigne, 2006:30. Mill to A. Fonblanque, 30/01/1838:XIII.370; *A*:I.110-1; Robson, 1968:76. Irwin (1998:443ff) excellently shows the limitations of both Mill's and Grote's views.

85. GP:XI.427; Mill to A. Bain, 07/01/1863:XV.818; also, Sotelo, 2006:367-8. Similarly, by tracing in the debate between Mill and Grote on Protagoras's *homo mensura* maxim a fundamental disagreement concerning their liberal outlooks, Giorgini (2009:643-6) does not take into account that Grote's analysis may have been indeed confusing and unconvincing (Kahn, 1996b:52-4).

86. Devigne, 2006:24-6, 30. Grote (1865:I.395n1) quoted Mill on Plato's dialectics (*OL*:XVIII.251-2). See, Demetriou, 2009 (cf. Turner, 1981:295-6, Burnyeat, 1998:361). It has gone unnoticed that Mill believed his *On Liberty* could 'free' and encourage Grote to take more risks in his interpretation of Plato (Mill to A. Bain, 15/10/1859:XV.639); Mill reported that Grote admitted to him being 'considerably outspoken' in Plato (Mill to Hel. Taylor, 04/02/1860:XV.670).

87. Mill to T. Carlyle, 02/08/1833:XII.170.

88. Devigne criticized Urbinati for identifying Mill with Grote (2006:242n5); still, Urbinati recognizes James Mill's influence (2002:133). See also, Borchardt, 1946:4-5, 15.

89. Burnyeat, 2001c:105; 2001a:20.

90. J. Mill, 1804:454; 1809a:199. J.S. Mill, Ph:XI.95. See also, Pappé, 1979:299.

91. GP:XI.410, 415-6. This was a side of Plato, Caird (1865:353-4) argued, to which Grote failed to do justice.

92. GP:XI.416-20, 419n, 410, 419; Sparshott, 1978a:xII.

93. GP:XI.432, 420-1, 403-4.

94. Schofield, 2006:140. Although Schofield seems unaware of it, his discussion of knowledge as 'geared to practice' echoes the views of both Mills, which makes his interpretation of J.S. Mill more credible. Villa associates Mill's attachment to Platonic governance with Plato's *Republic*, though without arguing that scientific governors would need to be out-of-this-world nor 'philosophical citizenship' out of reach (2001:75, 117, 121-4. See further, Sotelo, 2006:370-1).

95. GP:XI.432-9.

96. Mill published the translations of *Protagoras, Phaedrus, Gorgias* and *Apology*. Mill also translated Plato's *Charmides, Euthyphron, Laches, Lysis and Parmenides* but chose not to publish them.

97. J. Mill, 1809a:199; 1878:I.271. Grote wished he 'could concur with. . . [J. Mill] in exonerating Plato from these mystical visions, and imputing them exclusively to his successors' (in J. Mill, 1878:I.272n79).

98. Pr:XI.41; Glucker, 1987:173-4; 1996:386; Demetriou, 1996b:19-22.

99. Mill to G. Grote, 11/03/1865:XVI.1010; 18/06/1865:XVI.1068.

100. Mill to G. Grote, 04/02/1866:XVI.1145; to H. Taylor Mill, 07/02/1854:XIV.152.

101. Mill to G. Grote, 04/02/1866:XVI.1145.

102. Mill to J. E. Cairnes, 09/12/1872:XVII.192 and to G. Grote, 26/11/1865:XVI.1020 and 22/04/1866:XVI.1160.

103. *SOL*:VIII.938.

104. Coleridge, 1818-9:I.190; GP:XI.407.

105. GP:XI.387.

# CHAPTER SIX

## ON PLATO'S METHOD

John Stuart Mill viewed Plato as daring 'all things, however opposed to the common notions of his time, [...] if he could see his way to removing the rocks and shoals which threatened to be fatal to his commonwealth'.[1] Mill thought himself as having a similar role in England to that of Socrates in Athens.[2] At the same time, his attempt to reconcile the 'Platonic image of the happy society as one in which the people are willingly led by the wisdom of the Guardians' with his democratic claims has been a contentious subject in Mill scholarship. But as Alan Ryan has noted, Mill's time was not 'as sceptical as we are about the limits of expertise'.[3] What is more important, though Mill did praise Plato for recognizing 'that government is a Skilled Employment', he criticized him for asserting infallibility for his rulers—Mill's scepticism with regard to Plato's dogmatism was fuelled by Plato's own method.[4] He considered himself to be a true Platonist by being 'nourished in' and having 'endeavoured to practice Plato's mode of investigation'.[5]

## MILL'S INTELLECTUAL DEVELOPMENT AND PLATO

John Stuart Mill considered the 'crisis in [his] mental history' a central incident in his intellectual development. It enabled him, as he argued, to develop a 'broader' mode of thinking. As Mill's 'mental crisis' has indeed been 'over-explained ever since' the publication of Mill's *Autobiography*, this section focuses on its connection to Plato.[6]

Mill confessed that during his 'dejection' he tried to find 'strength and animation' in his favorite books. However, disenchanted and discouraged, no longer did he feel their *charm*. The Utilitarian end ('love of mankind') and the Platonic end ('excellence for its own sake') had worn themselves out. It was a state of depression, he argued, that only Romantic poetry had the means to capture and relieve. Some scholars argue that Mill's translations of Plato during this period played a major part in his recovery—something which left an indelible mark on his later views. What is more important, given Mill's description of events, it has been surmised that it was Samuel Taylor Coleridge's view of Plato, rather than James Mill's, who influenced important aspects of John Mill's 'enlargement' project. The underlying assumption is that his early education could not have had the means to do so.[7]

However, in his studies of the works of ancient Greek philosophers, Mill must have had contact with Epicurus' teachings. Epicurus had argued that sober reasoning (νήφων λογισμὸς) should guide one's life (in trying to make it as pleasant and as undisturbed by pain as possible) and one's deliberation of the causes of one's beliefs and choices—i.e., constantly checking for consistency in one's own conception of happiness and what were considered the best means to bring it about. This is relevant because Epicurus had set a question to serve as that guide to happiness: 'what will happen to me if what is sought by desire is achieved, and what will happen if it is not?'[8] The question Mill posed to himself was not much different: '[s]uppose that all your objects in life were realized, that all the changes in institutions and opinions which you are looking forward to, could be completely effected at this very instant; would this be a great joy and happiness to you?' Mill's reply was a resounding 'No'. What was worse, careful introspection showed no 'real desire for the ends which [he] had been so carefully fitted out to work for'—neither for pursuing excellence for its own sake nor promoting the general good. Since analysis attached ideas to things in an artificial way, Mill argued, the meaning of specific ideas was detached from the emotional faculties of individuals. Though he was convinced of the truth of his teachers' belief that the social feelings which aimed at the good of others 'were the greatest and surest sources of happiness', he now came to realize that 'to know that a feeling would make me happy if I had it, did not give me the feeling'.[9] And this intellectualism (identifying knowledge with happiness) constituted the main limitation of Benthamite psychology. But Mill did not have to go out of his way to find criticisms of such a limitation, since critiques of Socratic intellectualism and the effectiveness of dry argument in instilling virtue in individuals were subjects which constantly resurfaced in Plato's and Aristotle's works.[10]

In 1827, Mill identified motivating virtuous conduct as the 'grand problem' of political science.[11] However, according to Mill, the Benthamites persistently undervalued imagination and neglected emotional cultivation both in theory and in practice. Even if people came to know their 'true' interests through artificial means (e.g., public opinion), Mill argued, they would only be influenced if they already cared for what others thought. Transforming their feelings from selfish to social did not depend on the 'educated intellect', but on inspiration.[12] During the autumn of 1826, Mill felt the need of such inspiration; he found it in Wordsworth.

Commentators thus argue that Mill attempted his translations of Plato to rescue 'Greek humanism and the Socratic method of analysis' from 'the ruins of his father's teaching',[13] but also 'to recapture some of the glowing response which Plato's writings had formerly evoked in him'.[14] To this effect, Stanley Yake compares Mill's translations with other writings which expressed his reaction to Bentham's thought during the 1830s. Yake concludes that Mill was led to Plato because of the contrast between Plato's and Bentham's moral theories. He further suggests that Mill was unable to be inspired by Socrates, because Plato's dialectics were too much like Bentham's method. However, Plato's *Gorgias*, Yake argues, was instrumental to Mill's 'spiritual renewal' because of the 'passionate interest in the moral life' which *Gorgias* exhibited.[15]

Similarly, Robert Devigne argues that Mill, through the insights of ancient philosophers and romantic poets, reached a conclusion about which qualities of human nature ought to be encouraged 'if societies were to arrive at an ethics capable of fostering developed forms of individuality and human agency'. Such insights convinced Mill 'that the dominant "individualist" theories of his own school of empiricism were weak in comparison', by underestimating the capacity of individuals to 'shape and master their own character'. More importantly, Devigne argues that Mill was able to harmonize the ends of Plato, i.e., combining the cultivation of human faculties and higher modes of individualism with the pursuit of the common good 'as understood in an overarching morality of justice and more extended forms of social unity', by the romantic critique of empiricism. Devigne claims that Mill found this critique in Plato's *Gorgias*, which led him to embrace the Romantic view of Plato: that morality and ethics can only be justified selflessly with the power of imagination and art.[16] Devigne concludes that Mill reconciled human excellence and liberty through 'the romantic use of the imagination: the ability to frame and shape values that brings meaning to human existence'.[17]

However, only a part of Yake's and Devigne's discussions is supported by evidence. The paper Mill used to draft his translations was watermarked 1828.[18] This suggests that Mill did not begin translating Plato in the early stages of his 'crisis'. More importantly, Mill's notes were added later,[19] giving him much time to absorb Romantic ideas. Moreover, had John Mill turned to translating Plato to find relief, not only his choice of dialogues but also the focus of his translations would have been different—the Dreamer not the Radical Plato. But Mill remained firmly within the Radical reading of Plato's dialogues. For example, he considered the Romantic reading of Plato (e.g., Wordsworth's) 'bad philosophy'. Likewise, he claimed later on that 'the whole of German metaphysics'—which informed the Romantic view of Plato—was one of the most useless mental pursuits of his time.[20] Further, though Mill did note that his 'metaphysical creed' was different 'from that of the Condillac school', he concurrently admitted being nearest to Hartley and his father.[21] Finally, even if we were, for the sake of argument, to eliminate Mill's early education under James Mill as a source of his defence of the social worth of art, Mill became familiar with the thought of Henri de Saint-Simon in the late 1820s. Saint-Simon could be as likely a source as Coleridge for Mill's view that emotional cultivation offered cohesion to the community. Now, interestingly, some scholars argue that Saint-Simon was probably influenced, with regard to this and other aspects of his thought, by Plato.[22]

It cannot be denied that Coleridgean influences had led Mill to modify his old and develop new ideas as he discovered the 'other half' of the 'truth'. It cannot also be denied that Mill, soon after his reaction, returned to his utilitarian home, once he acquired the confidence of an independent thinker.[23] However, Fred Rosen seems right to suggest, only partly agreeing with John Robson, that Samuel Taylor Coleridge's influence was enduring.[24] Still, attributing key aspects of Mill's mature thought solely to Coleridgean influences ignores the similar lasting impact of Plato's dialectics; he did learn from Plato that 'disputed questions' ought to be treated with dialectical, rather than rhetorical, spirit.[25] All of Mill's works exhibit his intent to search for 'truth at the bottom' of common beliefs.

## The Worth of Plato as a Philosopher

John Stuart Mill argued that 'subsequent [to Plato's and Socrates'] times have been [...] much indebted' to Plato's dialectics 'for whatever intellectual clearness they have attained'. From early in his youth, Mill had associated Plato's method with logic and the validity of arguments.[26] As we saw in passing, there were two main aspects of Plato's method. First, in *A System of Logic* (1843), Mill pointed to the utility of the Socratic *elenchus* in extracting suppressed steps in arguments, which altered the reasoning process and conclusion.[27] Precise meaning begins by seeking the meaning of abstractions in experience, Mill argued. Thus, the negative leg of Plato's dialectics, Socrates' method, involved dissecting 'large abstractions', by 'fixing down to a precise definition the meaning which as popularly used' and by 'questioning and testing the common maxims and opinions in which they bear a part'. As we saw, for Mill, Plato's *Gorgias* and *Protagoras* were dialogues highly illustrative of this kind of enquiry.[28] But Plato's dialectics had a positive or corrective function as well. The positive part of Plato's method cleared up the confusions of an understanding 'which has made up all its bundles of associations under the guidance of popular phraseology', according to Mill. Thus, the value of Plato's method was not confined to 'drilling' and 'dissecting' bad arguments. Though often an exercise in logic, it was not limited to formal logic. Formal logic, Mill noted, 'only aims at removing one of the obstacles to the attainment of truth', i.e., consistency; but, he argued, it was 'of no importance whether we think consistently or not, if we think wrongly'. Plato's method could be applied on shared as well as frequent misconceptions, ascertaining truth with 'the more accurate mode of sifting opinions'.[29] Accurate classification of objects of 'popular phraseology', extending beyond the received notions to their proper sense, their original idea, was a required addition to the method of dissection of arguments.[30]

Plato, according to Mill, belonged in the elite group of reformers. He had applied a rigid mode of interrogation to the 'vague generalities' of his own time. He could not have been 'the master manufacturer of nonsense' as Jeremy Bentham had once argued; rather, Mill claimed, he was much like Bentham himself.[31] Plato's enemy, Mill claimed, was Commonplace—'the acceptance of traditional opinions and current sentiments as an ultimate fact'. Thus, Plato's Socrates struggled to find what quality lay underneath those 'vague generalities' upon which approbation and disapprobation in social affairs depended.[32] There was an 'urgent need, at the present and at all times, of such a teacher', according to Mill, to effect the 'intellectual renovation' which was essential to the 'grand moral and social improvements'. He detached Plato's method from Plato's metaphysics, as the dialectical method was quite efficient in its deconstructive and reconstructive tasks, without necessarily having to 'depend on the possession of positive scientific knowledge' or of metaphysical 'nonsense'.[33]

As we saw, Athenian culture encouraged Socrates' pursuits of 'truth'. At the same time, it also created a need as much to clear up the confusion caused by 'popular phraseology' as to break 'loose from received prejudices'. Mill did not underestimate the force of tradition in people's mind, which resulted in limitations to the degree of openness: '[t]o break entirely with the religion of their forefathers would have been a disruption of old feelings, too painful and difficult for the average strength even of superior minds'. Plato's 'almost perfect examples of the preparatory process of comparison and abstraction' led the way.[34]

However, freethinking was not only a matter of method. Socrates showed that it was possible to reach true opinion, but more certainly to weaken error, without the presumption of infallibility.[35] More importantly, knowledge required, first, both self-observation and self-interrogation.[36] This meant, according to Mill that Socrates did not take upon trust that the received opinions expressed the 'truth'. Socrates had been the living example, or the animating force, which pervaded Mill's belief that '[e]ach person's own reason must work upon the materials afforded by that same person's own experience' and that '[k]nowledge comes only from within; all that comes from without is but *questioning*, or else it is mere *authority*'. That was why Mill argued that a man of genius was an original thinker.[37] Socrates broke free from the fixed opinions of his time and questioned many of the established 'truths'; he discovered that popular phraseology contained and maintained distorted ideas. Thus, as Dana Villa notes, the '"examined life" [...] is a ceaseless struggle against the received truths of one's own society'.[38] Socrates tried to find 'truth' beyond the distorted images of belief—as in Plato's cave—to enable his interlocutors to do so themselves— 'hinting' to them 'what questions to ask', and stopping them when they were going in the wrong direction.[39] Thus, with the 'aid of suitable culture', Mill seemed to argue, everyone could become a Socrates.[40]

Socrates was a hero, by being 'ready, for a worthy object' to do what was 'painful and disagreeable'. It was painful and disagreeable, because Socrates disrupted the 'old feelings' that tradition had created; it was heroic because, Socrates was willing to 'brook ridicule' and 'brave evil tongues', without 'torpidity and cowardice'.[41] Plato's Socrates was thus happy at the moment when he broke 'loose from error'—being that kind of person who 'would just as gladly be refuted as refute', in order to combat prejudice or ignorance. But Socrates was a rare exception, as was Mill.[42]

Thus, even when Plato's works contained vague generalities, inconsistencies or fallacies,[43] their value was not negligible. According to Mill, they illustrated 'the whole unanalysed experience of the human race'. However, it requires, Mill added, a 'superior intellect' to focus on the 'truth at the bottom' and exhaust every possibility of consistency before rejecting a fallacious argument.[44] Mere 'logicians', Mill noted, fail to look beyond the surface of, or appreciate what germs of truth might be found in, fallacious arguments, assuming that there is nothing to learn from them.[45] Similarly, James Mill had noted in his *Commonplace Books* that 'the philosopher loves the truth for its own sake' and employs a 'philosophical method' to find it—little does it matter where truth is found: condemned or celebrated; 'defended by a famous author or [...] hidden in the work of an obscure' one.[46] Socrates embodied this love for truth; a discursive mode of reaching and preserving 'truth' that was defended in John Stuart Mill's *On Liberty*.

## MILL'S DIALECTICAL METHOD

The primary 'aid of suitable culture', as we saw in chapter four, was acquiring habits of 'reason' rather than 'routine'.[47] In this chapter, Mill's attempt to instill such critical habits through dialectics comes to the fore. Frederick Rosen has suggested recently that John Stuart Mill's 'Philosophy of Error', as was developed in *A System of Logic*, was primarily an offspring of his early education in logic and in the Socratic *elenchus*.[48] '[L]urking in the background', Rosen notes, Mill's philosophy of error 'fed into his other writings', 'encouraging the beneficial dialogue between truth and error, which enabled truth ultimately to replace error in inference, deduction, and in argument generally'.[49] However, Rosen does not notice that the negative leg of Plato's method—extracting suppressed steps in arguments, which altered the reasoning process and conclusion—was but one aspect of Plato's method—just one part of the 'twofold obligation, to be able to maintain our opinions against the criticism of opponents and refute theirs, and never to use a term in serious discourse without a precise meaning'.[50] As we just saw, the positive leg of Plato's method aimed to clear up confusions of an understanding 'which [had] made up all its bundles of associations under the guidance of popular phraseology'. Socrates, in Plato's dialogues, tried to go beyond the received notions of certain ideas to their 'proper' or 'original' sense—through the analytic and synthetic operations—and so did John Mill, taking after his father's example.[51]

In Book V of *A System of Logic* John Stuart Mill focused on the intellectual sources of erroneous opinions, i.e., fallacies. However, he did make a note of the moral sources of 'reasoning ill'. Both indifference to truth and bias act indirectly, according to Mill, by taking insufficient or inconclusive evidence to be sufficient or conclusive. This happens primarily because most people, who willingly or unwillingly 'blind themselves to the light of the truth', are not 'strongly fortified to the intellectual side'. More importantly, in the case of bias, individuals 'unfairly, giv[e] a larger share of [their attention] to the evidence which seems favourable to the desired conclusion, a smaller to that which seems unfavourable'.[52]

Proper examination of 'apparent evidence' to decide whether it is 'real' or not was the habit that John Stuart Mill's philosophy of error aimed at inculcating.[53] However, in so doing, Mill found himself in the company of Jeremy Bentham and James Mill. In 1826, while John was preoccupied with editing Jeremy Bentham's *Rationale of Judicial Evidence* (originally published in 1827 in 5 vols.),[54] James Mill noted that '[w]hen we come to the investigation of any question, the first thing required is, a process of self-examination', to decide whether there is both 'fullness of collection' and 'equality of reception' of evidence, or not:

> When the mind bestows an equal attention upon the evidence on both sides of a question, by that victory over affection and interest, which is one of the noblest exertions of virtue, because it is the source from which almost every laudable action proceeds, it does so by creating to itself a counteracting interest; the interest of truth and fairness. This is the tutelary principle. This is the safeguard of virtue. If a man loves truth and fairness more than he loves either side, he will inquire and judge virtuously. If he loves either side better than he loves truth and fairness, he is ready to decide dishonestly, whether he himself is aware of it, or not.[55]

The habit of 'mental partiality', 'the master vice of the understanding', James Mill noted in his *Commonplace Books*,

> depraves the judgement, makes men bad reasoners, both for speculation, and for practice—Makes men bad husbands, bad fathers, bad judges, bad legislators, bad every thing. This is the very source of injustice.—Strength of mind consists in the vigilant habit of attending to evidence, and estimating accurately its force.[56]

John Mill seemed to agree with his father.

Though Jeremy Bentham and James Mill wrote extensively on fallacies (though the latter almost exclusively in his *Commonplace Books*), John Mill's discussion of fallacies owed little to their views. For example, in *The Book of Fallacies* (originally published in 1824), Bentham was interested only in what he termed 'political fallacies', i.e., fallacies in connection to the 'decision procuring the adoption or rejection of some measure of *government*'[57]—a limited focus shared by James Mill. However, as Rosen seems right to suggest, '[a] more general and pervasive influence of Bentham on [John] Mill's treatment of fallacies might be found in the conceptions of evidence'.[58] The quotes from James Mill show that the same was true with regard to James Mill's influence—especially given that James Mill often made such remarks commenting Francis Bacon's 'Idols' which, as Rosen has acknowledged, influenced John Stuart Mill's philosophy of error.[59]

The educational aspect of John Stuart Mill's discussion of *Logic* is amply illustrated in his 'Inaugural Address'. For example, going into the value of studying logic, Mill made special mention that '[l]ogic is the great dispenser of hazy and confused thinking; it clears up the fogs which hide from us our own ignorance, and make us believe that we understand a subject when we do not'.[60] Similarly, for James Mill, '[o]ne of the grand objects of education should be, to generate a constant and anxious concern about evidence; to accustom the mind to run immediately from the idea of the opinion to the idea of its evidence, and to feel dissatisfaction till it is known that the evidence has been all before the mind, and fairly weighted'.[61] It is well known that in *On Liberty*, John Stuart Mill associated 'Socratic dialectics' with the understanding doctrines and their evidence:

> They were essentially a negative discussion of the great questions of philosophy and life, directed with consummate skill to the purpose of convincing any one who had merely adopted the commonplaces of received opinion, that he did not understand the subject—that he as yet attached no definite meaning to the doctrines he professed: in order that, becoming aware of his ignorance, he might be put in the way to attain a stable belief, resting on a clear apprehension both of the meaning of doctrines and of their evidence.

According to Mill, 'the powerful dialectics which formed the intellects of the "Socratici viri"' led them to never settle with opinions that originated in authority and routine.[62]

The abovementioned educational aspect of logic—both ratiocinative and inductive—highlights its connection to Plato's dialectics. It is well known that Plato's Socrates, in his search for the constituents of the virtuous life, went after definitions—e.g., what is justice, what is virtue, and so on. According to John Stuart Mill, 'a just and unambiguous definition of the subject-matter' could

> only be arrived at by an operation which we should call a philosophical analysis, and which [Socrates] describes as a process of composition and decomposition, or rather decomposition and recomposition, first distinguishing a whole into its kinds or parts, and then looking at those kinds or parts attentively, in such a manner as to extract from them the idea of the whole.[63]

However, what is more important, in that process of 'analysis and synthesis', Socrates would demonstrate to his interlocutors, 'much to their annoyance'—it being contrary to what they themselves believed—'that their culture (or any culture) had [not] taught them [...] to be virtuous and live well'.[64] The 'intellectual renovation' Mill sought for would only be possible through inculcating such reflective habits of thought and behavior—going after the 'real' meaning of the objects of 'popular phraseology' that affect the 'practical business of life', not being satisfied with their apparent or 'vulgar' meaning.[65] To illustrate the dialectical aspect of Mill method of investigation, I focus on two examples of Mill's method of 'decomposing and recomposing' with regard to the notions of 'nature' and 'justice'. At the same time, not only will the discussion of Mill's method when dealing with matters of definition demonstrate that he thought that Plato's Socrates had a method, but also it will highlight what he considered the 'essential and unique elements' of 'a single, unified procedure for interrogating and arguing', that is, what Mill considered Socrates' method to be—which are still very ambitious and contentious claims to make.[66]

## Nature

The brief definition of Socrates' method mentioned earlier appears right at the outset of John Stuart Mill's essay 'Nature'.[67] Mill notes that '[t]he most important application of the Socratic Elenchus, as exhibited and improved by Plato', first 'consists in dissecting large abstractions' of words which have

> become entangled in so many foreign associations, mostly of a very powerful and tenacious character, that they have come to excite, and to be the symbols of, feelings which their original meaning will by no means justify; and which have made them one of the most copious sources of false taste, false philosophy, false morality, and even bad law;

second, 'fixing down to a precise definition the meaning which as popularly used they merely shadow forth', and, third 'questioning and testing the common maxims and opinions in which they bear a part'. Mill then went on to note that

> It is to be regretted that among the instructive specimens of this kind of investigation which Plato has left, and to which subsequent times have been so much indebted for whatever intellectual clearness they have attained, he has not enriched posterity with a dialogue περὶ φύσεως. If the idea denoted by the word had been subjected to his searching analysis, and the popular commonplaces in which it figures had been submitted to the ordeal of his powerful dialectics, his successors probably would not have rushed, as they speedily did, into modes of thinking and reasoning of which the fallacious use of that word formed the corner stone; a kind of fallacy from which he was himself singularly free.[68]

While making these comments, Mill had already been writing about Socrates and thinking about writing on Plato.[69]

Being guided by Plato's method, Mill proceeded with its first step.[70] He went on dissecting the 'large abstraction' called 'nature'. However, to find what such a vague term means, according to Mill, we must turn from the 'abstraction' to the 'concrete'—from the 'universal' to the 'particular'. So what is the 'nature' of a thing? Mill answered that it is the aggregate of its powers and properties—its entire capacity of exhibiting phenomena. Thus, going from the particular to the universal, Mill noted that

> Nature in the abstract is the aggregate of the powers and properties of all things. Nature means the sum of all phenomena, together with the causes which produce them; including not only all that happens, but all that is capable of happening; the unused capabilities of causes being as much a part of the idea of Nature, as those which take effect.

Language being, according to Mill, 'the atmosphere of philosophical investigation, which must be made transparent before anything can be seen through it in the true figure and position', the word 'nature' 'is a collective name for all facts, actual and possible'—his use of the technical term 'collective name', suggests that Mill was putting his theory of names in *A System of Logic* to work.[71]

Following after the second step of Plato's method, Mill turned to the ways in which 'nature' was popularly used. To this effect, the contrast between Nature and Art commonly made suggested to Mill another meaning of the word 'nature'. Since art 'is the employment of the powers of Nature for an end', and since such an understanding of art cannot come into conflict with the 'true scientific sense' of nature noted earlier, he argued, we may distinguish between two main meanings of the word:

> In one sense, it means all the powers existing in either the outer or the inner world and everything which takes place by means of those powers. In another sense, it means, not everything which happens, but only what takes place without the agency, or without the voluntary and intentional agency, of man.

Both the phenomena which are produced human agency, 'the volition which designs, the intelligence which contrives, and the muscular force which executes', and those which are not, Mill pointed out, 'depend on the properties of the elementary forces, or of the elementary substances and their compounds'.

Mill then proceeded to the third step, that is to question and test a common practical maxim in which 'nature' bears a part: i.e., that 'any mode of thinking, feeling, or acting, is "according to nature" is usually accepted as a strong argument for its goodness'. However, as both senses of the term noted earlier correspond to 'what is', and the practical maxim of 'following nature' refers to 'what ought to be', Mill asked himself whether this means that we can distinguish a third sense of 'nature'. His answer was no:

> Those who say that we ought to act according to Nature do not mean the mere identical proposition that we ought to do what we ought to do. They think that the word Nature affords some external criterion of what we should do; and if they lay down as a rule for what ought to be, a word which in its proper signification denotes what is, they do so because they have a notion, either

clearly or confusedly, that what is, constitutes the rule and standard of what ought to be.

Without going into the details of his argument, Mill's own summary of it ran as follows:

> In the first of these senses, the doctrine that man ought to follow nature is unmeaning; since man has no power to do anything else than follow nature; all his actions are done through, and in obedience to, some one or many of nature's physical or mental laws.
>
> In the other sense of the term, the doctrine that man ought to follow nature, or in other words, ought to make the spontaneous course of things the model of his voluntary actions, is equally irrational and immoral.
>
> Irrational, because all human action whatever, consists in altering, and all useful action in improving, the spontaneous course of nature;
>
> Immoral, because the course of natural phenomena being replete with everything which when committed by human beings is most worthy of abhorrence, any one who endeavoured in his actions to imitate the natural course of things would be universally seen and acknowledged to be the wickedest of men.[72]

Mill's synopsis is suggestive of his use of Socrates' *elenchus*, the negative part of Plato's method, and there is no need to track further his argument or his use of the *elenchus* here.

The maxim that people should follow the spontaneous course of nature was one of the two 'conflicting theories' on whether artifice or spontaneity originates political institutions. Mill explored the two theories, aiming to 'get down to what is at the root of each' theory to try to find out 'the amount of truth which exists in either'.[73] The allusion to Plato's dialectics seems clear: 'going down to the roots and fundamentals of a matter', Mill noted in a private letter praising John Austin's habits of analysis—a praise he repeated when he compared Austin's discussion of the meaning of justice that of Plato in the *Republic*—is 'calculated [...] to give clear ideas and to correct vague feelings and confused notions on that particular subject'.[74] The early chapters of Mill's *Considerations on Representative Government* (1861) tried to correct the vague feelings and confused notions that are associated with the two theories of government. First, that government, as a practical art, is wholly a question of adapting means to ends: institutions, 'being made by man, it is assumed that man has the choice either to make them or not, and how or on what pattern they shall be made'. Second, that government, as a spontaneous product of history, is merely a question of discovering its natural properties and adapting ourselves to them: institutions are 'a sort of organic growth from the nature and life of that people: a product of their habits, instincts, and unconscious wants and desires, scarcely at all of their deliberate purposes'.[75] The germs of truth that can be found in both, very crudely, are that though institutions 'are made what they are by human voluntary agency' their stability depends upon certain conditions that must be met: a system of education, loyalty to a common ideal and an active principle of cohesion, i.e., nationality.[76]

## Justice

In the final chapter of *Utilitarianism*, Mill went into an investigation with regard to the nature of justice, trying to remove the 'obstacles to the reception of the doctrine that Utility or Happiness is the criterion of right and wrong' created by the belief that human beings are endowed with natural feelings of justice which allow them to spontaneously judge what is right and what is wrong. As was noted earlier, Mill's investigation of the meaning of 'nature' was an exemplary application of the Socratic *elenchus*, the negative aspect of Plato's dialectics. Mill's inquiry into the meaning of justice was an attempt to discover whether 'in everything which men are accustomed to characterize as just or unjust, some one common attribute or collection of attributes is always present'.[77] However, the 'direct search for the common feature of things that are classed together, or, in other words, for the meaning of the class-name' was the 'positive arm of Plato's dialectics, of which he and Sokrates may be regarded as the originators'.[78]

As Mill argued, 'the meaning of a name must always be sought in the distinctive qualities of the thing named: and these are only to be detected by an accurate study of the thing itself, and of every other thing from which it requires to be distinguished',[79] i.e., 'to find the common attributes of a variety of objects, it is necessary to begin by surveying the objects themselves in the concrete'.[80] With Plato's method then in hand, Mill proceeded to survey various *paradeigmata* or *exempla*, i.e., testimonies of just or unjust modes of action or arrangements of human affairs. Mill's mode of arguing seems to follow that of Plato's Socrates, 'gather[ing] and adduc[ing] a series of testimonies pointing to an inconsistency within the overall position of an opposing litigant'.[81] The opposing litigant in the case at hand was the same as always: the school of philosophy which holds '[t]he doctrine that truths external to the mind may be known by intuition or consciousness, independently of observation and experiment',[82] creating 'the greatest speculative hindrance to the regeneration so urgently required, of man and society'.[83]

The connecting link between the different cases of legal and moral rights and the various demands for rewards according to dessert, for promise-keeping, for impartiality and for equality, i.e., in all those everyday modes of action or relationships which we call just or unjust—where failure to act in a just manner causes some kind of harm—according to Mill, is

> that we call any conduct wrong, or employ, instead, some other term of dislike or disparagement, according as we think that the person ought, or ought not, to be punished for it; and we say that it would be right to do so and so, or merely that it would be desirable or laudable, according as we would wish to see the person whom it concerns, compelled, or only persuaded and exhorted to act in that manner.[84]

Punishment serves to disassociate these modes of actions and arrangements of affairs from respective actions and affairs that fall within expediency and worthiness, not those within morality,[85] when the desire to punish in retaliation or in self-defence, as Mill noted, becomes moral when it 'only acts in the directions conformable to the general good'.[86]

Having defined the connective link between acts within the domain of Morality—a rule of conduct which is 'common to all mankind, and intended for their good'—Mill tried to define the link that distinguishes just actions or affairs from other actions or affairs in the class-name Morality. The narrow sphere of justice is demarcated from the broader sphere of morality not in the need to punish for a wrong done—which may take expression in various forms, other than legal punishment—but in that there is an assignable person who is wronged:

> Justice implies something which it is not only right to do, and wrong not to do, but which some individual person can claim from us as his moral right. No one has a moral right to our generosity or beneficence [which comprise along with justice the domain of morality], because we are not morally bound to practise those virtues towards any given individual.

The outcome of Mill's process of classification and abstraction was that 'the two essential ingredients in the sentiment of justice are, the desire to punish a person who has done harm, and the knowledge [...] that there is some definite individual [...] to whom harm has been done'.[87] Just like in the case of 'following nature' as a maxim of individual conduct, subsequently to his conclusion with regard to the definition, i.e., the 'essential ingredients', of the notion of justice, Mill went after its connection to utility as the standard of morality.[88]

## CONCLUDING REMARKS

Students of *On Liberty* are well aware that discovery of truth, by one's own means, as well as perseverance in questioning established opinions was important to Mill—[89] exhibiting these qualities, Socrates became to Mill a model of 'ideal excellence'.[90] According to Mill, even if the world had reached truth beyond doubt—having no need for intellectual devices in clarifying errors—Plato's method would still retain its importance in the practical affairs of human life, satisfying the need to reach truth, in contrast to receiving it.[91] Plato's method was an invaluable 'means to attaining any positive knowledge or conviction worthy the name'—which was the reason why it was an 'indispensable education for dogmatic thinkers' as well.[92] Since dialectics do not train only dialecticians according to Mill, as we saw, the underlying condition for questioning established opinions is primarily a 'mood of mind', i.e., being aware of one's own limitations, being open in learning from others and thus seeking to rectify possible errors by finding parts of truth either in less accepted opinions or even in conflicting views. This 'mood' is owed to 'a quality of the human mind, the source of everything respectable in man either as an intellectual or as a moral being, namely, that his errors are corrigible. He is capable of rectifying his mistakes, by discussion and experience'.[93] These are the only ways that truth retains its vitality, its meaning and its effect on people holding an opinion, becoming 'a vivid conception and a living belief'.[94]

As we saw, an environment of freedom of opinion and discussion was another 'essential ingredient' for searching for, and maintaining a living apprehension of, truth. Unless such search could be freely and publicly pursued, Mill followed Plato, society would remain a corrupting influence in the intellectual development of its people:[95]

> The grand business of human intellect ought to consist in subjecting these [Justice, Virtue, Good] general terms to the most rigorous scrutiny, and bringing to light the ideas that lie at the bottom of them. Even if this cannot be done, and real knowledge be attained, it is already no small benefit to expel the false opinion of knowledge; to make men conscious of their ignorance of the things most needful to be known, fill them with shame and uneasiness at their own state, and rouse a pungent internal stimulus, summoning up all their mental energies to attack these greatest of all problems, and never rest until, as far as possible, the true solutions are reached.[96]

Such a great service seemed to be as much needed in Plato's time as in Mill's own. What option was then left open for Mill other than to try to put to the test the popular ideas concerning the proper domain of morality, the cultivation of virtue and the pursuit of happiness?[97]

## NOTES

1. GP:XI.436 (see also, PL:I.321). This was a view shared by James Mill as well (see J. Mill, 1835a:289).
2. See further, Demetriou and Loizides, 2013.
3. Ryan, 1974:130.
4. GP:XI.436-7. See further, Riley, 2007.
5. A:I.24-5.
6. A:I.136-9; Skorupski, 1989:13, 360n4. See further, Bain, 1882b:37-8; Robson, 1968:ch.2; Mazlish, 1975:12-43; Thomas, 1985:ch.2; Carlisle, 1991:63-79; Stafford, 1998:29-32; Vogler, 2001:ch.1.
7. A:I.139. See further, Packe, 1954; Yake, 1973, 2006; Devigne, 2006. I try to qualify this claim in Loizides, 2012.
8. Laertius, LOEP:X.130-2, 148; Inwood and Gerson, 1994:30, 34, 40; Arrigheti, 1960:155.
9. A:I.139, 143.
10. Plato, Rep:401b-2a, 548c, 590c-d; Aristotle, NE:1179b10-30 and Rhet:1356a1-30.
11. sUH:XXVI.395.
12. Go:XI.150; A:I.113.
13. Packe, 1954:136.
14. Borchardt, 1946:12.

15. Yake, 1973:3, 7-8. Borchardt, 1946:15. Anticipating F.E. Sparshott's criticism about those who make 'therapeutic' claims with regard to Mill's reading of Plato, Yake refers to Mill's admission that in his classic story of self-discovery he sketched mostly his 'new impressions' (Yake, 1973:7, 10; *A*:I.175; Sparshott, 1978a:xviii-xx).
16. Devigne, 2006:15, 27, 38.
17. *Ibid.* pp.146-7. See also, Burnham, 1977:204-7; Preyer, 1982:63ff.
18. Robson, 1978:lxxxi. Some leaves were watermarked 1825, but the Bekker edition of Plato was published in 1826.
19. Mill to W.J. Fox, 10/10/1833:XII.185.
20. Ph:XI.93-6; *A*:I.152-31; DE:07/02/1854:XXVII.642.
21. Mill to J.P. Nichol, 14/10/1834:XII.237.
22. Locke, 1986:20; McWilliam, 1993:61, 65. See also, Sharpless, 1967:128; Abrams, 1971:177-8.
23. Robson, 1968:76. See further, Thomas, 1979:186; 203-4. Thomas (1979:181); Sharpless (1967:128) and Abrams (1971:177-8) discuss Mill's attempt to balance old and new influences in reference to poetry.
24. Rosen, 2003b:19. As it is generally noticed, Coleridge influenced Mill primarily through John Sterling and Frederick Dennison Maurice (Thomas, 1979:174; 1985:46; Rosen, 2003b:19).
25. RPRB:XXV.1212.
26. TL:XXVI.147; LNL:XXVI.239; *A*:I.21-5.
27. *SOL*:VIII.744. Both Mills argued that logical analysis is a valuable exercise for a young mind (*A*:I.21-5; J. Mill, 1809a:199).
28. N:X.373; GP:XI.411; GA:XI.509; B:X.88.
29. *SOL*:VII.10-2, 206-8; *EHP*:IX.370; Pr:XI.44. The study of various argumentation schemes has developed into a distinct discipline; e.g., Walton, 1996, 2004, 2006, 2008.
30. *A*:I.25, 69; GG[5]:XXV.1163-4; Ph:XI.95. See further, Burnham, 1977:200ff.
31. GP:XI.387; GH[II]:XI.329. See also, *SOL*:VIII.677; B:X.88-90. Cf. Bentham, 1983b:135, 137.
32. GP:XI.403. As this was what the utilitarian project was all about (see J. Mill, 1835a:250), Turner (1981:402), it seems, was wrong in pointing out that there was a point of departure between Mill and Grote (see further, Demetriou, 2009).
33. GG[5]:XXV.1163-4; *ACP*:X.277-8.
34. *SOL*:VIII.677; T:X.441; GH[I]:XI.286.
35. SA[I]:XXII.233-4. See also, Plato, *Gor*:458a-b. See also, Mill to E.Bulwer-Lytton, 27/03/1843:XIII.578-9.
36. OG:I.330-2; GG[5]:XXV.1163-4; Plato, *Apol*:20c-3c.
37. OG:I.332; GH[II]:XI.320-1. It is frequently argued that the early 1830s constituted the time of Mill's most pronounced reaction against his father's views. However, 'On Genius' (1832) seems to draw much on Dugald Stewart (1814), his father's beloved teacher. Stewart's was a work that James Mill (1815) had reviewed and from which he collected a quote (Steward, 1814:I.23 at CPB:V.189r) which was very similar to the younger Mill's argument in 'On Genius'—John did say that he found many 'excellent remarks' on various subjects in Stewart's work (Mill to G.d'Eichthal, 07/11/1829:XII.43).
38. Plato, *Rep*:514a-20a; Villa, 2001:60.
39. OG:I.332; Plato, *Apol*:40a. Mill was quite familiar with Plato's simile of the cave (GP:XI.426; see also, PL:I.322; Mill to R.B.Fox, 10/3/1842:XIII.520). See also, J. Mill, 1811:421.
40. GP:XI.378; OG:I.334; *OL*:XVII.251-2. See also, Ryan, 1991:132-3; Villa, 2001:98.

41. Civ:XVIII.131-2. See also, Go:XI.149-50.
42. SA[I]:XXII.233-4. See further, BBTV:XI.269; Mill to E.Lytton-Bulwer, 27/03/1843: XIII.578-9.
43. E.g., GP:XI.395, 410, 415-6, 428; *SOL*:VIII.756, 812n, 815, 825; *ACP*:X.271.
44. B:X.90; UAPT:XVIII.6-7.
45. UAPT:XVIII.6-7. For Mill, Bentham's fault was that he did not look for truth in other people's thought (B:X.90). Mill mentioned the relation of dialectics to the examination of both sides of a question, even false ones, to ascertain truth; that he seemed to believe that Plato's *Parmenides* showed this (GA:XI.508) seems to explain his attempt to translate it.
46. J. Mill, CPB:III.105r-v. Interestingly, James Mill was drawing on Christian Wolff (1732:82-3).
47. Chapters seven and eight explore this in relation to John Stuart Mill's notion of an 'Art of Life' and character formation as the cultivation of virtue respectively.
48. Rosen, 2006:124-6. See also, *SOL*:VIII.737, 740ff; *A*:I.24-5.
49. Rosen, 2006:129. See in relation, *OL*:XVIII.ch.2.
50. GP:XI.411.
51. See further, Loizides, 2012.
52. *SOL*:VIII.737-9.
53. *SOL*:VIII.736.
54. See Bentham, 1838-43, vols. 6-7; J.S. Mill, *A*:I.119.
55. J. Mill, 1826b:9, 13.
56. J. Mill, CPB:III.101r, 208r-v.
57. Bentham, 1838-43:II.380-1.
58. Rosen, 2006:124.
59. Rosen, 2006:124, 129. See also, R.A. Fenn's editorial note in J. Mill, CPB:III and J. Mill's marginalia in his copy of Bacon's *Novum Organum*.
60. IA:XXI.239. See further, *ibid.* pp. 238-40; Rosen, 2006:121-3.
61. J. Mill, 1826b:14.
62. *OL*:XVIII.251.
63. Ph:XI.93.
64. Coleman, 2000:I.56.
65. For an example in Mill's translations of Plato, see Pr:XI.57, 59.
66. Scott, 2002:2.
67. For a fuller discussion of the affinities between Mill's and Plato's method in Mill essay on 'Nature', see Burnham, 1977:238ff.
68. N:X.373.
69. There is textual evidence to support that Mill's 'Nature' had already appeared in draft by October 1850. Mill began to rewrite it in August 1853 and it was finished by February 1854. In a letter to Walter Coulson, Mill noted:

> How can morality be anything but the chaos it now is, when the ideas of right & wrong, just & unjust, must be wrenched into accordance either with the notions of a tribe of barbarians in a corner of Syria three thousand years ago, or with what is called the order of Providence; in other words, the course of nature, of which so great a part is tyranny & iniquity all the things which are punished as the most atrocious crimes when done by human creatures, being the daily doings of nature through the whole range of organic life (Mill to Walter Coulson, 22/11/1850, XIV.53).

This passage echoes both Mill's view about Plato's battle against Commonplace on what is 'right & wrong, just & unjust' and his closing remarks in 'Nature' (see GP:XI.403;

N:X.402. See further, Robson, 1969:cxxvi-cxxviii). Both in 1850 and 1853 Mill commented on the need of a modern Socrates (to put into effect the 'intellectual renovation' that was noted earlier) in his reviews of Grote's *History* (GG[5]:XXV.503; GH[II]:XI.309). And just as he finished the essay on 'Nature', he immediately thought about writing on Plato, among other important subjects (See Mill to H. Taylor-Mill, 30/08/1853, XIV.111; 14/01/1854, XIV.131 and 7/02/1854, XIV.152).

70. For the following discussion, see N:X.373-7. Interestingly, Mill's discussion of 'nature' in 1854 does not show a very different view from the very brief discussion of the word in 1823 (see TWN:XXV.8-9).

71. N:X.378; *SOL*:VII.27-31. I discuss the implications of his theory of names for his ethical theory in chapter nine, where I argue that his *Utilitarianism* was an attempt to dissect another large abstraction: happiness.

72. N:X.401-2.

73. *CRG*:XIX.374-5. An idea he had already noted in his essay on Coleridge, see C:X.120.

74. Mill to A. Duff-Gordon, 27/01/1847, *CW*, XIII.706; AJ:XXI.175.

75. *CRG*:XIX.374-5.

76. *CRG*:XIX.375-6, 413ff; C:X.133-8. See further, Varouxakis, 2002a:ch. 4.

77. *U*:X.240, 241.

78. GP:XI.405.

79. AJ:XXI.175.

80. *U*:X.241.

81. Ausland, 2002:56

82. *A*:I.233. See further, *EHP*:IX.141-8.

83. Mill to T. Gomperz, 19/08/1854, XIV.239.

84. *U*:X.246.

85. *U*:X.247. Suffice it to say here that Morality, Expediency and Aesthetics are the three general departments of ends on human conduct, according to Mill. I explore Mill's Doctrine of Ends, and its relation to Plato, in chapter seven.

86. *U*:X.249.

87. *U*:X.247-8.

88. See, *U*:X.249ff.

89. Though the influence of Mill's *On Liberty* on Grote's *Plato, and the other Companions of Sokrates* has recently been discussed (Demetriou, 2009), as we saw it is not noticed that Mill thought that his *On Liberty* would encourage Grote to take more risks in his interpretation of Plato (Mill to A.Bain, 15/10/1859, XV.639; Mill to Helen Taylor, 04/02/1860, XV.670).

90. *A*:I.49.

91. OG:I.332.

92. *OL*:XVIII.252. GP:XI.410.

93. *OL*:XVIII.231.

94. SA[I]:XXII.233-4; *OL*:XVIII.247ff. See further, Rosen, 2004.

95. GP:XI.400.

96. *Ibid.* p. 404.

97. For a variety of takes on Mill's role as a British Socrates, see Demertiou and Loizides, 2013.

# PART THREE

## JOHN STUART MILL'S

## PLATONIC HERITAGE

# CHAPTER SEVEN

## THE ART OF LIFE[1]

In an attempt to revise the 'traditional' interpretations of John Stuart Mill, many studies in the last sixty years have explored the implications of an 'Art of Life', as developed in his *A System of Logic*, for his ethical and political thought. By advancing a theory of living as a *technê*, with happiness as its *summum bonum*, Mill helped himself to the rich depository of ideas of the Stoic tradition of the *ars vitae*. However, the ancient Greek echoes of Mill's 'Art of Life' have been widely ignored, even when his Greco-philia is taken under consideration.[2] Not only does a study of its Greek origins shed light on Mill's pithy sketch of the 'Art of Life', but also it highlights its connection to character formation and taking the 'higher ground' with regard to happiness.

## REASON AND ACTION

### J.S. Mill on Art and Science

John Stuart Mill's discussion on the 'Art of Life', as part of the logic of practice, appears in the final chapter of his *System of Logic* (1843). There are recurrent allusions to various 'arts of life' in Mill's works; he most frequently meant 'to dig, to plough, to build'.[3] However, in the 1851 edition of his *Logic*, Mill presented a rather different 'Art of Life'; it brought neatly together Mill's old ideas on the relation of science and art in the sphere of human practice, by defining an 'architectonic' *technê* of living in the ancient Greek sense.

That the 'Art of Life' did not appear in the first edition, but in the third—much revised—edition of the *Logic* is something of a puzzle. A clue to how Mill came to his new argument may be found in a brief notice on Alexander Bain's lectures regarding the applications of physical science to human well-being. Writing in late 1848, Mill cited extensively Bain's comments on the sections on the 'Arts of Life' and the 'Art of Living'. There, Bain had defined the former as 'man's powers in farming, building, manufacturing and trading' and the latter as 'his ability to apply the results of all these to his own life and well-being'; the 'Art of Living' was 'the final intention of [the] manifold labours' of the 'Arts of Life'.[4]

More importantly, in Mill's notice, Bain argued that '[t]he Art of Living is the method of stretching out the resources of the world to the measure of human wants, desires, and capabilities'. Despite being defined in such practical terms, the 'Art of Living' pointed to a method that finds and applies 'good and useful' means (that form the ends of other arts) 'in proper measure, and in well-timed arrangement to the highly complex structure and constitution of our living framework'. Through such an 'Art of Living', Bain drew his readers' attention to an example of employing a scientific method to 'making our lives joyous rather than grievous, powerful and benignant, rather than empty and hurtful'.[5]

The same principle pervaded Mill's own account of the 'Art of Life'. Echoing both earlier and later themes concerning theory and practice, Mill's 'Art' employed the 'powers of nature'—human nature—for the promotion of happiness.[6] In *Principles of Political Economy* (1848) the connection of this 'Art' to mental cultivation was more evident: any progress of such an 'Art of Living', according to Mill, was part of the moral and social progress and the overall progress of mental culture. It turned life, Mill added, into something more than just 'getting on'.[7] But incorporating intellectual cultivation in living as part of an art brought Mill closer to the ancient conception of *technê*. Four years earlier, Mill argued that '[a]n art would not be an art, unless it were founded upon a scientific knowledge of the properties of the subject-matter: without this, it would not be philosophy, but empiricism; *ἐμπειρία*, not *τέχνη*, in Plato's sense'.[8]

As Mill reported in his *Autobiography*, the connection between theory and practice was an early—rather unpleasant—lesson. Mill came to believe, as we saw in chapter four, that keeping in mind the relation between theory and practice had an important role in education, by preventing 'theory from degenerating into vain and idle refinements'.[9] Mill argued that science examines and determines the most appropriate means to the end which is supplied by art. Both the subject-matter of the art (human conduct) and its desired end (happiness) can be then used to define its nature and its relation to other arts.[10]

Furthermore, according to Mill, '[s]cience takes cognizance of a *phenomenon*, and endeavours to discover its law' and 'art proposes to itself an end, and looks out for *means* to effect it'. The best means could only follow from a careful examination of the causal laws of all phenomena at work—this would not exclude the examination of human nature.[11] Thus, science or theory is as much an integral part of art as is action or practice. However, Mill argued, art is distinguished from science in the same way that *will* is distinct from *understanding* and, in grammar, the way the imperative mood differs from the indicative mood (*ought* and *is*, respectively). Concurrently, as a result, art examines whether the means, as defined by science, are desirable and practicable (i.e., attainable, being in human power)—only then, Mill maintained, does art create a rule.[12]

While art transforms those theoretically grounded means into practical rules, which can be used to direct one's actions, Mill noted that the *whole* of knowledge of a *specific* subject was necessary for the proper formation of rules, since any premature formation might fail to bring about the intended outcome. John Mill added that art, though comprehensive, utilizes only the part of knowledge that can be condensed in general rules. However, even if these rules are imperfect and provisional, art consists of those 'truths of Science, arranged in the most convenient order for practice'.[13]

Moreover, science examines one cause to its diverse effects, Mill argued, and art, drawing from different sciences, seeks the 'multiplied and diversified causes and conditions' of one effect. A group of 'intermediate scientific truths' fill the gap between practical rules and different sciences. The first step is to set the effect to be produced and, in the most comprehensive manner, the body of conditions its production depends upon. Then, extensive propositions that express the relation of that end to its means (i.e., of the effect to be brought about and the available resources for its production) are pointed out. These extensive propositions comprise the rational account, the *logos* or the 'general scientific theory', of the art. From these, the practical methods 'follow as corollaries'.[14]

*Technê* was not 'a passive enterprise' in Mill; pursuits which follow the rules of art were by definition required to 'pass through practice'—just like in Plato's *Protagoras*.[15] Still, 'the complicated affairs of life' involved too many combinations of circumstances for an *ad hoc* thorough scientific consideration. Establishing precise procedures which lead to successful pursuits of ends,[16] and which people can learn and practice to a high level of competency,[17] was thus quite necessary.

However, Mill's discussion on the role of rules in the 'Art of Life' should not be mistaken for a rule-worshiping position. The connection with Plato helps to show that Mill thought that understanding the theory behind the rule was equally, if not more, important—otherwise it was mere 'uncalculating routine'.[18] Thus, he pointed to a distinction between 'cases in which individuals are bound to conform their practice to a pre-established rule' and cases 'in which it is part of their task to find or construct the rule by which they are to govern their conduct'. Anyone who goes, Mill argued, 'by rules rather than by their reasons, like [...] the physician who preferred that his patients should die by rule rather than recover contrary to it, is rightly judged to be a mere pedant, and the slave of his formulas'. When someone reasons upon rules, s/he proceeds to an interpretation of the formulas. Mill insisted that 'general principles are not intended to dispense with thinking and examining, but to help us to think and examine'.[19]

Thus, Mill used *art* in the 'older' meaning which preserved the connection between theory and practice.[20] In the ancient texts, life becomes part of an art, *technê,* only when *askisis,* practice, is not distinguished from *logos,* theory or science. Thus, this suggests that Mill was not merely 'cast in the mould' of Plato's dialectics. He was also part of the tradition of the Socratic 'Art of Living', which, in turn, does much to show that Mill's *Utilitarianism* (1861) was indeed 'intended partly as a guide to how to live'.[21] Living, and securing the best conditions which living well calls for, were central features—not just any part— of his utilitarian theory.

## The Ancient Art of Living

'Is it worth living that way?' is the most important question asked in the tradition of the 'Art of Living'. For Socrates, the examined life was the only life worth living. Stemming from the Socratic and Stoic tradition of the philosophic way of life, it is not surprising that today the 'Art of Living' has been formulated, more or less, as 'a conception of philosophy as a way of life'. Alexander Nehamas argues that contrary to pure theory, which searches for answers to important questions irrespective of what kind of a person one becomes, theories that discuss modes of lives incorporate truth and character as vital aspects. In this way, Nehamas adds, 'those who practice philosophy as the art of living construct their personalities through the investigation, the criticism, and the production of philosophical views'. In today's transformed *agora,* the mode of life inspired by Socrates is reflected primarily in the life of writing, rather than of conversing.[22]

Though the phrase 'Art of Living' ('technê tou biou') does not appear in ancient writings, it still serves as a summary to the ancient philosophy of the art that is concerned with life or ways of living (*technê peri ton bion*).[23] The 'Art of Living' in antiquity referred to a view of philosophy as 'something primarily expressed in an individual's actions (ἔργα) and way of life [...] rather than something restricted to written doctrines and arguments (λόγοι)'.[24] As John Sellars argues, the philosophy of the 'Art of Living' was perceived as a personal journey to happiness, or whatever constituted the conception of living or faring well; but, at the same time, despite the differences in the particular circumstances of each person, individuals recognized some general theoretical underpinnings or principles that would serve as means to reaching that end. Whether an 'Art of Living' would be successful or not, depended on action as well as on thinking— on *erga* as well as *logoi.*[25]

In Plato's *Apology,* Socrates' 'examined life' referred to the critical analysis of those matters that could bring about the highest welfare or excellence of the soul (τῆς ψυχῆς ὅπως ὡς ἀρίστη ἔσται).[26] In *Gorgias,* Socrates stated that he was the only man who practiced the true political art: leading a philosophical life, guided by what he thought to be right or just for the good of both himself and his fellow citizens; even if that meant endangering his own welfare or 'dying many deaths'.[27] On both occasions, Socrates had failed to convince his interlocutors.

Socrates argued that refraining from unjust actions or being committed to justice was the best protection that one can provide to himself from being harmed.[28] But acting in a right or just way, Socrates argued, presumes knowledge of what right or just is. In addition, throughout Plato's *Alcibiades I*, Socrates tries to explain that knowing what is right or just requires first to know one's own self; a knowledge that is also requisite in taking care of one's self. Thus, the philosopher's life points to a correlation between oneself, the criterion of right or just and one's good—which is found by self-examination. Concurrently, Plato's Socrates was convinced that only through the pursuit of virtue or human excellence can one take care of their self both for personal and social benefit.[29] Since such a mode of living did not allow one to do whatever one willed (ποιεῖν ὅτι ἂν βούλῃ) irrespective of justice and temperance, any sign of incontinence (*akratia*) was a sign of lack of freedom.[30] Socrates thus searched for definitions, seeking what the life of virtue consisted in, and showed to his contemporaries, 'much to their annoyance', that their unreflective habits of practice and behavior did not constitute, in contrast to what they thought, living well.[31] Thus, like everything else in the polis that had to be done well (and, more importantly, for good), living also required an art.[32]

Plato's *Gorgias* defined the subject-matter of the master art which deals with the soul as being what is good and bad, admirable and shameful, just and unjust.[33] Charles Kahn provides an apt summary of the relevant conclusion in *Gorgias*:[34]

> Such an art will have investigated the nature (*phusis*) that it cares for and the causal explanation (*aitia*) of its procedures, so as to be able to give a rational account (*logos*) of both, just like the doctor who has studied the nature of the body and the causes of disease, and so can give an explanation of his treatment [...] [J]ust as the doctor's procedures are teleologically subordinated to the goal of bodily health, so the theory and practice of the political art are rationally structured by their relation to the *telos*.

Scientific knowledge differs from practical knowledge (doing from experience) in the former's ability to provide a rational account (*logos*) of the principles—that is, the causal relations—that underlie practice. Unless an art is accompanied with such *logos*, it will simply be considered a skill acquired by mimesis, a routine, without knowledge of the principles that are involved. Not only is such an understanding of the principles involved central to the universality, teachability, precision, and explanation of the art, but also it is central to the commitment of its practitioners to the end as well as to their ability to adapt means to ends rationally as circumstances vary. Taking care of one's self called for a transformation of one's condition of the soul into a good condition (εὐεξία). The aim of Plato's 'art' was thus 'the moral welfare of the citizens, 'putting justice and temperance in their souls,' making their mind (dianoia) as noble as it can be', which adds an *aesthetic* quality to the life of the virtuous individual; the person who is *dikaios* and *agathos* but also *kalos*—an excellence which is the primary means to secure the happiness of the society.[35]

Thus, in the Socratic tradition of the 'Art of Living', a person's life required proper guidance of activity, guidance offered by knowledge (acquired through dialectics), to transform the condition of her/his soul into a good one; by achieving excellence, one makes her/his life worth living. However, to achieve expertise in this, as in any, craft, the role of *exercise* cannot be overestimated. Simply, one cannot lead the philosophical life, even if one knows its principles, without *askisis*.[36] This entails that the Socratic way of life could not be manifested through a mere list of principles in a book, since, as Martha Nussbaum has put it, 'philosophical books are to philosophizing as tennis manuals are to tennis [...] They can't do it; and they are no substitute for the live activity'.[37] Thus, the person who practices the 'Art of Life' achieves excellence in, and by, doing what is good, admirable and just; becoming, as David Hume put it in his essay 'The Stoic', that 'master workman who puts those several parts together [i.e., the subordinate arts of life], moves them according to just harmony and proportion [as cogs in a machine], and produces true felicity as the result of their conspiring order'.[38]

# MILL AND THE ART OF LIFE

## Plato and Mill on the 'Art of Life'

As we saw, arts define the end that is aimed at by individuals—different ends correspond to different arts. The final end, i.e., the end that cannot be for the sake of any end other than itself, is the subject matter of the most comprehensive art. This can be no other than the 'Art of Life'—the art that incorporates all aspects of human conduct. As art follows certain rational principles or rules, carefully constructed in such a way that when followed the agent is enabled to achieve the end, there is a need to develop a scientific method of establishing such rules.

The practice of an art affirms, Mill argued, the desirability of the end. The latter calls for further scrutiny on whether the course of action (based on rational principles) proposed is suitable for practice: '[f]or the purposes of practice, everyone must be required to justify his approbation'. This means that ends and their required means (i.e., specific arts) need to be tested against a higher standard or a more general premise. When the higher standard approves these specific arts, another test must be made: whether there are other objects available to the agent that may take precedence over the proposed end. In essence, these tests determine 'whether the special aim of any particular art is worthy and desirable, and what is its place in the scale of desirable things'.[39]

There are three domains of ends or general principles, which can test particular instances of conduct. These general action-guiding principles form the 'Art of Life': its end is the ultimate standard or first principle, the *telos*. The two tests mentioned above define the precise order of principles of conduct in relation to the final end. Here we reach a significant conclusion: there is a striking similarity with the central conclusion of Plato's *Gorgias*: that 'the theory and practice of the political art are *rationally structured by their relation to the telos*.[40] Similarly, while preparing his translations of Plato's dialogues for publication, Mill noted incidentally: a central idea or purpose saves different pursuits from 'incoherency and vain caprice', by making them '*one, harmonious, and a whole*'.[41]

The end of the 'Art of Life', Mill argued, is the promotion of happiness of mankind (a rather more general scope from the one Socrates assigned in the *Apology*); an end that must be clearly and precisely defined.[42] However, he added, there would be cases where 'on the whole more happiness will exist in the world, if feelings are cultivated which will make people, in certain cases, regardless of happiness'. But, still, the promotion of happiness, the final end, was the justification and the controller of subordinate ends, without itself being the sole end of all actions.[43]

As we saw, Mill recurrently turned to Plato's dialogues and ancient Greek thought in general during his early education. During the period which preceded his publication of his *Logic*, Mill was preoccupied with translating, discussing and reviewing works of, or on, Plato. It seems that the former experience left its mark on Mill's belief that living can be an art. Plato, according to Grote, in dialogues such as *Laches*, *Charmides* and *Protagoras*—dialogues which Mill translated—'dimply indicated' a 'Science of Ends', or Teleology: 'the truly regal art of life, upon which the attainment of Good depends'.[44] Though earlier, I suggested that Mill may have been inspired by Bain's lectures on the arts of life and of living, Bain himself claimed that it was George Grote, who had 'instigated Mr. Mill to compose that striking chapter'.[45] And perhaps he did. But what is of interest here is how Mill developed this art.

Like Plato's Socrates in *Apology*, Mill felt that '[t]here is no doctrine really worth labouring at, either to construct or to inculcate, except the Philosophy of Life. A Philosophy of Life, in harmony with the noblest feelings and cleared of superstition is the great want of these times'.[46] According to Mill, the 'Art of Life' is divided into three domains: morality (the right), prudence (the expedient) and aesthetics (the beautiful, noble). These three departments correspond exactly to the three distinct ends that constituted the subject-matter of the *politikê technê* as defined in Plato's *Gorgias*: morality (just or unjust—δίκαιον ἤ ἄδικον), prudence (advantageous or harmful—ἀγαθὸν ἤ κακόν) and aesthetics (noble or shameful—καλὸν ἤ αἰσχρὸν).[47]

However, it has recently been claimed that there is 'not much help to be found elsewhere in Mill's works', besides Mill's *Logic*, regarding the content of the three domains of ends of Mill's 'Art of Life'.[48] But, not only did Mill not ignore these 'spheres' of action in his translation of Plato's *Gorgias*, it seems that that he directly appropriated Socrates' argument concerning the 'superordinate craft'. Mill defined these 'departments of ends' in such a way as for them to complement each other. Like in Plato's *Statesman* (but not *Gorgias*), Mill did not consider the 'master art' to coincide with the domain of morality.[49]

Taking his cue from Grote, in his 'Grote's Plato', Mill discussed these ends of 'human action and qualities', in relation to the 'complicated' ancient Greek sentiments 'on matters of conduct and character'. He once again juxtaposed the aesthetic along the useful and the dutiful. More importantly, he argued that the English are incapable to understand what the aesthetic branch of conduct entails because of their 'practical turn of thought', whereas the French capture the aesthetic element of the Hellenic feeling but 'sometimes indeed out of due proportion to the prudential and the dutiful'.[50] Even though 'το καλόν' and the emotions that are attached to it (which form the domain of aesthetics) did not have a modern counterpart (it being a 'complex idea' or a 'mixed mode'—unlike 'Virtue, Justice, Courage, Knowledge, Law'), the key to unfolding its meaning was provided by Plato's dialectical method.[51]

While linguistic and cultural differences kept Plato's and Mill's worlds apart, superstition about the pursuit of the philosophical life had remained unaltered. For the proper guidance of life, Mill noted, commenting on Plato's project, knowledge of 'Good and Evil, Just and Unjust, Honourable and Shameful' was required, not the prescriptions of 'Commonplace'. As we saw in the previous chapter, dialectics drew out the common property of these abstract terms, allowing people to define a standard to regulate and make consistent their ideas about human conduct: '[t]he grand business of human intellect ought to consist in subjecting these general terms to the most rigorous scrutiny, and bringing to light the ideas that lie at the bottom of them'. This was the 'Platonic test' for the life 'worth having'; a test that Mill thought applicable to his own time. Dialectics were, Mill thus argued, an integral part of the 'Art of Living'.[52]

However, Plato's Socrates failed to convince his interlocutors in Gorgias about the worth of the philosophical life—an impossible task, Mill tried to explain, when attempted with mere argument. The belief 'that a wicked man would be happy if he could succeed in his wickedness' was rather commonplace in ancient Greece. An act that did not involve harm to others could not be called immoral, no matter how harmful or shameful it was for the person herself/himself.[53] This formed a problem for Plato's Socrates' conception of happiness—one that is fully developed in the Republic—because he argued that a person should not merely appear just but be just, otherwise he would not be happy.[54]

According to Mill, even if individuals have the ability to rationalize their actions and calculate benefits and costs, they cannot be held accountable to others when their calculations fail in actions that involve only themselves. Distinguishing between moral, expedient and aesthetic principles of conduct could show how a particular act can be inexpedient and yet be approved for practice—i.e., so long as it was conducive to the pursuit of happiness when one views life as a whole. Taking these departments of ends to be always and in all cases identical results in classifying an instance of human conduct as inexpedient and expedient concurrently (which was exactly what Socrates did in the Gorgias, leading Callicles to accuse him of contradiction).[55] This does not suggest that there are no cases of overlap between these domains, but it does suggest varying degrees of conduciveness to attaining happiness. Without muddling these domains, Mill tried to show how some instances of human action failed the tests of the 'Art of Life'. The truth that lay at the bottom of Socrates' noble—but fallacious[56]—claims needed to be extracted.

## Disentangling John Stuart Mill's 'Art of Life'

John Stuart Mill's 'Art of Life' has justifiably led studies of his thought to a number of directions, since a student of Mill's works has most likely by now identified themes from his better known writings.[57] However, this is not the place to explore any other direction than a basic one, i.e., the subject matter and function of the 'departments of ends'.

As discussed, that Mill turned to an 'Art of Life' in the third edition of the *Logic* and not earlier, may be related to his having recently reviewed Bain's lectures on the value of scientific methods to well-being. In any case, Mill attempted to transfer the familiar and imprecise language of 'theory *and* practice' into a consistent, scientific form. His 'Bentham' (1838) and his comments on Arthur Helps's 'The Art of Living with Others' suggest that Mill had already done much thinking on how to set a utilitarian framework to regulate issues of social interaction and interference. For example, such a framework would settle matters of acceptable and unacceptable social inequality by the cultivation of a 'high principle'—one that would protect free use of one's natural powers, despite the inequality this created, for the *greater* good. Any other inequality, i.e., a 'sway' of one person or group over others, Mill argued, would be made immoral, inexpedient and shameful.[58]

However, Mill's analysis of an 'Art of Life' in his *Logic* was very brief, if not sketchy. As we saw, he distinguished between three departments of ends of human action, secondary to the *final* end of human action. Moral, expedient and aesthetic ends were subordinated to the promotion of happiness; specific actions of human conduct were classed according to which principle of conduct they followed. The primary function of the ultimate principle was that of an 'umpire', i.e., a regulator of the secondary ends. It was not invoked unless in cases of conflict between them.[59]

Concurrently, neither was the relation between these departments of ends nor their connection to other areas of Mill's thought made clear. Thus students of Mill's works have tried to develop a rough framework through the various formulations of these distinct departments of ends that appear in Mill's other writings. In 'Bentham' and in the *Logic*, Mill offered two examples of human conduct which were supposed to assist his readers understand how actions are appraised and how these departments of ends interact as well as function against the background of the ultimate end of life, happiness. However, it is generally supposed—wrongly, as I hope to show—that Mill, in these two works, had the same purpose in mind, despite the difference in formulation.

In the *Logic*, Mill argued that happiness is the *final* end, but not the *sole* end of human conduct. He attempted to demonstrate a case in which happiness was better achieved without directly aiming at it, that is by postulating a different end to be pursued for itself which could even *seem* to go counter to the final end:

> the cultivation of an ideal nobleness of will and conduct, should be to individual human beings an end, to which the specific pursuit either of their own happiness or that of others (except so far as included in the idea) should, in any case of conflict, give way.

This example, to which this section will return several times, points to a case of priority of the aesthetic department over the other departments and the level of secondary principles, as Mill immediately argued that happiness *is* the justification, and *ought* to be regulator of these secondary ends of life:

> But I hold that the very question, what constitutes this elevation of character, is itself to be decided by a reference to happiness as the standard. The character itself should be, to the individual, a paramount end, simply because the existence of this ideal nobleness of character [...] in any abundance, would go further than all things else towards making human life happy.

Mill then proceeded to define two senses of a 'happy life': first, a 'humble' sense, i.e., pleasure and freedom from pain; second, a 'higher' sense, i.e., life 'as human beings with highly developed faculties can care to have'.[60]

Alan Ryan was one of the first to attempt to draw out the implications of Mill's concept of the 'Art of Life' for Mill's particular view of liberty and happiness.[61] By assigning different spheres of influence, Ryan defined the departments of the 'Art of Life' as follows: first, the department of *Morality* provides the general principles that deal with matters of *right* or *wrong* in *other-regarding* conduct. The end of this department is to produce *interpersonal* goods (e.g., peace, justice and honesty). Morality, Ryan argues, is the 'chief and most basic component' of Mill's 'Art of Life'.[62] Second, the department of *Prudence*, in agreement with the common use of the term, provides the general principles that deal with matters of *good* or *bad* in *self-regarding* conduct. The end of this department is to produce *personal* goods. Third, the department of *Aesthetics*, on the other hand, provides the general principles that characterize human conduct as beautiful or shameful. The end of this department is to *reflect* the quality in one's pursuits—in a perceptive, critical and revisionary way, rather than by calculating either social or private benefits. Thus, aesthetics are involved in the *evaluation* of pleasures and an agent's worth.[63]

Ryan's interpretation aptly shows that Mill's elaborate theory of the 'Art of Life' enabled an agent to distinguish between different kinds of judgment or standards. Mill opted, Ryan argues, for limiting punishment to the other-regarding sphere, i.e., the moral department of ends, which allowed individuals to move freely and experiment within a self-regarding sphere to enrich and ennoble their lives in any way they saw fit.[64] Ryan's interpretation has deservingly been very influential and has changed the way many think of Mill's *On Liberty* and *Utilitarianism*.

However, applying Ryan's position to the example mentioned above (from the last page of the *Logic*) shows that it is somewhat narrow, reducing the three spheres of actions to two. Ryan seems to read the above example, as a case of individuality, aesthetically noble, located in the department of prudence. If it is an end, it is self-regarding. But first, as critics argue, limiting prudence to a self-regarding sphere and morality to the other-regarding sphere fails to account for Mill's requirement of impartiality between self and others.[65] Second, Mill had clearly argued that there is a *better* conception of expediency rather than simple self-interest. Utilitarianism was usually considered to equate morality with expediency;[66] thus, Mill's solution was to argue for a 'higher degree' of expediency, not simply discern between self- and other-regarding spheres. In the aforesaid example, the higher degree referred to pursuing other ends for *themselves*, even if these are temporarily irrelevant or even harmful to happiness, since in the long run they will not be irrelevant in reference either to *personal* happiness (when one views life as a whole) or to *general* happiness (when everyone acts in a similar manner).[67]

Jonathan Riley has produced the most elaborate reconstruction of Mill's teleological doctrine. Riley's reconstruction of the 'Art of Life' through a close study of Mill's main texts expands on Ryan's brief treatment of Mill's 'Art' and avoids some of its problems. Riley does this by accommodating the claims of a self-regarding sphere of complete liberty, a social sphere of morality and law as well as a social sphere of competitive freedom—a sphere that Ryan did not set apart.[68] In this respect, first, the domain of *Morality* provides the general principles that secure social harmony. These refer to the cultivation of 'a feeling of moral obligation to make other-regarding choices': right other-regarding actions point to those choices whose consequences promote a person's 'permanent interest in social harmony [...], conceived as part of his own happiness'; wrong other-regarding actions point to those choices whose consequences undermine social harmony.[69]

Second, the domain of *expediency* provides a generalized, and straight-forward, consequentialist principle: '[a]ny person should evaluate the desirability of actions on the basis of their consequences'. This is co-extensive with all human conduct;[70] thus, unlike Ryan, Riley argues that this domain includes the other two domains and involves both self- and other- regarding actions.

Third, the department of *aesthetics* provides the general principles that enable people to develop their individuality. These refer to the cultivation of 'a feeling of aesthetic obligation [...] to *exercise* [one's] liberty of self-regarding actions'. Individuals have a special duty to themselves to exercise this liberty to promote their self-improvement. There is an aesthetic quality in such an exercise, whereas failure to exercise it, signals an individual's 'self-corruption'.[71] Riley allows that this department has both a self- and an other-regarding dimension; he also incorporates Ryan's 'reflective' aspect. In some cases, Riley argues, aesthetics overlap with the sphere of morality (just as Mill's example in the *Logic*, in which the happiness of others or social harmony could be pursued by cultivating a noble character); in others aesthetics manifest themselves in the (familiar) self-regarding sphere of complete liberty or in the social sphere of competitive freedom.[72] Riley's view of the department of aesthetic ends broadens the one-dimensional, i.e., reflective, character Ryan has argued for. He illustrates how this department can offer action-guiding principles on the level of the principles of the domains of morality and expediency. However, the aesthetic domain of ends is made to partake of all spheres of conduct without a clear view of its relation to the other domains.

On the other hand, Wendy Donner has on several occasions examined Mill's utilitarianism through the prism of the tradition of virtue ethics. This reading has enabled her to draw attention to the role of virtue and character in Mill's moral philosophy and attempt to supply the rationale that pervades the connection of aesthetics to the other two domains of conduct. Donner argues that in Mill's 'Art of Life' the department of *Morality* has authority over those 'rules of duty or obligation, whose violation calls for coercive moral sanctions'. A morally wrong act is that which is 'liable to punishment and coercion'. Thus, this is the province of (other-regarding) Duty, in which morally right acts may fail to maximize the good but whose 'perpetual practice' is indispensable to 'general well-being'.[73] These remarks highlight both the role of punishment (politically, socially or self-inflicted) and the suspension of the general consequentialist principle of maximization of the good.

Secondly, the department of general *Expediency* refers to the all-inclusive category of the general promotion of the good.[74] But, there is also the more limited sense of *simple* expediency, or prudence, which corresponds to Ryan's self-regarding sphere.[75] Thirdly, the department of *Aesthetics* encompasses the self-regarding *virtues*. These are not properly called 'duties to one's self', Donner argues, since they lack coercive influence. This is the province of Virtue, Nobility, Beauty and positive Worthiness, which has jurisdiction over acts, including forms of social interaction, which are not properly subject to coercion and punishment or intolerance. Here, supererogatory acts find their place.[76]

The principle of utility, Donner notes, supplies a 'general value ought'—not a *moral* ought—people *ought* to promote happiness, which makes the principle of utility an axiological principle. Such a 'great axiom' stipulates that 'happiness alone has intrinsic value' and does not have direct influence at the practical level of morality, but only at the critical level—'it cannot by itself impose obligations or yield judgments about right action'. Thus, Donner argues, it is general expediency that provides the maximizing consequentialist principle.[77] Mill defined these departments as 'essential components' of the 'Art of Life' and, Donner adds, they are 'not to be thought of as hierarchically arranged in all cases, but as interconnected domains that complement each other'.[78]

Donner lays emphasis on the importance of a proper demarcation of the domains of morality and aesthetics. Like both Ryan and Riley, Donner shows that Mill had a complex moral philosophy and theory of value to which many critics of his writings have failed to do justice. Still, like both Ryan and Riley, Donner seems to run into some trouble with Mill's domain of aesthetics. Though Donner does argue that virtue is not simply supererogation, saying that it is an element of a 'well-lived life' adds little if anything. It fails to capture Mill's more nuanced use of virtue; his example in the last page of the *Logic* seems to point to an 'ancient' sense of virtue, i.e., the ideal of human excellence (*kalos*), which can include Donner's more 'modern' sense, i.e., the sacrifice of personal interest. In addition, as Donner focuses on the other two domains of the 'Art of Life', the distinction between *general* and *simple* expediency (i.e., Riley's consequentialist principle of maximizing the overall good and Ryan's prudential principle of maximising self-regarding goods) as well as their relation to the *final* end, are not clear enough.

It is telling that Mill's example in the *Logic* of a case of priority of the aesthetic domain has led to so many misunderstandings. Thus, Mill may have been right to suggest that to the practical turn of mind of the moderns, the ancient Greek notion of the *kalon* was difficult to understand. James Mill, who also considered acts to be 'hurtful or beneficial' (prudence), 'moral or immoral' (morality), 'virtuous or vicious' (aesthetics), argued that it was 'only an abuse of language to call them beautiful or ugly'.[79] That John Mill did call them that, must count for something.

To move to the second example, the younger Mill's 'Bentham' has made it even more difficult to untangle his 'Art of Life' (especially in reference to aesthetics), by referring to the story of Lucius Junius Brutus.[80] As the story goes, not only did Brutus not prevent the beheading of his sons, Titus and Tiberius, for being part of the plot to restore the tyrannical power of the exiled Tarquinian family, but moreover 'he shut up his heart to his children with obdurate severity', fulfilling his duty as a consul and administering the appropriate punishment to those who endangered liberty.[81]

Mill employed this example not in order to explain the three departments of ends he was to develop thirteen years later, but to indicate how particular acts affect the people that witness or observe them—it was common enough in the Scottish tradition to separate the moral sentiments of the actor from those of the spectator.[82] A person's conduct in a given situation, Mill tried to explain, can be *appraised* according to the feelings it stimulates—and not just be deconstructed and transferred into different categories of ends. These feelings can be of three sorts: moral, aesthetic and sympathetic. The similarity with the departments of the 'Art of Life' has led some commentators to argue that Mill was talking about the same thing—inconsistently—and that these departments were later modified to morality, aesthetics and prudence (the last occupying the place of sympathy).[83]

But it seems that his objective was to show that moral and psychological theories need to consider these different ways in which people *estimate* particular actions and agents, since 'the moral view of actions and characters', though unquestionably it has priority, 'is not the sole one [...] it is only one of three, by which our sentiments towards the human being may be, ought to be, and without entirely crushing our own nature cannot but be, materially influenced':

> The first addresses itself to our reason and conscience; the second to our imagination; the third to our human fellow-feeling. According to the first, we approve or disapprove; according to the second, we admire or despise; according

to the third, we love, pity, or dislike. The morality of an action depends on its foreseeable consequences; its beauty, and its loveableness, or the reverse, depend on the qualities which it is evidence of.[84]

All three are critical or reflective.

With Mill's comments on Plato's *Gorgias* in mind (having been made just four years earlier), one may identify Mill's intent here: he did not seem to believe that people are influenced by a mode of action simply by approving it, unless they already desire the ends such an action advances. For people to be influenced into acting similarly, when they are *not already inclined* to act so, actions have to be admirable and loveable, to work on their imagination and excite care for the well-being of others—not to work on their rational faculties alone.

Thus, Mill argued, Brutus' actions can be *approved* because, in 'executing a law essential to the freedom of his country, against persons of whose guilt there was no doubt', he exhibited 'a bent of character from which useful [...] actions are likely to arise'.[85] At the same time, the choice to administer the sentence was '*admirable*, because it evinced a rare degree of patriotism, courage, and self-control'. These were important virtues (only the latter two can be self-regarding in Donner's sense), which Livy's and Niebuhr's narratives seemed to approve.[86] However, Brutus' choice could not be loveable because it excluded any sympathetic qualities for its pursuit—Brutus had managed to make that choice because he had suppressed the sympathetic feelings toward his sons.[87]

Commentators mistake Mill's example here as a discussion of the departments of the 'Art of Life', because it can be easily translatable in those terms. Brutus' course of action was moral because he executed a law of his country. However, it went against what his own temporary interest would command—not only was his choice not pleasurable, it must have been very painful. But the promotion of the happiness of the commonwealth was much more important than his own, and this was secured by protecting liberty from the power of a tyrant—despite the licenses many would enjoy under such a regime. It was also a noble choice for Brutus adhering to his role as a consul, despite the personal misfortune this would cause.

Mill explicitly employed this example to reply to the 'morality-intoxicated' thinkers whom he had in mind (Bentham and Comte),[88] by showing that the moral standard was neither the 'sole master of all our actions' nor 'even of all our sentiments'. More importantly, it shows that Mill did not seem to set the department of aesthetics as a sphere of licence. 'Base' actions may not be immoral or harmful, but they cannot be part of a 'noble' character. Though some types of conduct were not to be interfered with in matters that caused no harm to others, no conduct could be beyond 'praise or condemn': 'as if men's likings and dislikings, on things in themselves indifferent, were not full of the most important inferences as to every point of their character'.[89] This concern with what kind a character a person forms suggests that Mill's 'Art of Life', like all ancient theories which defined the best life, was directly related to what kind of person one becomes and what kind of truths one accepts.

To round off the main findings of this section, the 'Art of Life', Mill argued, is a 'Philosophia Prima' or *ultima* which consists in the first principles (the 'widest generalisations') of conduct.[90] As such, the 'Art of Life' deals with questions which concern the final and intermediate ends of conduct, how acts (and their ends) can be grouped according to some common attribute (and how they are further subdivided according to other common attributes) and how they relate within a hierarchy, both at the level of each domain separately and at that of the 'Art of Life' generally.

A person's chosen course of action aims to produce a certain end. An end, or the object of desire, is considered to be the product of the intended and foreseen consequences of the specific act. The principle of expediency will propose a course of action that, most surely (and directly), will bring about that end. Without such a plan of action, individuals are 'mere gamblers'. The common attribute of expedient actions is knowledge of the remote causes which with proper foresight, calculation and application of appropriate means will produce the desired end—incorporating questions 'of time, place, and circumstance'. Distinguishing between *immediate* and *ultimate* interests differentiates between simple and general expediency.[91]

Thus, Mill argued that 'there are different orders of expediency; all expediencies are not exactly on the same level'. More importantly, he argued that considerations of justice are a branch of expediency of the highest level.[92] If a course of action of simple expediency can be distinguished and separated from the domain of morality, only then ought the agent to pursue it without any further consideration. But, if a course of action has an other-regarding aspect, for the sake of ultimate interests, then individuals ought to incorporate the action-guiding principle of morality in their intended plan of action. They are required to choose the best possible course of action, without superseding the principle of morality.[93] How does one know what distinguishes morality from the other departments? As we saw, the common attribute that moral obligations have, Mill added, including the more limited sense of justice, is the 'punishability' of action (either by law, opinion or self-guilt)—this distinguishes the dutiful from the *simply* expedient. However the emotions associated with justice, Mill argued, make the difference between morality and expedience not one of *degree* but of *kind*, which further makes morality incommensurable to considerations of simple expediency.[94] In choosing a course of conduct, which gives due weight to these considerations, the outcome may be that the course of action may be moral but inexpedient—but ultimately it is still the best course of action. It is the best course of action from both the prudential standpoint and the standpoint of social harmony in Riley's terms. Fulfilling thus the 'proportionality' criterion,[95] the two tests mentioned earlier rank the moral act higher than the expedient act. However, there are extreme cases (e.g., social control or injustice), when other principles are involved (e.g., liberty or equality)—that for the sake of ultimate interests (e.g., the 'permanent interests of man as a progressive being'), a moral act may be ranked lower in the hierarchy (e.g., allow harm to avoid producing 'evils, greater than those which it would prevent' or to allow an injustice to correct an inequality). In such cases, direct recourse to the first principle is required—after all Mill did argue that 'Morals and Politics require those principles ['the general principles of Teleology'] at every step'.[96]

In contrast, the principle of aesthetics refers to acts as ends in themselves, not done as obligations or because they are expected.[97] However, the connection between Mill's 'Art of Life' and Socrates' politikê technê shows that Mill distinguished what is 'noble' from what is 'dutiful' or 'useful', because, of all three modes of conduct, it is the only one which can maintain an emotional impact—even life-changing—on other people when the other two fail to do so.[98] But, as in the case of morality, the outcome of the test of ordering between aesthetic and expedient ends may be that the course of action may be noble but immediately inexpedient. This may explain why Mill argued that, though a noble action is an end in itself, there is a need for more social incentives for 'le vrai, le beau, et le bien', which, unlike 'l'utile', 'have an inward reward, and whose 'external fruits [appear] only in a distant future'.[99] As aesthetics are still subject to the test of the final end, in case of conflict with morality, the latter has lexical priority.[100] However, Mill's use of the 'older' meaning of art, which by definition brought about only good, made it more likely for Mill to think that no such conflict was possible.[101] In any case, if the order of precedence is not justified by the ultimate standard of the promotion of the happiness of mankind, then such a scheme of action cannot be a part of an 'Art of Life'. Thus, the 'leading departments of human life', Mill argued (on a different subject, though having just mentioned the art of life), 'do not develope themselves separately, but each depends on all, or is profoundly modified by them'.[102]

## AN EDUCATION FOR THE ART OF LIFE

According to Mill, the secondary principles of conduct, whose importance most people agree about, define 'the real character of any man's ethical system'.[103] It is thus imperative to be able to make the conduct, which these action-guiding principles aim to bring about, desirable to individuals. This is what the art of education aims to do, with the means discovered by the science of ethology: distinguishing between reason, imagination and feelings, establishing a connection to the different domains of conduct, and working upon each domain with suitable influences to develop an emotional attachment to a rational plan of action.[104]

In Plato's Gorgias, Callicles (Socrates' last interlocutor) claimed that it is unnatural both to pursue and desire general happiness, since this end was formed for the preservation (and promotion of the well-being) of society; for this reason, such a desire is merely a submission to the prejudices of society.[105] But 'unnaturalness' was not an objection that could convince Mill. He argued that the injunctions of nature are to be conquered: 'All praise of Civilization, or Art, or Contrivance, is so much dispraise of Nature; an admission of imperfection, which it is man's business, and merit, to be always endeavouring to correct or mitigate'.[106]

Therefore, the natural state of human beings is not at all what defines humanity; society and education are necessary for the improvement of mankind:

> [T]he duty of man is to co-operate with the beneficent powers [germs of which can be found in human nature], [...] by perpetually striving to amend the course of nature—and bringing that part of it over which we can exercise control, more nearly into conformity with a high standard of justice and goodness.[107]

Both self- and other-regarding virtues can be cultivated so that they become consistently present in human conduct. When such virtues are cultivated 'the most elevated sentiments of which humanity is capable become a second nature, stronger than the first, and not so much subduing the original nature as merging it into itself'.[108] This was one of the first conclusions of the discussion between Socrates, Glaucon and Adeimantus in Plato's *Republic* as well, since a widely diffused process of education was deemed necessary for people to develop such 'elevated sentiments'. This requires the formation of habits from very early on in a person's life, '[f]or it is then that it is best molded and takes the impression than one wishes to stamp upon it'.[109] Early in his youth, Mill was taught that human improvement consists in having a 'high degree of virtue'.[110] However, to find out how to impress the 'stamp' of virtue, Mill argued, the artist must turn to the scientist.

In his inaugural address at the University of St. Andrews, Mill tried to develop such an educational scheme. Education, Mill maintained, was '[w]hatever helps to shape the human being, to make the individual what he is, or hinder him from being what he is not'; that is, everything done with 'the express purpose of bringing us somewhat nearer to the perfection of our nature'—or 'to the mental, moral, and aesthetic stature of which [our] nature is capable'.[111]

Mill's argument in his rectorial address evolved around the need to have a comprehensive education. If the debate between scientific and literary education prioritised thinking over expressing one's thoughts respectively, then it was problematic. An individual, Mill replied, requires equal development of both.[112] For this reason, Mill did not consider the division between scientific and literary education to be useful, but dividing between branches or departments of education, which, complementing each other, would offer an educational process of a more comprehensive nature, one that is pertinent to the 'Art of Life'.

If individuals have an education that makes them intelligent and sensible, whatever their occupation and their place in society, they will function intelligently and sensibly—philosophic shoemakers differ from skilled ones in that the first 'demand, and are capable of apprehending, principles, instead of merely cramming their memory with details', whereas the latter simply act from routine with a minimum understanding of principles.[113] More importantly, such an education enables them to lead a better life, become better citizens and better persons. As Mill noted, '[i]t really is of importance, not only what men do, but also what manner of men they are that do it. Among the works of man which human life is rightly employed in perfecting and beautifying, the first in importance surely is man himself'.[114] As this suggests, Mill was indebted to Socrates' call for life as an art, dialectics as the means to the discovery of its rational principles as well as the Socratic call for self-examination and self-development, i.e., transforming one's soul into a good one for the inherent pleasure of pursuing excellence for itself. However, Mill was aware that his considerations perhaps could 'not suffice to convince those who most need[ed] convincing', just like Plato's Socrates had failed to do so in *Gorgias*. For this reason, he also pointed to the extrinsic usefulness of cultivated individuals.[115]

Moreover, Mill divided education into intellectual, moral and aesthetic braches. In the university curriculum, intellectual education, which occupied most of Mill's speech, primarily referred to 'scientific instruction'. As moral (and religious) education concerned private values and convictions, Mill argued, it ought to be taught by the family to a greater extent and society to a lesser one, rather than by institutionalized education. Aesthetic education aimed at the 'education of the feelings, and the cultivation of the beautiful'.[116] Both the moral and aesthetic branches highlighted the need for training a person's non-cognitive faculties. These branches trained the faculty of reason, the moral faculty and the faculty of imagination; knowledge, conscience and feelings respectively. Even with a superficial glance, there seems to be a connection between these branches and the 'Art of Life'.

Intellectual education centered on 'the properties of the things which we have to work with, and to work among, and to work upon'. Knowing the laws of physical phenomena, Mill noted, keeps the world around us from being a 'sealed book', 'uninteresting because unintelligible'. Still, this knowledge, he added, is not the most important feature of intellectual education; the 'ascertainment of truth' of all those matters that are *vital* to us is the most important. Whatever truths one may seek, Mill added, 'the methods of getting at truth, and the tests of truth, are in all cases much the same': either by observation or reasoning. Intellectual education afforded the 'ability to judge correctly of evidence'.

> To do this with effect needs all the resources which the most perfect system of intellectual training can command. Those resources [...] are but of three kinds, first, models, secondly rules, thirdly, appropriate practice. The models of the art of estimating evidence are furnished by science: the rules are suggested by science, and the study of science is the most fundamental portion of the practice.[117]

Mill discussed the sciences of mathematics, physics, logic, physiology and psychology. Ethics and politics came next. While direct instruction is of great importance in intellectual education generally, Mill argued, for ethics and politics individuals need to be their own teachers. As intellectual education prepares the mind chiefly for moral and political ends, it can only describe and not prescribe—students need to decide for themselves. In the study of history, political economy, jurisprudence and international law, students can learn about the major works and problems in these disciplines, works and issues that will help them develop their own ideas.[118] In this branch, one witnesses the formation of a 'scientist', competent to observe, draw correct inferences from, physical as well as social phenomena and verify them in the annals of history. As he noted in his essay 'Nature', 'to know and take heed of the properties of the things we have to deal with, so far as these properties are capable of forwarding or obstructing any given purpose', i.e., the knowledge of things is an essential part of the skilful use of circumstances (which is a mark of free will),[119] is an act of prudence (which does much to explain the place of science in intellectual education).[120]

On the other hand, moral and religious education, according to Mill, did not properly fall within the realm of institutionalized education. Training the feelings and habits begins at home and is developed (often for the worse) by society in general. Institutionalized education can only be indirect, by presenting 'all knowledge as chiefly a means to worthiness of life. Given for the double purpose of making each of us practically useful to his fellow creatures, and of elevating the character of the species itself, exalting and dignifying our nature'.[121] Any instruction on ethical issues in educational institutions needs to remain, Mill maintained, strictly professional and as least dogmatic as possible, since 'it is not the teacher's business to impose his own judgment, but to inform and discipline that of his pupil'.[122] Thus, individuals become competent to form and judge worthy ends and, at the same time, are able to find and apply the proper means. At all times, they need to keep at heart the importance of other fellow travellers in life—either fellow citizens, or, more importantly, the human species itself.

The 'artistic' aspect, which complements the 'scientific', is provided by aesthetic education. Suffice it to note here, the aesthetic branch of education had direct bearing on human conduct. Those who limit Plato's influence to Mill's method consider Mill's rectorial address to be influenced by the Coleridgeans; however, in light of Mill's 'Art of Life', the Platonic elements of the aesthetic branch of education suggest an earlier influence:

> There is besides, a natural affinity between goodness and the cultivation of the Beautiful. When it is real cultivation, and not a mere unguided instinct. He who has learnt what beauty is, if he be of a virtuous character, will desire to realize it in his own life—will keep before himself a type of perfect beauty in human character, to light his attempts at self-culture.[123]

Mill captured the aesthetic quality present in the character of the *kalokagathos*, which is usually translated simply as 'virtuous man'.[124] To this effect, aesthetic education, Mill argued, attempts to lead individuals beyond considerations of expediency: life should be viewed as any work 'which is done as if the workman loved it, and tried to make it as good as possible, though something less good would have answered the purpose for which it was ostensibly made'.[125]

The development and cultivation of personal worth that such a comprehensive education leads to was considered by Mill as a reward of its own:

> there is one reward which will not fail you, and which may be called disinterested, because it is not a consequence, but is inherent in the very fact of

deserving it, the deeper and more varied interest you will feel in life, which will give it tenfold its value, a value which will last to the end.[126]

The gain of character formation as the cultivation of virtue was 'obvious without being specified'.[127] Only an educational scheme that trains one's rational and the affective faculties enables individuals to lead a life worth living—not only for one's own self but also for others.

## CONCLUDING REMARKS

In light of the above discussion, Mill's 'Art of Life' is closely related to ancient Greek thought. In the Stoic tradition, the task of the philosopher was to examine the inter-relation between the principles of *logos*, in order to understand precisely what each amounted to, and 'to understand *in what way*, they hang together'— what followed naturally was 'the correct use of this *logos*'.[128]

At the start of this chapter it was noted that the most important question of the tradition of the 'Art of Living' was: 'Is it worth living that way?' As we saw, Mill noted that the question of worth fell within the aesthetic department of ends.[129] The pleasures of such a life, Mill argued, have no limit.[130] To put it in the terms of Plato's *Republic*, for the cultivated individual a life of virtue does pay— 'in Art, the perfection is itself the object' and that is why a life in pursuit of excellence can only be understood in aesthetic terms.[131] This aesthetic quality was exhibited in the last pages of Mill's *Logic*.

As we saw, the self-modeling question, i.e., 'what to make of oneself?' highlights this interrelation of theory and practice in the care for the 'soul' but also in considering the consequences of what kind of a person one becomes. But there is a need to distinguish between the two distinct parts of the self-modeling question, that is, 'What should I take myself to be?' and 'What should I fashion myself into?' and then attend to them separately: '[y]ou can hardly undertake to fashion yourself without some preconception of what you are or could be, and you can hardly have a preconception of what you are or could be without also having some strong motivation or purpose'.[132] The 'Art of Life' both requires that kind of knowledge and, by Mill's definition, supplies this motivation. But it also requires that a person has the capability for self-development. Mill argues that one does. It is perhaps here that the Scientist meets the Artist.[133]

However, the tradition of the 'ars vitae' had stumbled upon five objections, brought forward by Sextus Empiricus' *Outlines of Pyrrhonism*: a. there are competing 'Arts of Living'; b. the 'Art of Living' cannot be taught; c. it presupposes adequate impressions; d. it produces no distinctive actions; and e. it cannot be put into practice due to the way societies function.[134] Viewing Mill's 'Art of Life' in light of these objections may serve as a summary.

To begin with, there simply cannot be any competing 'Arts of Living', according to Mill. The final end served as an umpire to settle potential conflicts. If clashes do appear, they result from conflicting *intermediate* ends; but the two tests of the 'Art of Life' correct any temporary mistake in priorities. Second, unlike some Stoics, Mill argued that the 'Art of Life' being, more technically, a craft, is comprised of rational principles, which constitute its scientific part or its *logos* and which can be the subject of teaching. On the other hand, Mill did accept that the end of the 'Art of Living', being subject to feelings rather than reason, would not be something that could be taught rationally, but it could be developed through the faculty of the imagination and the cultivation of feelings (which formed one of Mill's arguments against the 'narrowness' of the theory of his utilitarian predecessors). Third, Mill noted that the ends of the 'Art of Life' are pursued through means that science discovers. Scientific methods of correct inference from observation (including experience and experiment) and proper methods of reasoning assist in distinguishing reliable from unreliable impressions and draw precise conclusions regarding the causal laws at play. These are then made into rules of action, precise enough for the practical purposes of life. Fourth, Mill drew on Plato to distinguish between art and knack. Thus, the 'Art of Life' produced actions based on rational principles, which consistently led to an end. Such actions are discernible from actions without principles or without regard to the ultimate end, since the latter are random and incoherent and they do not point to settled character dispositions. Coming to the fifth objection, Mill's *On Liberty* primarily dealt with such a need for securing spheres of practice that would allow the 'Art of Life' to be developed in society. Mill thus in a sense recognized the force of Sextus' fifth objection that no society seems to have enough tolerance for the practitioner of the 'Art of Living' (e.g., the examples of Socrates and Jesus). But Mill, instead of abandoning the notion of an 'Art of Life', employed it to highlight the need to reform society. By distinguishing between domains of ends and spheres of human conduct, Mill had managed to separate between direct interference and indirect influence. He tried to construct a valid argument for this art, being aware of any historical and social limitations.

In conclusion, scholars point to three genres in the tradition of the 'Art of Living'.[135] A first genre can be constructed after the image of the Socrates of Plato's early dialogues: the one that 'urges people to join him in the examined life he considers the only life worth living for a human being' but 'has no means by which to prove that he is right'. In this respect, such an 'Art of Living' attempted to become universalist but merely remained 'tentative and protreptic'. A second variety of the 'Art of Living' can be advanced from Plato's middle works—Nehamas points to Plato's *Phaedon* and *Republic*. In such works Plato, inspired by Socrates, attempted to prove that *one* mode of life, the philosophical life, is best for all. In this genre of the 'Art of Living', Plato shared Socrates' ideal but departed from his method, becoming universalist. The third genre specifies that there is no single mode of life that is best for all—people need to find the one that suits them, and find their true self in the process. Inspiration is thus important and individuality is the central concept of this genre which makes it the least universalist.

Mill's view combines elements of all these genres in the attempt to set out the life that is worth living. It is evident that Mill's *On Liberty* develops an argument of the third genre, in reference to the expression of one's individuality—happiness was the ultimate end, but Mill argued it could not be pursued directly. It is individualistic as there are as many potential modes of living as there are individuals. At the same time, Mill's construction of the 'Art of Life' is universalist in that it urges people to principled living through a dialectical method, as we saw; that is, by seeking those reasoned beliefs that can make their life meaningful. Finally, for those who are not already convinced that the promotion of the happiness of mankind is the final end, Mill's account can only be tentative and protreptic. It at least points to a way of life in which individuals think for themselves and find new meaning in old beliefs. Within the limits set by these criteria (principled life, reasoned beliefs), individuals are *encouraged* not to imitate others and to find inspiration in a way of life that is truly felt to be their own. Only then can their life be regarded as a work of art. But life as a work of art, 'done as if the workman loved it', requires a person 'to make it as good as possible', even when 'something less good' can be sufficient for the ends at hand—opting for the 'higher', rather than the 'humble', sense of happiness.

## NOTES

1. A shorter version of this chapter appeared in K.N. Demeriou and A. Loizides, eds. (2013) *John Stuart Mill: A British Socrates* (Basingstoke: Palgrave Macmillan) reproduced with permission of Palgrave Macmillan.
2. E.g., Fitzpatrick, 2010:46-8, 101-4; Urbinati, 2011:240-2.
3. N:X.381.
4. Bain, 1848:6-8; BSH:XXV.1119-20 (for similar uses, see, e.g., Graham, 1828; Duhring, 1843). See also, Robson, 1998:349.
5. Bain, 1848:6-8, 10-11 (BSH:XXV.1119-20).
6. *SOL*:VIII.943-8; N:X.375.
7. *PPE*:III.756-7.
8. Plato, *Gor*:463b (J. Mill, CPB:I.112v); DPE:IV.312; Go:XI.109. See further, Haralsson, 2011. Interestingly, only after being praised by E. Bulwer-Lytton for novelty, did Mill cite Plato's *Gorgias* in the 1844 edition of his essays on political economy (Mill to E. Bulwer-Lytton, 27/03/1843:XIII.578-9).
9. *A*:I.35; OG:I.336.
10. Mill believed that his use of the word 'Art' (*SOL*:VIII.943-8) was commonplace 'at bottom' (Plato, *Gor*:464a-5a; *Char*:175b; *Ethm*:289a-b. See also, Bentham, 1983a:61); rather modestly, he noted that he had simply restated it in 'new language' (Mill to E. Bulwer-Lytton, 27/03/1843:XIII.578-9).
11. DPE:IV.312, 319-20. See also, Eggleston, Miller and Weinstein, 2011:3-5.
12. *SOL*:VIII.949, 943-5. Thus, studies on 'duties' were not scientific, since they went beyond the study of natural phenomena by being expressed in the imperative, rather than the indicative mood.
13. *Ibid.* pp. 945-7; TPV:I.357 (see also, MPE:IV.225). Cf. J. Mill, 1826c:13-4.
14. *SOL*:VIII.943-8. See also, DPE:IV.331n; *EHP*:IX.350-2. Mill's theory included all ancient criteria of art: a. universality, b. teachability, c. precision and, d. concern with explanation (Nussbaum, 2001:95).

15. Contra Lianeri, 2007:183.
16. *SOL*:VIII.945-6. This precision was achieved by dialectics (GP:XI.405).
17. This was a concern as much in Mill as in Plato (for Plato, see Nussbaum, 2001:98-111).
18. See for example, Go:XI.132; Pr:XI.59.
19. *SOL*:VIII.943-4; CFR:XX.161 (see also, WMP :X.179). See also, Baker, 1971. But this insistence made Mill vulnerable to the 'incoherence objection' (Miller, 2011:95. See also, Eggleston, 2011; Weinstein, 2011).
20. *SOL*:VIII.943n.
21. Contra Crisp, 1997:39.
22. Nehamas, 1998:2, 6-9.
23. Sellars, 2003:5. Both Sellars (2003:5, 5n25) and Long (2001:33) point to Foucault (1986) for drawing attention to the ancient concept of the 'art of living'. See also, Nehamas, 1998:ch. 6.
24. Sellars, 2003:31-2.
25. *Ibid.* pp. 20-32.
26. Plato, *Apol*:38a, 29d-30b.
27. Plato, *Gor:*521d-2d (see also, Coleman, 2000:I.53); *Apol*:30b-c.
28. Plato, *Gor:*522c-d; *Apol*:25c-e.
29. Plato, *Alc I*:129a, 130c, 134c-d. See also, Sellars, 2003:36-7, 37n20.
30. Plato, *Alc I*:134c, 122a. See also, Skorupski, 1989:254.
31. Coleman, 2000:I.56.
32. Sparshott, 1978b:289-90; Sellars, 2003:39.
33. Plato, *Gor:*521d, 459d. Though similar in breadth and purpose, Aristotle's 'architectonic' science has different criteria for choice (*EN:*1104b30-3): το καλόν (fine), το συμφέρον (beneficial), το ἡδύ (pleasant). As we will see, Mill follows Plato's 'royal science', i.e., the 'superordinate craft' that uses the products of the 'subordinate crafts' (Plato, *Ethm*:289a-b; Irwin, 1995:60).
34. Kahn, 1996a:130.
35. Kahn, 1996a:130-1; Plato, *Gor:*464a, 504e, 514a; also, Plato, *Rep*:420b. See also, Sellars, 2003:40-2, 42n46.
36. Sellars, 2003:42-50. See also, Kahn, 1996a:133.
37. Nussbaum, 2001:125. See also, Coleman, 2000:I.53-4.
38. Hume, 1826:III.167-8. See also, Stewart, 1991:279.
39. *SOL*:VIII.949-52. See also, NPE:V.443; *U*:X.207.
40. *SOL*:VIII.949ff; Kahn, 1996a:130 (italics added).
41. OG:I.333; GP:XI.404.
42. *U*:X.206.
43. *SOL*:VIII.952. Mill did not accept that there was only 'one road to happiness', but argued for a multiplicity of ends for multiple human beings (*ACP*:X.337).
44. Grote, 1865:II.208; also *ibid.* pp. 148, 169.
45. Bain, 1873: [119]
46. DE:23/01/1854:XXVII.645. See also, Plato, *Apol*:38a.
47. *SOL*:VIII.949; Plato, *Gor:*459d (Aristotle, *Rhet:*1358b20-8; Kahn, 1996a:129n3; Cooper 1999:34n6). The translation in the brackets is Kahn's (1996a:129). Mill's (Go:XI.105) translation was: 'just and unjust', 'good and evil', 'noble and disgraceful'.
48. Contra Eggleston, Miller and Weinstein, 2011:6-7. Similarly, they argue that the domain of aesthetics simply came to replace the 'science of education', which added little sense of what Mill originally meant (*ibid.*). But in 'Phaedrus', Mill (Ph:XI.95) pointed out

that the 'genera which form the basis of our moral and emotional' classifications and constitute 'excellence' (i.e., Justice, Courage, Holiness, Beauty), are called aesthetic by 'the Germans', and the pursuit of 'excellence for its own sake' was a problem to be solved by the science of character formation, i.e., ethology.

49. Kahn, 1996a:129. In *Statesman* (295e-7b), in which Mill found Plato's notion of scientific government, one also finds a view of the Good, the Just and the Noble as 'independent values' (Schofield, 2006:164). Still, Mill seemed to believe that they do become identical in virtuous conduct. To this effect, Werner Jaeger (1948:435) has argued that the 'Socratic-Platonic' theoretic life had received 'its moral dignity and its sacred rights' by its 'services to actual living'. This consisted in combating beliefs that viewed happiness independent of being good, just or noble.

50. GP:XI.409 (see also, *A*:I.61). In Mill's discussion of 'to kalon', perhaps one can notice a similarity with M. Arnold's *Culture and Anarchy* (1869:ch. 4; see also, Collini, 1988:82). See also Irwin (1992), for Sidgwick's and Green's different views of the 'kalon' in Aristotle. That England was a 'practical country' seemed to be a frequent complain amongst intellectuals; one which touched on various aspects of their works (See also, Blackie, 1857:5-6; Pattison, 1870:53 in Jones, 2007:57). For Mill's discussion of the French and English national character as 'completing counterparts', see Varouxakis, 2002a; 2002b.

51. GP:XI.409 (see also, J. Mill, 1804:II.578).

52. GP:XI.403-5.

53. Go:XI.97, 149; GP:XI.395-6.

54. Socrates and his interlocutors held two different conceptions of happiness, directive and additive respectively. See chapter nine for more details. On Plato, see further Russell, 2005.

55. See, Plato, *Gor:*482c-6d.

56. GP:XI.395.

57. See further, Eggleston, Miller and Weinstein, 2011.

58. B:X.112-3; Mill to A. Helps, c1847::XVII.2001-2. For Helps's published essay, see Helps, 1847:ch. 7.

59. *SOL:*VIII.949-52.

60. *SOL:*VIII.952 (see also, GP:XI.415-6).

61. Ryan, 1964:258-9. An even earlier attempt was made by D. D. Raphael (1955:345n1).

62. Ryan, 1965:164-5; 1974:106.

63. Ryan, 1965:164-5; 1970:216; 1974:105-6. See also, Brown, 1972:154.

64. Ryan, 1965:162, 165-7. See also, Gray, 1996:17.

65. Brown, 1972:154; see also, Gray, 1996:40. However, I think this criticism misses the mark, as Ryan carefully refers to 'interpersonal' goods.

66. Coleridge, 1854:II.141, 403-4.

67. *U*:X.223. See also, RBP:X.7-8; B:X.112-3.

68. Riley, 2011:139-41. See further, Riley, 2010.

69. Riley, 1988:198. In this way there is not a sharp distinction between one's own happiness and the happiness of others—social harmony benefits all.

70. *Ibid.* p. 196; 183.

71. *Ibid.* p. 227.

72. Riley, 2011:139-41.

73. Donner, 2007:269-70; 2010:89, 92-3 Donner and Fumerton, 2009:42, 44.

74. Donner, 2007:269; 2010:91; Donner and Fumerton, 2009:37.

75. Donner, 2010:92, 96 (see also, *U*:X.241).

76. Donner, 2007:271-2; 2010:89, 92, 95; Donner and Fumerton, 2009:42-3.
77. Donner and Fumerton, 2009:42; Donner, 2010:86-7 (see also, Gray, 1996:22, 25). See also, RBP:X.10.
78. Donner, 2010:96; Donner and Fumerton, 2009:53-4.
79. GP:XI.409; J. Mill, 1835a:263. James Mill's 'tripartite' view of the principles of conduct, shows that John Mill had—contrary to what to he said to Thomas Carlyle—these 'secondary principles in common' at least with one utilitarian (Mill to T. Carlyle, 12/01/1834:XII.207).
80 B:X.112-3. This example appeared several times in the utilitarian tradition (e.g., D. Hume; A. Smith; C. A. Helvétius. See, Rosen, 2003a:84-5).
81. Anon. , 1836:498; Niebuhr, 1851:I.497-8; Plutarch, *PL*: 984. I.1 (Perrin, 1918:VI.126-7); Livy, *HoR*:II.v7-v9 (Foster, 1919:433-5).
82. J. Mill (1835a:5-9) offers a brief history of this distinction as it is found in Smith, Hutcheson, Reid, Stewart and Brown.
83. Robson, 1998:348; Ryan, 1970:215. See also, Brown, 1972:154n11.
84. B:X.112. Thus, individuals have other 'beauties of character'—the moral point of view is not the sole one (*U*:X.221).
85. In *Utilitarianism* (X.220n, 220-1), Mill showed how the *morality* of the act and the *moral estimation* of the agent differ. That Mill noted that the moral aspect 'addresses itself to our reason and conscience' (B:X.112) allows for considerations of expediency as well. Riley (1988:188) argues that Mill had not yet conceptualized that self-regarding actions could not be considered to be immoralities; however, Mill's translation of Plato's *Gorgias* and his later comments regarding that dialogue in 'Grote's Plato' (XI.404-5) seem to undermine Riley's position.
86. Livy, *HoR*:II.v7-v9 (Foster, 1919:433-5); Niebuhr, 1851:I.497-8.
87. B:X.112-3. Plutarch attributed Brutus's disposition, hard by nature, to not being 'softened by letters', i.e., by philosophy (Plutarch, *PL*:984. I.1; see Perrin, 1918:VI.126-7).
88. Eggleston, Miller and Weinstein, 2011:9-11. See futher, Donner and Fumerton, 2009; Donner, 2010.
89. B:X.113. See also, *U*:X.221-2; *OL*:XVIII.263; RBP:X.7-8. Hamburger (1999:185-9, 191-3) argues that 'contempt', even by morally superior individuals, can be painful and thus akin to punishment, undermining the attempt to distinguish a sphere of liberty from a moral sphere. But, in the letter to Helps (c1847:XVII.2000-2), preserving the distinction between these three different sentiments that aspects of actions give rise to, Mill argues that actions that do not harm the general good (they are approved by sufficient reason) but create hate (opposite of sympathy) or even quiet distaste (opposite of an aesthetic sentiment), are not to be decided by a 'just sway' of someone superior.
90. *SOL*:VIII.951 (see also, *U*:X.234); *EHP*:IX.417.
91. *U*:X.206; *SOL*:VII.107; PCCD:IV.113-4; WMP:X.180-1; PQF:XXIII.342; *PPE*:II.162-3; C:X.154; CCP:IV.195-6; CoI [20]:XXIV.956; TS:XIX.636.
92. sAWF:XXVIII.152.
93. Persons are required to test their theories, by being able 'to make an estimate of means and of obstacles habitually a part of all [their] theories that have for their object practice, either at the present or at a more distant period' (AC:XX.174)—moral principles are such obstacles.
94. *U*:X.246, 251, 255, 259 (see also, *EHP*:IX.459n;462n ).
95. See further, Berger, 1984:105-20.
96. *OL*:XVIII.224-5; *U*:X.254; *SOW*:XXI.264; *SOL*:VIII.950.

97. *ACP*:X.337-8; TLC:V.650-1. Often noble actions of uncommon virtue, Mill noted, are above custom.
98. *SOL*:VIII.840-1.
99. *U*:X.235-7; *SOL*:VIII.853 (see also, Donner, 1998:258); Cen:XIX.595-6.
100. *U*:X.220-1. See further, Riley, 2010, 2011; Donner, 2010, 2011.
101. Sparshott, 1978b:289-90. This recognition seems to contradict T. H. Green's (1906:298-9) argument that 'the essential principle of all virtue [i.e., 'a direction of a man's will to the highest possible realisation of his faculties is the common ground of every form of true virtue'] at once distinguishes the doctrine of Plato and Aristotle from any form of Hedonism, or of Utilitarianism so far as Hedonistic'. As we saw, Mill draws on Plato's ends of action rather than Aristotle's, where the 'moral' is distinct from the 'fine', whereas the 'pleasant' is not a distinct end—thus, Mill was able to both retain the hedonistic foundation and be close to Plato.
102. *PPE*:III.758nb-b. Conflicts between the secondary ends of action may occur, but the second-order end can harmonize them in favor of general happiness. Nicholas White calls this line of argument 'Hegelian *harmonising eudaimonism*' (1999a:501), in which individual happiness is *fused* with general happiness (1995:260).
103. BHMS:X.29; B:X.110-1.
104. IA:XXI.223-4. 'The great business of this place', Mark Pattison noted with regard to Lincoln College, was 'the art of life, the self-formation, the building up of a high-principled character' (quoted in Jones, 2007:157). Similarly, the end 'to which the scholar is particularly called', R. W. Emerson argued (1841:176), and to which the 'Art of Life' above all other ends 'directs our attention', was '*self-culture*—the perfect unfolding of our individual nature'.
105. Plato, *Gor:*482d-4c.
106. N:X.381.
107. *Ibid.* p. 402.
108. *Ibid.* pp. 393-6.
109. Plato, *Rep*:376c-7a (trans. P. Shorey).
110. sPrf:XXVI.430.
111. IA:XXI.217; *OL*:XVIII.270.
112. IA:XXI.221.
113. IA:XXI.218. See also, sPSL:XXVI.410; OG:I.335-8; *A*:I.35; GAEI:XXIV.786-7; sU[1]:XXVI.351.
114. *OL*:XVIII.263; see also, RBP:X.7-8; B:X.112-3; *U*:X.221-2. Although there is much merit in Colin Heydt's study of the aesthetic terms of Mill's view of 'life as an art' (2006:13-46; 2011), it neglects to consider the connection between Mill and Plato as well as the Socratic underpinnings of Mill's 'Art of Life'. For example, Heydt, trying to highlight the link between art, life and character, quoted Mill (IA:XXI.256):

> Art, when really cultivated, and not merely practiced empirically, maintains [...] an Ideal Beauty, to be eternally aimed at, though surpassing what can be actually attained; and by this idea it trains us never to be completely satisfied with imperfection in what we ourselves do and are: to idealize [...] every work we do, and most of all, our own characters and lives.

But failing to take notice of 'not merely practiced empirically' and 'surpassing what can be actually attained', which illustrates the continuity of this account with Mill's earlier accounts of art (primarily the one in Mill's *Logic*), Heydt failed to see the connection between 'life as an art' and the *indirect* pursuit of happiness, which undermines his attempt to show that these two may be incompatible at times (Heydt, 2006:32-6).

115. *OL*:XVIII.267. So did Plato (*Rep*:bk. 7)

116. IA:XXI.251.

117. *Ibid.* p. 235.

118. *Ibid.* pp. 233-47.

119. N:X.380; *SOL*:VIII.840; *A*:I.177.

120. N:X.379-80

121. IA:XXI.248

122. *Ibid.* pp. 247-51.

123. IA:XXI.255. See also, Plato, *Sym*:212a; *GrH*:296d. One should keep in mind that Mill had just reviewed Grote's *Plato*—one of the reasons why he postponed his Rectorial Address.

124. Perhaps here Mill anticipated John Dewey (see further, Garrison, 2004), though as F. Bourriot (1995) discusses, the concept of *kalokagathia* is much more complex than is usually assumed.

125. IA:XXI.256.

126. *Ibid.* p. 257. The similarity with Plato's *Republic* (585d-7b) cannot be missed.

127. T:X.489.

128. Mansfeld, 2003:123-4;129-30. Interestingly, a strikingly similar view has been attributed to Mill more than 80 years ago, as Street (1926:49) notes that to Mill 'Philosophy [...] was the Science of Life'.

129. *U*:X.246-7.

130. APHM:XXXI.226.

131. IA:XXI.255-6. See further, Heydt, 2011.

132. Long, 2001:19-20.

133. See Mill's comments on Harriet (*A*:I.194-5); on himself and Carlyle (Mill to T. Carlyle: 17/06/1832:XII.113; 05/07/1833:XII.163; 02/08/1833:XII.183); and on Plato (GP:XI.410). See further, Robson, 1960; 1966; 1968:ch. 6.

134. Sellars, 2003:88-101. Mill was familiar with Sextus' book (*EHP*:IX.383n).

135. Nehamas, 1998:9-10.

# CHAPTER EIGHT

## CHARACTER, ETHOLOGY AND VIRTUE

No study of ideas pertaining to character and its formation of a 'Greek-intoxicated' thinker such as John Stuart Mill can be complete without a discussion of the connections between his ideas on character and his reading of ancient texts. By reading Mill through the prism of Plato, or Aristotle, his ideas on character, character formation and self-development come to the fore in the attempt to clarify the role of virtue in his notion of happiness. Such an exploration might also explain why Mill seemed to take a different route than the predominant 'trends' of Victorian times. Here, I focus on those individuals who are capable of harmonizing the ends of the 'Art of Life' and on how they can develop this ability according to Mill. His conception of character seemed to bring out another aspect of his indebtedness to ancient Greek thought, as the question of character formation becomes a question of cultivating virtue.

## DEFINING CHARACTER

### Character in Nineteenth-Century Britain

From early on in the nineteenth century, preoccupation with character formation had a practical aim: to prevent the formation of characters that 'fill society with crimes'. According to Robert Owen, whose views were in vogue in the first quarter of the century, by applying specific means—which are (or can be) controlled by the government—any character can be given to anyone: the 'plastic nature' of young people can be so moulded as to form ideal 'rational wishes and desires'.[1]

Taking his argument a step forward, Owen argued that individuals do not form their own characters—it is always formed for them, as all ideas and habits are given, and these 'govern and direct [...] conduct'. For this reason, individuals could not be held 'accountable for all [their] habits and sentiments'.[2] However, in its most important respects, Owen's take on character formation was primarily a call for reform. The improvement of educational practice was an essential condition, if not for the well-being of the uneducated, at least for social well-being.[3] In the 1830s, the flow of these ideas to the working classes by Owenites was not 'an unknown gospel; it had already been spread by the radical movement as a whole'. Consequently, education was viewed as the way to combat 'drunkenness, brutality, and other social evils' to achieve social improvement. The mid-nineteenth-century 'social tranquillity', some argue, owed much to these attempts.[4]

In nineteenth-century Britian, the public experienced an unprecedented amount of public deliberation about reform. But the call for expansion of the 'access to the public sphere' was not attempted regardless of who benefited. Thus, in the years between the two Reform Acts (1832 and 1867), as Rohan McWilliam notes, several attempts were made 'to construct a virtuous working-class public sphere worthy of the franchise'.[5] Virtue and worth were key words for all parties concerned. First, there was the question of moral excellence: would those included in the franchise be guided by social or selfish interests? In response, second, many (including John Stuart Mill) argued that the vote was more of a matter of trust than a right; thus individuals needed to possess some 'qualities' (e.g., education, property) which justified that trust and secured against ill-advised or misguided use.

During this time, character formation was increasingly being studied with 'scientific' ambitions. Anthropology, psychology, phrenology and Mill's proposed ethology were claiming expertise for working out the principles of character formation. Character was no longer perceived as something static: character originated desires and it could thus be trained to 'dominate rather than be buffeted by circumstances' (i.e., to subdue and order desires)—a dynamic view of character ascended to a prominent position in Victorian political thought.[6] These insights were not new. They formed the subject matter of James Mill's *Analysis of the Phenomena of the Human Mind* which, according to John Stuart Mill, 'followed up the deepest vein of the Lockian philosophy, that which was opened by Hartley, to still greater depths',[7] but it goes back to Thomas Hobbes and even further back to at least Aristotle. By 1859, psychology—associationist or not—was receiving so much attention that John Mill was confident that '[t]he sceptre of psychology has decidedly returned to this island' [i.e., Britain].[8]

In one of the first comprehensive treatments on the subject of character formation, Samuel Bailey defined five basic constituents of character: first, the 'predominance of certain feelings, propensities, and desires in [one's] mind over others which, although existing there, are less marked'. The second feature referred to 'being able to perform certain intellectual operations better than other operations' and, third, being 'able to perform these and other intellectual operations much better in respect to certain objects than in respect to other objects'. The fourth feature concerned the 'energy or feebleness of [one's] volitions—[one's] acts of willing'. The fifth referred to the 'physical endowments or the qualities of [...] bodily constitution'. Thus Bailey argued that nature, instruction, habits and the influence of the social environment were all responsible for the formation of character.[9]

The discussion on character, according to Steffan Collini, outlined the moral sensibility of Victorian intellectuals. This, first, took the shape of an antipathy to selfishness. Egoism and altruism stood sharply on opposite grounds. Victorian moralists, second, became extremely concerned with stirring 'adequate motivation' in moral agents. Third, as this inevitably led to prioritizing the emotions over the intellect as a source of action, they became increasingly preoccupied with cultivating 'appropriate feelings'. Fourth, they assumed that these feelings could not only be compatible with each other but could also be 'productive of socially desirable actions'. Finally, Collini adds, Victorian moralists were very concerned with 'the possibility of sinking into a state of psychological malaise', because of self-absorption.[10] Thus, Victorians seemed to assign a 'causal role' to character, as actions were 'essentially the expression of character'.[11] Discussing the work of Samuel Smiles (1859) and Alexander Bain (1861), Janice Carlisle notes that choice, action and behavior exhibited the constituents of character: thoughts, desires and impulses.[12] Carlisle argues that, in this burst of public deliberation, 'character' denoted roughly the same thing, despite appearing in dissimilar subjects.[13] However, as Collini shows, one can distinguish between descriptive and evaluative uses of the term. The former referred to settled dispositions, i.e., 'the sum of mental and moral qualities' that make an individual 'a homogenous whole'. The latter referred 'to the possession of certain highly valued moral qualities', which met with 'ethical approval'—for example, cultivating an altruistic character was perceived to be the only security against a will which yielded to the pursuit of 'individual satisfactions'.[14]

Samuel Smiles used the evaluative sense of the term when he noted that character is the 'moral order embodied in the individual'—the test being one's attitude toward others. An ideal character was noble and benevolent; one whose powers reached their fullest potential and exhibited a 'warm sympathy' of either an admiration for what is 'good and gracious in human nature' or a 'sense of pity for human beings suffering under misfortune'.[15] Conversely, the answer to Alexander Bain's test 'how does a man spend his days' is descriptive. Carlisle does note that Bain's account 'could not be more removed from Smiles's concern for the moral ingredients of worldly success', but does not see a difference in kind.[16] However, the evaluative sense of character is directly connected to uses of character in antiquity—as Samuel Taylor Coleridge argued: manliness, strength of character and energy of will closely resemble the ancient Greek sense of virtue.[17]

# J.S. Mill, Êthos and Character

The 'spirit of the age', as we saw, associated character formation with reform—good character was conducive to actual social benefits. John Start Mill contributed to this trend.[18] But Mill had a second, more personal, reason to be concerned with character formation: his own character had been completely another man's work. He was a living proof of the soundness of Owen's theory. As this thought sank him into a state of depression, he tried to qualify the Owenite doctrine to make room for some kind of self-transformation. Both concerns (i.e., social reform; self-culture) informed Mill's attempt to examine the process of character formation.

Mill argued that the ancient Greek concept of *êthos* (ἦθος) corresponded more closely to the concept of character as he meant to use it in his science of character formation. *Êthos* was Mill's response to the prevailing Victorian and Romantic visions of character, combining 'self-restraint' with 'an exploratory attitude towards one's own individuality and potential'.[19] This invites one to define the ancient Greek notion of *êthos*—especially given that this is a connection to the ancients that has not been explored. Plato and Aristotle are the usual suspects.

In *Nicomachean Ethics*, Aristotle argued that happiness is an activity of the soul in accordance with virtue over the range of a whole life. Virtue is the excellent performance of the human function. Instruction develops intellectual excellence (through experience and time); habit forms moral excellence: as in Plato, *êthos* had much to do with the ability to take pleasure in the *right* things.[20] In *Rhetoric*, êthos was also associated with a person's intellectual qualities. Studying the effective speaker, Aristotle argued that a person's ability to persuade depends not only upon the content of one's speech, but it also depends upon the feelings one excites and the qualities one possesses (practical wisdom—φρόνησις; virtue—ἀρετή; good will—εὔνοια).[21] Though necessary, no one quality was sufficient to persuade an audience. What concerns us here, the êthos of the speaker was manifested by means of his virtue, which, in Aristotle's earlier sorting of the virtues, included temperance, prudence and wisdom among others.[22]

Aristotle's *Eudemian Ethics*, clarifying the connection between reason and emotion, defined êthos as a disposition or quality of the mental constitution of human beings that makes the affective or non-rational part to follow or to listen to the rational part of the soul: 'διὸ ἔστω <τὸ> ἦθος τοῦτο ψυχῆς κατὰ ἐπιτακτικὸν λόγον <τοῦ ἀλόγου μέν,> δυναμένου δ' ἀκολουθεῖν τῷ λόγῳ ποιότης'—êthos 'is the mediator in the soul between reason and desire; it brings the unruly impulses and emotions under the sway of reason'.[23] Similarly, in the tripartite view of the soul presented in Plato's *Republic*, êthos pointed to the bond between the spirited part (θυμοειδές) and the rational part (λογιστικόν). By proper training, a strong spirit could follow reason and learn to control the ἐπιθυμητικόν (appetitive part of the soul), which did not listen to reason—at the same time, a strong reason could also create new desires.[24]

Thus, character refers to both moral and intellectual qualities. Reason itself is not character. Character is rather found in the emotional part of the soul that can be persuaded and guided by reason (i.e., feelings and desires being directed by rational principles).[25] Still, how much knowledge one possesses, necessarily affects how one will be disposed to act: '[t]o be able to choose well in the sphere of action involves both a certain mode of thought [...] and a certain habituated and stable disposition of character which desires and finds pleasure in doing well'.[26] In addition, the etymological link of êthos to habit, suggests that character is not innate or fixed. If it was, character would not be susceptible to alteration by habituation in certain practices.[27] Human beings, Aristotle claimed, are by nature capable of acquiring the virtues, but with habitual practice they fully develop them. Human excellence is 'acquired by *the training of behaviour to desire the right end*'.[28]

If, as I am proposing, we focus on Mill's definition of character as *êthos*, we come to see that Mill did develop a systematic notion of character, which runs counter to Carlisle's argument that he did not. Mill considered character, Carlisle argues, to be 'a thoroughly conditioned phenomenon known by its "powers or properties"' which 'comprises one's thoughts, desires, and impulses'. Character involves how a person acts or is acted upon by other human beings as well as by their shared circumstances and it is 'known most accurately through one's choices and actions'. Carlisle notes (with *On Liberty* in mind) that character is one's desires and impulses as the expression of one's own nature developed by self-culture. According to Mill, Carlisle argues, character more often is comprised by the qualities that distinguish one's 'entire capacity of exhibiting phenomena'—be it a person or a group of individuals.[29] However, first, 'character' as one's 'entire capacity of exhibiting phenomena' seems to be too broad to give a meaningful description of a person's character. Second, by focusing on action and choice, Carlisle does not recognize the possibility that there might be a discrepancy between appearance and reality in reference to one's actions and character—which adds an evaluative dimension.

First, following Mill's preferred method of analysis, one needs to find the meaning of the universal (character) in the concrete (e.g., John's character). That John finds pleasure in eating sugary food, though it gives us information about him, is not a part of his character; but eating three bars of chocolate while suffering from type-one diabetes may be. If John's diet is always well-regulated and his eating chocolate was a momentary weakness of will, this particular action is not enough for either a change in our perception of his character or a change in his character itself. Only if this reckless regard of one's own well-being is a stable disposition would such changes in our perception be justified.

However, Mill made a stronger claim: a person's desires or impulses must be the expression of one's own nature developed and modified by one's own efforts. Thus, character referred to a set of stable dispositions (of feelings and desires) that have been developed or modified (to follow reason) by one's own self.[30] This mention of 'one's own nature' has been identified with the romantic belief of 'an essence that awaits discovery'. But it is rather a reference to a person's natural capacities for certain tasks.[31] As Fred Berger convincingly argues, people have faculties and capacities (and corresponding needs and desires) which are the 'distinctive endowment' of human beings—e.g., higher faculties and noble capacities which require exercise for their development (in a suitable social environment). Since capacities for feelings and sources of pain and pleasure differ between human beings, 'nature' seems to refer to 'unique kinds or combinations of desires, enjoyments, and so on' rather than an inner unique essence. An abstract destiny, a fixed and unchangeable inner essence that awaits discovery means that an individual cannot escape this inner determinism. Such a unique essence would suggest development of something that one has no control over (i.e., having only procedural control).[32]

Second, Mill shared Plato's worry about the possibility of appearing virtuous, without really being one, i.e., having 'a reputation for virtue, without the trouble of deserving it'.[33] Mill's 'Art of Life' and his critique of Bentham expanded on his belief that a person's worthiness is not always manifested in a particular action, as a right action does not always indicate a virtuous person. Actions, being frequently socially constrained, indicate how a person 'desires to be thought' (by others or one's self). Action is the test of character from the perspective of the world at large only in what people can expect from others— i.e., actions of the moral domain of the 'Art of Life'. However, as Mill added, 'to [the agent's] intimates, who care about what he is and not merely about what he does, the involuntary indications of feeling and disposition are a much surer criterion of them than voluntary acts'. Since actions create moral, aesthetic and sympathetic estimations of the *agent* rather than of the *act*, some actions might lead to wrong estimations of what kind of a person one is—by exclusive focus on the moral criterion—i.e., those acts which affect the interests of others. Bentham, according to Mill, failed as much to distinguish between one's voluntary actions and the involuntary indications of feelings that precede the act as to define a self-educating part of morality (i.e., self-training of the affections and will).[34]

Furthermore, Mill followed his utilitarian predecessors in taking intention, not motivation, to constitute the morality of an act. If the bad consequences of an action were intended, even if they were not desired (i.e., irrespective of dispositions and habits), then the act is immoral.[35] Mill was concerned with individuals who foresaw and brought about good consequences without desiring them (or desiring only a part of them)—their actions being 'materially' rather than 'formally' good.[36] Worthiness does not depend upon the morality of voluntary actions alone, but also upon the actor's feelings and dispositions. Virtuous persons can select and pursue worthy ends; more importantly, they can create habits that can slowly change their feelings, dispositions and even desires. Thus, defined as êthos, character shows how acting in accordance with reason (i.e., the principles of the 'Art of Life') leads one to take pleasure in the 'higher' type of life, the life of 'a clear and comprehensible unity, a deliberately shaped life-pattern'.[37]

# On Ethology

John Stuart Mill argued that the laws of character formation had only been studied cursorily in his time. According to Mill, ethology was '*la théorie de l'influence des diverses circonstances extérieures, soit individuelles, soit sociales, sur la formation du caractère moral et intellectuel*'.[38] He argued further that the science of character formation was the foundation of education, clearly distinguishing ethology from the art of education.[39] With August Comte's help, he developed a three-level analysis of the individual—psychology, ethology and sociology.[40] His sketched an inverse deductive method dialectically combining the strengths of both the geometrical and historical methods. Trying to avoid the limitations of these two methods in politics and ethics, he sought to find *which* type of science was suitable to study *what* kind of aspect of human life.

Associationism was criticized, John Mill noted, because it set the nobler parts of human nature, the higher endowments of the human mind, as outgrowth and offspring of lower mental states. Even if those nobler parts of human nature are not 'self-sown and original' but are created or create themselves, irrespective of what kinds of materials, Mill argued, understanding 'as much as possible of the process by which the materials are put together' was still 'highly important' for education and the improvement of character.[41] Ethology studied this process. It could determine 'the kind of character produced [...] by any set of circumstances, physical and moral', always in compliance to the general laws of the human mind, studied by psychology. The knowledge of these circumstances would afford the 'power as to establish in the mind of every individual an indissoluble association between his own happiness and the good of the whole'.[42] As we saw, this in antiquity meant training one's behavior to desire the 'right end'.

However, society has a claim to what the 'right ends' of behaviour are, leading Mill to warn about the potential harmful effects of character formation. A person's character develops by being habituated in certain social practices. And even if education enables people to reason upon principles as well as social practice, such practices are likely to habituate individuals into pursuing, in some way or another, those 'right ends'. But if those ends or those practices are corrupted then character is not likely to be good, since habitual bad social practice is likely to corrupt one's ability to reason.[43] This was what Radicals and Owenites claimed with regard to educational practice in early nineteenth-century, as we saw. Exploring an example of such distorted habituation of character in *The Subjection of Women* (1869), Mill pointed to three causes which led 'the object of being attractive to men' in becoming 'the polar star of feminine education and formation of character': first, the natural attraction between the two sexes; second, the complete dependence of wives on their husbands; and third, that only through men could women obtain or achieve their happiness.[44] A combination of corrupted habitual practice, unproven assumptions about human nature and obsolete views on what the 'rights ends' of women were had led to the subjection of women.

In cases such as these, not only were external influences not conducive to self-development, but 'forced repression' and 'unnatural stimulations' had artificially created characters 'entirely distorted from [their] natural proportions'. Like in Plato, Mill did not seem to believe that the mental differences between the two sexes are innate, but the result of education and external influences: '[a]ll causes, social and natural' combine to turn women into willing slaves.[45] Thus, what were socially accepted as the 'right ends' concerning the character of women required radical reconsideration. Ethology could show how 'a change in character is possible through changes in institutions and relations'.[46] This was a case in which Mill used a 'familiar [...] vocabulary [i.e., character formation] for new and unexpected purposes'.[47]

Contrary to Carlisle's argument, Mill did not *invent* ethology 'to authorize', with a science, his own belief in reform.[48] The earlier discussion on êthos should contribute toward a better understanding of what this science was about. It was the science that discovered those general laws of human nature, which can be used in training and instruction, to regulate the development of stable dispositions that direct one's feelings and desires in accordance to what they have reason to value. Physical and moral as well as social and individual circumstances are important, since they affect the different aspects as well as the different directions of character formation. Ethology studied both the rational and the emotional nature of man. Furthermore, Mill argued that causal laws rather than empirical laws (i.e., approximate generalizations) provide the 'really scientific truths' that enable ethology to afford sufficiently reliable inferences. Empirical laws can be used to verify the conclusions of a theory based on causal laws. The combination of universal laws with the particular facts of different cases can produce 'the whole of the phenomena of human action and feeling'. Ethological laws are deduced from the general laws of the mind and are verified by observation.[49] Though the complexity of each case forbids the collection of all the data required for a precise prediction, the degree of prediction that can be achieved is not devoid of practical worth: '[i]t is enough that we know that certain means have a *tendency* to produce a given effect, and that others have a tendency to frustrate it'.[50]

Thus, a careful formation of opinions on matters such as these may not offer, Mill maintained, absolute certainty, but, without claiming infallibility, there could be 'assurance sufficient for the purposes of human life'. Differences in education and outward circumstances afforded 'adequate explanation of by far the greatest portion of character'. By qualifying the predictive power of ethology, Mill had managed to ease the determinism that was inherent in the Owenite view of character formation, while still allowing ethology to remain a 'secure basis for art or practice'.[51]

It was essential for Mill that ethology was not detached either from an analysis of surrounding circumstances or from the more general laws of human mind. Thus, ethology reached conclusions through a double process: first, the deduction of 'ethological consequences of particular circumstances of position', which would then be tested against experience; and, second, a 'reverse operation': a careful collection of experiential data regarding different types of human nature which with the help of psychological laws will account for the different characteristics by the peculiarities of the circumstances. It was a safe foundation and 'a more deepened theory of human nature' for the more comprehensive Social Science, as it attempted to include the many levels and many sides of social reality. [52]

However, Mill did not further develop his 'cherished' ethology; perhaps because it never 'assumed any definite shape' in his mind.[53] David Leary pointed to a number of reasons why ethology, in Mill's time, did not acquire the scientific status Mill desired. Under the influence of evolutionism, mid-nineteenth-century social science changed focus. Not social circumstances of character formation, but racial and physical factors seemed to answer the questions of origin and development of different social groups. Also, the main opponent to Mill's (and Bain's) theory was phrenology, whose decline as a valid theory of character formation rendered Mill's and Bain's views uninteresting. In addition, there were inherent problems in Mill's account as well. Mill's proposal, Leary argues, was neither systematic nor biological enough. Ethology seemed to require a more emotional and empirical orientation to gain scientific credibility.[54] But Mill knew that little had 'been done, and that little not at all systematically, towards forming' this science. Not even in 1859 did he feel himself ready to tackle the details of ethology.[55] Still, he never lost his belief in its importance.[56]

## MEANS AND ENDS OF CHARACTER FORMATION

### Society, Self-Development and Virtue

As we saw, Mill argued that unless people develop independence of thought and sentiment, they have no character.[57] Individuality of character was contrasted with adherence to custom and conformity.[58] A decided character exhibited individuality by being 'free from halfness of all sorts' and by bringing to fruition one's own ideas ('the only source of real progress').[59] But it takes strong feelings to follow a direction away from social convention and escape the 'domineering' social principles—i.e., it takes a strong individual character (which is often perceived as 'a proof of madness').[60]

Though Mill's concern with the tendency to 'bear down' on individuality, 'circumscribing the exercise of the human faculties within narrow limits' imposed by 'the despotic yoke of public opinion', is usually attributed to the influence of Alexis De Tocqueville, De Tocqueville was certainly not the only possible source.[61] However, finding Mill drawing on Plato to provide a metaphor for individuality under the 'yoke of public opinion', speaks volumes about Mill's reading of Plato. For example, just before his first review of *De la Démocratie en Amérique* (1835), Mill published his translations of Plato's dialogues. While he was preparing those translations for publication, in a letter to Thomas Carlyle (before Mill read Tocqueville), Mill used a Platonic image to capture what he thought was so special about Paris: 'individualities of character are there *unchained*, not being kept down and fashioned to a model by a common overruling Belief'.[62]

Character formation was part of the discussion on whether human volition is determined by antecedent circumstances or whether it determines itself. Individuality presupposed that one is not a 'helpless slave of antecedent circumstances'. As character is not solely formed by agencies beyond one's control, the formation of one's own character, Mill argued, is within one's power. This power made the doctrine of free will 'really inspiriting and ennobling'—the doctrine of Philosophical Necessity 'weighed on [Mill's] existence like an incubus' no more. Thus, in a letter to Carlyle in 1833, Mill announced that he was 'throwing off' a part of his former character, the deficiency of which he was now doing much to mend. The possibility of self-development was implied. He no longer held that people *cannot* be 'made to love their neighbours better than themselves'; but also he qualified his father's teaching that 'in proportion as the people are better instructed, in that very proportion prudential habits prevail'.[63]

It was true, Mill argued, that having the knowledge of all those circumstances that come into effect in a particular case could allow a prediction of the outcome of their interaction. Thus, with knowledge of the motives and the character of an individual, he added, one can predict how that individual will act on a given occasion. The frequent inability to predict with accuracy the effects, Mill maintained, owed not to it being impossible, but to one's having inaccurate and deficient knowledge of causes and circumstances.[64] In contrast, advocates of Owen's theory pointed to the 'utter absurdity and fallaciousness of free will'.[65] But prediction, Mill argued, did not necessarily mean that one cannot *counteract* the habitual susceptibility to motives, since human actions are never 'ruled by any one motive with such absolute sway, that there is no room for the influence of any other'.[66] It is one thing to argue that actions spring from characters and that characters result from a person's individual circumstances, and quite another to argue that people have no power to effect any change.

A person's own desire to shape her/his character in some way is an important circumstance that can influence the process of character formation: 'We are exactly as capable of making our own character, *if we will*, as others are of making it for us'. By working on some of the means of character formation, individuals can do much to modify their 'future habits or capabilities of willing'.[67] Individuals may will to change their character once they experienced the painful consequences to which their character led or once they experienced a strong feeling of admiration. Unless individuals, Mill argued, wish to alter their character, they do not feel the desperation that they cannot. True freedom lies in going after the improvement of one's own character; it is thus important that individuals are not 'passive instruments of some other will', but have their own purposes, plans and ideas.[68]

Irrespective of what original circumstances influenced the formation of their character, individuals ought to strive by education and training to direct their conduct toward virtuous pursuits—it is 'paralysing to our desire of excellence' to feel unable to do so.[69] Like in Plato, vivid and powerful impulses are the source 'for the passionate love of virtue, and the sternest self-control'.[70] Since an internal force is necessary to escape old habits and inclinations, individuals are free in the degree they can achieve the character they desire—when for some reason they come to feel that who they are and who they want to be conflict. Mill did not argue, like Plato's Socrates, that reason was an independent source of such a motivation. Yet, he did argue that once such a desire develops, reason can create those circumstances that will slowly work upon the feelings to make, in James Mill's words, the associations and values correspond.[71] 'And hence', John Mill concluded, 'it is said with truth, that none but a person of confirmed virtue is completely free'.[72]

Mill tried to envisage a tolerant society which fosters self-development, by providing the conditions that enable individuals to develop 'liberty and spontaneity, duly balanced with self-government'.[73] Individuality, still, needed to be supplemented by 'mutual criticism', which encourages people to stimulate each other, thereby increasing the exercise of their higher faculties and affording 'increased direction of their feeling and aims towards wise instead of foolish, elevating instead of degrading objects and contemplations'.[74]

Only wise and elevating objects and contemplations were suitable for Mill's ideal character. Broadly speaking, as we saw, Mill seemed to argue that education aimed to form a character most suited to the 'Art of Life'.[75] Ethology supplies the knowledge necessary for placing anyone in the most suitable circumstances in order to achieve this excellence. The art of character *education* referred to the application of scientific—ethological—means to produce intellectual and moral excellence—an excellence of character that was an end in itself as well as a means to happiness. Mill did argue that there is 'hardly a single point of excellence belonging to human character' that is not 'decidedly repugnant' to the uncultivated human nature.[76]

## Reason and Emotion

Mill was early acquainted with the 'particulars' of character formation. In a youthful debating speech, he defended himself against the criticism that his speech lacked feeling. Mill was afraid that *he* was charged with being destitute of feeling—not just his speech (a common charge against Benthamites).[77] Mill retorted:

> Feeling has to do with our actions, reason with our opinions; it is by our reason that we find out what it is our duty to do; it is our feelings which supply us with motives to act upon it when found. Let these two operations be kept as they always ought to be kept, separate, and let feeling no more encroach upon the province of reason, than reason upon the province of feeling. The gentleman has quoted Plato, he must be well aware that this maxim holds a distinguished place in the ethical system of that great philosopher; of which system in truth it

is the very foundation; but I do not adopt it because it is the language of Plato but because it is the language of truth.[78]

This 'very foundation' of Plato's ethical thought, I am arguing, was also Mill's. As we saw in passing, Mill claimed that supplying 'motives sufficient to keep [...] men within the line of virtue' was the 'grand problem of political science'.[79] Ethology could solve this 'grand problem'. The person of 'sublime character', Mill argued, was one 'whose whole soul was so strictly under the dominion of principle that he had not one wish which did not center in the happiness of mankind'. Ethology was charged with the discovery of *how* desires and impulses can be directed by reason.[80]

In line with the ancient Greek conception of *êthos*, Mill recurrently pointed to *direction* as the key constituent of human character. In his early public activities, Mill reiterated the belief that the direction which early impressions give 'decides the whole character, the whole life of the man'.[81] He later clarified how new impressions can be used to give a different direction. But education, Mill argued, required not only the training of the intellect but of feelings as well. Like his father, Mill noted that a good character required both proper motives and rational principles. The relation of feelings to reason, i.e., whether it was in the direction reason pointed to or against it, defined strong or weak character. Unlike his father, Mill did not believe that emotion 'could take care of itself'.[82]

In the following decades, Mill developed the theme of the cultivation of reason and emotion on the basis of the above outline regarding their relation. Rational human beings, Mill argued, are not 'governed by the utterly senseless modes of feeling and action'.[83] He never questioned the 'rectitude of the intellect and the right direction of the actions and will'; but there was a higher expediency—one that was achieved by 'an ideal nobleness of will and conduct'. The question of how this ideal is cultivated—its ethological principles, had never received a suitable answer. But he was certain that emotion ought to be cultivated with equal force with that of 'severe reason', for the sake of social and personal improvement.[84]

Character formation considers the questions of *how* (ethological means) reason and emotion are trained and *which* direction they ought to follow (educational ends), without underestimating the importance of self-education, of one's own training of one's will and affections. 'Much thought and little feeling', Mill noted in his diary, make a person 'a mental voluptuary who wastes life in intellectual exercise for its own sake'; while, '[m]uch feeling and little thought are the common material of a bigot and fanatic'.[85] Mill tried to find the middle ground. On the one hand, 'strength of intellect' is required, Mill noted, to calculate correctly the circumstances of actions and warn against false steps; but 'strength of character', 'a still rarer endowment', is what makes the individual to dare to retrace such false steps,[86] because feelings, not the intellect, determine the will.

Thus, feelings are particularly important in producing action in accordance with virtue. Defining those circumstances that have produced the 'best' persons of the human race, will allow 'to make all or most men as virtuous as those' were. But the belief that moral excellence is possible without cultivation of the feelings, displays a narrow view of human nature. Mill had already argued in 1828 that feelings can be converted into auxiliaries of moral principles by a well-regulated moral education, 'because it is they which furnish the active principle, the moving force; passions are the spring, the moral principle only the regulator of human life'.[87] '[T]he stronger a feeling is', Mill noted, 'the more quickly and strongly it associates itself with any other object or feeling'.[88] Bentham, Mill argued, had ignored the need to cultivate the feelings as much as he had ignored diversities of character and deeper springs of action.[89] Though indeed powerful, self-interest does not have the hold of the mind, Mill noted, that people usually assign to it. It is possible to combine authentic 'private affections' with a 'sincere interest in the public good' in well-designed education.[90]

Moral, religious and aesthetic education aimed to cultivate the feelings and create virtuous habits. On one hand, Mill argued, individuals were habituated in social values at home and by the society. On the other, art provided timeless ideals of virtue that could act forcefully on a person's imagination—Mill attached more value to those forms of art that conduce to the development of those feelings that lead to a stern pursuit of the improvement of mankind.[91] There is a close parallel with Plato's *Republic*, in which emotional cultivation 'is designed to present [norms of right and wrong] in every available medium, and to ensure by a kind of aesthetic habituation that these norms become ingrained in the ψυχή [psyche]'.[92]

Plato's Socrates in *Republic* tried to promote 'independent capacity for analytic thought, the ability to formulate and defend one's conception of abstract notions', i.e., to think for oneself, through a variety of theoretical courses.[93] As we saw, according to Mill, this system of education was established in ancient Greece, through 'a series of exercises to form the thinking faculty itself, that the mind, being active and vigorous, might go forth and know'.[94] As ideas have the power to take hold of people's mind and be part of their character, it is important for individuals to be intellectually equipped both to produce certain ideas and to resist others when they tend to 'mislead'. However, despite its advantage over emotional cultivation, intellectual cultivation was equally deficient, according to Mill.[95]

Plato's *Gorgias* suggested to Mill that over-reliance on rational faculties does not inevitably lead to virtuous actions; inspiration and a habitual love for virtue are prerequisites. But *Gorgias* pointed to no method of cultivating the non-rational faculties of individuals; only in *Republic* was there anything close to a psychological theory, and a scheme of training both the feelings and the intellect. Well-developed feelings, Mill noted, 'work with, and not against, the outward motives to care for others'.[96] For Mill, it was the work of literature to achieve such a balance between rational analysis and feelings. As Parvin Sharpless argues, this can be achieved in four different ways: first, literature can provide individuals with new experiences, instances of life, instances that can inspire individuals that have been tired of the conventional way they are living. Second, literature can balance the scale of a materialistic or rationalistic mind with feelings and sympathy. More importantly, literature can inspire people in a moral course of action as well as, finally, 'provide ideal examples of excellence which could inspire men in the struggle toward goodness'.[97]

Moreover, virtuous conduct can be achieved, as we saw, only by one's feelings and dispositions. If one's conduct is wholly influenced by external circumstances then virtue (but not morality) is lost. For such inward circumstances to be worked upon there must be 'a firm unwavering confidence', Mill noted, 'in man's capability of virtue'. People, he added, are not the cool, 'thoughtful calculators' Bentham expected. They are not swayed solely by their intellect, which is 'only a part of the inducements which really actuate them'. More importantly, what is valuable in a character, according to Mill, develops out of a person's emotions, where all the capacity for happiness comes from.[98]

A confirmed character, Mill quoted from Carlyle, is a 'completely fashioned will'; one that can separate ends and purposes from the emotions that originally stimulated them; one that can create those circumstances that will develop their affective faculties toward rational ends.[99] Plato had taught Mill that virtuous individuals were 'not found, but made'. He too seemed to believe it required subjecting them, or their subjecting themselves, in 'every kind of tuition and training, intellectual, emotional, and practical'.[100] Such training allowed the pursuit of personal happiness and became conducive to the happiness of society. But individuals, Mill was convinced, ought to strive for the happiness of mankind.

## Self-Development, Self-Government and Happiness

As we saw, like in Plato, Mill argued that reason and emotion are not mutually exclusive; equal—and to a high standard—cultivation leads individuals to excellence.[101] The cultivated individual, Mill added, could be anyone whose 'fountains of knowledge have been opened' and has learned to exercise both affective and rational faculties. Such persons can find 'sources of inexhaustible interest in all that surrounds' them—be it objects of nature or achievements of art, poetry or even history and the past and present ways of mankind as well as their prospects in the future.[102]

However, as we saw, Mill argued that character education was in most ways a habituation in established social standards: '[t]o train the human being in the habit, and thence the power, of subordinating his personal impulses and aims, to what were considered the ends of society'.[103] As we already saw, Mill perceived a danger in this process. The power of society to habituate individuals in certain standards had enormous potential to lead to tyranny, and there was need for protection 'against the tendency, of society to impose, by other means than civil penalties, its own ideas and practices as rules of conduct on those who dissent from them'. Such social tyranny suppressed any individuality, any person 'not in harmony with its ways, and compel all characters to fashion themselves upon' the prevailing social models, opinions and feelings.[104]

To counter such tendencies, Mill argued that people need to develop their own character.[105] Education ought to enable individuality, not shun it, but at the same time, it ought to habituate individuals toward social ends. This does not suggest a contradiction. A person should not take the established social standards upon trust, but analyse them critically, to *discover* their reasons, rather than going routinely by tradition. Producing an independent understanding of social standards of belief and action was an educating principle to which Plato's Socrates also subscribed.[106] Mill did not say that people should not benefit 'by the ascertained results of human experience'. But he argued that 'it is the privilege and proper condition of a human being, arrived at the maturity of his faculties, to use and interpret experience in his own way' and strengthen her/his rational faculties.[107] Like in *Republic*, this kind of training predisposed the individual to the pursuit of virtue, as it offered the basis of self-development, allowing individuals to go by doing 'their own work'.[108]

As we saw, character referred to one's stable emotional disposition to follow rational principles. The art of education defined the ends that the development of such stable emotional dispositions needed to serve. What is more, ethology was responsible to find the scientific means for the formation of those qualities that Mill considered being 'interesting to us'. Since Mill himself was discussing about which combination of the 'laws of the mind' and the actual 'general position of our species in the universe', produce these qualities, these must be qualities that benefit us as a species and as a society.[109] Since Mill defined individuality as being able to choose one's own life-plan, it involved making the choices which most exercise '[t]he human faculties of perception, judgement, discriminative feeling, mental activity, and even moral preference'. Once the 'deliberate decision' has been made to follow one path rather than another, 'firmness and self-control' are required to hold it—strong intellect, will and character that have been developed by habits of acting to bring about certain ends.[110] As a Utilitarian, for Mill the final end was the happiness of mankind.[111]

While such a final end moves Mill away from Plato (and ancient Greeks more generally), what Mill did share with Plato was the belief in the intrinsic worth of individuality and virtue. Mill argued that self-development and self-government make for a fuller existence; an existence which brings individuals 'nearer to the best thing they can be'. Character formation was the cultivation of individuality; the formation of 'well-developed human beings'.[112] This cannot be descriptive; it is evaluative. It is a particular ideal of human nature. This development was not merely connected with the moral and prudential branches of the 'Art of Life' but with the aesthetic as well: 'He who has learnt what beauty is, if he be of a virtuous character, will desire to realize it in his own life—will keep before himself a type of perfect beauty in human character, to light his attempts at self-culture'.[113] Such an understanding of character formation brought Mill closer to the ideals of ancient Greece: not only being *Dikaios* and *Agathos* but *Kalos* as well. Mill's was an account of nobility that did not require a choice between 'individual flourishing' and 'communal well-being'.[114]

There is a way of enabling individuals to create and act upon motives directed toward the greater good, Mill argued, without hindering the freedom of acting in 'innumerable and conflicting directions'.[115] Since human beings cannot be as well-proportioned as buildings—they cannot be 'rounded off and made symmetrical'—he added, a 'bold, free expansion in all directions is demanded by the needs of modern life and the instincts of the modern mind'.[116] But by arguing that 'man' is a 'living thing' and 'requires to grow and develope itself on all sides', Mill escaped the limitations of French and German classicism. Indeed, self-development was the core of Mill's ethics, as John M. Robson has argued.[117]

Mill's 'Art of Life' provided a general outline for human conduct; not in the sense of one ideal mode of living, but rather in the sense of an ideal method. In this way, 'harmony' should not be taken to mean 'uniformity'. As long as others are not harmed, individuals are encouraged, and are free, to make their life worth living. Their character depends on how they guide their impulses toward rational ends, not on fixing their desires upon one object.[118] Character formation and self-development aimed at making individuals capable of self-government and enabling them to shape their own will. That was why Mill argued that the ideal of self-government blends with, but does not supersede, the ideal of self-development.[119]

Mill's ideal of character referred to strong impulses guided by a vigorous reason; strong feelings strongly controlled by a conscientious will. However, 'control' should not be mistaken for 'coercion'. Given that character was defined in reference to a stable disposition of feelings to follow the direction reason affords, the Platonic and Christian ideal of self-government seems to refer to the ability of individuals to use their reason to set their own direction.[120] At the same time, it points out that individuals need a strong will to control strong feelings or resist external coercion. In the *Principles of Political Economy* (1848), Mill defined self-government as σωφροσύνη.[121] This ancient Greek virtue included 'all the qualities or habits which were considered most contrary to *licentiousness* of morals and manners'. Temperance, continence, modesty, moderation and even sobriety, he noted, 'are all short of the mark'. Mill did think 'self-restraint' and 'self-control' more precise, but, as we saw, they imply coercion; and 'what is required is rather a character not needing coercion'. He added '[u]nobtrusiveness' as an essential part of the concept' as well as 'Judgment or Intelligence (let us say Reasonableness)'.[122] At once, Mill argued, *sophrosunê* implied ideas of order, measure and deliberateness; these fitted well with his approval of Von Humboldt's and Plato's end on man: 'the highest and most harmonious development of his powers to a complete and consistent whole'.[123] In light of Mill's definition of *sophrosunê*, his remark 'that none but a person of confirmed virtue is completely free' begins to make sense.[124] Thus, Mill's 'moral inculcations' were at all times those of the 'Socratici viri'.[125]

Though to the virtuous individual, as we saw, virtue was an end in itself, the social gains were not negligible. Society and the world at large benefit from virtue. In order to maintain 'all kinds and amounts of good' that is already present in a society as well as increase it, societies need to actively engage in the education of their citizens—virtues such as industry, integrity, justice and prudence, serve the improvement of society—such an education, Mill noted, 'in the long run makes them claim to have control of their own actions'.[126] Whatever the state could do, it could not do it all; it ought to allow people 'to provide themselves with all helps necessary for their individual devotions'. However, these could be achieved solely by 'the general spirit of its institutions'. At the same time, that it has the power to 'instruct, and by instruction it can not only form the intellect but develop the moral perceptions', called for critical and inquisitive habits.[127]

In appropriate social conditions, self-development and self-government enable individuals to be self-dependent; 'a virtue which is one of the first conditions of excellence in the human character—the stock on which if the other virtues are not grafted, they have seldom any firm root'.[128] Individual improvement can only be possible and durable, Mill noted, as long as it is in one's own hands. Active characters possess the 'self-benefiting qualities', by struggling 'against evils' and endeavouring 'to make circumstances bend to' themselves, they neither give way to 'natural powers and tendencies' nor are they satisfied with the existing level of improvement. Since society is an aggregate of its citizens, 'the habits and conduct which promote the advantage of each [...], must be at least a part of those which conduce most in the end to the advancement of the community as a whole'.[129] In 1861, Mill argued that he was writing against the 'commonplaces of moralists, and the general sympathies of mankind', when he extolled the active, self-helping character against the passive type. But the British public had already witnessed the commercial success of Samuel Smiles' *Self-Help* (1859). An ideal of self-dependence was gaining ground among the British public; self-shaping character and the well-being of others became among the highest priorities.[130]

However, being self-dependent was not enough for social well-being; the latter required individuals who cared for other people and aimed at unselfish goods. The well-being of society and mankind required the formation of characters with

> a disinterested regard for others, and especially for what comes after them, for the idea of posterity, of their country, or of mankind, whether grounded on sympathy or on a conscientious feeling, which ever directs the minds and purposes of classes or bodies of men towards distant or unobvious interests.[131]

As we saw, virtue was defined as acting in the 'right' way, setting and following 'distant or unobvious interests', without being forced to do so. What differentiates morality and virtue, as we saw in chapter seven, is that 'uncommon virtue' cannot be extracted as a debt; it lies beyond the moral domain. But, like in ancient ethical theories, for the practitioner of the 'Art of Life' practical reasoning is not divided into moral, prudential or aesthetic—it is one and the same. Virtuous conduct does not mean acting in morally neutral ways (though some instances of conduct do mean so)—that is why Mill argued that in improving societies the moral domain widens, turning virtue from 'uncommon' to 'common' (i.e., expected) and why Mill also argued that virtue was a permanent interest of progressive beings.[132]

## CONCLUDING REMARKS

Nineteenth-century Britain was greatly concerned with the idea of character, which pervaded many aspects of the public life, especially debates on reform. John Stuart Mill's view of the means and ends of character formation was also influenced by ancient Greek thought. This chapter supported the argument that Mill's ideas of virtue and character were an integral part of his radicalism.[133]

Plato, and Aristotle, influenced Mill in his conception of character as *êthos* and the need to cultivate both the affective and rational faculties of human beings. For both Plato and Mill, this necessitated a unifying theory of living—'a clear and precise conception of what we are pursuing' as the first thing needed in any calculation of action. The pursuit of happiness was connected with the development of human excellence, even if the latter became an intrinsic end itself.[134] In ancient Greek thought, no less than in Victorian times, noble action was considered an end in itself as well as a means for social unity. Like Plato's Socrates, Mill argued that character was not innate or fixed. Through self-examination and training one's habits, Mill was convinced that individuals could form their own character in accordance with the 'greater good'. People needed to have this choice in order to develop their character and be morally responsible. Mill was not surprised to find that in a society of intolerance, like that of Plato's Socrates, free individuals are misunderstood, feared and, ultimately, silenced.

This called for a change in social practices. Like in Plato's *Republic*, Mill noted that the current social structure unjustifiably perpetuated unequal opportunities in the development of character. A blatant example was the treatment of women. For both Plato's Socrates and Mill, individuals were as much responsible for the formation of their character as society; the latter for fostering the appropriate conditions so that the former can know and be who they want to be—to enable people to find and do their 'own work'.[135] To be able to find their own path in life, individuals require free scope to question established beliefs and values, and if those values and beliefs are indeed true, then they will follow them. Not blind trust, not routine but reason and discussion preserve the vitality of truth and its connection to feelings. Here as well, Mill moved beyond Plato: what is taken to constitute 'truth' especially needed to be questioned.

The nature of Plato's dialogues makes it difficult to make direct comparisons with Mill's works. That is why Aristotle is of great use. Aristotle noted three conditions that prove someone's virtue: a. acting with foreknowledge (not by accident or by coercion); b. acting virtuously for its own sake (not as a means to an end); and c. acting from a firm and stable disposition of the emotions to follow reason (not by caprice or impulse).[136] All three elements appeared in Mill's move from what he saw as 'narrow' Benthamism to a broader foundation for happiness. Thus, Mill did return to the Greeks and a conception of utility as *eudaimonia*.[137]

Still, one should not overestimate the importance of convenient definitions found in Aristotle. It was Plato, not Aristotle, that Mill had called the 'Great Teacher'. Plato, Mill argued, had the power of combining moral enthusiasm with logical discipline, making his readers *feel* what he felt. As we saw, according to Mill, Plato was the only example 'once in all literature, of the union between an eminent genius for philosophy and the most consummate skill and feeling of the artist'.[138] All the dialogues that Mill had translated dealt with or touched upon, either directly or indirectly, issues of character formation.

Concurrently, Mill was aware of the (cultural and philosophical) limitations of many Platonic ideas. The habitual selective reading of ancient texts in his time made it easy for Mill to retain the ideas he thought most useful. Thus, he found much usefulness in Plato's discussions on character formation, i.e., the attempt to cultivate the feelings in the direction rational principles afford. However, in Plato's scheme, the desired end was the happiness of the society; for Mill, it was the happiness of mankind. For both, the desire end was achieved through the happiness of the individual when that individual aimed not at the satisfaction of her/his selfish desires but when the cultivation of virtue was an end in itself.

## NOTES

1. Owen, 1813:9, 22, 27. See also, Bennett, 1846.
2. Owen, 1991:43, 64.
3. Owen, 1813:13, 53-4. See also, T. Arnold, 1858:193 (also Plato, *L:*87b).
4. Tholfsen, 1971:77; McCord, 1991:236-7.
5. McWilliam, 1998:47.
6. Collini, 1991:94; Jones, 2000:31.
7. BP:XI.342.
8. Ibid. p. 341.
9. Bailey, 1858:266-7; see also, Bain, 1861:10-3 (see also, Bain, 1859:ch. 10).
10. Collini, 1991:65. See further, Dixon, 2008.
11. Bradley, 1905:10 (in Collini, 1991:96-7). The ancient Greeks shared this belief (see, Stough, 1978:211-3; Rist, 1972:92-9; Bobzien, 2006:219-22).
12. Carlisle, 1991:1, 4.
13. Ibid. pp. 3-6. These included, for example, moral, scientific, economic, religious discussions.
14. Collini, 1991:96, 74.
15. Houghton, 1957:265-6.
16. Carlisle, 1991:4. See, Bain, 1961:192; Smiles, 1871:18.
17. Coleridge, 1854:I.228 (also, Smiles, 1859:317; T. Arnold, 1858:349).
18. Exhibiting 'the connection of philosophical speculation with the practical business of life', for which J.S. Mill especially had a talent (Ward, 1843:349), was of great importance to both Mills (see, *A:*I.232-3; APHM:XXXI.228).
19. *SOL:*VIII.869. Also, Collini, 1991:103. Put into the terms of chapter seven, *êthos* combined the *dutiful* with the *noble*; in Matthew Arnold's terms, *êthos* combined the *Hebrew* with the *Hellene*.

20. Aristotle, *EN*:1098a15-20, 1103a7, 1103a14-7, 1104b10-5; Plato, *L*:653a-c; *Rep*:401e-2a. Thus, education was 'a process of turning the mind in the right direction' (Barrow, 1975:32).
21. Aristotle, *Rhet*:1377b21. See further, Gill, 1984:153-5; Schütrumpf, 1970.
22. Aristotle, *Rhet*:1378a (also, 1366b); Plato, *Gor*:487a-b (Fortenbaugh, 1992:217-20).
23. Aristotle, *EE*:1220b5; Chamberlain, 1984:181.
24. Plato, *Rep*:439a-40d, 442a-c. See also, Rorty, 1998:172. Though Aristotle seems to think in terms of a bipartite soul (e.g., *Pol*:1333a16ff), there are some similarities with Plato (see, Cooper, 1999:119n2). Bain noted that a tripartite view allowed for a better psychology (in J. Mill, 1878:II.182n).
25. Aristotle, *EN*:1103a7; Coleman, 2000:I.157.
26. Coleman, 2000:I.158; Aristotle, *EN*:1139a32-7.
27. Aristotle, *EN*:1103a19-21. See, *A*:I.270; Mill to J. P. Nichol, 30/09/1848:XIII.739.
28. Aristotle, *EN*:1103a26-30; Coleman, 2000:I.158 (italics added). Also, Chamberlain, 1984:182.
29. Carlisle, 1991:1. However, human drives (which habit and training counteract), Mill argued, and 'nervous susceptibility' also influence behavior (N:X.398; *PPE*:II.367; TP:I.413; APHM:XXXI.220ff).
30. N:X.373ff; *OL*:XVIII.264. See further, Skorupski, 1994:96-99; Miller, 2010:21-2.
31. TP:I.413; *U*:X.213. See also, Plato, *Rep*:370a-b. See further, Riley, 1988:228-9; Donner, 1991:120-1; Garforth, 1980:80-1 (contra Gray, 1996:73).
32. *U*:X.212; N:X.396-7 (see also, Bailey, 1858:266-7); Berger, 1984:236.
33. PL:I.323-4 (see also, Civ:XVIII.133); Plato, *Rep*:359a-60d. Once again, Coleridge, rather than Plato, is credited with a particular aspect of Mill's critique of modern society (Semmel, 1984:91). In 1824, Mill argued that actions and choices do portray one's character; still he qualified this by noting that 'fine feelings and acute sensibilities' motivate and guide conduct pursuant to virtue, when being regulated by rational principles (BHBE:VI.4). Bentham was reluctant to use 'virtue' in the place of 'good', because the association of virtue with reputation, he argued, might lead self-regarding vices (which are harmful only to one's self)—to be considered, and be punished as, a crime (other-regarding harm) (Bentham, 1996:125n; Nussbaum, 1999:167).
34. *U*:X.221; DE:02/03/1854:XXVII.658; RBP:X.7ff; Mill to W.G. Ward, 28/11/1859: XV.649; B:X.98, 112 (see also, Miller, 1998:79-81). Heydt (2006:58-9) does not distinguish between aesthetic and moral evaluations or between virtue and morality; still he, like Robson (1968:131), more than Donner (who makes the distinction; e.g., 2010; 2011), brings out the evaluative 'character-viewpoint' of actions, which was ancient in origin (Gill, 1983:470-1). See also, Kamtekar, 2004.
35. WMP:X.188; *U*:X.219, 219n; APHM:XXXI.252-3 (see further, Bentham, 1996:chs. 8, 10). See also, Ridge, 2002.
36. SD:X.69. Mill refers to *objective* and *subjective* goodness, a scholastic distinction that Henry Sidgwick (1874:180n2) traced back to ancient Stoics. See further, Prior, 1951.
37. Jaeger, 1946:II.46. With such a view of character, Mill would accept the basic grounds of virtue ethics (Nussbaum, 1999:170; also, Jones, 1992:299ff).
38. Mill to Comte, 30/10/1843:XIII.604 and 08/12/1843:XIII.616. This was strikingly similar to James Mill's view on character formation (see, J. Mill, 1825:VII. Contra Ball, 2011).
39. Mill to Comte, 30/10/1843:XIII.604; *SOL*:VIII.869, 889.
40. Ball, 2000:32 (see further, Capaldi, 1973). Skorupski (1989:260) added a forth level of observations in social and historical circumstances.

41. BP:XI.348-9. See further, Skorupski, 1989:22-3. See Garthforth, 1979:46-66 and 107-41 for the fullest discussion of the associationist foundation of John Stuart Mill's ethological theory.
42. *SOL*:VIII.869; *U*:X.218.
43. For this argument, as it relates to the cultivation of virtue, see Coleman, 2000:I.158-9.
44. *SOW*:XXI.272; see further, Ball, 2000:37-40.
45. *SOW*:XXI.276, 271 (also, Mill to Nichol, 30/09/1848:XIII.739); Plato, *Rep:*453d, 454d-e, 455d-6e. Like in Plato, Mill argued that well-developed individuals could *combine* what were considered traditionally the highest feminine qualities (emotion) with the highest masculine ones (reason)—good character was not a question of sex (Mill to Carlyle, 05/10/1833:XII.184; Plato, *Rep:*456c-d). Interestingly, Mill's argument was about the inherent injustice of the subjection of women (*SOW*:XXI.261), whereas Plato's seemed to be utilitarian (Annas, 1976; Lesser, 1979). Thus, Jenkyns' (1980:230) claim that Plato's feminism guided and encouraged Mill may be exaggerating. See further, Urbinati, 1991; 2002:180ff; Annas, 1977; Okin, 1988:viii-x; Morales, 2005.
46. Carlisle, 1991:142; see also, Ball, 2000:37-40.
47. See, Jones, 2000:x; 1992:292.
48. Carlisle, 1991:142. Physical circumstances may mean those inherent in the body (part of one's natural constitution) or beyond the control of individuals (*SOL*:VIII.869; Mill to H. Taylor Mill, 07/02/1854:XIV.152 and to Comte, 08/12/1843:XIII.616). Also, J. Mill, 1825:VII.21.
49. *SOL*:VIII.862, 864, 869; also, DPE:IV.327-9; SD:X.56n.
50. *SOL*:VIII.847, 869-70.
51. *OL*:XVIII.231; *SOL*:VIII.859; Carlisle, 1991:141.
52. *SOL*:VIII.873-5; also, Mill to Comte, 26/03/1846:XIII.398; Bain, 1843:453; Feuer, 1976:87. Political ethology, the science of national character (πολιτείας ἦθος in Plato, *Rep:*549a; πόλεως ἦθος in Isocrates, *AN*:31), was the most important branch of sociology (Varouxakis 2002a:54-60). James Mill did not ignore it (1813b:102, 114; 1826a:I.401 and V.308n, 506); but, according to John Mill, Bentham did (RBP:X.9; B:X.99, 105).
53. Bain, 1882a:78-9. Also, Mill to A. Bain, late 1843:XIII.617. Elijah Millgram suggests that 'no science could have done what Mill needed' of ethology to do—having realized that, Mill 'quietly let ethology lapse' (Millgram, 1995:351-2).
54. Leary, 1982:155-7, 159-62 (See also, Garforth, 1979:65; Wilhoite, 1971). See also, Anon., 1828.
55. *SOL*:VIII.872-3; Mill to A. Bain, 14/11/1859:XV.645.
56. The lack of substantial revision of the comments on the ethology, in the various editions of the *Logic*, has been used to highlight Mill's belief in its importance (even if only to be then criticized; see, Ward, 1891:447).
57. TDA[I]:XVIII.81, 88-9.
58. See further, Smith, 1989:132; Riley, 1991.
59. Mill to T. Carlyle, 17/09/1832:XII.118; *PPE*:III.940.
60. ACJ:XXIV.866; GL:XX.384.
61. TDA[I]:XVIII.81 (see also, TDA[II]:XVIII.189; *PPE*:III.940). See also, Varouxakis, 1999:306ff.
62. Mill to T. Carlyle, 05/09/1833:XII.175; Plato, *Rep:*514a-20a. That education can be used as an instrument to create minds 'in perpetual bondage', was an early lesson for Mill (sPR[2]:XXVI.274), probably given by James Mill's study of Staël's *De l' Allemagne* (1813:I.32-4 in CPB:III.35r; V.64r. ). Also, J.S. Mill mentioned Plato's *Gorgias* (513a-c)

while discussing the tendency of public opinion in democracies to diminish individuality (*CRG*:XIX.508. See also, COS:V.746; *PPE*:II.209-10; *A*:I.260).

63. *A*:I.175-7; Mill to Carlyle, 05/10/1833:XII.183; sPRT:XXVI.304-6. For an excellent discussion of Mill's 'incubus' see Millgram, 2011.

64. *SOL*:VIII.836-7; also, ATCC:I.426-7.

65. Chas, 1827:62.

66. *SOL*:VIII.837-9. See also, *EHP*:IX.452-4, 458-9, 465; *U*:X.252.

67. *SOL*:VIII.840; *A*:I.177. It is interesting that Mill never acknowledged the connection of his theory at least to Aristotle's very similar view (e.g., *EN*:1114a20; see further, Ott, 2006).

68. *SOL*:VIII.840-1; *EHP*:IX.466; NN:VI.152 (Also, J. Mill, 1878:II.348ff). See further, Ryan, 1970:ch. 7.

69. *SOL*:VIII.838 (also, Plato, *Rep:*381c; *U*:X.212).

70. Plato, *Tm*:87b; *Rep:*442a-4e. Also, *OL*:XVIII.264. Mill argued that a strong character can be used for good as well as bad purposes, depending on the direction of reason. Mill credited his insight about the role of emotions in virtue to Wordsworth (sWB:XXVI.441).

71. Plato, *Rep:*441e, 442c (see further, Copper, 1999:ch. 4); *SOL*:VIII.840-1. Also, J. Mill, 1878:II.259.

72. Col[25]:XXIV.973; *SOL*:VIII.841. See, Plato, *Alc I*:134c, 122a; *Rep*:562c (see further, Barrow, 1975:37).

73. Villa, 2001:75; Riley, 1998:82. Riley calls this ideal of character Periclean; Socratic seems a better fit, given Mill's insistence about the importance of the examined life as the one worth living (see further, Villa, 2001:60; Ryan, 1997:xxxv; Hamburger, 1999:36-37).

74. Mill to the New York Liberal Club, 20/01/1871:XVII.1801-2; *OL*:XVIII.277. Unless an advanced state of civilization exists, Mill argued, being 'ready recipients of ideas and modes of action from all sides' may serve to unite a heterogeneous society (*PPE*:III.754; FWNI:XXI.118-9; MHF:XX.237-8).

75. IA:XXI.217-8; DE:23/01/1854:XXVII.645. Self-development also requires freedom of tastes and pursuits as well as a strong intellect with poetic cultivation to frame 'the plan of our life to suit our own character' (*OL*:XVIII.226; TP:I.417).

76. *SOL*:VIII.952; N:X.393. Also, *SOL*:VIII.842; B:X.95; *U*:X.236-7.

77. Mill's other possible interpretation was that, in Aristotle's terms, he had exhibited *êthos* and *logos* but lacked *pathos* (displaying his own feelings and exciting those of the audience). He was aware that it 'was not altogether untrue' of him at the time being merely a 'reasoning machine' (*A*:I.111).

78. sPRT:XXVI.307. Also, J. Mill, 1835a:42-7.

79. sUH:XXVI.395. The problem was keeping the ruling few within the line of virtue.

80. sCM:XXVI.396; Go:XI.149.

81. sPSL:XXVI.410-1. James Mill's influence is evident, since at this time the elder Mill was still preparing his *Analysis*, a work that John Mill studied and discussed thoroughly (*A*:I.70-1, 124ff) and, forty years later, with Bain's and Grote's help attempted to update its doctrines. Interestingly, some argue that Plato also tried to update Socrates' 'purely rationalistic account of education' (e.g., Gill, 1985:6).

82. sWB:XXVI.434; *A*:I.112-3.

83. CL:IV.378.

84. T:X.483. See also, SD:X.50; WMP:X.172; *A*:I.147.

85. DE:11/03/1854:XXVII.660.

86. WI:VI.147. See also, DE:13/01/1854:XXVII.642-3; SA[IV]:XXII.293-4.

87. sPrf:XXVI.430, 432. Though Mill had not yet developed the 'Art of Life', we can still see that he used the principle of utility in the same sense with that of the much later 'directive rule' (*U*:X.213).
88. TPV:I.357.
89. SD:X.50; B:X.98, 93, 96.
90. C:X.131; *U*:X.216. See also, COS:V.740; Mill to H. Taylor, 21/03/1849:XIV.19.
91. IA:XXI.247-57; *A*:I.147-9; TPV:I.350-1; WAV:I.499-500. See further, Robson, 1968:26; Sharpless, 1967:179-81; Plato, *Rep:*390a-b.
92. Gill, 1985:11. See, Plato, *Rep:*401b-2a (see further, bks. 2-3).
93. Plato, *Rep:*bks. 6-7 (see, Gill, 1985:16-9).
94. OG:I.335-6.
95. TDA[II]:XVIII.198-9; *SOL*:VIII.737-9; UAPL:XVIII.304. See also, GAEI:XXIV.786; IA:XXI.233-7.
96. *U*:X.233. See also, TPV:I.363-4; *A*:I.142-3.
97. Sharpless, 1967:218.
98. RBP:X.12-3, 15-7; *A*:I.144.
99. *SOL*:VIII.842-3 (also, Carlyle, 1840:II.242).
100. GP:XI.437 (see further, Irwin, 1977:191-5).
101. DE:11/03/1854:XXVII.660 and 17/02/1854:XXVII.655. See also, Plato, *Rep:*442a-4d.
102. *U*:X.216.
103. This function of education was the first condition of the permanence of a political community (C:X.133). Like James Mill (CPB:V.62r on Plato, *Prot*:327b; 1835a:259ff), John Mill noted that history exhibited the power of education in habituating a person in the society's moral values (UR:X.409).
104. *OL*:XVIII.220. James Mill (CPB:III.36v) was aware that Socrates recognized this tyrannical social influence and sought ways to counteract it (*Rep:*492aff, 527d-e; see further, Rorty, 1998:177; Gill, 1985:5).
105. Otherwise, Mill argued, they do not develop character, any more 'than a steam-engine has a character' (*OL*:XVIII.264 contra Donner, 1991:95).
106. OG:I.332-5 (see further, Wilson, 1998:234-5); Gill, 1985:2; Rorty, 1998:163ff (see also, Annas, 1978).
107. *OL*:XVIII.262-3; also, SD:X.65-6, 74; NN:VI.227-8.
108. See, Gill, 1985:6. Mill seemed indeed unconscious of his Platonizing in this case (O'Brien, 1958:458).
109. *SOL*:VIII.873-4; also, IA:XXI.247-51.
110. *OL*:XVIII.262-3; Mill to J. Austin, 13/04/1847:XIII.712.
111. Just as developed human beings can be of use to the undeveloped in a society, so can more advanced societies to the undeveloped ones. *OL*:XVIII.267-8 (also, *CRG*:XIX.ch. 18). See further, Riley, 1998:84ff.
112. *OL*:XVIII.266-7. It seems that Mill paid more attention to the extrinsic worth of individuality, as it was more likely to convince others on account of its social benefits (contra Hamburger, 1999:148).
113. IA:XXI.255. See further, Robson, 1968:121, Valls, 1999:256. Jones (2000:35-7) associates Mill's evaluative take on character with a positive rather than a negative conception of liberty.
114. Bartlett, 2002:525-6. Developmental theories of education seem to focus on moral education (e.g., Carr, 2002; 2007) and even when examining the connection to virtue (e.g.,

Carr, 2008), the aesthetic aspect is absent. Both the notions of *Paideia* and *Bildung* retain that aesthetic aspect.

115. *OL*:XVIII.263; *A*:I.259.
116. DE:06/02/1854:XXVII.651-2. See futher, Habibi, 2001:ch. 2.
117. Robson, 1968:140.
118. ACP:X.337; Valls, 1999:256. See further, Donner, 2007.
119. *OL*:XVIII.266.
120. Ibid. pp. 263, 265-6, 271-2; TPV:I.364.
121. *PPE*:III.763. Smith (1989:125-8) connects this with a positive conception of freedom.
122. Pr:XI.53; Ch:XI.175n; GP:XI.408.
123. *OL*:XVIII.261 (see further, Valls, 1999); Plato, *Rep*:442c-4a; *Gor*:503d-4b.
124. *SOL*:VIII.841. Robert Devigne (2006:38) ignores Mill's reference to the non-coercive function of emotions in his discussion concerning the role of feelings in Mill's thought. Moreover, Mill may have held a version of the 'compatibility view' of virtues, i.e., that 'the development of one virtue does not threaten or set limits to the development of any of the others' (Walker, 1989:349). Thus, by highlighting self-development and self-government as distinctive human functions, Mill appears to have held a 'self-realization' theory (Sidgwick, 1907:90-3; see further, White, 1979, Nussbaum, 2004).
125. Mill did so, following after his father's footsteps (*A*:I.48-9). Concurrently, placing 'virtue in utility' and linking it to 'proper guidance of affections' reveals Mill's Scottish background (see further, Rosen, 2003a:78).
126. *CRG*:XIX.385, 390, 403. Col[20]:XXIV.955. Plato, *L*:bk. 2.
127. NN:VI.227 (also, FB:XXI.107; J. Mill, 1825:VII.44-6). Also, RBP:X.9.
128. *PPE*:III.763-5; II.282.
129. *CRG*:XIX.406-7 (also, APHM:XXXI.226); CL:IV.383. See further, Eisenach, 1989:253.
130. IC:XXIII.398; Collini, 1991:133. 'Self-dependence vs. social conditions' appeared often in Mill's essays: Col[2]:XXIV:887; Col[11]:XXIV:916; Col[20]:XXIV:955; Col[25]:XXIV:973. Also, SMWC:V.415.
131. *CRG*:XIX.444-5; also, RBP:X.8.
132. *OL*:XVIII.235; *ACP*:X.338; Berkowitz, 1999:147. See further, Annas, 1995; Donner, 2010, 2011.
133. Jones, 1992:289.
134. *U*:X.206.
135. See also, Plato, *Rep*:451e-2a, 540c-e; *SOW*:XXI.271-2, 276
136. Aristotle, *EN*:1105a27-30.
137. Levi, 1959:40.
138. GP:XI.410, 415.

# CHAPTER NINE

## EUDAIMONIA AND UTILITY

Ever since it first appeared in *Fraser's Magazine* in late 1861 as a series of essays, John Stuart Mill's *Utilitarianism* has been under attack. The 'traditional' critique of Mill's 'qualitative hedonism' is familiar. Hedonism requires that pleasure alone is good as an end—i.e., is desired for its own sake. When Mill introduced qualitative differences in the estimation of pleasures, he essentially postulated that there are other good-making properties, not just pleasure. Henry Sidgwick thus concluded that 'all qualitative comparison of pleasures must really resolve itself into quantitative' otherwise one is mixing 'Intuitionism with Hedonism'. Mill was either a bad logician or not a hedonist.[1]

Philosophical reconstructions of the argument in Mill's 'little volume', less or more charitable, have led to a number of directions in the attempt to make his various claims with regard to happiness consistent. Mill's appropriation of Platonic ideas was one of the less promising directions.[2] But perhaps it is not. For this reason, a conception of happiness present in Plato's works is here put to use to disentangle that of Mill. No scholarly consensus with regard to Mill's view of happiness is required for this interpretation. On the other hand, a particular interpretation of Plato's notion of happiness is being adopted here, although no pretension is being made that there is consensus about it.

Though it has become common knowledge that Mill attempted to revise his utilitarian inheritance, I argue that he took on this task by reconfiguring the place of reason and pleasure in life as a whole. However, to do so I try to trace the 'historical sources'[3] of Mill's ideas on happiness to his reading of Plato. I also attempt to sift through interpretations of Mill's thought which focus on deliberation and inclusiveness to argue that Mill held a conception of happiness in which pleasure was neither just an ingredient among many nor the sole end of action. To this effect, the discussion begins by defining some basic features of *eudaimonia* and by discussing how they may have been introduced to Mill's early inculcation in Benthamism, i.e., in a conception of utility. Then, once the conceptual framework is established, Mill's notion of happiness is examined against some possible objections and recent interpretations. The plausibility of this interpretation derives from the suggested centrality to Mill's thought both of a Socratic 'Art of Life' and of character formation as the pursuit of excellence.

## UTILITY OR EUDAIMONIA?

### An Impossible Choice?

As we saw, Mill commonly returned to the texts of ancient Greeks for instruction, and, more frequently, for corroboration of various ideas. Mill's 'intoxication' has led Geraint Williams to claim that 'Mill was a Greek before he was a nineteenth-century utilitarian disciple of Bentham'.[4] However, this soon changed, according to Williams. Mill's attachment to ancient Greece was sidetracked by reading Jeremy Bentham's *Traités de Législation* (1802) in his teens. Still, Mill's Greek influences re-emerged to a prominent position, Williams has argued, during his 1826 'crisis'. But, as Williams suggests, in the attempt to conciliate the Greek with the Utilitarian project Mill was led to a notion of happiness that could not, without problems, adjust the claims of both. However, Mill being 'Greek' before being 'Utilitarian' is somewhat exaggerating the case, as it was James Mill who guided John's learning of ancient Greek thought.[5] John Mill's *Autobiography* (1873) points to several lessons in ancient Greek moral thought (e.g., the 'Choice of Hercules'), with which the elder Mill strove to teach his son that virtue may be accompanied by great pains. More importantly, John Mill noted that the principle of utility in Bentham's *Traités* had given '*unity* to [his] conceptions of things', falling 'exactly into its place as the *keystone* which held together the detached and fragmentary component parts of [his] knowledge and beliefs'.[6] Perhaps, John was not as 'torn between' utility and eudaimonia, as is usually claimed.[7]

In the *Traités*, Bentham set three prerequisites so that the principle of utility could provide a common ground in ethics and in politics: first, utility needs to be clearly and precisely defined; second, its unity is established once it assumes control of all other principles; third, its consistency is guaranteed by finding a sort of 'moral arithmetic'. So utility, first, was taken to be an abstract term. It referred to the 'property' of things, or actions, which tends to prevent some evil (pain or cause of pain) or produce some good (pleasure or cause of pleasure). Bentham attached no metaphysical meaning to the sensations of pleasure and pain—'*il ne faut consulter ni Platon, ni Aristote*'—everyone was susceptible to pleasurable or painful mental states. Second, the principle of utility was axiomatic; just as with mathematical principles, utility cannot be proved directly; yet, it would be 'absurd' to reject it. Third, it was necessary to be able to calculate pleasures and pains in all operations of judgment; Bentham recognized no good in moral (or other) acts or things unless there was some good in felt-experience (i.e., pleasures of the 'soul' or of the 'senses'). Appearing in the first pages of the *Traités*, these ideas burst upon Mill 'with all the force of novelty'.[8]

Bentham defined a number of attributes of pleasures to take into account in calculations of consequences, but never a procedure of interpersonal calculations.[9] So calculating pleasures could ostensibly conflict with the claims of conventional morality, which provided grounds for reform of the latter. For example, virtue was a good only in so far as it promoted pleasure. Virtue, Bentham argued, was the sacrifice of a smaller interest for a greater one. The principle of utility was not opposed to the just or the honest; if it ever did, it was due to miscalculation: '[s]i *un homme calcule mal, ce n'est pas l'arithmétique qui est en défaut, c'est lui-même*'. Bentham argued that to suppose that one would pursue advantages against virtue, '*c'est supposer que le Bonheur peut être ennemi du Bonheur même*'. Thus, utility was simple and intelligible; it reduced all matters of ethics and politics, including virtue, to a function of reason—calculation.[10] This was not an unknown thesis to Mill. It constituted Socrates' argument in Plato's *Protagoras*, which goes some way toward confirming that his early education had indeed been 'in a great measure, a course of Benthamism'.[11]

However, the cultivation of virtue was the first thing Mill came across in ancient discussions on eudaimonia.[12] A virtuous person is disposed to act in a virtuous way (i.e., to act according to the virtue that is involved in the act—as such it is also a matter of experiencing the virtues). As a disposition, virtue develops from repeated choices and from certain habits of choosing—virtue is exercised in choice, by acting on reasons. In this way, the virtues have both an affective aspect and an intellectual aspect. The affective aspect means that virtue involves feelings (particularly the feelings of pleasure and pain); developing a virtue requires the development of feelings in a certain (i.e., supportive) way. The intellectual aspect refers to having a good grasp of what is the right thing to do in a given situation (according to the virtue at hand) and, then, to do it. A virtuous person has developed the affective and intellectual aspects into a harmonious whole.[13] Thus, it was about character and its proper development.

In Plato's *Republic*, Socrates initiated the discussion on how character affects happiness by asking Thrasymachus to think better about the way one ought to live ('περὶ τοῦ ὄντινα τρόπον χρὴ ζῆν').[14] Julia Annas begins her inquiry into the ancient concept of eudaimonia by trying to answer this question. It is primarily a question about one's life as a whole. The answer calls for some degree of introspection about how one has become the person one is: first, 'how past plans, successes and failures have produced the person who now has the present projects and attitudes'; second, where these present projects and attitudes lead to; and, third, whether the end these are leading to is worthy of reaching.[15]

Ancient Greek philosophers viewed 'life as a whole as some kind of unity', since 'the final good unifies and organizes all [...] other aims and goods'. The final end was considered to be both *complete* (i.e., comprehensive; being both the ultimate object of desire and the good that gives shape to all other aims and ends) and *self-sufficient* (i.e., making the life of the agent self-sufficient without needing any further adding into; one that incorporates all subordinate aims, projects and attitudes). Objectivity was introduced into the concept, when what the final end is was associated with what is considered to be the specific function, or the most fundamental facts, of human nature. As Annas points out, 'happiness in ancient theories is given its sense by the role it plays; and the most important role it plays is that *of an obvious, but thin, specification of the final good*.[16] But, what is the exact relation between the final good and other goods? It is either a *collection* of first-order goods or, Annas adds, their connection lies *in the way of collecting* or *using* them—the former being primarily passive, the latter primarily active.[17]

There is thus an underlying assumption that 'action and choice have an end-directed structure'. Deliberating about action and choice refers to the attempt to *bring about* a certain outcome, one that achieves the end sought. For the ancient Greeks, according to Annas, 'our motivations, of all kinds, are so structured that there is something "ultimate" which *forms them into an organized whole* by being the end towards which they all tend'. Reflecting on one's own life as a whole, an agent sets a hierarchy of ends; the successful pursuit of secondary ends will lead—somehow—to the final end.[18] However, Mill criticized Plato for exactly such indeterminacy in his dialogues: '[o]ur life is to be regulated, but we are not told what it is to be regulated by'.[19] Thus, it is not difficult to see why, at fifteen, Mill saw in Bentham a force of novelty, and felt that all previous moralists had been surpassed. The principle of utility could indeed become the keystone to Mill's thought—assuming a place on top of all aims, offering comprehensiveness, stability and objectivity (i.e., an external criterion).

When Mill read the newly published edition of Bekker's *Plato's Works* (1826)—while trying to assert his independency and originality as a thinker[20]—Plato's dialogues and Bentham's works seemed to advance conflicting theses. According to Mill, Plato favored 'the opinion that certain qualities of mind are good or evil in themselves, independently of all considerations of pleasure or pain'[21]—common morality promulgated similar views. However, deep in his 'mental crisis', Mill saw the flaws in Benthamite intellectualism. Moreover, not only was Mill by that time committed in dialectically extracting whatever 'truth' lay at the bottom of conflicting opinions,[22] but also his new influences, his early education having laid the groundwork,[23] brought out the importance of emotional cultivation for virtuous exertion. Eventually, as a way out of crisis, Mill developing a notion of happiness, in which happiness was not pursued directly but indirectly, through character, various projects, and a hierarchy of ends. Though the principle of utility remained at the top those ends, Mill thought the theory of his utilitarian predecessors required a more nuanced psychological basis, i.e., one which captured the importance of 'co-ordination' between thought, feeling and will, i.e., about the importance of character.[24]

The question for Mill was how to incorporate goods, in the jargon of the Greeks, or pleasure, in that of Bentham, and the importance of active self-development in a consistent notion of happiness—with the principle of utility as the keystone of the arch. Recent interpretations argue that Mill failed to achieve such consistency.[25] Such a view asserts that Mill had to choose between a conception of happiness which considered pleasure as the sole of action (the only good) and one in which pleasure as one of the ends of action (one among many goods)—and though he chose the second, he still defined happiness in terms of pleasure and pain. However, it seems that Mill did not think that happiness consisted in a *collection* of first-order goods; rather, he seemed to think that happiness consisted *in the way of collecting* or *using* them,[26] that is a directive rather than an additive conception of happiness.[27] The former offered a 'higher' ground upon which a notion of happiness, that allowed 'gradations in pleasures' and in lives, could be built without inconsistency—unlike his father,[28] John Mill did not merely experiment with such an idea, but tried to make it work.

## Additive and Directive Conceptions of Happiness

The simplest way to define an additive conception of happiness is that 'the more goods you have, the happier you should be'.[29] Several 'ingredients' can then be said to make up happiness, and as Socrates, in Plato's *Euthydemus*, argued, individuals are considered to do and fare well by having *plenty* of those ingredients, i.e., things that are considered to be good (or objects of desire). Thus, typically, when such a notion was articulated, an enumeration of goods ensued, of which greater amounts (or the capacity to acquire greater amounts of those goods) meant more happiness.[30]

Being much more specific, with his typical 'exhaustive method', Bentham moved much further into the discussion regarding the sources and kinds of pleasure.[31] Instead of talking about ingredients, Bentham talked about the pleasures various goods afford. These are the pleasures of sense, wealth, skill, amity, good name, power, piety, benevolence, malevolence, memory, imagination, expectation, the ones dependent on association, of relief—each having a corresponding kind of pain. The value of pleasures depends upon their intensity, duration, certainty, propinquity, fecundity, purity and extent. Bentham's principle of utility points to an additive view of happiness: actions are approved or disapproved according to their tendency to *augment* or to *diminish* happiness.[32] Thus, the additive conception is about sums of pleasures that various goods bestow. Sources of pleasures are not valued in themselves; pleasure is the only thing valuable in itself. Virtue and wisdom, for example, were valuable only in so far as they enabled someone to use goods with skill and intelligence and produce, in some way, more rather than less pleasure.

The famous examples against the claims of hedonism, as they appear in works such as Aldous Huxley's *Brave New World* (1932) and Robert Nozick's *Anarchy, State, and Utopia* (1974), elucidate another aspect of the additive conception: it may be rational for an individual to consume 'soma' and feel pleasure without the prospect of pain or to be hooked on an experience machine and live all through those activities or projects that one finds pleasurable, without actually living them. The pleasure of arriving at happiness by one's own means or the number of people affected would be taken into account, but the intensiveness, duration, certainty, propinquity, fecundity and the purity of pleasure could be made to outweigh all other considerations, suggesting that nothing other than pleasure is valued *for its own sake*. John Mill put it thus: mental over bodily pleasures were indeed preferred in the theory of his utilitarian predecessors; but only because of 'the greater permanency, safety, uncostliness, &c. of the former—that is, in their circumstantial advantages rather than in their intrinsic nature'.[33]

In contrast, in the directive conception of happiness, happiness is determined by rational or intelligent agency which is the source of all proper direction in one's life. But here intelligence receives a different role in life as a whole than the one intelligence or rationality has in additive conceptions. For example in the additive view, wealth can make one happy, but it would make one happier if one used it with intelligence, *ceteris paribus*, rather than ignorance. In the directive view, wealth itself cannot make one happy, no matter how intelligently one uses it, but it can be *part* of a person's happiness given the direction it receives and its place in one's life as a whole. Thus, though happiness depends on the intelligent or virtuous use of goods, happiness still depends on goods. In the latter case, happiness depends on the intelligence of giving goods an appropriate place in one's life, that is, by formulating attitudes and priorities with respect to such goods.[34]

Furthermore, in the additive view, happiness is determined by goods and projects in which one engages in an intelligent way, but in the directive view happiness is determined by the intelligence with which one engages with goods and projects. In the latter, goods and projects 'require direction from a holistic skill of living that grasps all of one's priorities and values and puts them together in the right sort of way'.[35] In the additive view, the ability to calculate what things can be pleasurable and what kind of use produces more pleasure is a very valuable *tool*. Goods, projects and intelligence have extrinsic worth and instrumental roles—once they cease to confer pleasure, they are no longer useful. In the directive view, certain goods, attitudes and projects gain intrinsic worth, as they cannot be dispensed with, even if they no longer have any ostensible usefulness; pleasure itself is not pursued, but rather accompanies a certain way of living.

Perhaps Plato can lend a hand here. In *Euthydemus*, Socrates proposed a definition of happiness with which his interlocutors could concur: having plenty of good things is an indication that one is happy and fares well. But then he argued that good things need to be used, and used in a *right* way, in order to bestow benefit to their possessor: things which people traditionally consider good are intrinsically neither good nor bad. These things become goods with knowledge ('the guide which directed the action')—rational agency is the only good-making property, the only unconditional good; all other things are conditional goods.[36] In *Gorgias*, Socrates argued that 'the goodness of anything, whether implement or body or soul or any living thing, does not best come to it by merely haphazard, but through a certain rightness and order and through the art that is assigned to each of them' (i.e., 'the presence of some excellence'). Things acquire their proper place in one's life, and thus become good, by 'sound-minded' individuals (σώφρονες), when they integrate their various concerns and projects 'into a rational whole'.[37]

# DIRECTION, PLEASURES AND LIVES

For the ancient Greeks how people incorporate their projects into a larger structure of ends was directly related to what kind of persons they are and what kind of life they lead. Lives differ, Daniel Russell argues in reference to Plato, in the ways that the emotional and the appetitive part of the soul co-operate with reason: 'there are ways that it is good to be passionate, and ways that it is good to be desirous'. What is more, it is reason alone that leads passion and desire into such good ways—'their fulfilled and healthy condition'—Russell adds, by finding out how they can function in the best way possible and by actually bringing that way about. The person that leads the best kind of life has managed to harmonize conflicting desires, and, thus, is 'first in happiness'.[38]

According to Mill, the argument that 'reason has a rightful authority over desire and affection' was common. What Mill changed was making utility the 'directive rule' of conduct—setting the rules by which reason guides and governs the desires and affections. However, this claim, with the concurrent definition of happiness as 'pleasure, and the absence of pain', seemed to come into conflict with his acknowledgment of various ingredients of happiness, each being pursued for their intrinsic worth (e.g., virtue, power, fame, wealth), not as means to more pleasure.[39] Thus, any agreement on whether Mill developed a consistent view of happiness diminishes when it comes to question of the role of pleasure in it. Here, I develop the theme of a directive conception of happiness, in search of a conceptual framework in which pleasure retains a central place, while allowing a variety of ends to acquire intrinsic worth.

## Deliberation, Inclusiveness and Mill on Happiness

As we saw, what is at stake is how Mill's notion of happiness incorporates rational agency and pleasure. In this section, I focus on the former. Bentham did not object to viewing life in terms of satisfying long-term, low-risk or even high-brow pleasures, since he considered their value greater.[40] Still, at the bottom, Martha Nussbaum argues, individuals were viewed as 'large containers of sensations of pleasure or satisfaction. Their capacity for agency is of interest only in the sense that it makes them capable of choosing actions that produce utility'.[41]

The same did not seem to be true of Mill. Thus, David Brink, in an excellent paper on Mill's utilitarianism, argues, among other things, that Mill advanced a deliberative view of happiness. It was *deliberative* in the sense that happiness primarily consisted in the exercise of the higher capacities (i.e., distinctively human function), which included the 'capacities for practical deliberation': reflective choice and implementation of structured plans. The content of these plans was important only in so far as it allowed for the exercise of one's higher capacities, i.e., to 'form, revise, assess, choose, and implement one's own set of plans and projects'. Brink argues that Mill's conception was also *objective* in the sense that the preference of competent judges showed that deliberative activities are valuable because of their 'intrinsic nature and independently of their being the object of desire' of any one person in particular; in this way, 'the swine is failing to realize higher pleasures even if he is meeting self-imposed goals and satisfying his own desires'.[42]

Though Mill's language was misleading (i.e., defining happiness in terms of pleasure), Brink notes, it still highlighted his commitment to a type of life of practical deliberation.[43] To explain Mill's misleading language, John Lachs points to conflicting loyalties in Mill. Thus, instead of focusing on those specified features of happiness which make Mill's 'official' conception part of his father's legacy, Lachs shows how Mill 'unofficially' viewed happiness from a holistic point of view—that of a happy life: one that is ordered and meaningful, deriving its value 'from the specific interplay of person and action, the individual, his beliefs and his behaviour'; one that cannot dispense with a condition of liberty which allows for 'an ongoing process of voluntary self-expression, [...] continued generation and appropriation of its actions and acceptance of its fortunes by the self'.[44] Mill's commitment to 'self-realisation' is more marked in Lachs's rather than Brink's analysis, though both bring out the importance of deliberation.

However, it is not as easy as usually asserted to find out at what point James Mill would not be willing to follow his son's notion of happiness. In the *Analysis of the Phenomena of the Human Mind* (1829), the elder Mill defined the pursuit of ends as a matter of *suitably* making *appropriate* associations of ideas. Using the example of writing, he argued that the end or ends of a discourse cannot be achieved without a proper combination of its many subordinate ideas: '[i]f every thing in the discourse tends to the accomplishment of the end, the Discourse is said to be coherent, appropriate, consistent'.[45] This is a striking example because James Mill argued that living requires a similar ordering of ideas—some people actually manage to exhibit such 'steady direction of their actions, through the course of their lives, to some general end, or ends'.[46] Then, happiness, he argued, is said to predominate and control 'the associations in every part of the process'; it is the 'grand suggesting principle' and the 'grand selecting principle'—suggesting which trains of ideas are connected with happiness and selecting which particular ideas can operate as causes to its attainment. This was what it meant to the elder Mill to have control over one's own ideas and actions.[47] Thus, as we saw, happiness consists in pursuing what one 'deliberately approves'.[48] This remarkable similarity between father and son regarding the need for a rational plan of living according to two tests of happiness has been largely ignored. Both Mills thus committed themselves to 'a conception of virtue or the good life, [...] the basic constituent [of which] was an ideal of rationality'.[49] However, if John Mill argued for an 'enlightened' additive notion of happiness, in which rational agency is valuable because the pursuit of pleasure is made more efficient when other things than pleasure are directly pursued as ends, then he departed little, if at all, from his father's utilitarianism.

The younger Mill distinguished between two senses of happiness: the 'humble' and the 'higher' sense. As James Mill had made clear, the former sense reduces 'all the elements of happiness [...] to the simple sensations' of pleasure and pain. For the younger Mill, the latter sense defined the happy life with regard to the kind of life that 'human beings with highly developed faculties can care to have'. John's focus on the 'higher' sense was a conscious choice. Assuming that he had conflicting loyalties makes it easy to refrain from attempting to find consistency in his thought; but he argued that his use of the 'higher' did not conflict with the 'humble' sense.[50] Thus, to do him justice, one must try to find out what he meant.

If someone fails to incorporate reason and emotion in his conception of happiness in a way that pain could *precede* immoral acts, then, Mill argued, 'the man is not really virtuous'. Deliberation about consequences causes pains '*consequent* upon the act', and those who deliberate thus are 'in imminent danger of being lost'. A 'life of circumspect and cautious selfishness' may secure pleasure and freedom from pain, but the life of ideal nobleness of will and conduct, disinterestedly pursed, does more for general happiness. That was the reason why Mill tried to define a 'higher meaning' or find a 'higher ground', even though there was much usefulness in the 'humble' sense of happiness.[51]

This 'higher ground' had much to do with nobility and dignity, the aesthetic aspect of virtue, which Mill found originally in the works of ancient Greeks. To separate him from the parent flock, it is the aesthetic aspect, not the deliberative, of his notion of happiness that needs to be highlighted. Otherwise Mill did not go beyond an 'enlightened' additive notion of happiness: goods (e.g., liberty, security), rationally and hierarchically structured, still 'swell an aggregate'. Though I believe Lachs's and Brink's readings are correct, I simply draw attention to the need to exhibit the difference in *kind* between the additive and the directive conceptions in Mill's view of happiness. It is not enough to point out that John Mill argued for a deliberative notion of happiness—the elder Mill had done so too.

A more promising line of interpretation to Mill's conception of happiness introduced the hermeneutic tools which first appeared in the debate on Aristotle's final good: 'inclusiveness' and 'dominance'. Inclusive ends refer to those ends that combine or include a plurality of goods or those ends that have different components of roughly *equal* value. Dominant ends either refer to those ends that consist of only *one* valued good (strong sense) or those ends that consist of a *plurality* of valued goods, but in which one good is of paramount importance (weak sense).[52]

Robert Hoag argues that Mill defines happiness in 'terms of the successful, long-term *organisation* of some specified element(s) of life'. For Hoag, dominant conceptions (e.g., Bentham's) set life-plans which seek to maximize a single element which is considered to be a superior activity or state of affairs. Inclusive conceptions (e.g., Mill's) define life-plans which harmoniously integrate a plurality of elements of happiness, all being recognized as superior activities or states of affairs.[53] Thus, Mill had a broad notion of means, in which the specified elements of happiness were pursued both as means to happiness and as ends in themselves.[54] The famous passage on the definition of the creed of Utilitarianism, Hoag argues, (drawing on Fred Berger), shows Mill's intent to modify the utilitarian tradition by arguing that the prospect of pleasure is not the *only integral* part of happiness, since people develop desires regardless of consequences. Mill's *Utilitarianism* is thus discussed from the standpoint that Mill provided 'supplementary explanations' which differentiated him from classical utilitarianism.[55]

Hoag is aware that his inclusivist reading does not fit Mill's texts well; but attributes this to 'a fundamental tension within Mill's utilitarianism'. As we saw, Mill thought it possible to have a plurality of ends (moral, prudential, aesthetic) and yet for them to be part of a hierarchy, in which utility served as an umpire. Just as Bentham did, Mill offered a procedure for assigning value to acts and ends by calculating consequences, making the ingredients of happiness comparable and measurable; but, according to Hoag, this created tension between his commitments to pluralism and to Bentham's 'monolithic' end.[56]

Hoag neglects to consider a weak sense of dominance, in which one end is paramount and other ends are non-dominant.[57] First, such a conception anticipates the objection that an inclusivist view of happiness fails to work out conflicts between self-regarding and other-regarding ends.[58] Second, the usefulness of the weak sense of dominance lies in maintaining the connection between happiness and the 'Art of Life'. To use Plato's *Republic* as an example, Socrates, according to Terence Irwin, 'took happiness to comprehend all goods that are worth pursuing': justice was the *dominant* component but it included other goods as non-dominant components and regulated their interaction—as we saw in chapter seven, Mill seemed to hold a similar view.[59] Third, as in Plato's *Republic*, Mill criticized common beliefs about what it means to take happiness to consist in pleasure; common views with respect to the ends of a happy life were granted a hearing (e.g., that there are other ends than 'pleasure'; base pursuits lower human life; certain vital social interests are not to be traded off with 'pleasure'), but it was then admitted that it was necessary to put such beliefs on a proper basis.[60]

Moreover, as we saw, Hoag broadens Mill's conception of happiness so that other things than pleasure can be included in it. Similarly, Geoffrey Scarre cites several scholars in refutation of Roger Crisp's hedonistic reading of Mill.[61] Scarre argues that Mill advanced a eudaimonistic conception of happiness, in which the role of pleasure differed from the role of pleasure in classical utilitarianism. However, Scarre argues that Mill conflated what Aristotle had distinguished: virtue and pleasure were 'categorically different kinds of end'.[62] But Mill followed Plato's, not Aristotle's departments of ends (which indeed recognized pleasure as a distinct end of action). Like in Plato, virtue was defined as a harmonizing, coherent and consistent functioning of the domains of the 'Art of Life'; pleasure was inherent in their harmonious integration, not a distinct kind of end.[63]

Hoag and Scarre ignore Mill's caveat that his 'supplementary explanations' did not affect the end-result of the theory of life of earlier utilitarians. An 'enlightened' additive notion of happiness does confer great value to certain pursuits that many people engage in—even if only for their 'circumstantial advantages'. What is more important, it systemizes and makes coherent the pursuit of happiness. However, as we saw, a 'higher ground' for the principle of utility could be reached, Mill argued, by a 'comprehensive formula' that took under consideration that people seek to achieve happiness in their life, but also that they may have ends other than pleasure. Like in Plato's *Republic*, Mill added an intermediate stage between *means* and *ends*: those goods that are good both for their consequences (leading to happiness) and for their own sake (disinterestedly valued).[64] This may be called an 'intermediate stage' only because of Mill's own Teleology—the 'Art of Life', i.e., his view of the 'doctrine of ends'.[65] But what is more important to note, Mill argued that strictly speaking, 'it is a physical and psychological impossibility to desire anything, except in proportion as the idea of it is pleasant'.[66]

For this reason, instead of broadening his conception of happiness away from pleasure, Mill reconfigured the role of pleasure within it. He built upon his belief that what pleasure and pain meant was, to a great extent, an 'open question'.[67] Brink, Hoag and Scarre argue that Mill identified pleasure as just one of the intrinsic goods that people desire. But this, I intend to argue, was not what Mill did.

Perhaps it is useful to attempt to summarize the argument so far. Mill noted in his *Autobiography* that he came to the conclusion that one's own happiness is not something that one can pursue directly. Though he still considered happiness all-inclusive, it required defining something else rather than pleasure as its dominant component; it was not a distinct end in itself.[68] Here, suffice it to say that Mill introduced to the utilitarian tradition of adding up *sensate* pleasures, i.e., the actual feeling when something is done or happens, Plato's and Aristotle's concept of *modal* pleasures, i.e., the feeling that accompanies activities done in a certain way.[69]

Mill's 'little volume' expanded on the principle of utility—'the directive rule of human conduct'. Utility, Mill argued, provides the rules with which reason guides and governs the desires and affections; but '[r]eason is not an end in itself'. Reason teaches individuals the *right* ends and the *right* way to them—desiring these ends depended on emotional cultivation. Thus, it was important 'to give to the imagination that direction which will exercise the most beneficial influence upon the feelings'.[70] The directive notion of happiness highlights Mill's concern with giving *rational* direction to *feelings* (in accordance with the happiness of mankind) by a self-transformation process, which forms the end of character formation.[71] At the same time, Mill's 'Art of Life' came to provide the same coherence, consistency and hierarchy of ends as that of an 'enlightened' additive conception of happiness, despite a plurality of objects or pursuits desired for their intrinsic worth. Thus, Mill specified that the dominant end both justifies and controls the subordinate ends, without itself being the sole end of all actions.[72] The good that results from pursuits located in the non-dominant domains of ends is not added up to make a person happy; happiness is determined by the structure of those ends in relation to the final end; i.e., in other words, it consists in their harmonious integration in life as a whole. As we saw in the previous chapter, not only did rational agency mean being able to control one's natural instincts, it meant also *enlightening* them—desire itself is passive, but one can come to desire what one wills to desire. In Plato's *Republic*, Socrates argued that reason did not simply restrain or pursue efficiently emotional or appetitive desires but also created desires in pursuit of what was taken to be the overall good. 'Right action', Mill argued, 'must mean something more and other than intelligent action'.[73] Thus, training *behavior to desire the right end* was an essential part of happiness, for both Mill and Plato's Socrates. Unlike the additive view, a directive view of happiness does capture this nuanced distinction—the practitioner of the 'Art of Life' must be *kalos* as well as *phronimos*.[74]

## Linguistic and Psychological Premises of Mill's Theory

This section turns to John Stuart Mill's rather cryptic remarks about ingredients and parts of happiness, since some of Mill's clarifications on means and ends of happiness seem to put into doubt the rejection of the additive conception of happiness suggested here. Interestingly, this is a part of Mill's *Utilitarianism* that classicists turn to with the intention of clarifying some ambiguities in Plato's and Aristotle's conceptions of happiness.[75]

In one of the earliest and most influential attempts to rescue Mill's *On Liberty* from inconsistency, James Bogen and Daniel Farrell have argued that Mill did not take happiness to be a simple mental state, but a 'set of all those things that are intrinsically desirable'.[76] For them, Mill rejected the 'common language' about ends that are competing to happiness; he incorporated these ends (virtue, health, etc.) as parts or ingredients of happiness: 'what is intrinsically desirable on Mill's view is not some one thing—some simple, non-composite whole, that is, such as 'happiness', conceived as a mental or psychological state of some sort—but a whole set or collection of things'.[77] Though Bogen and Farrell are not much concerned with resolving the problems of ranking between goods,[78] they have provided textual evidence suggestive of a utilitarian defence of liberty.

However, Bogen's and Farrell's argument that happiness is a collection of things that are intrinsically good anticipates the contrary position advanced here that Mill was working with a directive notion of happiness. Indeed, in Mill's works we come across phrases such as 'the ingredients of happiness are very various' (e.g., virtue, power, fame, wealth) or that individuality is one of the 'principal ingredients' of happiness. Mill also noted that with the possession of such goods individuals are made happy or 'made unhappy by failure to obtain' them.[79] Given that James Mill also talked about 'ingredients of happiness',[80] it becomes imperative to examine how the talk about ingredients and means and ends affects the proposed interpretation of John Stuart Mill's conception of happiness.

Mill argued that each of the various ingredients of happiness is 'desirable in itself, and not merely when considered as swelling an aggregate'. Even if certain goods or ends are desired for their own sake (independently of pleasure) they remain parts of a person's happiness. Thus, he argued that, first, these 'ingredients' are not to be understood simply as 'means to a *collective something* termed happiness'; happiness, Mill noted, 'is not an *abstract idea*, but a *concrete whole*'. These remarks pointed to the adoption of a particular terminology with regard to happiness, on which Mill did not expand in *Utilitarianism*, but in *A System of Logic*. Second, he argued that some people become happy by the possession of such goods or think they would be happy by their possession, adding however, *depending on their associations*—an aspect of his theory on which his *Utilitarianism* did expand.[81]

As we saw in chapter six, Mill, 'cast in the mould of [Plato's] dialectics', was in the habit of attempting to clarify the meaning vague generalities—utility, justice, theory, interest, nationality, etc.—by cross-examining the 'commonplaces of received opinion' (and their respective 'bundles of associations' which were created 'under the guidance of popular phraseology'). The reason for doing so was that individuals, 'becoming aware of [their] ignorance, [they] might be put in the way to attain a stable belief, resting on a clear apprehension both of the meaning of doctrines and of their evidence'.[82] The name 'happiness' called for a similar clarification. Though I have already suggested why such a clarification was necessary, James Mill's *Analysis of the Phenomena of the Human Mind*— and John Mill's comments on his father's views—may make it more explicit.

James Mill argued that we create classes, for convenience's sake, of objects (considered either synchronically or successively) and of feelings: 'Experience teaches what sort of grouping answers the purposes of naming best; under the suggestions of that experience, the application of a general word *is tacitly and without much of reflection regulated*[.]'[83] However, John Stuart Mill argued that the application of general names should not be regulated 'tacitly and without much of reflection', except in those cases when the objects grouped together resemble each other obviously. As he noted, 'there are other resemblances which are not superficially obvious; and many are not brought to light except by long experience, or observation carefully directed to the purpose.' As these 'more recondite resemblances are often those which are of greatest importance to our interests', careful analysis is indispensable.[84] The meaning of general terms—'as a vehicle of the communication'—is not found in the multitude of distinct simple ideas that each individual super-adds to the association of a complex idea which a general name denotes, but in the 'association common to all', that is in 'the nucleus of more closely associated ideas, which is the constant element in the complex idea of the class, both in the same mind at different times, and in different minds'.[85] In *Utilitarianism* Mill tried to define the 'nucleus' of the complex idea of happiness.

In the passages from *Utilitarianism* quoted earlier Mill used three different phrases in reference to happiness ('collective something', 'abstract idea' and 'concrete whole'), trying to explain how virtue or fame or wealth, etc. become 'desired and desirable in and for themselves; besides being means, they are a part of the end'. What he meant was not readily evident in *Utilitarianism*, but Mill's theory of names developed in his *Logic* did define these terms.[86] The focus is on the individual who 'is made, or thinks he would be made, happy by its mere possession; and is made unhappy by failure to obtain it'—i.e., the possession of virtue, fame or wealth.

According to Mill, names can be general or singular, concrete or abstract, connotative or non-connotative, positive or negative, relative or absolute and can be employed univocally or equivocally. With regard to the first 'fundamental' distinction, that between general and singular names, Mill argued that a general name 'is capable of being truly affirmed, in the same sense, of each of an indefinite number of things', whereas a singular or individual name 'is only capable of being truly affirmed, in the same sense, of one thing'. Therefore, the name 'soldier' can be assigned to an indefinite number of individuals, all possessing those qualities which the word 'soldier' expresses, whereas the name 'Paul' does not express certain qualities which are said to be possessed by all those individuals who bear that name.

Furthermore, Mill noted that general names may be distinguished from collective names. A collective name can be predicated by taking all individual instances together, whereas a general name 'can be predicated of *each* individual of a multitude'. However, the aforesaid multitude can be a multitude of collective names. To use Mill's example, the 76th regiment is a collective name, as it is 'predicated of a multitude of individual soldiers taken jointly'—Privates John, Private Paul, Private George (and so on up to a thousand soldiers) are the 76th regiment— but 'it cannot be predicated of them severally'—i.e., 'Private John is the 76th regiment'. The name 'regiment' is both a general name and a collective name: 'General with respect to all individual regiments, of each of which separately can be affirmed: collective with respect to the individual soldiers of whom any regiment is composed'.

As we saw, Mill said happiness is not a collective something —as such it is not predicated to a multitude of individuals, taken together (as it was in the case of the 76th regiment). John may be happy because he is wealthy, famous or virtuous.[87] But this does not mean that John's happiness tell us everything about what is included in the name happiness. Paul may have nothing of these individual elements and still we can predicate as 'happy'—just like we can speak of the 77th regiment, which does not have Privates John, Private Paul, Private George, but Private Ringo and Private Pete. Happiness as a collective and a general name (as in the case of 'regiment') predicates John's happiness (76th regiment), Paul's happiness (77th regiment), George's happiness (78th regiment), and an indefinite number of such instances. However, as such, these collective names may differ in what individual elements they take together (as regiments have different individual soldiers), but still they express certain qualities which enable us to predicate them with the same name (i.e., regiment)—John is happy; Paul is happy; George is happy.

The last remark above brings us to the second and third phrases Mill used. Mill was clear that abstract names are names of *attributes* of subjects; concrete names are names of subjects. Thus, while one might take happiness to name an attribute, Mill specifically said that it is a 'concrete whole', not an 'abstract idea'. Thus, as a concrete name, which is also a general and collective name, happiness is a connotative name. Connotative names denote subjects, and imply attributes:

> The word white, denotes all white things, as snow, paper, the foam of the sea, &c., and implies [...] the attribute whiteness. The word white is not predicated of the attribute, but of the subjects, snow, &c.; but when we predicate it of them, we convey the meaning that the attribute whiteness belongs to them. The same may be said of the other words above cited. Virtuous, for example, is the name of a class, which includes Socrates, Howard, the Man of Ross, and an undefinable [sic] number of other individuals, past, present, and to come. These individuals, collectively and severally, can alone be said with propriety to be denoted by the word: of them alone can it properly be said to be a name. But it is a name applied to all of them in consequence of an attribute which they are supposed to possess in common, the attribute which has received the name of virtue.

Similarly, happiness denotes a class of particular subjects, but also connotes that these possess certain attributes in common. In this way, Mill could maintain that despite differences in the peculiar circumstances of individuals (John who is famous; Paul who is wealthy; George who is virtuous), they can still be predicated with the name 'happy'. But what are those shared qualities or attributes which are implied by the name 'happiness'? These individuals are called 'happy' 'either because the consciousness of [fame, wealth, virtue] is a pleasure, or because the consciousness of being without [them] is a pain, or for both reasons united'.[88] Thus, pleasure is the connective link which unites the different *testimonies* of what constitutes happiness—i.e., it is the 'constant element', the 'nucleus' of the complex idea of happiness.

In the second case noted at the start of this section, i.e., the psychological premise, father and son followed the same line of argument: associationism. For example, John Mill argued that it was consistent with the utilitarian psychological theory to accept that virtue is 'a good in itself, without looking to any other end beyond it'. Mill was not hiding behind 'vague generalities'— experience showed that money, power or even fame become paramount ends for some individuals, irrespective of the pleasures they bestow. Though Mill also mentioned reasons why virtue is to be preferred, he tried to stress that the laws of association show how things other than pleasure can become desired for their own sake.[89] Still, since some things, though instrumental to the final end, are desired for their intrinsic rather than extrinsic worth alone, one needs to differentiate between final vs. instrumental and intrinsic vs. extrinsic ends.

Again, James Mill's *Analysis* succinctly defined the 'psychological law' mentioned:

> It is [...] to be observed, that when a grand cause of pleasures has been associated with a great many pleasures, and a great many times, the association acquires a peculiar character and strength. The idea of the cause, as cause, is so lost among the innumerable ideas of the pleasures combined with it, that it seems to become the idea of pleasure itself.[90]

Similarly, John Mill argued, some human actions that are sources of pleasure to our own selves and others become 'inclosed in a web of associated ideas of pleasures or of pains at a very early period of life' and, thus, become disinterested (i.e., desired independently 'of any pleasures or pains actually expected to result to ourselves'). Thus, to the person of confirmed virtue (and 'all those who pursue deliberately and consistently any determinate end'), 'the habitual act of will in [some] individual instance is not in contradiction to the general intention prevailing at other times, but *in fulfilment* of it'.[91]

As we saw, the life of the practitioner of the 'Art of Life' went 'further than all things else towards making human life happy'. However, Mill did not deny the belief of his utilitarian precursors that disinterested sympathy and moral feelings 'were the greatest and surest sources of happiness'.[92] But he did point out that pursuing ends solely for their 'circumstantial advantages' ran the risk of ultimately reducing the utilitarian notion of happiness to psychological egoism.

Like Socrates in Plato's *Republic*, Mill in order to maintain that individual choices, when they are 'in fulfilment' of a noble character, reflect the higher quality inherent in certain (superior) activities (which other competent individuals concur in denoting them as such) had to prove that ends desired for their own sake (irrespective of pleasure), formed part of the desire for happiness.[93] As we saw, final ends are pursued for the sake of no other end and are valuable under all conditions. All other ends are extrinsically valuable, as their goodness depends upon certain conditions. For Mill, as in Plato, the conditions to be met are *conduciveness* and *right order* in relation to the final end.[94] When the association of such ends to the final end receives 'peculiar character and strength', extrinsically valued ends acquire *also* intrinsic value. As they become objectively good, their goodness does not depend on the condition of instrumentality—a 'noble character' thus is not pursued because it is pleasant.

Thus, the instrumental vs. final distinction implies the *way* in which one values things; the extrinsic vs. intrinsic distinction involves specific conditions in which things become objectively good.[95] Mill argued that the former was invoked only in cases of conflict of the latter kind of ends.[96] As we saw, there are three kinds of secondary ends that acquire intrinsic value: moral, expedient and aesthetic ends. But since these ends are not *originally* or *naturally* unconditionally good, they can conflict under some conditions. In such cases, their value is re-examined in reference to the final end, which serves as an umpire; then, some type of action assumes a position of superiority. For an example, one may pursue excellence for its own sake, but when such a pursuit conflicts with claims of justice by others (as in the case of Callicles' superhuman in Plato's *Gorgias*), to resolve the conflict one needs to invoke the instrumental vs. final distinction in order to find their respective place with regard to the final end of the 'Art of Life'.

## Pleasures, Lives and Happiness

Many students of Mill's works agree that he attempted on several occasions to dissociate both himself and the 'creed' of Utilitarianism from the 'school of Bentham'.[97] However, Mill's 'supplementary explanations' about pleasure remain a source of great dissension among them, not least because of his attempt to define a 'higher ground' for utilitarianism: one that was neither 'impracticably dry when the word utility precedes the word pleasure' nor 'too practicably voluptuous when the word pleasure precedes the word utility'.[98] It is suggested here that Mill argued primarily for the pleasure derived from different kinds of life; but the best kind of life was, at the same time, the pleasantest. This argument led Paul Shorey to claim that Mill's *Utilitarianism* had directly adopted the argument of Plato's *Republic*.[99]

Pleasure, Hoag argues, is not the only thing desirable according to Mill, because in his early critique of Bentham, he argued that some ends are not pursued in the *prospect* of pleasure.[100] However, what Mill specified was that individuals choose not to pursue certain ends because they recoil 'from the very thought of committing the act'. The prospect of pleasure is indeed absent (and, therefore, not desirable), but *pain* prevents virtuous individuals from '*dwell[ing] upon* it long enough to have even the physical power of perpetrating the crime'. The associations of virtuous individuals are too strong on the side of morality; a healthy mental state prevents them from committing anything contrary to it. Hoag ignored the importance that utilitarians assigned to the absence of pain.[101]

Hoag further argues that pleasure was just one of the parts of happiness that are intrinsically valuable.[102] However, Hoag fails to make his case consistent with Mill's belief that 'all desirable things [...] are desirable either for the pleasure inherent in themselves, or as means to the promotion of pleasure and the prevention of pain'. The discussion on Mill's linguistic and psychological theory affirmed the pervasive role of pleasure, even when individuals come to desire things irrespective of their being sources of pleasure. Mill's psychological theory allowed him to argue that some 'desire what they will'. For example, virtuous persons create habits of willing irrespective of the prospect of pleasure or pain—but the consciousness of being virtuous remains a source of pleasure to them as much as becoming vicious is a source of pain.[103]

The last point above is connected to Mill's claim that certain pleasurable states of consciousness, like the ones experienced by pigs, 'do not satisfy a human being's conception of happiness'—a similar discontinuity exists within the human species (i.e., some confound *contentment* with *happiness*). The discontinuity of perception is produced by either the sensation itself or the attributes of pleasurable objects, since different kinds of objects cause different sensations. Still, the shared attribute 'pleasantness' includes facts about both the quality and the quantity (in some relational sense) of the sensation pleasant things excite.[104]

A theory on the 'fundamental law' of pleasure, Mill argued, must be able to account for why some things, having a level of intensity which makes other things pleasant, fail to excite pleasure; saying the right kind of object if experienced in a right kind of way causes pleasure is not enough: pleasure or pain is made to depend on 'the perfect or imperfect action of the sense, when there was no criterion of imperfect or perfect action except that it produced pain or pleasure'. Searching for the 'law' by which the phenomena of pleasure and pain 'are governed in all their manifestations' seems to be searching for a unity of cause, where there may be a multitude of different causes.[105] A better theory, Mill thus argued, needs to account for qualitative as well as quantitative differences. But his *Utilitarianism* did little to clarify this dichotomy. Like Francis Hutcheson more than a century earlier, Mill saw no reason to deny the 'reality' of kinds of pleasures.[106] In the *Logic*, Mill argued that if the difference felt in the sensation is a question of degree, then the difference is quantitative: one gallon is felt to be different from ten gallons of water; a gallon of water is felt to be the same with a gallon of wine, when all that matters is volume. The difference is qualitative when the difference felt is a question of the nature of the object. The only way to feel qualitative differences lies in the sensation objects excite; this is all that can be proved. Ten gallons of water and a gallon of wine differ both quantitatively and qualitatively. Superiority, which is just one form of relation, involves questions about both objects as well as the percipient.[107]

Mill argued that kinds are divided by 'an unfathomable chasm' that cannot be bridged.[108] Hoag correctly infers that 'not all persons are equally qualified to sort things into kinds'; people with natural aptitude, equipped with sufficient capabilities of observation, memory and 'extensive experience' know the difference by 'observation and experiment upon the kind itself'.[109] The preference of competent percipients is *evidence* of which kind of two pleasures is more valuable, having experienced both (i.e., drawing on their sensation, emotions, thoughts and volitions)—the criterion is the actual experience itself.[110]

Like most of his contemporary critics, seldom do students of Mill's *Utilitarianism* today consult any other of his works to decrypt his brief remarks about kinds of pleasures. This has resulted in widely different interpretations about Mill's definitions of 'quantity' and 'quality'. The meaning of 'quality' and its relation to 'quantity' is frequently considered to make or break Mill's case for consistency. There are, of course, some who disagree. Hoag, for example, is puzzled by the recent revisionist attempts to illustrate the centrality of qualities of pleasures to Mill's moral theory.[111] This is a legitimate claim to make for someone who, as we saw, defines happiness as an inclusive end, of which pleasure is but one part. Though this is not the place for a detailed stock-taking of every argument on this aspect of Mill's thought, the discussion of some recent readings brings out some of the dangers of attempting to reconcile eudaimonia with utility, i.e., downgrading pleasure, without a suitable conceptual framework.

Usually Mill's agreement with Bentham's definition of happiness as pleasure is made only nominal: scholars argue that Mill, like Aristotle, 'holds certain activities intrinsically desirable because they are pleasures (i.e., for the pleasure inherent in them, as opposed to the mental state produced by them)'; a happy life is made up by a variety of activities, each intrinsically desirable, and not by pleasurable mental states. Thus, scholars such as Ben Saunders and David Brink draw on Aristotle's *Nicomachean Ethics* to argue that activities are pleasures.[112] However, this interpretation of Aristotle is in no way uncontested. I agree with those who read Aristotle to argue that pleasures *complete* or *perfect* activities.[113] As Francis Sparshott notes, 'when conditions are right, pleasure "completes" activity, not by any *causal contribution* [...] *pleasure is no more and no less separable from its associated activity* than beauty is from the physical features of the beautiful person'. Thus, pleasure accompanies an activity done in a certain way, which makes clear, not why someone does it, but why that activity prevents them from desiring to do anything else.[114] In contrast, Roger Crisp notes the ambiguity in Mill's text and reads 'pleasure'—drawing on the utilitarian tradition—as the actual pleasurable experience, not as a pleasure-source activity.[115]

Mill was aware that the term 'pleasure' denotes 'indiscriminately the sensation and the attribute'. However, drawing on Plato and Aristotle, one can distinguish between sensate and modal pleasures which can assist in the attempt to examine the bearing of higher and lower pleasures on Mill's theory.[116] Sensate pleasures 'are the feelings that result from what is done or happens'.[117] This is an example of what Mill called a 'bodily feeling' ('the class of feelings which are immediately occasioned by bodily states'). In contrast, modal pleasures refer to feelings that result from things that are done or happen in a certain way. This is an example of 'complex emotion', formed by a coalition of several simple pleasures or pains, of which it is the result without being the aggregate, or in any respect homogeneous with them. The product, in these cases, is generated by its various factors; but the factors cannot be reproduced from the product.[118]

Furthermore, Roderick Long argues that Mill considered the pleasantness of a noble character to provide the quantitative superiority to higher pleasures. However, as we saw, Mill argued that indications of involuntary feelings rather than actions reveal a person's character. Thus, pleasures cannot be identified with activities; exercising one's higher capacities does not automatically turn one into a noble being or to someone capable of experiencing the higher pleasures. Though I agree with Long's argument that '[w]e choose to be a certain kind of *person*, namely, one who chooses the higher pleasures', Mill did not say that 'one chooses the higher pleasures as a *result* of' a noble character. To my understanding, Mill seems to mean that a person makes choices, acts and takes pleasure in certain things *in fulfillment* of a noble character, as some activities grow to be pleasurable and some cease to be so, but done by habit.[119] If pleasure 'inevitably ensues' when certain conditions are met and one of the conditions is that actions are in fulfilment of a noble character—'not imposing upon him by *express definition*, a prescribed mode of action'[120]—then pleasure neither is a distinct nor the sole end of action. Pleasure does not accompany the exercise of the higher capacities of all, but of those who lead a higher 'mode of existence'.[121] This does not mean that these individuals either experience all the higher pleasures or none at all. As was already noted, the position of superiority of a given kind of pleasure has to do with the recipient's experiences—for some, 'the pleasures of the intellect' (i.e., solving a mathematical problem) may rank higher than the pleasures 'of the feelings and imagination' (i.e., reading Kavafis) or even 'of the moral sentiments' (i.e., volunteering at a homeless shelter).[122]

I have been arguing that in order to understand properly Mill's conception of happiness, Mill's notion of an 'Art of Life' and character formation as the cultivation of virtue must be granted an integral role in it. As we saw, in Mill's 'Art of Life', the right conditions of certain ends depend on their having a rational structure in proportion to their conduciveness to the *telos*. This criterion of rational deliberation was common in the utilitarian tradition. But, at the same time, not only are ends required to be hierarchically structured, but also they must form part of a kind of life that enables individuals to enjoy the highest of pleasures. Pleasure was an inevitable concomitant of the activities 'in fulfilment' of the higher lives, but the final 'product' was irreducible to its originating factors. In this way, given that human life is neither infinite nor homogeneous, a person's happiness depends on which ends dominate her/his mode of living and on what kind of individual one is (i.e., what pleasures a person becomes capable of experiencing and evaluating).

Mill was thus clear that we come to know that a pleasure is 'higher' by the verdict of competent judges, who prefer the enjoyment of those activities that exercise their higher (realized) capacities.[123] It made sense for Mill to talk about qualitative superiorities, since pleasures of a lower kind could never be preferred to those of a higher kind, as an 'unfathomable chasm' which 'cannot be bridged' keeps the two kinds apart.[124] He accepted no trade-offs between happiness and 'grades of existence', since beings of *lower* grades of existence are incapable of true happiness. Mill seemed indeed to draw on Plato's *Republic*: Socrates had argued that only the philosophical life (which develops the highest faculties) can produce the pleasures of happiness, and not what *appears* as happiness.[125] Thus, neither did Plato's Socrates nor Mill accepted that a person could exchange a 'higher' for a 'lower' kind of life, in 'promise of the fullest allowance' of the pleasures of the latter.[126] Similarly, Socrates had also argued that only philosophers are capable of experiencing the *true* pleasures and, thus, they are the most competent to decide which pleasures *are* preferable, and, as such, *ought* to be more desired in a happy life as a whole.[127]

Since Mill argued that only 'observation and experiment upon the kind itself' creates the ability to form preferences, and since this experimentation needs to accord with the conditions of the 'Art of Life' (conduciveness and right order with regard to the final end), experiments in living seem to be the only way.[128] However, there is always the danger of failing to choose distant goods because of 'infirmity of character'. Some 'pursue sensual indulgences to the injury of health though perfectly aware that health is the greater good'; others try with all their powers 'for everything noble' but 'as they advance in years sink into indolence and selfishness'.[129] This is the reason why character formation as the cultivation of virtue (training behavior to desire the right end) is equally important. Thus, only a process of self-discovery and self-transformation allows individuals to develop different modes of life, which will then enable them to experience different kinds of pleasure.

## CONCLUDING REMARKS

Mill argued that defining happiness as the end of life does not mean 'a life of rapture; but moments of such, in an existence made up of few and transitory pains, many and various pleasures, with a decided predominance of the active over the passive, and having as the foundation of the whole, not to expect more from life than it is capable of bestowing'.[130] Happiness does not consist in *adding up* pleasurable incidents, activities or various other elements without apparent end; happiness is found in life as a whole, one whose secondary ends are pursued for their own sake and form part of the final end—pleasure inevitably follows a certain mode of acting rather than being pursued as a distinct end.[131]

Pleasure is rationally incorporated in the virtuous life, by being inherent in the actions that are in fulfilment of the virtuous life, i.e., in the exercise of the higher capacities. This 'function' entails all that is distinctively human. That is why a predominance of higher pleasures can lead to a higher mode of life which is preferable to a life in which lower pleasures predominate. The higher pleasures may of course vary. What is more important, like in Plato's *Philebus*, Mill pointed to the need for a 'mixed life'.[132] This was a life in which 'higher' predominate over 'lower' pleasures as much as 'active' over 'passive' pleasures. A life of passive pleasures does not meet Mill's criteria for varied activities which require effort and concentration and actions that test one's character and skill—not even when they are higher pleasures and intrinsically valuable or when they are not appreciated in lower kinds of life.[133] But in any case, Mill was right in arguing that his analysis was consistent with the traditional utilitarian theory.

Direction comes from the higher capacities of human nature, just like in Plato's *Republic*, in which the 'rational part of the soul' provided direction in accordance to the final end (through a holistic skill of living), by *guiding* existent as well as *creating* new desires. However, the pursuit of 'rational desires' (e.g., loving virtue disinterestedly) demands emotional cultivation to attach ourselves to what he have reason to value.[134] The higher kinds of life are associated with a strong *sense of dignity*, which makes it imperative that nothing that conflicts with the chosen mode of life can be desirable except momentarily. Individuals who cannot rationally structure their pursuits for the sake of a 'greater expediency' are incapable of happiness, even though they may experience many pleasures.[135]

Thus, Mill's *Utilitarianism* complemented his *On Liberty*; as John Gray notes, 'the forms of happiness which are almost distinctively human are unachievable except against a background of autonomy and security'.[136] Virtue was a higher pleasure, sitting high on Mill's hierarchy, as it presupposed the fulfillment of the ideals of self-development and self-government—a fulfillment contingent upon suitable social conditions. Not only is the consciousness of leading such a life a source of pleasure itself; but it also brings about the dominant end of the 'Art of Life'.[137] Its value for the utilitarian did not consist in that it was 'perfected' by pleasure, but because such a life was the best security for general happiness—but being perfected by (higher) pleasure made this mode of life preferable to those who experienced it. Scholars have suggested that when Mill argued that certain states of being are good for their own sake, he had abandoned the hedonistic premise of his utilitarian predecessors. However, Mill's conception of utility, as his linguistic and psychological theory suggests, appeared to be consistent with his 'qualitative hedonism'.

Trying to explain Mill's argument that 'not all pleasures are equally valuable *when considered in relation to their possessor's happiness*',[138] Fred Berger has pointed to 'autonomy' and 'security' as the two permanent elements of Mill's notion of happiness. The first refers to an individual's sense of being her/his own person and of developing one's life as one chooses; the second refers to the sense that others fulfil the rules of justice and respect our rights. Their being associated with certain human capabilities, requirements and needs makes them *natural* goods. In contrast, *acquired* goods are those which *become* requisites for happiness when an individual moves beyond any association to pleasure and pursues them for their own sake (e.g., virtue).[139] However, Roger Crisp has very thoroughly showed how Mill refused to conceive nobleness of character independently of enjoyableness—a requirement which makes Mill's conception hedonistic. Enjoyment, then, seems to be a *natural* good; which makes *acquired* goods, goods only if they are also enjoyable, or, at least, not overall painful. Regardless of its being higher or lower, Crisp maintains, pleasure remains the only good-making property; a pleasure is valuable, not because it is higher, but because it is still a pleasure—it is preferable to lower pleasures, and that is why is more valuable.[140]

Thus, Mill, like in Plato, seemed to argue that people in their lives always seek a surplus of pleasure over pain; and, again like in Plato, Mill tried to prove that the virtuous life was preferable to the vicious life, *even* when all that matters is pleasure.[141] In *Utilitarianism*, Mill tried to focus on the intrinsic worth of rational agency, virtue and ways of living, which left unclear the relation of pleasure and happiness. Crisp is more likely to prove that Mill was a hedonist, when all that matters are goods—either natural or acquired. In an additive notion of happiness, the hedonist holds the vantage ground. Crisp noted that when Mill posed virtue as an end in itself, he actually meant the 'enjoyable experience' of being virtuous or acting virtuously;[142] and, after all, Mill was well aware of the long tradition on the importance of pleasure. In the very first sentences of Bentham's *Introduction to the Principles of Morals and Legislation*, we read: 'Nature has placed mankind under the governance of two sovereign masters, *pain* and *pleasure*. It is for them alone to point out what we ought to do, as well as to determine what we shall do'.[143]

As we saw, Plato's dialogues did not deny the importance of pleasure, pain and desire; human nature depended upon these more than upon anything else.[144] In Plato, the life of a virtuous person was argued to be the most pleasant mode of life; anyone who experienced the higher modes of life would indeed prefer them to the rest.[145] Mill also accepted that the happiest life must be the most pleasant, as there is a limit to the pleasures that the contented life (the one comprised predominantly of lower pleasures) is susceptible to, whereas the higher pleasures, especially aesthetic ones, were considered to be limitless.[146] By such premises, the conclusion seems to be necessarily hedonistic.

Mill argued that '[a]ll acts suppose certain dispositions, and habits of mind and heart, which may be in themselves states of enjoyment or of wretchedness'. However, not all acts may form part of a *character* that is essentially excessive or 'essentially deficient in some quality eminently conducive to the "greatest happiness"'.[147] When pleasure guides action, actions, more frequently than not, conflict; thus, living requires setting a rational principle to provide structure and a method of resolving conflicts. When pleasure receives its proper place in someone's life, it rather accompanies or completes it, as opposed to guiding it.

Mill's critique of Bentham indicated that the discussion regarding pleasure and pain was not a simple one and that character needed to be awarded a central place in the utilitarian conception of happiness.[148] But since not only do pleasures denote sensations (i.e., caused by certain objects), but they also denote affective attitudes toward things (i.e., how a person is disposed to feel experiencing certain things),[149] pleasures are not unconditionally good. It is the right pleasure if and only if it is about the right thing. In a complex emotion, pleasure may either be added or even removed.[150] A self-developed, self-regulated individual takes pleasure in pursuits guided by moral, prudential and aesthetic ends; but the condition of their goodness is supplied by social happiness. Thus, the happiness of mankind, the final end, is an aggregate of those 'happy' individuals, who train their behavior to desire to be part of a class of individuals, whose mode of life promotes the 'permanent interests of man as a progressive being'.[151]

Mill did not question the common belief that reason has authority over pleasures and desires. However, he was not so easily persuaded about which rule or rational principle should guide and govern the desires and affections: '[t]he point in dispute is [...] whether we ought to take the feelings as we find them, as accident or design has made them, or whether the tendency of actions to promote happiness affords a test to which the feelings of morality should conform.'[152] It was here that the 'Art of Life' entered the discussion: feelings need to be shaped and directed toward the pursuit of the secondary ends of action as ends in themselves. The principle of utility intervenes only to correct any disharmony. As I have been arguing, to be able to pursue certain ends for their own sake, people need to make them their 'own'. Not only is there a danger that things that have been singled out by the society as valuable are not valuable for some individuals, more importantly, unless people come to value them as part of their own nature, as an expression of their individuality and in fulfilment of their character, their attachment will only be artificial and superficial; conflicts with other goods will then certainly ensue.

So did Mill believe that one's own pleasure *brings* good direction or *requires* good direction in one's life as whole? I have argued the latter. As long as action is rationally structured in relation to the final end and in fulfilment of 'an ideal nobleness of will and conduct', pleasure need not be the dominant end. Thus, Mill's notion of happiness was of a *holistic* nature, and a calculation of pleasures and pains could not account for all the aspects of our lives—'our choices, our pursuits, our relationships, our fears and emotions'. Similarly, for Plato, D.C. Russell argues, 'it is the wholeness, completeness, and integration of the entire person that makes for happiness'— it depends on a person's whole existence and not just a facet of it.[153] I have argued that the same was true of Mill.

Socrates, in Plato's *Republic*, argues that judging between types of lives (and pleasure) requires experience, intelligence and discussion. In Mill's terms, it rests on the judgment of competent judges; judges that are familiar with the pleasures of each type of life.[154] Given these conditions, only members of the first type of life, i.e., 'the lovers of wisdom' can have an authoritative say on which life is the most pleasurable. Because, of all three types, only they have the experience, intelligence and dialectical ability to distinguish between kinds of pleasures. They are the only ones capable to experience the highest types of pleasures— either those of 'the intellect, of the feelings and imagination, and of the moral sentiments'—since the rest are inexperienced in true pleasure.[155] Though the poet may not find as much pleasure as a mathematician in solving a mathematical problem, but both leading higher mode of existence, in their own way, add to the happiness of mankind.

By distinguishing between pleasures of the soul and those of the body, Socrates, like Mill, sought to find which one is more suitable for the nature of each type of human life.[156] From the premise that mind rather than body is more real and that the pleasures of the mind rather than those of the body are more real, Socrates reaches the conclusion that the pleasures of the mind rather than those of the body will be more satisfying. Only pleasures of the mind can offer a real fulfilment and actualization to human beings.[157] Rather than being discarded, pleasure is rationally incorporated into the higher type of life—higher pleasure is associated with a higher type of living. Thus, these kinds of pleasure are comparable and measurable and the pleasures of the mind always rank higher than the pleasures of the body. These considerations point to a life which at the same time enjoys more dignity, beauty and excellence;[158] one which no one would willingly give up for a lower kind of life.[159]

The 'Art of Life' refers primarily to a mode of life, which is reasoned, principled or contemplated upon and impossible to disconnect from practice or activity—in short, it is a theory of life that requires the agent to test the validity and viability of its principles through actions and life itself. Mill's works expanded on such a theory of life, in which 'truth' and character were very important, as the first was connected with the validity of the theory, and the second with its viability, i.e., sufficiently associating happiness, the final end, with its moral, prudential and aesthetic means, by making them ends in themselves. Mill did not develop the 'Art of Life' as a strategy to gain happiness—as we saw, he considered such a strategy to undermine happiness itself, which is perhaps the reason why he set the elevation of character as a 'paramount end' in life as a whole.[160]

Unlike Plato's Socrates, Mill distinguished three departments of ends that account for a complete existence and not just one; however, for Mill, a virtuous character was a mode of life, one that harmonized all three departments of ends—even if individuals moved in different directions—that is, moral, prudential and aesthetic ways of living. Thus, Mill's conception of happiness does not seem to refer to a 'whole set or collection of things',[161] in which virtue or individuality are parts just like wealth and health may be. There is a rational principle that judges the agent's relation to, and use of, these things and directs her/his actions; a rational principle which is manifested in the agent's character, and which rationally structures her/his course of life in relation to the final end. Lewis Campbell was thus right to argue that Mill's utilitarianism was able to comprehend the subtleties of Plato's conception of the Good.[162]

The directive notion of happiness reflects the pervasive role of pleasure, a role that revisionist interpretations reject, out of fear of giving in to a view of happiness according to which dignity, beauty and excellence have a place solely as means to an end. I have argued that Mill, like some of Plato's dialogues,[163] argued that the choice was between kinds of lives rather than kinds of pleasures. Again like in Plato, this choice was achieved through a master art that harmonized the domains of morality, prudence and aesthetics,[164] through stable dispositions of character, which direct one's feelings and desires in accordance to reason. As Marcus Singer underlines: '[t]he goal of all this activity, or one main goal, is to make the world "all that, if will and knowledge were not wanting, it might easily be made"',[165] that is, a place where individual happiness flourishes.

## NOTES

1. Sidgwick, 1907:94. See also, Bain, 1882b:113-4; Bradley, 1876:108; Moore, 1903:62; Green, 1906:183-5. See further, Schneewind, 1976.
2. Williams, 1996; Irwin, 1998.
3. Irwin, 1998:456.
4. Williams, 1996:6.
5. See also, J. Mill to J. Bentham, 28/07/1812 (in Bain, 1882a:119-20. See also, Bentham, 1838-43:X.472-3).
6. *A*:I.48-9, 68-9 (italics added). As Kinzer (2007:18) notes, Bentham's 'transformative' effect on Mill suggests that Mill's education had not been doctrinaire (i.e., 'rigidly Benthamite').

7. Nussbaum, 2004:61. See also, Nussbaum, 2005; Williams, 1996; Saunders, 2010.

8. Bentham, 1802:I.1-5; *A*:I.67.

9. Bentham, 1802:I.1-5; 1996:38-41.

10. Bentham, 1802:I.27, 29-30.

11. *U*:X.205; *A*:I.66-7.

12. See *A*:I.48-9 for Mill's early inculcation in the Socratic virtues.

13. Annas, 1993:47-84.

14. Plato, *Rep*:352d.

15. Annas, 1993:27-9. See also, Cooper, 1986:92, 96.

16. Annas, 1993:46 (italics added). See further, Plato, *Phl*:20d-1a.

17. Annas, 1993:30, 35-8. See also, Copper, 1986:96-7, 97n6.

18. Annas, 1993:30, 35-8 (italics added).

19. GP:XI.420.

20. *A*:I.122-3.

21. Pr:XI.61.

22. See also, sCo:XXVI.319; SA[1]:XXII.234.

23. See Loizides, 2012.

24. B:X.90 (also, RBP:X.18n); *A*:I.137ff.

25. E.g., Williams, 1996:14; Nussbaum, 2004:62; Saunders, 2010:52.

26. For the distinction in Mill, see *PPE*:II.105.

27. For the present task, Daniel C. Russell's (2005) distinction between additive and directive notions of happiness itself is important, rather than his rendering of Plato's view based on this distinction.

28. J. Mill, *CPB*:IV.4v-6r. See further, chapter three.

29. Annas, 1993:393.

30. Plato, *Ethm*:279a; *Gor*:482c-6d. Aristotle (*Rhet*:1360b20; see also, Sidgwick, 1907:153) mentions among others, health, wealth, social position and friendship as goods (or sources of happiness).

31. Bentham, 1996:chs. 4-5. Though it did not offer a procedure of interpersonal comparisons, this 'sort of common measure' was indispensible to the legislator (Williams, 1994:8).

32. Bentham, 1996:ch. 1.

33. *U*:X.211.

34. Russell, 2005:17-8.

35. Ibid. p. 35.

36. Plato, *Ethm*:280b, 280e-1e (trans. W. H. D. Rouse).

37. Plato, *Gor*:506c-e, 507a-c (trans. W. D. Woodhead). Also, Russell, 2005:50-1, 66-71.

38. Russell, 2005:132ff; Plato, *Rep*:580b-1c, 439c-d, 442c. See also, Irwin, 1977:191-5.

39. *U*:X.210, 213, 235-7; WMP:X.172. See also, *OL*:XVIII.261; HPD:XXII.285.

40. At least, this is what Mill (*U*:X.211) tells us about his utilitarian predecessors.

41. Nussbaum, 2004:63.

42. Brink, 1992:79-82.

43. Ibid. pp. 79, 82-3.

44. Lachs, 1973:19.

45. J. Mill, 1878:II.370 (see also, J. Mill, 1835a:270).

46. It is quite interesting that the end does not have to be just one—this idea is usually associated with John not James Mill.

47. J. Mill, 1878:II.371, 377-8.

48. J. Mill, 1825:VII.15. See also, Fenn, 1987:51.

49. Jones, 1992:288.
50. J. Mill, 1825:VII.17; *SOL*:VIII.952; *U*:X.210-1.
51. RBP:X.12-3; Go:XI.150; *SOL*:VIII.952; *U*:X.211.
52. Ackrill, 1980:17. See also, Hardie, 1965:279; White, 2006:90.
53. Hoag, 1987:422. See also, Scarre, 1996:139.
54. Hoag, 1987:422-6; *U*:X.235; B:X.12.
55. *U*:X.210; Hoag, 1987:426-8, 427n22; Berger, 1984:37-8.
56. Thus, Brink's (1992:83) argument, when he says that rational deliberation is a dominant component in Mill's conception, is more plausible than Hoag's.
57. Hoag, 1987:429-31; also, Ackrill, 1980:17. Scarre (1996:140) noted that 'Mill believed that happiness was the dominant end of life but was itself an inclusive end having several components', which corresponds to the weak sense of dominance used here.
58. White, 1995:268. It is insufficient to say that happiness is inclusive, White argues, since without a sufficient basis for disinterested other-regarding ends it may be reduced to egoism.
59. Irwin, 2007-9:I.90ff.
60. *U*:X.ch. 2. See also, Annas, 1978.
61. Scarre, 1999:493-4. See also, Crisp, 1996; 1997.
62. Scarre, 1999:497; Aristotle, *EN*:1176b5-10.
63. See also, *SOL*:VIII.949ff; Plato, *Gor*:459d; Aristotle, *EN*:1104b30-3.
64. *U*:X.208, 210, 235-8. See also, Plato, *Rep*:357b-d. Thus, White (1999b:155-6) was wrong to argue that Mill identified extrinsic with intrinsic usefulness.
65. As we saw in chapter seven, Bain thought that Grote's reading of ancient Greek philosophers may have instigated Mill in writing the final chapter of his *A System of Logic*, where Mill's referred to 'Teleology' and 'Doctrine of Ends' (Bain, 1873: [119]).
66. *U*:X.238.
67. Ibid. pp. 209-10.
68. *A*:I.144-7. If it is made so, Mill noted, no longer is a person happy.
69. For the distinction in Plato, see Rudebusch (1999:68).
70. SD:X.50; T:X.483. Ryan (1991:123) claims that Mill guided his own life in this way.
71. *SOL*:VIII.949ff; *U*:X.206, 213; WMP:X.172.
72. *ACP*:X.337; *OL*:XVIII.chs. 3-4. See also, SD:X.56, 69.
73. *U*:X.238-9, 240; N:X.380, 392. See also, Plato, *Rep*:441b-c.
74. *U*:X.238. This addresses White's (1994:71-2) second objection to the inclusivist view: not only are ethical activities obligatory in a way that prudential ones are not—regardless of motivation—but the former also acquire *aesthetic* and *sympathetic* worth when they are an expression, or are 'in fulfilment', of noble character traits which have an emotional bond with the 'good of the species'.
75. E.g., Irwin, 1977:341; 1995:290ff; White, 1995:270ff.
76. Bogen and Farrell, 1978:329.
77. Ibid. p. 331.
78. Ibid. pp. 335-8.
79. *U*:X.235-6; *OL*:XVIII.261.
80. See, J. Mill, 1835a:192, 272.
81. *U*:X.235-6 (italics added).
82. *OL*:XVIII.251; *A*:I.24-5. See about 'utility' in *U*:X.209; 'justice' in *U*:X.241; 'theory' in *SOL*:VIII.812; 'interest' in RBP:X.14; 'nationality' in C:X.135. As we already saw, Mill did refer to Plato's method in B:X.88 and AJ:XXI.175-6.
83. J. Mill, 1878:I.268-9 (italics added).

84. APHM:XXXI.143.

85. Ibid. p. 145.

86. The following discussion draws on *SOL*:VII.27-32. Robert Hoag (1992) explores Mill's theory of names, but with regard to pleasure, not happiness.

87. *U*:X.235.

88. Ibid. p. 237.

89. Thus, contra Semmel (1984:177), desiring virtue for itself 'even if in a particular case it produced unhappiness' was a 'sound Benthamite doctrine': unlike with wealth, power or fame, when virtue is a dominant end, there can be no conflict between the individual and the society (*U*:X.235ff).

90. J. Mill, 1878:II.266.

91. APHM:XXXI.232; *SOL*:VIII.842-3; *U*:X.238 (italics added). See Robson, 1968:147-8.

92. APHM:XXXI.232; see also, *A*:I.143.

93. *U*:X.208, 210, 235-8 (see also, *PPE*:II.10). Plato, *Rep*:357b-d.

94. *SOL*:VIII.949; Plato, *Ethm*:280e; *Gor*:468c; *Mn*:88c-d.

95. See Korsgaard (1983:170-2) for a more detailed discussion on these two distinctions.

96. White (1999b:153) argues that Mill failed to develop a theory that deals with conflicts, and thus shows himself ignorant of what Mill considered to be the primary advantage of utilitarianism.

97. See further, SD:X.52; *U*:X.210. See also, Priestley, 1969.

98. *U*:X.210-11, 209 (quoting Peacock, 1827:375 (not identified in Mill's *CW*)).

99. Shorey, 1938:231. See also, Gibbs, 1986; R. Long, 1992.

100. Hoag, 1987:425; see also, Berger, 1984:36ff.

101. Semmel (1984:88) also ignored this aspect. See further, RBP:X.12; *U*:X.238 (Go:XI.150).

102. Hoag, 1987:426-8.

103. *U*:X.210, 237-8. See also, APHM:XXXI.232; *SOL*:VIII.842-3.

104. *U*:X.210ff; *SOL*:VII.55-65.

105. *EHP*:IX.430-1, 434-5; *U*:X.213.

106. *A*:I.229; Hutcheson, 1969:V.117 (in Edwards, 1979:70; Gibbs, 1986:32).

107. *SOL*:VII.65-69, 73-5 (also, APHM:XXXI.182, 189-90). See also, J. Mill, 1878:II.44-61. Hoag (1992:265) considers quantity and quality parts of the intrinsic nature of substances. But there is nothing intrinsically different to the chemical compounds of water ($H_2O$), when it is one gallon or ten. Likewise, Hoag (1987:429-31) argues that Mill's (*U*:X.258n) view 'that the truths of arithmetic are applicable to the valuation of happiness, as of all other measurable quantities' may cause problems. But Mill noted that 'the quality of whiteness ascribed to the object snow, is grounded on its exciting in us the sensation of white'—but to be able to excite sensations, snow must exist in some quantity.

108. *SOL*:VII.123 (also, VIII.787-8); see also, *U*:X.251.

109. Hoag, 1992:268-70 (see further, Cohen, 1980); *SOL*:VIII.719, 659.

110. *U*:X.211; *SOL*:VII.123; *EHP*:IX.430ff.

111. Hoag, 1992:259n49.

112. Saunders, 2010:53-6; Brink, 1992:72-3 (also, Williams, 1996:11-3; Irwin, 1998:454-5; Scarre, 1999:492; Nussbaum, 2004:65); Aristotle, *EN*:1153a9-13.

113. Aristotle, *EN*:1174b14-5b1, 1175b32-5.

114. Sparshott, 1994:312ff (italics added); Owen, 1971-2:145ff. See also, Plato, *Phl*:51d.

115. Crisp, 1997:27; 1996:373.

116. D. E. Miller (2010:chs. 3-4) refers to this distinction as the 'internalist' view and 'externalist' view of pleasure.

117. *SOL*:VII.52. See also, Rudebusch, 1999:68. This differs from what Rem Edwards (1979:35ff) calls 'localized' / 'non-localized' pleasures in that a sensate, but simple, pleasure may be non-localized.

118. *SOL*:VII.53, 442. George Harris (1983:510) argues that 'it is conceptually puzzling to try and understand virtue as *part* [and not simply as a cause] of a sensation or a feeling [...] that could be described as pleasurable', but Mill did provide the means to solve this puzzle.

119. R. Long, 1992:279, 285-6. See also Riley (1993) for some other criticisms.

120. Mill to J. Sterling, 24/05/1832:XII.101 (italics added). See also, Scarre, 1996:89-90.

121. See also, Berger, 1984:36.

122. *U*:X.211.

123. Saunders, 2010:56-60; Brink, 1992:98; Crisp, 1997:36; Donner and Fumerton, 2009:22.

124. *SOL*:VII.123; *U*:X.251. See also, Gibbs, 1986:36-7, 39n. See further, Riley, 1993 and 1999 contra Saunders, 2010:60-6.

125. *U*:X.211-2; Plato, *Rep:*583b-7e.

126. Plato, *Rep:*582a-3a (also, Aristotle, *Rhet*:1365a2-4; *EN*:1174a1-3; *EE*:1235b35ff); *U*:X.211ff.

127. Plato, *Rep:*581c-3a; *U*:X.234ff (also, *SOL*:VIII.949ff).

128. Thus, Mill's was not an *a priori* reasoning in the way Sidgwick (1907:121-2) pointed out concerning Aristotle's notion of the 'best life', since the 'best life' was suggested by the experience of competent judges not from 'its moral attributes and from its consequences' (*U*:X.213). However, Mill's notion of experiments in living, as John Gray (1996:144) has argued, seems to require people to be able to choose lives as easily as they can choose certain activities or habits.

129. While the first choice is to some extent voluntary, Mill noted, the second is not: 'they addict themselves to inferior pleasures, not because they deliberately prefer them, but because they are either the only ones to which they have access, or the only ones which they are any longer capable of enjoying' (*U*:X.213; *OL*:XVIII.264-5). In *On Liberty*, Mill argues quite similarly in reference to custom and personal inclinations. The similarity between these two passages, as far as I know, has gone unnoticed. See also, *CRG*:XIX.444.

130. *U*:X.215.

131. *U*:X.213; *SOL*:VII.949ff. Whether this indirect pursuit makes Mill's notion an indirect, strategic, rule, act, or of act-multi-level utilitarianism, is a long discussion and cannot be pursued here.

132. *U*:X.215 (Plato, *Phl*:22a). Life cannot consist solely of altruistic actions; thus, some 'egoistic propensities', Mill noted, are also required for a joyful life (*ACP*:X.339; contra B. Semmel (1984:178) and S. Blackburn (2006:141).

133. *U*:X.215, 217. See further, Gibbs, 1986:39-40; Singer, 2000:30, 33; Martin, 1972:147. Thus, to adapt Mill's economic theory, 'a certain quantum of enjoyment' is here 'classed among necessaries, since anything short of it would not be consistent with the greatest efficiency of labour' (*PPE*:II.52).

134. Plato, *Rep:*580c-3a, 440ff. Also, Irwin, 1977:191-5; Russell, 2005:119.

135. *U*:X.212, 231.

136. Gray, 1996:70.

137. *U*:X.235ff. See further, Riley, 2010. These two reasons contradict Martin's (1992:149) conclusion that Mill was inconsistent because life is not a pleasure, and, thus, cannot be desirable.

138. Berger, 1984:37, 39.
139. Berger, 1984:40-2; also, Singer, 2000:32.
140. Crisp, 1997:34-5; 1996:370.
141. Plato, *L:*663a-d.
142. Crisp, 1997:87.
143. Bentham, 1996:11 (1838-43:I.1). See also, J. Mill, 1878:II.377-8.
144. Plato, *L:*732e.
145. Plato, *L:*663d, 733e-4a; *Rep:*583a. See futher, Irwin, 1995:344-5.
146. APHM:XXXI.226.
147. RBP:X.7-8.
148. RBP:X.12-3; B:X.95-6. Also, *U:*X.210ff.
149. Miller, 2010:35-6. See further, Russell, 2005:4-5.
150. APHM:XXXI.214
151. Mill to H. Jones, 13/06/1868:XVI.1414; *OL:*XVIII.224.
152. WMP:X.172.
153. Russell, 2005:75.
154. Plato, *Rep:*582a; *U:*X.211-3.
155. Plato, *Rep:*582e-5a; *U:*X.211.
156. Plato, *Rep:*585d-e. For Mill's argument, see *U:*X.209-12
157. Plato, *Rep:*583b-8a. See Russell (2005:121ff) for a discussion of both arguments.
158. Plato, *Rep:*588a: 'εὐσχημοσύνη τε βίου καὶ κάλλει καὶ ἀρετῇ'. Notice here εὐσχημοσύνη, which can be translated as dignity, decency or nobility. I have chosen the first to allude to Mill's own mention of the sense of dignity in human beings (*U:*X.212).
159. Plato, *Rep:*381c; *U:*X.212.
160. *SOL:*VIII:949ff; *U:*X.206, 213; WMP:X.172. See further, Singer, 2000:44-7.
161. Bogen and Farrell, 1978:331.
162. Campbell, 1866:129-30, 42-3.
163. Plato, *L:*733d-4e (see also, Stalley, 1983:68); *Rep:*583aff.
164. *SOL:*VIII.949-52; Plato, *Gor:*459d.
165. Singer, 2000:33-5 (quoting *U:*X.217).

# CONCLUSION

Parts one and two of this book explored the cultural and biographical contexts of John Stuart Mill's engagement with ancient Greek thought in general, and with Plato's writings in particular. I have presented the main trends in classical reception, with which Mill was in dialogue throughout his life. As we saw, 'knowing Greek' provided access to a closed society of 'cultivated' individuals. For many years the Radicals tried to fight such aristocratic prejudices, which extended to viewing the 'uneducated' public as unsuitable to participate in the affairs of the state, by attacking classical studies from the outside (i.e., by questioning their place in education). However, the two Mills and George Grote followed a different tactic. They employed the dialogues of Plato and the history of ancient Greece—then the stronghold of the *élite*—to undermine the prevailing aristocratic prejudices. They thus highlighted the usefulness of Plato's dialectical method in exposing the 'vague generalities' which perpetuated those very prejudices. Concurrently, they showed how the British Constitution was anything but 'mixed'—the interests of the people hardly being protected from 'sinister interests'. To this effect, the history of Athens served to support the radical demands for wider participation, which could be achieved without endangering either property or person.

However, in exploring the uses of Plato in the early nineteenth century, I have argued that Plato's dialogues, at least in the case of James Mill, were more than just a device for polemical application. While Plato's authority was indeed employed to corroborate radical claims, something from Plato's dialogues did also penetrate the elder Mill's utilitarian theory. And though James Mill did not explore it all the way, it seems to offer an opportunity to study the corresponding effect on John Mill.

In the second part, I argued that John Stuart Mill's views on Athens and Plato, though obscured by his eclecticism, were a direct product of his education

207

under the supervision of his father. However, his was not an education of cram. The younger Mill added to his father's ideas as much as he received from them. Still, given the place of classics in nineteenth-century Britain, Mill's views on Athens and on Plato were not abstract exercises in historical or philosophical analysis; they served a highly polemical cause: reform. And as social and political circumstances changed with the passage of time, Mill's argument for reform mirrored that change.

Whether it was about educational, social or political reform, Mill argued that individuals need to develop critical habits, to go by reason rather than routine—a statement which had educational, social and political implications. Not only were rote and cram unsuitable educational principles; but also the ability to discover or pursue something for one's own self called for a social setting of individual liberty. However, though being able to question established opinions did not always lead one to choose to overthrow them, this capability had direct bearing on how people perceived and were affected by established or popular opinions. What is more, going by reason rather than routine was of vital political importance; thus, 'Civil or Social Liberty' was associated with political institutions in which individuals were called to choose their ablest fellow-citizens to manage the interests of all. However, concurrently, *caring* for the interests of all is not an affair of the mind; such *care* requires specific circumstances which encourage the creation of a desire for the well-being of others. Thus, appropriate educational, social and political conditions, which promote both intellectual and emotional cultivation, may encourage a person to not only to define, but also put into effect her/his own life-plan—without any presumption of infallibility on the part of society about what the 'right' ends of life are.

It seems that Mill's *Autobiography* served its purpose well: seldom is John Stuart Mill read as not an *independent* thinker (i.e., as one who did not add anything to what he found in others). But there is a cost: charges of inconsistency still dominate the discussion on Mill's conception of happiness. In the third part, I have argued that what most scholars regard as a tension in Mill's theory of utility—namely the role of pleasure in a happy life—may be resolved when viewed through the prism of his ancient Greek influences. However, 'great questions are not accessible directly'; rather, as Mill posited, they are accessed through 'a very circuitous route'. To this effect, I have argued that his 'Art of Life', which prioritised between ends of life (defining those secondary ends through which Mill considered the 'ultimate end' to be 'attainable, and should be pursued'); his theorising on character formation, which would supply the scientific means for creating the desire to bring about those ends; and his notion of happiness, which defined the corresponding kind of bond between individual pleasure and social happiness, would, taken together, help formulate a coherent utilitarian theory.[1] I have thus tried to make a case for consistency in Mill's conception of happiness by examining his views with regard to the two senses of happiness he himself identified: the 'humble' and 'higher' senses. I discussed these two senses in terms of additive and directive conceptions of happiness respectively, in accordance with ancient theories on *eudaimonia*, while relating the former notion to James Mill's view of happiness and the latter notion to John Mill's.[2]

As we saw, though tempted to do so, James Mill refused to abandon the surefootedness of pleasurable experience as the foundation of happiness,[3] trying to ground the pursuit of social interests—or duty—on 'enlightened' self-interest—perhaps in fear of inconsistency. However, John Mill, in his early comments on Plato's *Gorgias*, as we saw, pointed out that '[i]t is impossible, by any arguments, to prove that a life of obedience to duty is preferable, so far as respects the agent himself, to a life of circumspect and cautious selfishness'.[4] Similarly, later in the nineteenth century, Henry Sidgwick would identify a 'contradiction in our apparent intuitions of what is Reasonable in conduct': it was indeed rational to choose to promote the happiness of mankind—when it offered more pleasure to the agent herself/himself—from the standpoint of either self-interest or duty. But when 'enlightened' self-interest came into conflict with duty, Sidgwick argued, the choice ultimately rested on non-rational impulses. This suggested, Sidgwick concluded, the duality of practical reason and hence its limits.[5] In *The Methods of Ethics*, Sidgwick elaborated upon all the implications of this claim, in a much more systematic, and perhaps more consistent, manner than Mill. But as Mill anticipated Sidgwick's doubt with regard to practical reason, he also tried to solve the problem, with which his utilitarian predecessors and successor were faced. He tried to set a 'higher ground' for happiness—as did Socrates, in Plato's *Gorgias*, by defining 'the cultivation of a disinterested preference of duty for its own sake, as a *higher state* than that of sacrificing selfish preferences to a more distant self-interest'.[6] Thus, character formation as the cultivation of virtue was the key: '[w]hat it is the man's interest to do or refrain from, depends less on any outward circumstances, than upon what sort of man he is'.[7]

The linguistic and psychological premises of Mill's notion of happiness brought him closer to the tradition of Jeremy Bentham and James Mill—it is not easy to justify why Mill retained hedonistic elements in his theory, if he held a non-hedonist one. Still, he distanced himself from his utilitarian predecessors in arguing for the *aesthetic* worth of pursuing the virtuous life for its own sake—especially when something less good would have sufficed for general happiness. But experiments in living, and the pleasure that inevitably follows the best kind of living, would keep a person from desiring any other kind of life than that which promotes social happiness.[8]

Thus, as Mill himself made clear, the 'alpha and omega' of his creed was that 'the good of the species (or rather of its several units)' is the *ultimate* end of action; as such, it claimed 'authority over the whole of human life'. Though he was aware that 'every mode of life has its drawbacks', he 'believe[d] with the fullest Belief that this end can in no other way be forwarded but by [...] each taking for his exclusive aim the developement of what is best in himself'. Not only was this to be achieved deliberately through subordinating secondary ends to the ultimate end; but also by associating a feeling 'sufficiently powerful to give it in fact, the authority over human conduct to which it lays claim in theory'.

To this effect, the essence of Mill's theory was 'the strong and earnest direction of the emotions and desires towards an ideal object, recognized as of the highest excellence, and as rightfully paramount over all selfish objects of desire'—Mill came to call this theory the Religion of Humanity.[9] And, it being a religion, it ultimately rested on non-rational impulses, just as Sidgwick suspected it would. Guiding these non-rational impulses in the direction which rational principles point out (i.e., in accordance with the happiness of mankind) *fulfilled* Mill's criterion for a 'confirmed character'—that view of character with which friends and foes alike would be comfortable in Victorian Britain.

Mill thus came to the conclusion that 'utility in the largest sense, grounded on the permanent interests of man as a progressive being', was the solution to the paradox he first experienced around 1826-7.[10] Unsatisfied with 'merely tracing the laws' of *any* progressive movement—not just that of economic progress—he asked the question: 'to what goal' do such movements aim? His 'ideal of life' was not 'that of struggling to get on' or 'drudging from early morning till late at night for bare necessaries'; the 'existing type of social life', he argued, was not 'the most desirable lot of human kind'. Thus 'the well-being of a people', he argued, 'must exist by means of the justice and self-government, the δικαιοσύνη and σωφροσύνη, of the individual citizens'.[11]

Social well-being depended upon cultivating individual excellence which, in turn, rested upon intellectual, moral and aesthetic education: 'the highest & most important of these purposes [i.e., to which '[t]he united forces of society [...] [are] directed' for 'man's good'] is the improvement of man himself as a moral and intellectual being'.[12] Ultimately, what was required for the pursuit of self-culture was 'a good state of society and education'; however, such a state entailed, as has been correctly remarked, 'a radical reordering of society and the typical outlook of individuals'. By trying to find the means to that 'reordering', according to his own definition, Mill remained a 'Philosophic Radical' to the end.[13]

As I have argued, Mill's view on the 'Art of Life', his preoccupation with 'confirmed character' and his discussion concerning the means and ends of happiness made him—to that extent—part of the tradition of Plato, and the other companions of Socrates. But here we reach a telling difference between the two Victorian utilitarian thinkers whom I have been discussing in this conclusion; though both Mill and Sidgwick felt that they were pupils of Plato 'beyond any modern' that they knew of, Sidgwick perhaps was not as willing as Mill to follow Plato to the end—that is, to the extent of accepting the belief that virtue was conducive to social happiness, even when it seemed counterintuitive to believe so.[14] I have tried to show why Mill was willing to do so; I have also tried to show what his doing so entailed for his conception of happiness.

## NOTES

1. GP:XI.379; BHMS:X.29; *SOL*:VIII.764, 949ff.

2. See, *U*:X.213; *SOL*:VIII.952; J. Mill, 1825:VII.17.

3. J. Mill, CPB:IV.4r.

4. Go:XI.149. Cf. Miller, 2010:53.

5. Sidgwick, 1907:508-9 (see further, Schneewind, 1977; Frankena, 1976, 1992; Skorupski, 2001).

6. GP:XI.416 (italics added).

7. *CRG*:XIX.444.

8. Mill to H. Jones, 13/06/1868:XVI.1414. See also, *U*:X.211, 215, 237; DE:09/04/1854:XXVII.66; *OL*:XVIII.267; Go:XI.150.

9. *A*:I.85; *ACP*:X.332; Mill to T.Carlyle, 12/01/1834:XII.207-8; UR:X.422.

10. *OL*:XVIII.224; sUH:XXVI.395. See also, *A*:I.139; WAV:I.469; Ph:XI.95.

11. *PPE*:III.752, 754, 763; II.367.

12. Mill to G. d'Eichthal, 08/10/1829:XII.36-7.

13. IA:XXI.251; FE:VI.353; Singer, 1992:69. See also, IC:XXIII.398.

14. *A*:I.24; Sidgwick, 1907:375n1. See further, Irwin, 1992.

# BIBLIOGRAPHY

## I.

Adams, G. (1746) *The Heathen Martyr or, The Death of Socrates; an Historical Tragedy* (London. N.P.).

Alison, A. (1837) 'The Athenian Democracy', *Blackwood's Edinburgh Magazine* 42 (261): 44-50.

Anon. (1759) 'A Synopsis or a General View of the Works of Plato', *Critical Review or Annals of Literature*, part I in 8 (Dec.): 421-7; part II in 10 (Sep., 1760): 194-202.

———. (1794) 'Taylor's Translation of Plato's *Cratylus*, etc.', *Monthly Review* 14 (July): 248-54.

———. (1804a) 'Taylor's Works of Plato', *Annual Review and History of Literature* 3 (Jan.): 337-47.

———. (1804b) 'Taylor's Plato', *Critical Review or Annals of Literature* 3rd Series, parts I&II in 2 (2): 121-33, 270-89; parts III&IV in 3 (1): 1-19, 132-46.

———. (1804c) 'Taylor's Works of Plato', *Imperial Review* 1 (Mar.): 321-6.

———. (1806) 'Taylor's Translation of Plato', *British Critic* 27 (June): 577-92.

———. (1821a) 'Manners of Athenians', *Quarterly Review* XXIV (47-48; October and January): 419-61.

———. (1821b) 'Mitchell's Comedies of Aristophanes', *The British Review and London Critical Review* 17: 50-88.

———. (1822) 'Republic of Plato', *New Monthly Magazine and Literary Review* 3, part I in (1): 512-17; parts II and III in (2): 69-76 and 152-7.

— —. (1828) 'Address to Phrenologists', *Co-Operative Magazine* 5 (3): 98-111.

———. (1836) 'Brutus, Lucius Junius', *The Penny Cyclopaedia of the Society for the Diffusion of Useful Knowledge*, V (Blois—Buffalo): 498-9.

————. (1837a) 'Mr. Bulwer's Athens', *Metropolitan Magazine* 19 (74): 209-19.

————. (1837b) 'Bulwer's Athens', *Fraser's Magazine for Town and Country* 16 (93): 347-56.

————. (1837c) 'Bulwer's Athens', *Examiner* 1544: 565-6.

————. (1837d) 'Bulwer's Athens', *Monthly Review* 2 (2): 185-95.

————. (1838) 'National Education, State of the Question in Parliament', *British Magazine* 14: 567-73.

————. (1880) 'Miscellanea', *Westminster Review* 57 (1): 301-12.

Arnold, M. (1869) *Culture and Anarchy* (London: Smith, Elder and Co.).

Arnold, T. (1858) *The Miscellaneous Works of Thomas Arnold*, 2nd ed. (London: B. Fellowes).

Axon, W. (1890) *Thomas Taylor, The Platonist* (London).

Bacon, F. (1645) *Novum Organum* (LVGD.BAT: Adrianum Wijngaerde and Franciscum Moiardum).

Bailey, S. (1858) *Letters on the Philosophy of the Human Mind, Second Series* (London: Longman, Brown, Green, Longmans, and Roberts).

Bain, A. (1843) '*A System of Logic* by John Stuart Mill', *Westminster Review* 39 (2): 412-56.

————. (1848) *On the Applications of Science to Human Health and Well-Being* (Glasgow: Richard Griffin).

————. (1859) *The Emotions and the Will* (London: John W. Parker and Son).

————. (1861) *On the Study of Character; Including an Estimate of Phrenology* (London: Parker, Son, and Bourn).

————. (1865) 'Grote's Plato: The Negative or Search Dialogues' and 'the Affirmative or Exposition Dialogues', *MacMillan Magazine* 12 (May-October): 193-208, 457-72.

————. (1873) 'Estimate of Character and Writings', in *The Minor Works of George Grote*, ed. A. Bain (London: John Murray): [1]-[170]

————. (1882a) *James Mill: A Biography* (London: Longmans, Green).

————. (1882b) *John Stuart Mill: A Criticism with Personal Recollections* (London: Longmans, Green).

Baines. M.A. (1856) *A Comprehensive View of National Education Schemes: Their Past Fallacies and Future Prospects: Being a Review of Education Measures During the Session of 1856* (London: Wertheim and Macintosh).

Bartley, G.C.T. (1871) *The Schools for the People* (London: Bell & Daldy).

Bekker, I. (1826) *Platonis et quae vel Platonis esse feruntur vel Platonica solent comitari scripta Graece omnia*, 11 vols. (Londini: A.J. Valpy).

Benn, A.W. (1906) *The History of English Rationalism in the Nineteenth Century*, 2 vols. (London: Longmans, Green).

Bennett, W.J.E. (1846) *Crime and Education: The Duty of the State Therein* (London: W.J. Cleaver).

Bentham, J. (1802) *Traités de Législation Civile et Pénale*, 3 vols., trans.; ed. E. Dumont (Paris: Bossange).

————. (1834) *Deontology*, 2 vols., ed. J. Bowring (Edinburgh: William Tait).

————. (1838-43) *Works of Jeremy Bentha*m, 11 vols., ed. J. Bowring (Edinburgh: William Tait).

————. (1983a) *Chrestomathia*, eds. M.J. Smith, W.H. Burston (Oxford: Clarendon Press).

————. (1983b) *Deontology, together with A Table of the Springs of Action and An Article on Utilitarianism*, ed. A. Goldworth (Oxford: Clarendon Press).

————. (1996) *An Introduction to the Principles of Moral and Legislation*, eds. J.H.Burns, H.L.A. Hart; intr. F. Rosen (Oxford: Clarendon Press).

Blackie, J.S. (1852) *Classical Literature in its Relation to the Nineteenth Century and Scottish University Education* (Edinburgh and London: Sutherland and Knox; Simpkin, Marshall and Co).

Blackie, J.S. (1857) 'Plato', in *Edinburgh Essays by Members of the University 1856* (Edinburgh: Adam and Charles Black).

————. (1866) 'Letter to the Author', in *Classical Instruction: Why?—When?— For Whom?*, W.B. Hodgson (London: C.F. Hodgson & Son).

Blackstone, W. (1771) *Commentaries on the Laws of England*, 4th ed., 4 vols. (Dublin: John Exshaw, Henry Saunders, Boulter Grierson, and James Williams).

Bradley, A.C. (1905) *Shakespearean Tragedy* (Greenwich: Fawcett Publications, 1965).

Bradley, F.H. (1876) *Ethical Studies* (London: Henry S. King).

Bulwer-Lytton, E. (1837) *Athens: Its Rise and Fall*, Knebworth ed. (London: George Routledge and Sons, 1874).

————. (2004) *Athens: Its Rise and Fall*, ed. O. Murray (London; New York: Routledge).

Caird, E. (1865) 'Plato and the Other Companions of Socrates', *North British Review* 43 (Sept.-Dec.): 351-84.

Campbell, L. (1866) 'Grote's Plato', *Quarterly Review* 119 (237): 108-53.

Carlyle, T. (1840) *Critical and Miscellaneous Essays*, 5 vols. (London: Fraser).

Chas, R.R. (1827) 'On the Formation of Moral Character', *Co-operative Magazine and Monthly Herald* 2 (2): 60-74.

Clark, A. (1806) *An Account of the English Translations of All the Greek and Roman Classics and Ecclesiastical Writers* (London: W. Baynes).

Clark, W.G. (1855) 'General Education and Classical Studies', *Cambridge Essays*: 282-308.

Coleridge, S.T. (1795) 'Lecture Five', in *Lectures 1795: On Politics and Religion*, eds. L.Patton and P.Mann (Princeton: Princeton University Press, 1970): 194-212.

————. (1818) *The Friend: A Series of Essays*, 3 vols., 2nd ed. (London: Fenner).

————. (1818-9) *Lectures on the History of Philosophy*, 2 vols., ed. R.J. de J. Jackson (Princeton: Princeton University Press, 2000).

————. (1854) *The Complete Works*, 7 vols., ed. W.G.T. Shedd (New York: Harper & Brothers).

————. (1895a) *Anima Poetae*, ed. E.H. Coleridge (London: W. Heinemann).

————. (1895b) *Letters of S.T. Coleridge*, 2 vols., ed. E.H. Coleridge (London: W. Heinemann).

Combe, G. (1848) *Lectures on Popular Education, Delivered to the Edinburgh Philosophical Association in April and November 1833*, 3$^{rd}$ ed. (Edinburgh: MacLachlan, Stewart, &Co).

Constant, B. (1819) 'The Liberty of the Ancients Compared with that of the Moderns', in *Political Writings*, trans.; ed. B. Fontana (Cambridge: Cambridge University Press, 1988): 309-28.

Cornwallis, C.F. (1851) *The Philosophy of Ragged Schools* (London: William Pickering).

Crawford, C. (1773) *A Dissertation on the Phaedon of Plato* (London: printed for the author).

Cudworth, R. (1743) *The True Intellectual System of the Universe*, 2 vols., 2$^{nd}$ ed. (London: J. Walthoe et al).

Cunningham, P. (1866) *The Letters of Horace Walpole*, 9 vols. (London: Bohn).

Donne, W.B. (1837) 'The Rise and Fall of Athens', *British and Foreign Review* 7 (13): 36-85.

Drummond, W. (1794) *A Review of the Governments of Sparta and Athens* (London: Nicol).

Duff, W. (1767) *An Essay on Original Genius and its Various Modes of Exertion in Philosophy and the Fine Arts particularly in Poetry* (London: Edward and Charles Dilly).

Duhring, H. (1843) *The Art of Living* (London: Longman, Brown, Green and Longmans).

Duncan, D. ed. (1908) *Life and Letters of Herbert Spencer* (London: Methuen).

Emerson, R.W. (1841) 'The Art of Life—The Scholar's Calling', *The Dial* 1 (2): 175-82.

Ferguson, A. (1768) *An Essay on the History of Civil Society*, 2$^{nd}$ ed. (London: A. Millar and T. Cadell).

Freeman, E.A. (1856) 'Grote's History of Greece', *North British Review* 25 (49): 141-72.

Geddes, J. (1748) *An Essay on the Composition and Manner of Writing of Ancients, Particularly Plato* (Glasgow: Robert Foulis).

Gillies, J. (1786) *The History of Ancient Greece*, 2 vols. (London: Strahan and Cadell).

————. (1809) *The History of Ancient Greece*, 3$^{rd}$ ed., 4 vols. (London: Cadell and Davies).

Godwin, W. (1793) *An Enquiry Concerning Political Justice and its Influence on General Virtue and Happiness*, 2 vols. (London: G.G.J. and J. Robinson).

Goldsmith, O. (1774) *The Grecian History*, 2 vols. (London: Rivington et al.).

Graham, T.J. (1828) *Sure Methods of Improving Health and Prolonging Life, or A Treatise on the Art of Living Long and Comfortably by Regulating the Diet and Regimen*, 3$^{rd}$ ed. (London; Edinburgh: Simpkin and Marshall, Bell and Bradfute).

Gray, J. (1836) *Thoughts on Education; with a Particular Reference to the Grammar School System* (London: W. Marchant).

Green, T.H. (1906) *Prolegomena to Ethics*, 5th ed., ed. A.C. Bradley (Oxford: Clarendon Press).

Grote, G. (c1825-6) 'The Character of Socrates' (BL Add. 29522, vol. X), in 'Grote on Socrates: An Unpublished Essay of the 1820s in its Context', K. Demetriou, *Dialogos* 3 (1996): 43-7.

———. (1826) 'Institutions of Ancient Greece', *Westminster Review* 5 (Jan-Apr): 269-331.

———. (1846-56) *History of Greece; From the Earliest Period to the Close of the Generation Contemporary with Alexander the Great*, 12 vols. (New York: Harper and Brothers, 1875).

———. (1865) *Plato, and the Other Companions of Sokrates*, new ed., 4 vols. (London: John Murray, 1888).

———. (1872) *Aristotle*, eds. A. Bain, G.C. Robertson (London: John Murray).

———. (1873) *Minor Works*, ed. A. Bain (London: John Murrey).

Grote, H. (1873) *The Personal Life of George Grote*, 2nd ed. (London: John Murray).

Grote, J. (1856) 'Old Studies and New', *Cambridge Essays* II: 74-114.

Guizot, F. (1829) *Cours D' Histoire Moderne; Histoire de la Civilisation en France*, 5 vols. (Paris: Pichon and Didier).

———. (1847) *A Plea for Ragged Schools* (Edinburgh; Glasgow; London: J.Elder; W.Collins and J.Nisbet and Co.).

Guthrie, T. (1860) *Seed-time and Harvest of Ragged Schools* (Edinburgh: A.& C. Black).

Harris, W. T. (1879) 'The Place of the Study of Latin and Greek in Modern Education', *American Institute of Instruction* 50: 91-119.

Helps, A. (1847) *Friends in Council I* (London: William Pickering).

Hill, F. (1836) *National Education: Its Present State and Prospects*, 2 vols. (London: Charles Knight).

Hodgson, W.B. (1866) *Classical Instruction: Why?—When?—For Whom?* (London: C.F. Hodgson & Son).

Humboldt, W. Von (1791-2) *The Limits of State Action*, ed. J.W. Burrow (Indianapolis: Liberty Fund, 1993).

Hume, D. (1826) *The Philosophical Works of David Hume*, 4 vols. (Edinburgh: Adam Black and William Tait).

Hutcheson, F. (1969) *Collected Works*, 7 vols., ed. B. Fabian (Hildesheim: G.Olms).

Ireland, J. (1809) *Paganism and Christianity Compared* (London: Murray).

Jackson, J. E. (1802) 'On the Character and Doctrines of Socrates', *Oxford English Prize Essays* 5 (Oxford: Talboys, 1836): 299-336.

Jebb, R. (1907) *Essays and Addresses*, ed. C. Jebb (Cambridge: Cambridge University Press).

Jowett, B. (1892) *The Dialogues of Plato translated into English with Analyses and Introductions*, 5 vols., 3rd ed. (Oxford: Oxford University Press).

Kennedy, C.R. (1837) *Classical Education Reformed* (London: Green & Longman).

Lewes, G.H. (1845) *The Biographical History of Philosophy*, Library Edition (New York: D. Appleton and Company, 1857).

———. (1865) 'Mr. Grote's Plato', *Fortnightly Review* 2: 169-83.

Macaulay, T.B. (1824) 'On Mitford's History of Greece', *Knight's Quarterly Magazine* 3 (2): 285-304.

Macaulay, T.B. (1829) 'Mill's Essay on Government: Utilitarian Logic and Politics', *Edinburgh Review* 49 (97): 159-89.

———. (1837) 'Lord Bacon', *Edinburgh Review* 66 (132): 1-103.

Macfait, E. (1760) *Remarks on the Life and Writings of Plato* (Edinburgh: Millar; London: Kincaid and Bell).

Malkin, F. (1829) *History of Greece: From the Earliest Times to the Final Subjection to Rome* (London: Baldwin and Cradock).

Matthews, H. (1821) 'On the Character of Socrates', *New Monthly Magazine and Literary Journal* 1: 555-68.

Mill, J. (1802) 'Belsham's Elements of the Philosophy of the Mind', *Anti-Jacobin Review* 12 (47): 1-13.

———. (1804) 'Taylor's Translation of Plato', I. *Literary Journal* 3 (8): 449-461; and II. *Literary Journal* 3 (10): 577-89.

———. (1805a) 'Hints Towards Forming the Character of a Princess', *Literary Journal* 5 (8): 903-11.

———. (1805b) 'Forsyth's Principles of Moral Science', *Literary Journal* 5 (4): 381-92.

———. (1806) 'Colquhoun's System of Education for the Poor', *Literary Journal* 2 (5): 528-39.

———. (1809a) 'Taylor's Plato', *Edinburgh Review* 14 (27): 187-211.

———. (1809b) 'Fox's History of the Reign of James II', *Annual Review and History* 7 (for 1808): 99-114.

———. (1811) 'Chas, Sur la Souveraineté', *Edinburgh Review* 17 (35): 409-28.

———. (1812a) 'Marsh and Others against Lancaster', *Philanthropist* 2 (6): 57-108.

———. (1812b) 'Toleration', *The Philanthropist* 2 (6): 108-24.

———. (1812c) 'Persecution of Infidelity', *The Philanthropist* 2 (7): 209-26.

———. (1812d) 'On the Poor, and the Poor Laws', *Philanthropist* 2 (8): 309-38.

———. (1812e) 'Bentham's *Théorie des Peines et des Récompenses*', *Eclectic Review* 8 (1): 77-87.

———. (1812f) 'Education of the Poor', *Eclectic Review* 8 (2): 651-68.

———. (1813a) 'Education of the Poor', *Edinburgh Review* 21 (41): 207-19.

———. (1813b) 'Essays on the Formation of Human Character', *Philanthropist* 3 (10): 93-119.

———. (1813c) 'Schools for All, not Schools for Churchmen Only', *Philanthropist* 3 (10): 154-79.

———. (1815) 'Stewart's Philosophy of the Human Mind', *British Review* 6 (11): 170-200.

————. (1825) *Essays: I. Government; II. Jurisprudence; III. Liberty of the Press; IV. Prisons and Prison Discipline; V. Colony; VI. Law of Nations; VII. Education; Reprinted from the Supplement of Encyclopaedia Britannica* (London: J. Innes).

————. (1826a) *History of British India*, 3rd ed., 6 vols. (London: Baldwin, Cradock and Joy).

————. (1826b) 'Formation of Opinions', *Westminster Review* 6 (2): 1-23.

————. (1826c) *Elements of Political Economy*, 3rd ed. (London: Baldwin, Cradock and Joy).

————. (1830) 'Thoughts on Moderate Reform in the House of Commons (The Ballot)', *Westminster Review* 13 (25): 1-39.

————. (1835a) *A Fragment on Mackintosh* (London: Baldwin and Cradock).

————. (1835b) 'State of the Nation', *The London Review* 1 (1): 1-24.

————. (1835c) 'Ballot—A Dialogue', *The London Review* 1 (2): 201-53.

————. (1835d) 'The Church and its Reform', *The London Review* 1 (2): 257-95.

————. (1836a) 'Aristocracy', *The London Review* 2 (4): 283-306.

————. (1836b) 'Whether Political Economy is Useful', *The London Review* 2 (4): 553-71.

————. (1836c) 'Theory and Practice', *The London Review* 3 (1): 223-34.

————. (1878) *Analysis of the Phenomena of the Human Mind*, 2 vols., 2nd ed., eds. J.S. Mill, A. Bain, A. Findlater, G. Grote (London: Longmans, Green, Reader and Dryer; 1st ed., 1829).

Mitchell, T. (1820) *The Comedies of Aristophanes*, 2 vols. (London: Murray).

Mitford, W. (1808) *The History of Greece*, 8 vols. (London: Cadell and Davies).

————. (1836) *History of Greece*, 10 vols., new ed. (London: Cadell).

————. (1838) *History of Greece*, 8 vols., new ed. (London: Cadell).

Montagu, E.W. (1760) *Reflections on the Rise and Fall of Ancient Republicks* (London: Millar).

Montaigne, M. (1739) *Essais*, ed. P. Coste, 4th ed., 6 vols. (London: Jean Nourse; 1st ed., 1580).

Moore, G.E. (1903) *Principia Ethica* (Cambridge: Cambridge University Press).

Morell, T. (1827) *Elements of the History of Philosophy and Science From the Earliest Authentic Records to the Commencement of the Eighteenth Century* (London: B.J. Holdsworth).

Morgan, C. (1795) *An Investigation of the Trinity of Plato and of Philo Judaeus* (London: F. and C. Rivington).

Morley, J. (1908) *The Life of Richard Cobden*, 2 vols. (London: Macmillan).

Mouldon, C.W. (1901-4) *The Library of Literary Criticism of English and American Authors*, 8 vols. (New York: Moulton Publishing Company).

Napier, M. (1879) *Selections from the Correspondence of the Late Macvey Napier*, ed. M. Napier (London: Macmillan).

Newman, J.H. (1859) *The Scope and Nature of University Education*, 2nd ed. (London: Longman, Green, Longman, and Roberts).

Niebuhr, B.G. (1851) *The History of Rome*, 2 vols., trans. J.C. Hare and C. Thirlwall (London: Taylor, Walton and Maberly).

Owen, R. (1813) *A New View of Society: Essays on the Principle of the Formation of the Human Character and the Application of the Principle to Practice* (London: Cadell and Davies).

———. (1991) *A New View of Society and Other Writings*, ed. G. Claeys (London: Penguin Books).

Pakington, J.B. (1856) *National Education* (London: Hatchard).

Pater, W. (1866), 'Coleridge's Writings', *Westminster Review*, 29 (1): 106-32.

Pattison, M. (1870) 'The Characters of Theophrastus', *Academy* 2 (14): 52-4.

Payne, J. (1866) *The Curriculum of Modern Education* (London: Virtue Brothers).

Peacock, T.L. (1827) 'Moore's Epicureanism', *Westminster Review* 8 (4): 351-84.

Potter, J.H. (1831) *The Religion of Socrates* (London: B. Fellowes).

———. (1845) *Characteristics of the Greek Philosophers: Socrates and Plato* (London: John W. Parker).

Priestley, J. (1788) *Lectures on History and General Policy, to which is prefixed An Essay on a Course of Liberal Education for Civil and Active Life* (Dublin: P. Byrne).

Priestley, J. (1803) *Jesus and Socrates Compared* (Philadelphia: P. Byrne).

———. (1804) *The Doctrines of Heathen Philosophy Compared with Those of Revelation* (Northumberland: John Binns).

Pycroft, J. (1847) *Four Lectures on the Advantages of Classical Education as an Auxiliary to a Commercial Education* (London: Tyler and Reed).

Redding, C. (1860) *Literary Reminiscences and Memoirs of Thomas Campbell*, 2 vols. (London: Charles J. Skeet).

Redesdale, J.M. (1829) 'A Brief Memoir of the Author', in *The History of Greece*, W. Mitford, 8 vols, ed. Lord Redesdale (London: Cadell): I.vii-xlii.

Rigg, J.M (1898) 'Life of Thomas Taylor', *Dictionary of National Biography* 55: 468-70.

Robertson, W. (1778) *The History of Ancient Greece*, 2nd ed. (Edinburgh: C.Elliot; London: T.Cadell).

Sandford, D.K. (1837) 'Bulwer's Rise and Fall of Athens', *Edinburgh Review* 66 (132): 151-77.

Schleiermacher, F.D.E. (1833) 'The Worth of Socrates as a Philosopher', trans. C. Thirlwall, *Philological Museum* 2: 538-55.

Seeley, J.R. (1870) *Lectures and Essays* (London: Macmillan and Co.).

Sewell, W. (1830) *An Essay on the Cultivation of the Intellect by the Study of Dead Languages* (London: John Bohn).

———. (1841) *An Introduction to the Dialogues of Plato* (London; Oxford: Rivington and Parker).

Sidgwick, H. (1874) *The Methods of Ethics*, 1st ed. (London: Macmillan).

———. (1877) 'Hedonism and Ultimate Good', *Mind* 2 (5): 27-38.

———. (1907) *The Methods of Ethics*, 7st ed. (Indianapolis: Hackett Publishing Company, 1981).

Smiles, S. (1859) *Self-Help* (London: John Murray).

————. (1871) *Character* (London: John Murray).

Spens, H. (1763) *The Republic of Plato* (Glasgow: Robert and Andrew Foulis).

Staël-Holstein, Baroness de (1813) *Germany*, 3 vols. (London: John Murray).

Stanley, A. P. (1845) *The Life and Correspondence of Thomas Arnold*, 2 Vols., 5th ed. (London: B. Fellowes).

Stanyan, T. (1739) *The Grecian History*, 2 vols., 2nd ed. (London: Tonson and Draper).

Stedman, A.M.M. (1887) *Oxford: Its Life and Schools* (London: George Bell and Sons).

Stephen, L. (1950) *The English Utilitarians*, 3 vols. (New York: Pater Smith).

Stewart, D. (1814) *Elements of the Philosophy of the Human Mind*, 2 vols. (Boston: Wells and Lilly).

Swift, J. (1704) 'A Full and True Account of the Battle Fought Last Friday between the Ancient and the Modern Books in St. James's Library', *in The Works of Jonathan Swift*, ed. W. Scott, 19 vols. (Edinburgh: Constable; London: White, et al.; Dublin: Cumming, 1814): XI.213-60.

Sydenham, F. (1759) *A Synopsis or General View of the Works of Plato* (London: Nourse; Sandby; R.J. Dodsley).

Symonds, J. A. (1893) *In the Key of Blue and Other Prose Essays* (London and New York: Elkin Mathews & John Lane; Macmillan & Co).

Tate, T. (1857) *The Philosophy of Education* (2nd American ed. New York: Bardeen, 1885).

Taylor, T. (1790) *The Spirit of All Religions* (London: Hookham).

————. (1793) 'Preface', in *The Cratylus, Phaedo, Parmenides and Timaeus of Plato*, trans. T. Taylor (London: Benjamin and John White).

————. (1797a), 'Example of the Dialectic of Plato', *Monthly Magazine and British Registrar* 4 (24): 332-3.

————. (1797b) 'Atlantic History of Plato', *Monthly Magazine and British Registrar* 4 (25): 519-32.

————. (1804) *The Works of Plato*, 5 vols. (London: Taylor).

Temple, W. (1690) 'An Essay upon the Ancient and Modern Learning', in *Works*, 4 vols. (London: Rivington et al. 1814): III.444-518.

Thirlwall, C. (1835-47) *A History Of Greece*, 8 vols. (London: Longman et al., Taylor).

————. (1845-52) *A History Of Greece*, 8 vols., 2nd ed. (London: Longman et al., Taylor).

Thoreau, H.D. (1854) *Walden; or Life in the Woods* (Boston: Houghton Mifflin Company, 1910).

Thursfield, J.R. (1865) 'Mr Grote's Plato', *Westminster Review*, New Series 28 (October): 459-82.

Tocqueville, A. (1835) *De la Démocratie en Amérique*, 2 vols. (Paris: C. Gosselin).

Trevelyan, G.O., ed. (1876) *The Life and Letters of Lord Macaulay*, 2 vols. (New York: Harper and Brothers).

————. (1907) *Marginal Notes by Lord Macaulay* (London: Longmans, Green and CO.).

Ward, G.W. (1843) 'Mill's Logic', *British Critic, and Quarterly Theological Review*, 34 (68): 349-427.

Ward, J. (1891) 'J.S. Mill's Science of Ethology', *International Journal of Ethics* 1 (4): 446-59.

Westcott, B.F. (1866) 'The Myths of Plato', *Contemporary Review* 2 (May-Aug): 199-211, 469-81.

Whewell, W. (1838) *On the Principles of English University Education including Thoughts on the Study of Mathematics as part of a Liberal Education*, 2nd ed. (London: John W. Parker).

————. (1850) *On Liberal Education in General*, 2nd ed., parts I&II (London: John W. Parker).

————. (1859-61) *The Platonic Dialogues for English Readers*, 3 vols. (London: Macmillan).

————. (1866) 'Grote's Plato', *Fraser's Magazine* 73 (Jan.-Jun.): 411-23.

Wolff, Christian (1732) *Philosophia Rationalis sive Logica, Method Scientifica Pertractata et Ad Usum Scientiarum Atque Citae aprtata; Praemittitur Discursus Praeliminaris De Philosophia in Genere*, 2nd ed. (Frankfurt and Leipzig).

Wood, R. (1802) 'Taylor's Translation of Aristotle's *Metaphysics*', *Monthly Review* 37 (Mar.): 225-34.

Young, W. (1804) *The History of Athens*, 3rd ed. (London: Robson et al.).

# II.

Abrams, M.H. (1971) *The Mirror and the Lamp: Romantic Theory and the Critical Tradition* (Oxford: Oxford University Press).

Ackrill, J.L. (1980) 'Aristotle on Eudaimonia', in *Essays on Aristotle's Ethics*, ed. A.O. Rorty (Berkeley: University of California): 15-33.

Annas, J. (1976) 'Plato's *Republic* and Feminism', *Philosophy* 51 (197): 307-21.

————. (1977) 'Mill and the Subjection of Women', *Philosophy* 52 (200): 179-94.

————. (1978) 'Plato and Common Morality', *Classical Quarterly* 28 (2): 437-51.

————. (1992) 'Plato the Sceptic', in *Methods of Interpreting Plato and his Dilogues*, eds. J.C. Klagge, N.S. Smith (Oxford: Clarendon Press) [*Oxford Studies in Ancient Philosophy*, Sup. Vol. 1992]: 43-72.

————. (1993) *The Morality of Happiness* (Oxford: Oxford University Press).

————. (1995) 'Prudence and Morality in Ancient and Modern Ethics', *Ethics* 105 (2): 241-57.

Arrighetti, G. (1960) *Epicuro: Opere* (Torino: Giulio Einaudi).

Ausland, H.W. (2002) 'Forensic Characteristics of Socratic Argumentation', in *Does Socrates have a Method?*, ed. G.A. Scott (University Park: Pennsylvania State University Press): 36-60.

Baker, J.M. (1971) '*Utilitarianism* and "Secondary Principles"', *Philosophical Quartetly* 21 (82): 69-71.

Baldwin, A.; Hutton, S., eds. (1994) *Platonism and the English Imagination* (Cambridge: Cambridge University Press).

Ball, T. (1982) 'Platonism and Penology: James Mill's Attempted Synthesis', *Journal of the History of Behavioural Sciences* 18 (3): 222-29.

———. (1992a) *James Mill: Political Writings* (Cambridge: Cambridge University Press).

———. (1992b) 'Introduction', in *James Mill: Political Writings*, ed. T. Ball (Cambridge: Cambridge University Press): xi-xxviii.

———. (1995) *Reappraising Political Theory* (Oxford: Clarendon Press).

———. (2000) 'The Formation of Character: Mill's "Ethology" Reconsidered', *Polity* 33 (1): 25-48.

———. (2004) 'Mill, James (1773—1836)', *Oxford Dictionary of National Biography* (Oxford University Press; online edition, October 2007: http://www.oxforddnb.com/view/article/18709, last accessed 4 Feb. 2011).

———. (2010) 'Competing Theories of Character Formation: James vs. John Stuart Mill', in *John Stuart Mill: Thought and Influence*, eds. G. Varouxakis, P. Kelly (London; New York: Routledge): 35-56.

Barrow, R. (1975) *Plato, Utilitarianism and Education* (London: Routledge & Kegan Paul).

Bartlett, R.C. (2002) 'Socratic Political Philosophy and the Problem of Virtue', *American Political Science Review* 96 (3): 525-33.

Benson, H.H. (2006) 'Plato's Method of Dialectic', in *Blackwell Companion to Plato*, ed. H.H. Benson (Oxford: Blackwell Publishing): 85-100.

Berger, F.R. (1984) *Happiness, Justice and Freedom* (Berkeley; Los Angeles; London: University of California Press).

Berkowitz, P. (1999) *Virtue and the Making of Modern Liberalism* (Princeton: Princeton University Press).

Best, G. (1971) *Mid-Victorian Britain, 1851-1875* (London: Weidenfeld and Nicolson).

Biagini, E. (1996)'Liberalism and Direct Democracy: John Stuart Mill and the Model of Ancient Athens', in *Citizenship and Community: Liberals, Radicals and Collective Identities in the British Isles, 1865-1931*, ed. E. Biagini (Cambridge: Cambridge University Press): 21-43.

Blackburn, S. (2006) *Plato's Republic: A Biography* (London: Atlantic Books).

Bobzien, S. (2006) 'Moral Responsibility and Moral Development in Epicurus' Philosophy', in *The Virtuous Life in Greek Ethics*, ed. B. Reis (Cambridge: Cambridge University Press): 206-29.

Bogen, J.; Farrell, D.M. (1978) 'Freedom and Happiness in Mill's Defence of Liberty', *Philosophical Quarterly* 28 (113): 325-38.

Borchardt, R. (1946) 'Introduction', in *John Stuart Mill: Four Dialogues of Plato*, ed. R. Borchardt (London: Watts & Co.): 1-27.

Bourriot, F. (1995) *Kalos Kagathos-Kalokagathia* (Hildersheim: Georg Olms).

Bowen, J. (1989) 'Education, Ideology and the Ruling Class: Hellenism and English Public Schools in the Nineteenth Century', in *Rediscovering Hellenism*, ed. G.W. Clarke (Cambridge: Cambridge University Press): 161-86.

Brant, C. (1998) '"What Does That Argue for Us?": The Politics of Teaching and Political Education in Late Eighteenth-Century Dialogues', in *Pedagogy and Power; Rhetorics of Classical Learning*, eds. Y.L. Too; N. Livingstone (Cambridge: Cambridge University Press): 67-82.

Breisach, E. (1994) *Historiography; Ancient, Medieval and Modern*, 2nd ed. (Chicago; London: Chicago University Press).

Brink, D.O. (1992) 'Mill's Deliberative Utilitarianism', *Philosophy and Public Affairs* 21 (1): 67-103.

Brown, D.G. (1972) 'Mill on Liberty and Morality', *The Philosophical Review* 81 (2): 133-58.

Burnham, P.R. (1977) *Plato in Victorian Britain: The Response of Matthew Arnold, John Stuart Mill, and John Ruskin*, PhD Thesis (Madison: University of Wisconsin-Madison).

Burns, J.H. (1957) 'J.S. Mill and Democracy', *Political Studies* 5, part I in (2): 158-75; part II in (3): 281-94.

———. (1976) 'The Light of Reason: Philosophical History in the Two Mills', in *James and John Stuart Mill/ Papers of the Centenary Conference*, eds. J.M. Robson and M. Laine (Toronto: University of Toronto Press): 3-20.

Burnyeat, M.F. (1980) 'Aristotle on Learning to Be Good', in *Essays on Aristotle's Ethics*, ed. A.O. Rorty (Berkeley: University of California): 69-92.

———. (1998) 'The Past in the Present: Plato as an Educator of Nineteenth-Century Britain', in *Philosophers on Education: Historical Perspectives*, ed. A.O. Rorty (New York and London: Routledge): 353-73.

———. (2001a) 'Plato', *Proceedings of the British Academy* 111: 1-22.

———. (2001b) 'What was 'The Common Arrangement'? An Inquiry Into John Stuart Mill's Boyhood Reading of Plato', *Apeiron* 34 (1): 51-89.

———. (2001c) 'Introduction', *Apeiron* 34 (2): 101-10.

Burston, W.H. (1969) *James Mill on Education* (Cambridge: Cambridge University Press).

———. (1973) *James Mill on Philosophy and Education* (London: Athlone Press).

Butler, E. (1935) *The Tyranny of Greece over Germany: A Study of the Influence Exercised by Greek Art and Poetry over the Great German Writers of the Eighteenth, Nineteenth and Twentieth Centuries* (Cambridge: Cambridge University Press).

Capaldi, N. (1973) 'Mill's Forgotten Science of Ethology', *Social Theory and Practice* 2 (4): 409-20.

————. (2004) *John Stuart Mill: A Biography* (Cambridge: Cambridge University Press).

Carlisle, J. (1991) *John Stuart Mill and the Writing of Character* (Athens; London: University of Georgia).

Carr, D. (2002) 'Moral Education and the Perils of Developmentalism', *Journal of Moral Education* 31 (1): 5-19.

————. (2007) 'Moralized Psychology or Psychologized Morality? Ethics and Psychology in Recent Theorizing about Moral and Character Education', *Educational Theory* 57 (4): 389-402.

————. (2008) 'Character Education as the Cultivation of Virtue', in *Handbook of Moral and Character Education*, eds. L.P. Nucci, D. Narvaez (New York; London: Routledge): 99-116.

Carr, W.R. (1971) 'James Mill's Politics Reconsidered: Parliamentary Reform and the Triumph of Truth', *The Historical Journal* 14 (3): 553-80.

————. (1972) 'James Mill's Politics: A Final Word', *The Historical Journal* 15 (2): 315-20.

Cartledge, P. (2001) 'Introduction', in *George Grote: A History of Greece from the Time of Solon to 403B.C.*, eds. J.M. Mitchell and M.O.B. Caspari (London; New York: Routledge): ix-xx.

Chamberlain, C. (1984) 'Why Aristotle Called Ethics Ethics: The Definition of ἦθος - Eudemian Ethics 2.2', *Hermes* 112 (2): 176-83.

Chambers, M. (1996) 'Grote's *History of Greece*', in *George Grote Reconsidered*, eds. W.H. Calder, S. Trzaskoma (Hildesheim: Weidmann): 1-22.

Chroust, A.H. (1965) 'The Organization of the Corpus Platonicum in Antiquity', *Hermes* 93: 34-46.

Clarke, M.L (1959) *Classical Education in Britain 1500-1900* (Cambridge: Cambridge University Press).

Coburn, K.H. (1934) 'S.T. Coleridge's Philosophical Lectures of 1818-9', The Review of English Studies 10 (40): 428-37.

————, ed. (1971-2002) *Collected Works of Samuel Taylor Coleridge*, 16 vols. (Princeton: Princeton University Press).

Cohen, E.D. (1980) 'J.S. Mill's Qualitative Hedonism: A Textual Analysis', *Southern Journal of Philosophy* 18 (2): 151-8.

Coleman, J. (2000) *A History of Political Thought*, 2 vols. (Oxford: Blackwell Publishing).

Collini, S. (1988) *Arnold* (Oxford: Oxford University Press).

————. (1991) *Public Moralists: Political Thought and Intellectual Life in Britain: 1850-1930* (Oxford: Clarendon Press).

Collini, S.; Winch, D.; Burrow, J. (1983) *That Noble Science of Politics: A Study in Nineteenth-Century Intellectual History* (Cambridge: Cambridge University Press).

Cooper, J.M. (1986) *Reason and the Human Good in Aristotle* (Indianapolis: Hackett Publishing Company).

————. (1999) *Reason and Emotion: Essays on Ancient Moral Psychology and Ethical Theory* (Princeton: Princeton University Press).

Crisp, R. (1996) 'Mill on Virtue as Part of Happiness', *British Journal for the History of Philosophy* 4 (2): 366-80.

————. (1997) *Mill on Utilitarianism* (London and New York: Routledge).

Crook, D.P. (1965) *American Democracy in English Politics: 1815-1850* (Oxford: Clarendon Press).

Cumming, I. (1962) 'The Scottish Education of James Mill', *History of Education Quarterly* 2 (3): 152-67.

Cunliffe, K. (1994) 'Recollection and Recovery: Coleridge's Platonism', in *Platonism and the English Imagination*, eds. A. Baldwin, S. Hutton (Cambridge: Cambridge University Press): 207-16.

Degraff, T. B. (1940) 'Plato in Cicero', *Classical Philology* 35 (2): 143-53.

Demetriou, K.N. (1996a) 'Grote On Socrates: An Unpublished Essay of the 1820s in its Context', *Dialogos* 3: 36-50.

————. (1996b) 'The Development of Platonic Studies and the Role of the Utilitarians', *Utilitas* 8 (1): 15-37.

————. (1996c) 'In Defence of the British Constitution: Theoretical Implications of the Debate over Athenian Democracy in Britain, 1770-1850', *History of Political Thought* 17 (2): 280-97.

————. (1998) 'George Grote and the Platonic Revival in Victorian Britain', *Quaderni di Storia* 47: 17-59.

————. (1999) *George Grote on Plato and Athenian Democracy: A Study in Classical Reception* (Frankfurt and New York: Peter Lang).

————. (2009) 'Socratic Dialectic and the Exaltation of Individuality: J.S.Mill's Influence on George Grote's Platonic Interpretation', *Quaderni di Storia* 58: 33-59.

Demetriou, K.N.; Loizides, A., eds. (2013) *John Stuart Mill* (Basingstoke: Palgrave Macmillan).

Devigne, R. (2006) *Reforming Liberalism, J.S. Mill's Use of Ancient, Religious, Liberal, and Romantic Moralities* (New Haven and London: Yale University Press).

Dixon, T. (2008) *The Invention of Altruism: Making Moral Meanings in Victorian Britain* (Oxford: Published for the British Academy by Oxford University Press).

Donner, W. (1991) *The Liberal Self: John Stuart Mill's Moral and Political Philosophy* (Ithaca and London: Cornell University Press).

————. (1998) 'Mill's Utilitarianism', in *The Cambridge Companion to Mill*, ed. J. Skorupski (Cambridge: Cambridge University Press): 255-92.

————. (2007) 'John Stuart Mill on Education and Democracy', in *J.S. Mill's Political Thought*, eds. N. Urbinati, A. Zakaras (Cambridge: Cambridge University Press): 250-74.

————. (2010) 'John Stuart Mill and Virtue Ethics', in *John Stuart Mill: Thought and Influence*, eds. G. Varouxakis, P. Kelly (London; New York: Routledge): 84-98.

————. (2011) 'Morality, Virtue and Aesthetics in Mill's Art of Life', in *John Stuart Mill and The Art of Life*, eds. B. Eggleston, D.E. Miller, D. Weinstein (Oxford: Oxford University Press): 146-65.

Donner, W.; Fumerton, R. (2009) *Mill* (Malden, MA; Chichester: Wiley-Blackwell).

Dowling, L. (1994) *Hellenism and Homosexuality in Victorian Oxford* (Ithaca; London: Cornell University Press).

Edwards, P. (2004) *The Statesman's Science; History, Nature, and Law in the Political Thought of Samuel Taylor Coleridge* (New York: Columbia University Press).

Edwards, R.B. (1979) *Pleasures and Pains* (Ithaca: Cornell University Press).

Eggleston, B. (2011) 'Rules and their Reasons: Mill on Morality and Instrumental Rationality', in *John Stuart Mill and The Art of Life*, eds. B. Eggleston, D.E. Miller, D. Weinstein (Oxford: Oxford University Press): 71-93.

Eggleston, B.; Miller, D.E.; Weinstein, D. (2011) 'Introduction', in *John Stuart Mill and The Art of Life*, eds. B. Eggleston, D.E. Miller, D. Weinstein (Oxford: Oxford University Press): 3-18.

Eisenach, E.J. (1989) 'Self-Reform as Political Reform in the Writings of John Stuart Mill', *Utilitas* 1 (2): 242-58.

————, ed. (1998) *Mill and the Moral Character of Liberalism* (University Park: Pennsylvania State University Press).

Ellis, A.C.O. (1973) 'Influences on School Attendance in Victorian England', *British Journal of Educational Studies* 21 (3): 313-26.

Evangelista, S. (2009) *British Aestheticism and Ancient Greece* (Basingstoke: Palgrave Macmillan).

Evans, F.B. (1940) 'Thomas Taylor, Platonist of the Romantic Period', *PMLA* 55 (4): 1060-79.

————. (1943) 'Platonic Scholarship in Eighteenth-Century England', *Modern Philology* 41 (2): 103-10.

Fenn, R.A. (1972) *James Mill's Political Thought*, 2 vols., PhD Thesis (London: University of London).

————. (1987) *James Mill's Political Thought* (New York; London: Garland Publishing).

————. (1991) 'Journals and Debating Speeches by John M. Robson; John Stuart Mill' and 'Public and Parliamentary Speeches by John M. Robson; Bruce L. Kinzer; John Stuart Mill', *Victorian Periodicals Review* 24 (1): 49-50.

Feuer, L.S. (1976) 'John Stuart Mill as a Sociology: The Unwritten Ethology', in *James and John Stuart Mill/ Papers of the Centenary Conference*, J.M. Robson and M. Laine, eds. (Toronto: University of Toronto Press): 86-110.

Field, C.G. (1924) 'Socrates and Plato in Post-Aristotelian Tradition I', *The Classical Quarterly* 18 (3-4): 127-36.

Finley, M.I. (1973) *Democracy Ancient and Modern* (London: Chatto and Windus).

————. (2004) 'Athenian Demagogues', in *Athenian Democracy*, ed. P.J. Rhodes (Edinburgh: Edinburgh University Press): 163-84.

Fitzpatrick, J.R. (2010) *Starting with Mill* (Suffolk: Continuum).

Fontana, B., ed.; trans. (1988) *Benjamin Constant; Political Writings* (Cambridge: Cambridge University Press).

Forsdyke, S. (2005) *Exile, Ostracism, and Democracy: The Politics of Exclusion in Ancient Greece* (Princeton: Princeton University Press).

Fortenbaugh, W.W. (1992) 'Aristotle on Persuasion through Character', *Rhetorica: A Journal of the History of Rhetoric* 10 (3): 207-44.

Foster, B.O., trans. (1919) *Livy*, vol. 1 (LOEB 114; Cambridge: Harvard University Press; London: William Heinemann).

Foucault, M. (1986) *The Care of the Self*, trans. R. Hurley (New York: Random House).

Frankena, W.K. (1976) 'Sidgwick and the Dualism of Practical Reason', in *Perspectives on Morality*, ed. K.E. Goodpaster (Notre Dame: University of Notre Dame Press): 193-207.

————. (1992) 'Sidgwick and the History of Ethical Dualism', in *Essays on Henry Sidgwick*, ed. B. Schultz (Cambridge: Cambridge University Press): 175-98.

Friedman, R.B. (1968) 'An Introduction to Mill's Theory of Authority', in *Mill: A Collection of Essays*, ed. J.B. Schneewind (London: Macmillan): 379-425.

Garforth, F.W. (1979) *John Stuart Mill's Theory of Education* (Oxford: Martin Robertson).

————. (1980) *Educative Democracy* (New York: Oxford University Press).

Garrett, D. (2004) '"A Small Tincture of Pyrrhonism", Skepticism and Naturalism in Hume's Science of Man', in *Pyrrhonian Skepticism*, ed. W. Sinnott-Armstrong (Oxford: Oxford University Press): 68-98.

Garrison, J.W. (2004) 'The Aesthetics of Ethical Virtues and the Ethical Virtues of Aesthetics', *Interchange* 35 (2): 229-41.

Gibbs, B. (1986) 'Higher and Lower Pleasures', *Philosophy* 61 (235): 31-59.

Gill, C. (1983) 'The Question of Character-Development: Plutarch and Tacitus', *Classical Quarterly* N.S. 33 (2): 469-87.

————. (1984) 'The Ēthos/Pathos Distinction in Rhetorical and Literary Criticism', *Classical Quarterly* N.S. 34 (1): 149-66.

————. (1985) 'Plato and the Education of Character', *Archiv für Geschichte der Philosophie* 67: 1-26.

Gilmour, R. (1993) *The Intellectual and Cultural Context of English Literature 1830-1890* (London; New York: Longman).

Giorgini, G. (2009) 'Radical Plato: John Stuart Mill, George Grote and the Revival of Plato in Nineteenth-Century England', *History of Political Thought* 30 (4): 617-46.

Glucker, J. (1987) 'Plato in England. The Nineteenth Century and After', in *Utopie und Tradition: Platons Lehre vom Staat in der Moderne*, ed. H. Funke (Würzburg: Königshausen und Newmann): 149-210.

————. (1996) 'The Two Platos of Victorian Britain', in *Polyhistor: Studies in the History of Historiography and Ancient Philosophy*, eds. K.A. Algra, P.W. van Der Horst and D.T. Runia (Leiden; New York; Köln: E.J. Brill): 385-406.

Goldhill, S. (2002) *Who Needs Greek? Contests in the Cultural History of Hellenism* (Cambridge: Cambridge University Press).

Gooch, G.P. (1967) *History and Historians in the Nineteenth Century*, 2nd ed. (London: Longmans).

Gray, J. (1996) *Mill on Liberty: A Defence*, 2nd ed. (London; New York: Routledge).

Gray, J., Smith, G.W., eds. (1991) *J.S. Mill On Liberty in Focus* (London; New York: Routledge).

Gregory, A. P.R. (2002) *Coleridge and the Conservative Imagination* (Macon: Mercer University Press).

Güthenke, C. (2008) *Placing Modern Greece: The Dynamics of Romantic Hellenism, 1770—1840* (Oxford: Oxford University Press).

Haakonsen, K. (1985) 'James Mill and Scottish Moral Philosophy', *Political Studies* 33 (4): 628-36.

Habibi, D.A. (2001) *John Stuart Mill and the Ethic of Human Growth* (Dordrecht: Kluwer Academic Publishers).

Halévy, E. (1929) *The Growth of Philosophic Radicalism*, trans. M. Moris (London: Faber & Faber).

Hamburger, J. (1999) *John Stuart Mill on Liberty and Control* (Princeton: Princeton University Press).

Hansen, M.H. (1992) 'The Tradition of the Athenian Democracy A. D. 1750-1990', *Greece & Rome* 39 (1): 14-30.

Haralsson, R.H. (2011) 'Taking it to Heart: Mill on Appropriation and the Art of Ethics', in *John Stuart Mill and The Art of Life*, eds. B. Eggleston, D.E. Miller, D. Weinstein (Oxford: Oxford University Press): 215-35.

Hardie, W.F.R. (1965) "The Final Good in Aristotle's *Ethics*", *Philosophy* 40 (154): 277-95.

Hardwick, L.; Stray, C. (2008) 'Introduction: Making Connections', in *A Companion to Classical Receptions*, eds. L. Hardwick; C. Stray (Oxford: Blackwell Publishing): 1-9.

Harris, G.W. (1983) 'Mill's Qualitative Hedonism', *Southern Journal of Philosophy* 21 (4): 503-12.

Harris, J. (1993) *Private Lives, Public Spirit: A Social History of Britain 1870-1914* (Oxford: Oxford University Press).

Harrison, J.F.C. (1971) *Early Victorian Britain* (London: Weidenfeld and Nicolson).

Hartle, A. (2003) *Michel de Montaigne: Accidental Philosopher* (Cambridge: Cambridge University Press).

Harvie, C.; Matthew, H.C.G. (2000) *Nineteenth-Century Britain; A Very Short Introduction* (Oxford: Oxford University Press).

Haven, R. (1959) 'Coleridge, Hartley, and the Mystics', *Journal of the History of Ideas* 20 (4): 477-94.

Hedley, D. (2000) *Coleridge Philosophy and Religion: Aids to Reflection and the Mirror of the Spirit* (Cambridge: Cambridge University Press).

Heyck, T.W. (1982) *The Transformation of Intellectual Life in Victorian England* (London: Croom Helm).

Heydt, C. (2006) *Rethinking Mill's Ethics: Character and Aesthetic Education* (London: Continuum).

———. (2011) 'Mill, Life as an Art, and Problems of Self-Description in an Industrial Age', in *John Stuart Mill and The Art of Life*, eds. B. Eggleston, D.E. Miller, D. Weinstein (Oxford: Oxford University Press): 264-89.

Himmelfarb, G. (1974) *On Liberty and Liberalism: The Case of John Stuart Mill* (New York: Alfred A. Knopf).

Hoag, R.W. (1987) 'Mill's Conception of Happiness as an Inclusive End', *Journal of the History of Philosophy* 25 (3): 417-31.

———. (1992) 'Mill's Language of Pleasures', *Utilitas* 4 (2): 247-78.

Holmes, S. (2009) 'The Liberty to Denounce: Ancient and Modern', in *The Cambridge Companion to Constant*, ed. H. Rosenblatt (Cambridge: Cambridge University Press): 47-68.

Houghton, W.E. (1957) *The Victorian Frame of Mind 1830-1870* (New Haven and London: Yale University Press).

Hunt, B.C. (1976) 'Coleridge and the Endeavor of Philosophy', *PMLA* 91 (5): 829-39.

Huxley, A. (1932) *Brave New World* (London: Chatto and Windus).

Inwood, B.; Gerson, L.P., eds., trans.; Hutchinson, D.S., intr. (1994) *The Epicurean Reader* (Indianapolis: Hackett Publishing Company).

Irwin, T.H. (1977) *Plato's Moral Theory* (Oxford: Clarendon Press).

———. (1992) 'Eminent Victorians and Greek Ethics: Sidgwick, Green and Aristotle', in *Essays on Henry Sidgwick*, ed. B. Schultz (Cambridge: Cambridge University Press): 279-310.

———. (1995) *Plato's Ethics* (New York and Oxford: Oxford University Press).

———. (1998) 'Mill and the Classical World', in *The Cambridge Companion to Mill*, ed. J. Skorupski (Cambridge: Cambridge University Press): 423-63.

———. (2007-9) *The Development of Ethics*, 3 vols. (Oxford: Oxford University Press).

Jaeger, W. (1946) *Paideia: The Ideals of Greek Culture*, 3 vols., trans. G. Highet, 3rd ed. (Oxford: Basil Blackwell).

———. (1948) *Aristotle: Fundamentals of the History of his Development*, trans. R. Robinson, 2nd ed. (Oxford: Oxford University Press).

Jaffro, L. (2008) 'Which Platonism for Which Modernity? A Note on Shaftesbury's Socratic Sea-Cards', in *Platonism at the Origins of Modernity; Studies on Platonism and Early Modern Philosophy*, eds. D. Hedley, S. Hutton (Dordrecht: Springer): 255-67.

Jenkyns, R. (1980) *The Victorians and Ancient Greece* (Oxford: Blackwell).

Jennings, J. (2009) 'Constant's Idea of Modern Liberty', in *The Cambridge Companion to Constant*, ed. H. Rosenblatt (Cambridge: Cambridge University Press): 69-91.

Jones, H.S. (1992) 'John Stuart Mill as Moralist', *Journal of the History of Ideas* 53 (2): 287-308.

Jones, H.S. (2000) *Victorian Political Thought* (London: Macmillan Press).

———. (2007) *Intellect and Character in Victorian England: Mark Pattison and the Invention of the Don* (Cambridge: Cambridge University Press).

Kagan, D. (1961) 'The Origin and Purposes of Ostracism', *Hesperia* 30 (4): 393-401.

Kahn, C.H. (1996a) *Plato and the Socratic Dialogue* (Cambridge: Cambridge University Press).

———. (1996b) 'Grote's *Plato and the Companions of Sokrates*', in *George Grote Reconsidered*, eds. W.H. Calder, S. Trzaskoma (Hildesheim: Weidmann): 23-58.

Kamtekar, R. (2004) 'Situationism and Virtue Ethics on the Content of Our Character', *Ethics* 114 (3): 458-91.

Kellermann, F. (1956) 'Montaigne, Reader of Plato', *Comparative Literature* 8 (4): 307-22.

Kiesling, H.J. (1983) 'Nineteenth-Century Education According to West: A Comment', *Economic History Review* 36 (3): 416-25.

Kinzer, B.L. (2007) *J.S. Mill Revisited: Biographical and Political Explorations* (Basingstoke: Palgrave Macmillan).

Kitson, P.J. (2002) 'Political Thinker', in *The Cambridge Companion to Coleridge*, ed. L. Newlyn (Cambridge: Cambridge University Press): 156-69.

Korsgaard, C.M. (1983) 'Two Distinctions in Goodness', *The Philosophical Review* 92 (2): 169-95.

Lachs, J. (1973) 'Two Views of Happiness in Mill', *The Mill Newsletter* 9 (1): 16-20.

———. (1992) 'Mill and Constant: A Neglected Connection in the History of the Idea of Liberty', *History of Philosophy Quarterly* 9 (1): 87-96.

Lamm, J.A. (2000) 'Schleiermacher as Plato Scholar', *The Journal of Religion* 80 (2): 206-239.

Lane, M. (2001) *Plato's Progeny: How Socrates and Plato Still Captivate the Modern Mind* (London: Duckworth).

Leary, D. (1982) 'The Fate and Influence of John Stuart Mill's Proposed Science of Ethology', *Journal of the History of Ideas* 43 (1): 153-62.

Lesser, H. (1979) 'Plato's Feminism', *Philosophy* 54 (207): 113-7.

Levi, A.W. (1956) 'The Idea of Socrates: The Philosophic Hero in the Nineteenth Century', *Journal of the History of Ideas* 17 (1): 89-108.

———. (1959) 'The Value of Freedom: Mill's Liberty (1859-1959)', *Ethics* 70 (1): 37-46.

Lianeri, A. (2007) 'Effacing Socratic Irony: Philosophy and *Technê* in John Stuart Mill's Translation of the *Protagoras*', in *Socrates in the Nineteenth and Twentieth Centuries*, ed. M.B. Trapp (Hampshire: Ashgate Publishing): 165-84.

Locke, R.P. (1986) *Music, Musicians, and the Saint-Simonians* (Chicago; London: The University of Chicago Press).

Loizides, A. (2012) 'Taking their Cue from Plato: James and John Stuart Mill', *History of European Ideas* 38 (1): 1-20

————. (2013) 'The Socratic Origins of J.S. Mill's "Art of Life"', in *John Stuart Mill*, eds. K.N. Demetriou and A. Loizides (Basingstoke: Palgrave Macmillan).

Long, A.A. (2001) 'Ancient Philosophy's Hardest Question: What to Make of Oneself?' *Representations* 74: 'Philosophies in Time' (Spring issue): 19-36.

Long, R.T. (1992) 'Mill's Higher Pleasures and the Choice of Character', *Utilitas* 4 (2): 279-97.

Machor, J.L.; Goldstein, P. (2001) 'Introduction', in *Reception Study: From Literary Theory to Cultural Studies*, eds. J.L. Machor; P. Goldstein (New York; London: Routledge): ix-xvii.

Mansfeld, J. (2003) 'Zeno on the Unity of Philosophy', *Phronesis* 48 (2): 116-31.

Marback, R. (1995) 'The Phoenix of Hermes, or the Rebirth of Plato in the Eighteenth Century', *Rhetorica: A Journal of the History of Rhetoric* 13 (1): 61-86.

Marshall, A.J. (1976) 'Library Resources and Creative Writing at Rome', *Phoenix* 30 (3): 252-64.

Martin, R. (1972) 'A Defence of Mill's Qualitative Hedonism', *Philosophy* 47 (180): 140-51.

Martindale, C. (1993) *Redeeming the Text: Latin Poetry and the Hermeneutics of Reception* (Cambridge: Cambridge University Press).

————. (2006) 'Introduction', in *Classics and the Uses of Reception*, eds. C.A. Martindale, R.F. Thomas (Oxford: Blackwell Publishing): 1-13.

Mazlish, B. (1975) *James and John Stuart Mill: Father and Son in the Nineteenth Century* (London: Hutchinson).

McCord, N. (1991) *British History 1815-1906* (New York: Oxford University Press).

McCullagh, B.C. (1991) 'Can our Understanding of Old Texts be Objective', *History and Theory* 30 (3): 302-23.

McWilliam, N. (1993) *Dreams of Happiness: Social Art and the French Left, 1830-1850* (Princeton: Princeton University Press).

McWilliam, R. (1998) *Popular Politics in Nineteenth-Century England* (London; New York: Routledge).

Midwinter, E. (1970) *Nineteenth Century Education* (London: Longman).

Miller, D.E. (1998) 'Internal Sanctions in Mill's Moral Psychology', *Utilitas* 10 (1): 68-82.

————. (2010) *J.S. Mill* (Cambridge: Polity Press).

————. (2011) 'Mill, Rule Utilitarianism, and the Incoherence Objection', in *John Stuart Mill and The Art of Life*, eds. B. Eggleston, D.E. Miller, D. Weinstein (Oxford: Oxford University Press): 94-116.

Millgram, E. (2009) 'Liberty, the Higher Pleasures, and Mill's Missing Science of Ethnic Jokes', *Social Philosophy and Policy* 26 (1): 326-53.

————. (2011) 'Mill's Incubus', in *John Stuart Mill and The Art of Life*, eds. B. Eggleston, D.E. Miller, D. Weinstein (Oxford: Oxford University Press): 169-91.

Mitchell, L. (2003) *Bulwer Lytton; The Rise and Fall of a Victorian Man of Letters* (London: Hambledon and London).

Morales, M.H., ed. (2005) *Mill's The Subjection of Women* (Lanham: Rowman & Littlefield Publishers).

Muirhead, J.H. (1930) *Coleridge as Philosopher* (London; New York: George Allen & Unwin; Humanities Press).

———. (1931) *The Platonic Tradition in Anglo-Saxon Philosophy* (London: George Allen & Unwin; New York: The Macmillan Company).

Murray, O. (2004a) 'Introduction', in *Edward Bulwer Lytton; Athens: Its Rise and Fall*, ed. O.Murray (London; New York: Routledge): 1-34.

———. (2004b) 'Introduction to the Previously Unpublished Third Volume of Bulwer's *Athens*', in *Edward Bulwer Lytton; Athens: Its Rise and Fall*, ed. O.Murray (London; New York: Routledge): 527-32.

Nehamas, A. (1998) *The Art of Living: Socratic Reflections from Plato to Foucault* (Berkeley, Los Angeles and London: University of California Press).

Nelson, E. (2004) *The Greek Tradition in Republican Thought* (Cambridge: Cambridge University Press).

Norlin, G., trans. (1928) *Isocrates*, 3 vols. (London: William Heinemann).

Notopoulos, J.A. (1949) *The Platonism of Shelley: a Study of Platonism and the Poetic Mind* (Durham: Duke University Press).

Nozick, R. (1974) *Anarchy, State and Utopia* (Oxford: Basil Blackwell).

Nussbaum, M.C. (1986) *The Fragility of Goodness*, up. ed. (Cambridge: Cambridge University Press, 2001).

———. (1999) 'Virtue Ethics: A Misleading Category?', *The Journal of Ethics* 3 (3): 163-201.

———. (2004) 'Mill between Aristotle & Bentham', *Daedalus* 133 (2): 60-68.

———. (2005) 'Mill on Happiness: The Enduring Value of a Complex Critique', in *Utilitarianism and Empire*, eds. B. Schultz, G. Varouxakis (Oxford: Lexington Books): 107-24.

O'Brien, J. (2005) 'Montaigne and Antiquity', in *The Cambridge Companion to Montaigne*, ed. U. Langer (Cambridge: Cambridge University Press): 53-73.

O'Brien, M. (1958) 'Modern Philosophy and Platonic Ethics', *Journal of the History of Ideas* 19 (4): 451-72.

O'Neill, O. (2001) 'Sidgwick on Practical Reason', in *Henry Sidgwick*, ed. R. Harrison (Oxford: Published for The British Academy by Oxford University Press): 83-9.

O'Rourke, K.C. (2001) *John Stuart Mill and Freedom of Expression* (London; New York: Routledge).

Ogilvie, R.M. (1964) *Latin and Greek* (London: Routledge and Kegan Paul).

Okin, S.M. (1988) 'Editor's Introduction', in *John Stuart Mill; The Subjection of Women*, ed. S.M. Okin (Indianapolis: Hackett Publishing Company): iv-xiv.

Ott, W. (2006) 'Aristotle and Plato on Character', *Ancient Philosophy* 26 (1): 65-79.

Owen, G.E.L. (1971-2) 'Aristotelian Pleasures', *Proceedings of the Aristotelian Society* N.S. 72: 135-52.

Packe, M. (1954) *The Life of John Stuart Mill* (London: Secker and Warburg).

Pappé, H.O. (1979) 'The English Utilitarians and Athenian Democracy', in *Classical Influences on Western Thought: A.D.1650-1870*, ed. R.R. Bolgar (Cambridge: Cambridge University Press): 295-307.

Peardon, T.P. (1933) *The Transition in English Historical Writing 1760-1830* (New York; London: Columbia University Press; P.S. King & Son).

Perkins, M.A. (1997) 'Coleridge and the "Other Plato"', *European Romantic Review* 8 (1): 25-40.

———. (2002) 'Religious Thinker', in *The Cambridge Companion to Coleridge*, ed. L. Newlyn (Cambridge: Cambridge University Press): 187-99.

Perrin B. (1918) *Plutarch's Lives*, vol. 6 (LOEB 98; Cambridge: Harvard University Press; London: William Heinemann).

Perry, S. (2002) 'The Talker', in *The Cambridge Companion to Coleridge*, ed. L. Newlyn (Cambridge: Cambridge University Press): 103-25.

Popper, K.R. (1945) *The Open Society and its Enemies*, 2 vols. (London: George Routledge and Sons).

Potter, E.J. (2005) *Confronting Modernity: Ancient Athens and Modern British Political Thought, c1780's-1880's*, PhD Thesis (London: University of London).

Press, G.A., ed. (2000) *Who Speaks for Plato: Studies in Platonic Anonymity* (Lanham: Rowman and Littlefield).

Preyer, R.O. (1982) 'John Stuart Mill on the Utility of Classical Greece', *Browning Institute Studies* 10: 41-70.

Priestley, F.E.L. (1969) 'Introduction', in *The Collected Works of John Stuart Mill*, vol. 10, ed. J.M. Robson (Toronto: Toronto University Press): vii-lxii.

Prince, M.B. (1996) *Philosophical Dialogue in the British Enlightenment: Theology, Aesthetics and the Novel* (Cambridge: Cambridge University Press).

Prior, A.N. (1951) 'The Virtue of the Act and the Virtue of the Agent', *Philosophy* 26 (97): 121-30.

Raine, K. (1968) 'Thomas Taylor, Plato and the English Romantic Movement', *British Journal of Aesthetics* 8 (2): 99-123.

———. (1969) 'Thomas Taylor in England', in *Thomas Taylor the Platonist: Selected Writings*, eds. K. Raine; G.M. Harper (London: Routledge and Kegan Paul): 3-48.

Raphael, D.D. (1955) 'Fallacies in and about Mill's "Utilitarianism"', *Philosophy* 30 (115): 344-57.

Rawson, E. (1969) *The Spartan Tradition in European Thought* (Oxford: Clarendon Press).

Rees, J.C. (1985) *John Stuart Mill's On Liberty*, ed. G. Williams (Oxford: Clarendon Press).

Reeves, R. (2007) *John Stuart Mill: Victorian Firebrand* (London: Atlantic).

Richards, J. (2009) *The Ancient World on the Victorian and Edwardian Stage* (Basingstoke: Palgrave MacMillan).

Ridge, M (2002) 'Mill's Intentions and Motives', *Utilitas* 14 (1): 54-70.

Riley, J. (1988) *Liberal Utilitarianism* (Cambridge: Cambridge University Press).

————. (1991) 'Individuality, Custom and Progress', *Utilitas* 3 (2): 217-44.

————. (1993) 'On Quantities and Qualities of Pleasure', *Utilitas* 5 (2): 291-300.

————. (1998) *Mill on Liberty* (London and New York: Routledge).

————. (1999) 'Is Qualitative Hedonism Incoherent', *Utilitas* 11 (3): 347-58.

————. (2007) 'Mill's Neo-Athenian Model of Liberal Democracy', in *J.S.Mill's Political Thought*, eds. N. Urbinati, A. Zakaras (Cambridge: Cambridge University Press): 221-49.

————. (2010) 'Justice as Higher Pleasure', in *John Stuart Mill: Thought and Influence*, eds. G. Varouxakis, P. Kelly (London; New York: Routledge): 99-129.

————. (2011) 'Optimal Moral Rules and Supererogatory Acts ', in *John Stuart Mill and The Art of Life*, eds. B. Eggleston, D.E. Miller, D. Weinstein (Oxford: Oxford University Press): 119-45.

Ripoli, M. (1998) 'The Return of James Mill', *Utilitas* 10 (1): 105-21.

Rist, J.M. (1972) *Epicurus: An Introduction* (London: Cambridge University Press).

Roberts, J.T. (1994) *Athens on Trial: The Antidemocratic Tradition in Western Thought* (Princeton: Princeton University Press).

Robinson, E.W. (2004) 'Ancient Greek Democracy: A Brief Introduction', in *Ancient Greek Democracy: Readings and Sources*, ed. E.W. Robinson (Oxford: Blackwell Publishing): 1-6.

Robson, J.M. (1960) 'J. S. Mill's Theory of Poetry', *University of Toronto Quarterly* 29 (4): 20-37.

————. (1964) 'John Stuart Mill and Jeremy Bentham with some Observations on James Mill', in *Essays in English Literature Presented to A.S.P. Woodhouse*, eds. M. MacLure, F.W. Watt (Toronto: University of Toronto Press): 245-68.

————. (1966) 'Harriet Taylor and John Smart Mill: Artist and Scientist', *Queen's Quarterly* 73 (2): 167-86.

————. (1968) *The Improvement of Mankind* (London: Routledge and Kegan Paul).

————. (1969) 'Textual Introduction', in *The Collected Works of John Stuart Mill*, vol. 10, ed. J.M. Robson (Toronto: Toronto University Press): cxv-cxxxix.

————. (1978) 'Textual Introduction', in *The Collected Works of John Stuart Mill*, vol. 11, ed. J.M. Robson (Toronto: Toronto University Press): lxxvii-ic.

————. (1988) 'Introduction', in *The Collected Works of John Stuart Mill*, vol. 26, ed. J.M. Robson (Toronto: Toronto University Press): xi-lv.

————. (1998) "Civilization and Culture as Moral Concepts", in *The Cambridge Companion to Mill*, ed. J. Skorupski (Cambridge: Cambridge University Press): 338-71.

Rogers, P. (1994) 'Introduction', in *Platonism and the English Imagination*, eds. A. Baldwin, S. Hutton (Cambridge: Cambridge University Press): 181-5.

Rorty, A.O. (1998) 'Plato's Counsel on Education', *Philosophy* 73 (283): 157-78.

Rosen, F. (1981) 'William Thomas, *The Philosophic Radicals: Nine Studies in Theory and Practice*, 1817-1841', *The Bentham Newsletter* 5: 61-3.

———. (1992) *Bentham, Byron, and Greece: Constitutionalism, Nationalism, and Early Liberal Political Thought* (Oxford: Clarendon Press).

———. (2003a) *Classical Utilitarianism from Hume to Mill* (London; New York: Routledge).

———. (2003b) 'Mill on Coleridge', *Τέλος Revista Iberoamericana de Estudios Utilitaristas* 12 (2): 7-21.

———. (2004) 'J.S. Mill on Socrates, Pericles and the Fragility of Truth', *Journal of Legal History* 25 (2): 181-94.

———. (2006), 'The Philosophy of Error and Liberty of Thought: J. S. Mill on Logical Fallacies', *Informal Logic* 26 (2): 121-47.

———. (2007) 'The Method of Reform; J.S.Mill's Encounter with Bentham and Coleridge', in *J.S.Mill's Political Thought*, N. Urbinati, A. Zakaras (Cambridge: Cambridge University Press): 124-44.

Rudebusch, G. (1999) *Socrates, Pleasure and Value* (New York and Oxford: Oxford University Press).

Russell, D.C. (2005) *Plato on Pleasure and the Good Life* (Oxford: Clarendon Press).

Ryan, A. (1964) 'Mr. McCloskey on Mill's Liberalism', *The Philosophical Quarterly* 14 (56): 253-60.

Ryan, A. (1965) 'John Stuart Mill's Art of Living', *in J.S.Mill on Liberty in Focus*, eds. J.Gray, G.W.Smith (London and New York: Routledge, 1991): 162-8.

———. (1970) *The Philosophy of John Stuart Mill*, 2nd ed. (New Jersey: Humanities Press International, 1990).

———. (1974) *J. S. Mill* (London and Boston: Routledge and Kegan Paul).

———. (1991) 'Sense and Sensibility in Mill's Political Thought', in *A Cultivated Mind: Essays on J.S.Mill Presented to John M. Robson*, ed. M. Laine (Toronto: University of Toronto Press): 121-38.

———. (1997) 'Introduction', in *Mill: Texts; Commentaries* (New York; London: Norton and Company): ix-xlv.

———. (2011) 'J.S. Mill on Education', *Oxford Review of Education*, 37 (5): 653-67

Sachs, J. (2009) 'Greece or Rome?: The Uses of Antiquity in Late-Eighteenth- and Early Nineteenth-Century British Literature', *Literary Compass* 6 (2): 314-39.

Saunders, B. (2010) 'J. S. Mill's Conception of Utility', *Utilitas* 22 (1): 52-69.

Saxonhouse, A. W. (1993) 'Athenian Democracy: Modern Mythmakers and Ancient Theorists', *PS: Political Science and Politics* 26 (3): 486-90.

Scarre, G. (1996) *Utilitarianism* (London; New York: Routledge).

———. (1999) 'Happiness for the Millian', *Journal for the History of Philosophy* 7 (3): 491-502.

Schneewind, J.B. (1976) 'Concerning Some Criticisms of Mill's *Utilitarianism*', in *James and John Stuart Mill/ Papers of the Centenary Conference*, J.M. Robson and M. Laine, eds. (Toronto: University of Toronto Press): 35-54.

————. (1977) *Sidgwick's Ethics and Victorian Moral Philosophy* (Oxford: Clarendon Press).

Schofield, M. (2006) *Plato: Political Philosophy* (Oxford: Oxford University Press).

Schütrumpf, W. (1970) *Die Bedeutung des Wortes êthos in der 'Poetik' des Aristoteles* (Munich: Beck).

Schultz, B.; Varouxakis, G., eds. (2005) *Utilitarianism and Empire* (Lanham, Md.; Oxford: Lexington Books).

Scott, G.A. (2002) 'Introduction', in *Does Socrates have a Method?*, ed. G.A. Scott (University Park: Pennsylvania State University Press): 1-16.

Sellars, J. (2003) *The Art of Living: The Stoics on the Nature and Function of Philosophy* (Hants: Ashgate).

Semmel, B. (1984) *John Stuart Mill and the Pursuit of Virtue* (New Haven; London: Yale University Press).

————. (1998) 'John Stuart Mill's Coleridgean Neoradicalism', in *Mill and the Moral Character of Liberalism*, ed. E.J. Eisenach (University Park: Pennsylvania State University Press): 49-76.

Shannon, R.T. (2004), 'Seeley, Sir John Robert (1834—95)', in *Oxford Dictionary of National* (Oxford University Press; online edition, October 2007: http://www.oxforddnb.com/view/article/25025, last accessed on 1 June 2012).

Sharpless, F.P. (1967) *The Literary Criticism of John Stuart Mill* (Hague; Paris: Mouton).

Shorey, P. (1938) *Platonism; Ancient and Modern* (Berkeley: University of California Press).

Silver, H. (1965) *The Concept of Popular Education: A Study of Ideas and Social Movements in the Early Nineteenth Century* (London: MacGibbon & Kee).

Silver, H.; Lawson, J. (1973) *A Social History of Education in England* (London: Methuen).

Silver, H.; Silver, P. (1974) *The Education of the Poor: the History of a National school 1824-1974* (London; Boston: Routledge & K. Paul).

Simon, B. (1974) *The Two Nations and the Educational Structure 1780-1870* (London: Lawrence and Wishart).

Sinclair, R.K. (1988) *Democracy and Participation in Athens,* (Cambridge: Cambridge University Press).

Singer, M.G. (1992), 'Sidgwick and Nineteenth-Century British Ethical Thought', in *Essays on Henry Sidgwick*, ed. B. Schultz (Cambridge: Cambridge University Press): 65-91.

————. (2000) 'Mill's Stoic Conception of Happiness and Pragmatic Conception of Utility', *Philosophy* 75 (291): 25-47.

Skorupski, J. (1989) *John Stuart Mill* (London; New York: Routledge).

————. (1994) "J.S. Mill: Logic and Metaphysics", in *The Nineteenth Century* (Routledge history of Philosophy, vol. 6), ed. C.L. Ten (London; New York: Routledge): 81-100.

Skorupski, J. (2001) 'Three Methods and a Dualism', in *Henry Sidgwick*, ed. R. Harrison (Oxford: Published for The British Academy by Oxford University Press): 61-81.

Smith, G.W. (1989) 'Freedom and Virtue in Politics: Some Aspects of Character, Circumstances and Utility from Helvetius to JS Mill', *Utilitas* 1 (1): 112-34.

Sotelo, P.C. (2006) *The Platonic Experience in Nineteenth-Century England*, trans. Y. Giannaris (Lima: Pontificia Universidad Católica del Perú Fondo Editorial).

Sparshott, F.E. (1978a) 'Introduction', in *The Collected Works of John Stuart Mill*, vol. 11, ed. J.M. Robson (Toronto: Toronto University Press).

————. (1978b) 'Zeno on Art: Anatomy of a Definition', in *The Stoics*, ed. J.M.Rist (Los Angeles: University of California Press).

————. (1994) *Taking Life Seriously; A Study on the Argument of the Nicomachean Ethics* (Toronto: University of Toronto Press).

Stafford, W. (1998) *John Stuart Mill* (London: MacMillan Press).

Stalley, R. F. (1983) *An Introduction to Plato's Laws* (Oxford: Basil Blackwell).

Stanier, R.S. (1941) 'Latin or Greek?', *Greece & Rome* 10 (30): 97-104.

Stewart, M.A. (1991) 'The Stoic Legacy in the Early Scottish Enlightenment', in *Atoms, Pneuma, and Tranquillity*, ed. M.J. Osier (Cambridge: Cambridge University Press): 273-96.

Stillinger, J. (1991) 'John Mill's Education: Fact, Fiction and Myth', in *A Cultivated Mind: Essays on J.S.Mill Presented to John M. Robson*, ed. M. Laine (Toronto: University of Toronto Press): 19-43.

Stopper, M.R. (1981) 'Greek Philosophy and the Victorians', *Phronesis* 26: 267-85.

Stough, C. (1978) 'Stoic Determinism and Moral Responsibility', in *The Stoics*, ed. J.M. Rist (Berkeley and Los Angeles: University of California Press).

Stray, C.A. (1997) '"Thucydides or Grote?" Classical Disputes and Disputed Classics in Nineteenth-Century Cambridge', *Transactions of the American Philological Association* 127: 363-71.

————. (1998) *Classics Transformed: Schools, Universities, and Society in England, 1830-1960* (Oxford: Clarendon Press).

————. (1999) 'The First Century of the Classical Tripos (1822-1922): High Culture and the Politics of Curriculum', in *Classics in 19$^{th}$ and 20$^{th}$ Century Cambridge: Curriculum, Culture and Community*, ed. C. Stray (Cambridge Philological Society: Supplementary Volume 24): 1-14.

Street, C.L. (1926) *Individualism and Individuality in the Philosophy of J.S. Mill* (Milwaukee: Morehouse Publishing).

Sullivan, R.E. (2009) *Macaulay: The Tragedy of Power* (Cambridge, Massachusetts; London: Belknap Press).

Tarrant, H. (1993) *Thrasyllan Platonism* (Ithaca, N.Y.; London: Cornell University Press).

Taylor, A.E. (1949) *Plato, the Man and his Work*, 6th ed. (London: Methuen).

Taylor, J.S. (1984) *William Mitford and Greek History*, PhD Thesis (Oxford: University of Oxford).

Tholfsen, T.R. (1971) 'The Intellectual Origins of Mid-Victorian Stability', *Political Science Quarterly* 86 (1): 57-91.

Thomas, W. (1969) 'James Mill's Politics: The "Essay on Government" and the Movement for Reform', *The Historical Journal* 12 (2): 249-84.

―――. (1971) 'James Mill's Politics: A Rejoinder', *The Historical Journal* 14 (4): 735-50.

―――. (1979) *The Philosophic Radicals* (Oxford: Clarendon Press).

―――. (1985) *Mill* (Oxford: Oxford University Press).

Thompson, D.F. (1976) *John Stuart Mill and Representative Government* (Princeton: Princeton University Press).

Thomson, J.A.K., trans.; Tredennick, H., rev.; Barnes, J., intr. (2004) *Aristotle: The Nicomachean Ethics* (London: Penguin Books).

Tigerstedt, E.N. (1974) *The Decline and Fall of the Neoplatonic Interpretation of Plato* [Commentationes Humanarum Litterarum 52] (Helsinki: Societas Scientiarum Fennica).

Todd, R. B. (1999) 'Henry Sidgwick, Cambridge Classics, and the Study of Ancient Philosophy: The Decisive Years (1866-9)', in *Classics in 19th and 20th Century Cambridge: Curriculum, Culture and Community*, ed. C. Stray (Cambridge Philological Society: Supplementary Volume 24): 15-26.

Turk, C. (1988) *Coleridge and Mill* (Aldershot: Avebury).

Turner, F.M. (1981) *The Greek Heritage in Victorian Britain* (New Haven and London: Yale University Press).

―――. (1982) 'Antiquity in Victorian Contexts', *Browning Institute Studies* 10: 1-14.

―――. (1986) 'British Politics and the Demise of the Roman Republic: 1700-1939', *The Historical Journal* 29 (3): 577-99.

―――. (1989) 'Why the Greeks and not the Romans in Victorian Britain', in *Rediscovering Hellenism*, G.W. Clarke, ed. (Cambridge: Cambridge University Press): 61-81.

Urbinati, N. (1991) 'John Stuart Mill on Androgyny and Ideal Marriage', *Political Theory* 19 (4): 626-48.

―――. (2002) *Mill on Democracy: From the Athenian Polis to Representative Government* (Chicago: University of Chicago Press).

―――. (2011) "An Alternative Modernity; Mill on Capitalism and the Quality of Life", in *John Stuart Mill and The Art of Life*, eds. B. Eggleston, D.E. Miller, D. Weinstein (Oxford: Oxford University Press): 236-63.

Urbinati, N.; Zakaras, A., eds. (2007) *J.S. Mill's Political Thought* (Cambridge: Cambridge University Press).

Vaio, J. (1996) 'George Grote and James Mill: How to Write History', in *George Grote Reconsidered*, eds. W.H. Calder, S. Trzaskoma (Hildesheim: Weidmann): 59-74.

Valls, A. (1999) 'Self-Development and the Liberal State: The Cases of John Stuart Mill and Wilhelm von Humboldt', *The Review of Politics* 61 (2): 251-74.

Varouxakis, G. (1999) 'Guizot's Historical Works and J.S. Mill's Reception of Tocqueville', *History of Political Thought* 20 (2): 292-312.

————. (2002a) *Mill on Nationality* (London; New York: Routledge).

————. (2002b) *Victorian Political Thought on France and the French* (Basingstoke: Palgrave).

Varouxakis, G.; Kelly, P., eds. (2010) *John Stuart Mill: Thought and Influence—The Saint of Rationalism* (London; New York: Routledge).

Vigus, J. (2009) *Platonic Coleridge* (London: Legenda).

Villa, D. (2001) *Socratic Citizenship* (Princeton; Oxford: Princeton University Press).

Vivenza, G. (2001) *Adam Smith and the Classics: The Classical Heritage in Adam Smith's Thought* (Oxford: Oxford University Press).

Vogler, C.A. (2001) *John Stuart Mill's Deliberative Landscape; An Essay in Moral Psychology* (New York; London: Garland Publishing).

Walker, A. D. M. (1989) 'Virtue and Character', *Philosophy* 64 (249): 349-62

Wallace, J. (1997) *Shelley and Greece: Rethinking Romantic Hellenism* (London: Macmillan Press).

Wallas, G. (1898) *The Life of Francis Place 1771-1854* (London: Longmans Green).

Walton, D.N. (1996) *Argumentation Schemes for Presumptive Reasoning* (New Jersey: Lawrence Erlbaum Associates).

————. (2004) *Relevance in Argumentation* (New Jersey: Lawrence Erlbaum Associates).

————. (2006) *Fundamentals of Critical Argumentation* (Cambridge: Cambridge University Press).

————. (2008) *Informal Logic: A Pragmatic Approach* (Cambridge: Cambridge University Press).

Webb, T. (1982) 'Introduction', in *English Romantic Hellenism: 1700-1824*, ed. T. Webb (Manchester: Manchester University Press): 1-35.

————. (1993) 'Romantic Hellenism', in *The Cambridge Companion to British Romanticism*, ed. S. Curran (Cambridge: Cambridge University Press): 148-76.

Weinstein, D. (2011) 'Interpreting Mill', in *John Stuart Mill and The Art of Life*, eds. B. Eggleston, D.E. Miller, D. Weinstein (Oxford: Oxford University Press): 44-70.

West, E.G. (1965) "Liberty and Education: John Stuart Mill's Dilemma", *Philosophy* 40 (152): 129-42.

————. (1970) 'Resource Allocation and Growth in Early Nineteenth-Century Education', *Economic History Review* 23 (1): 68-95.

————. (1971) 'The Interpretation of Early Nineteenth-Century Education Statistics', *Economic History Review* 24 (4): 633-42.

Whedbee, K.E. (2004) 'Reclaiming Rhetorical Democracy: George Grote's Defense of Cleon and the Athenian Demagogues', *Rhetoric Society Quarterly* 34 (4): 71-95

———. (2007) 'An English Plato: J.S. Mill's "Gorgias"', *Rhetoric Society Quarterly* 37 (1): 19-41.

———. (2008) 'Making the Worse Case Appear the Better: British Reception of the Greek Sophists prior to 1850', *Rhetoric & Public Affairs* 11 (4): 603-30.

Wheeler, K. (1999) 'Blake, Coleridge, and Eighteenth-Century Greek Scholarship', *Wordsworth Circle* 30 (2): 89-94.

White, N.P. (1979) 'The Basis of Stoic Ethics', *Harvard Studies in Classical Philology* 83: 143-78.

———. (1994) 'Neoaristotelian Inclusivist Eudaimonism: Some of its Problems', *Internationale Zeitschrift für Philosophie* 3 (1): 57-72.

———. (1995) 'Conflicting Parts of Happiness in Aristotle's Ethics', *Ethics* 105 (2): 258-83.

———. (1999a) 'Harmonizing Plato', *Philosophy and Phenomenological Research* 59 (2): 497-512.

———. (1999b) 'Intrinsically Valued Parts of Happiness: Aristotle, Butler, and Mill', *Philosophiegeschichte und Logische Analyse* 2: 149-56.

———. (2006) *A Brief History of Happiness* (Oxford: Blackwell Publishing).

Wilhoite, F.H. Jr. (1971) 'Ethology and the Tradition of Political Thought', *The Journal of Politics* 33 (3): 615-41.

Williams, G.L. (1982) 'History and History: J.S. Mill on the Greeks', *Polis* 4 (2): 1-17.

———. (1994) 'The Early Utilitarians', in *The Nineteenth Century* (Routledge history of Philosophy, vol. 6), ed. C.L. Ten (London; New York: Routledge): 4-25.

———. (1996) 'The Greek Origins of J.S. Mill's Happiness', *Utilitas* 8 (1): 5-14.

Wilson, F. (1990) *Psychological Analysis and the Philosophy of John Stuart Mill* (Toronto: University of Toronto Press).

———. (1998) 'Mill on Psychology and the Moral Sciences', in *The Cambridge Companion to Mill*, ed. J. Skorupski (Cambridge: Cambridge University Press): 203-54.

Woodcock, M.B. (1980) 'Educational Principles and Political Thought: The Case of James Mill', *History of Political Thought* 1 (3): 475-97.

Woodruff, P. (1986) 'The Sceptical Side of Plato's Method', *Revue Internationale De Philosophie* 156-7: 22-37.

Woodward, E.L. (1962) *The Age of Reform, 1815-1870*, 2nd ed. (Oxford: Clarendon Press).

Yake, S.J. (1973) 'Mill's Mental Crisis Revisited', *The Mill Newsletter* 9 (1): 2-12.

———. (2006) 'J.S. Mill and Platonic Ideals of Public Life', paper presented at *J.S. Mill Bicentennial Conference, UCL* (April, 2006).

# INDEX

accountability, 132, 154

aesthetics: and Art of Life, 121n85, 131-44, 147n48, 167, 169, 186, 192, 199; and education, 68, 141-43, 165, 210; and happiness, 150n114, 199, 201; and worth, 137, 144, 158, 209; *see also*, beauty; character; education; ethology; nobility; virtue

altruism, 155, 205n132

arguments, 108-9, 128: insufficiency of, 87-88, 132, 209; *see also*, error; Socrates

Aristotle, 10, 26, 36, 38n29, 59n58, 67, 75, 99 106, 154, 170-171, 172n24, 174n77, 178; on character, 153, 156-57, 170; and happiness, 147n33, 150n101, 185-87, 188; and pleasures, 195, 202n30; *see also*, character; ethology; happiness; pleasure; virtue

art, 87, 114; craft (*technê*), 75, 125, 131; and imagination, 54-55, 107, 108; life as an, 150n114, 165; of living, 95, 128-30; older meaning of, 126, 128, 140; of measurement, 53-54, 89; of persuasion, 11, 28; and science, 51, 125-28; of statesmanship, 75, 115

Art of Life, 126, 130-33, 134-7, 144, 169; and Art of Living, 126, 145-46, 201; components of, 130, 139-40; and education, 140-44, 163, 167-68, 188, 199; and happiness, 131, 158, 186-87, 192, 196, 198, 200-201; *see also*, aesthetics; beauty; expediency; *kalon*; morality; virtue

associationism, 48, 52, 54-55, 154, 159, 163, 184, 189, 191-92, 193; and happiness, 195, 197, 198, 200-201, 209-10; and the need for dialectics, 108, 110, 112

Athens: and authority, 9, 27, 73; and democracy, 7-10, 12-13, 27-29, 32, 69, 74-75; 78; and equality, 8-9, 67, 74; and liberty, 69-71, 109; and reform, 6-8, 13-15, 28-29, 71-78; *see also*, citizenship; Cleon; Grote, George; Mill, John Stuart; Mitford,

William; Pericles; Plato; Socrates; Sophists; Sparta

Austin, John, 115

authority, 29, 73

autonomy, *see* individuality

Bacon, Francis, 26, 35, 42n133, 90-91, 112

Bain, Alexander, 92, 126, 131, 133, 155, 161, 172n24, 174n81, 203n65

beauty, 54, 68, 137-38; and humanism, 77; and man, 142-43, 150, 167, 200-201; *see also*, aesthetics; character; nobility; virtue

Bentham, Jeremy, 31, 47, 90-91, 111, 138, 172n33, 185-86, 198, 209; and James Mill, 44, 47, 50, 53, 56; and John Stuart Mill, 106, 107, 111-12, 120n45, 158, 165-6, 173n52, 178, 180, 186, 199; on pleasure, 181, 183, 193; and Plato, 41n104, 86, 109; school of, 10, 193; on utility, 178-79, 181; *see also*, Mill, James; Mill, John Stuart; happiness; pleasure

Brutus, Lucius Junius, 137-38

Bulwer-Lytton, Edward, 9-10, 11-12

capacities, 158; exercise of, 183-84, 195, 196, 197

Carlyle, Thomas, 161-2, 166

character, 138, 149n84, 150n114, 153-55, 160, 197, 201; and aesthetics, 135-36, 146; and Art of Life, 128, 140-44, 150n104, 179-80, 200-1; and classics, 16n12, 77, 87-88; English and French, 14, 132, 148n50; as *êthos*, 156-8, 167, 180, 195; and liberty, 162-63, 168-69; and happiness, 134, 197-99, 201; and individuality, 161-62, 166-70, 200, 210; *see also*, education; ethology; happiness; Mill, James; Mill, John Stuart; nobility; virtue

choice, *see* deliberation

Christianity, 26, 29, 30, 168; and Plato, 24, 26, 33-34, 42n152; sources alternative to, 14, 33, 35
citizenship, 31, 49, 70, 71-76, 98, 141, 169; *see also*, Athens
civilization, 76, 140
classification, 109, 117, 147n48
Cleon, 8-9, 74
Coleridge, Samuel Taylor, 10, 37, 155; influence on J.S. Mill, 78, 106, 108, 119n24, 143, 172n33; on Plato, 21, 33-37, 42n126, 42n152, 96-97, 99; and Thomas Taylor, 38n29, 42n123
Comte, Auguste, 138, 159
culture, 14, 90-1, 95, 156-57; Athenian, 13, 67-69, 109, 112; and classics, 5, 15, 22; and progress, 110, 126, 210; and self-development, 43, 88, 97, 143, 167; *see also*, Athens; character; ethology; self-development
custom, 67; and classics, 5, 11, 68, 92; reason vs. routine, 51, 56, 66-70, 75, 95, 110, 127, 129, 141, 167, 170; and conformity, 109-10, 112, 161; *see also*, education; ethology; liberty

deliberation, 52-54; and character, 157, 167; and choice, 106, 138, 115, 168, 179-80, 184; and consequences, 135, 185-86, 196; and happiness, 158, 177, 183-85, 192, 200-201
desire, 48, 52, 87, 93, 98 106, 115, 117, 126, 138-39, 140, 143, 154-68, 179-80, 183-84, 186-92, 193, 197, 199, 201, 208, 210
dialectic method, 32, 67, 90, 132, 146; and authority, 90, 109, 112; negative leg of, 93, 95, 108, 110, 112-13, 115-16; Plato's, 23, 24-25, 31-32, 35-36, 43, 45, 78, 86, 89-99, 107-10, 112-13, 115-17, 142; positive leg of, 95, 108, 110, 116; *see also*, Mill, John Stuart; Plato; Socrates
dignity, 13, 26, 87, 148n49, 185; and happiness, 197, 200-201
discussion, 58n39, 89-90, 110; freedom of, 15, 48, 69-71, 77, 170; *see also*, dialectic method; liberty
duty, 87, 97, 136, 163, 209; to one's self, 135, 141; of Socrates, 27-28, 30; *see also*, justice; morality; virtue

education, 37, 140-44, 154, 164; in Athens, 11, 69-70, 73, 76, 78; and classics, 3-5, 13-15; cram vs. mental cultivation, 35, 66-68, 70, 75, 77, 141, 208; and elites, 13, 73, 74; James Mill on, 45, 47-48, 51-55; Plato on, 31, 58n44; John Stuart Mill on, 66-69, 77, 112, 159-60, 163-65, 167, 169; *see also*, Art of Life; character; ethology; virtue
emotion, 15, 30, 137-39; cultivation of, 52, 68, 69, 74, 87-88, 93, 96-98, 106, 108-109, 140, 142-43, 145, 160-61, 187, 197, 208; and dialectics, 96, 113-15; and reason, 87, 155-57, 160, 163-71, 185, 199, 209; and virtue, 87-88, 131, 140, 154-58, 179-80, 192; *see also*, aesthetics; beauty; character; education; ethology; pleasure; virtue
ends: final vs. instrumental, 54, 87, 106, 126, 130-40, 143, 144-46, 179-80, 184, 187-93, 196, 199-201, 209-210; of government, 6, 16n29, 54, 59n56, 78, 106, 115; inclusive and dominant, 185-87, 194, 203n57, 204n89; of life, 54, 143-44, 150n102, 183, 197, 208; and means, 51-52, 127-29, 142, 145, 187; of Plato, 35, 78, 98, 107; social, 61, 66n97, 159-60, 166; and virtue, 157-58, 160-71, 198-99; *see also*, Art of Life; character; education; reason; virtue
Epicurus, 34, 46, 56, 106
equality and inequality, 133, 139, 140, 170
error, 70, 98, 118; and dialectics, 109-110, 117; philosophy of, 110-12
ethology, 107, 140-44, 153-55, 173n52, 178; and development, 156-70, 187; James Mill on, 47-48, 53, 172n38; and reform, 156, 160; and virtue, 147n48, 153, 162, 163-65, 171, 196-97, 208-209; *see also*, Art of Life; character; education; Mill, James, Mill, John Stuart; self-development
eudaimonia, *see* happiness
excellence, *see* virtue
expediency, 10, 88, 117, 131-34, 139, 143, 186, 192, 199, 201, 203n74; and consequences, 135-36, 137; simple vs. general, 135-37, 164, 169, 197; as

a virtue, 156, 162, 169; *see also*, aesthetics; Art of Life; morality
experience, 22, 25, 27, 37, 50, 51, 53, 60n89, 66, 108-109, 110, 118, 160, 167, 178-79, 189, 194, 196, 198-99; *see also*, competence; pleasure
experiments in living, 196, 209

fallacies, 45, 47, 111-12, 113; of Plato, 110, 133; of Sophists, 86, 97; *see also*, error; truth
feelings, *see* emotion
free will, 143, 162
freedom, *see* liberty

generosity, 52, 117
genius: in Athens, 12-13, 69-70, 78; and originality, 109, 119n37; Plato's, 22, 28, 37, 90-91, 171; Socrates', 29, 34
Gillies, John, 7, 9-10, 27-28, 39n63, 40n66
government, 105, 115; and education, 48, 153-54; *see also*, Athens; education; Mill, James; Mill, John Stuart; Plato
Grote, George, 21, 43, 65, 69, 70, 71, 72, 74, 77, 85, 88-89, 90, 102n86, 103n97, 131, 207; and Athenian reception, 9-10, 10-11, 12-13; on Plato and Socrates, 23, 30, 31-33, 34, 96-97, 98-99; reception of, 91-94

habit(s): Athenian, 10-11, 67, 69; fostered by classics, 46, 68, 189; and education, 48, 50, 52-53, 68-69, 95, 110-11, 113, 115, 141, 143, 154-55, 208; and virtue, 129, 156-59, 162-63, 165-70, 179, 192-93, 199; *see also*, character; custom, ethology; virtue
happiness: additive vs. directive, 181-83, 197-201; Aristotle on, 156, 185, 186, 187, 188, 195; and Art of Life, 125, 126, 128, 129, 131-35, 138, 140, 146, 187-88, 196; and associationism, 191-93; Bentham on, 181, 185, 186, 193, 195, 198-99; and character, 159, 163-64, 166, 170-71, 196; and conflict, 150n102, 150n114, 183, 192-93, 199; vs. contentment, 193-94, 197, 199; and deliberation, 184-85; eudaimonia vs. utility, 178-81;

186, 195, 208-209; of the greatest number, 30-31, 146, 167; inclusive vs. dominant, 136, 177, 185-87, 194; ingredients of, 176-77, 182-83, 186, 188-89; James Mill, on, 52-55, 56, 134, 184-85, 189; John Stuart Mill on, 50, 106, 116, 118, 133-34, 146, 177-78, 184; as a name, 188-91; Plato on, 27, 49-50, 78, 87-88, 97, 148n49, 171, 177; Socrates on, 26, 28, 100n11, 110; *see also*, aesthetics; Art of Life; Bentham, Jeremy; character; duty; education; ends; ethology; Mill, James; Mill, John Stuart; Plato; pleasure; utility; virtue;
harm, 116-17, 129, 132, 137, 138, 139, 149n89, 168
Hartley, David, 34, 37, 107, 154
hedonism, *see* pleasure
Helvetius, Claude, 31, 41n100, 149n80
Hume, David, 130, 149n80
Hutcheson, Francis, 149n82, 194

impartiality, 92, 96, 116, 135
individuality, 70, 107, 156, 158, 161-62, 163; and Art of Life, 135, 145-46; and happiness, 188, 200, 201; and self-development, 166-67; *see also*, character; ethology
infallibility, 90-91, 98, 105, 109, 160
introspection, 22, 106, 179
intuitionism, 111, 116, 129, 142, 177

Jesus, 30, 40n81, 42n152, 57n32, 145
justice, 48, 52, 59n55, 73, 112, 116-17, 118, 141, 120n69, 134, 139-40, 149n89, 169, 189, 193, 198, 203n82, 210; Plato on, 95-96, 97, 131-32, 147n47, 148n49, 186; Socrates on, 129-30; *see also*, Art of Life; expediency; morality

*kalon*, 137, 148n50; and *kalokagathos*, 129, 137, 143, 151n124, 167, 188; *see also*, aesthetics; beauty; nobility; virtue

liberty, 48, 80n41, 92, 96, 129, 137, 138, 139, 188, 208; ancient vs. modern, 69-71; in Athens, 6-7, 9-10, 65, 66, 69-71, 74-75, 77-78; of discussion, 15, 48, 69, 118; and happiness, 184, 185; John Stuart Mill on, 107, 134, 149n89, 162-63, 168, 174n75, 175n113; spheres of, 135-36; *see also*, Athens; character; culture; education; Mill, John Stuart

Locke, John, 26, 34, 37

logic, 4, 10; and Plato's dialogues, 24, 33, 35-36, 92, 95-97, 108-114, 171; of practice, 125-26; *see also*, dialectic method; Mill, John Stuart; Plato

Macaulay, Thomas Babington, 8, 11, 17n36, 40n96, 41n102, 41n112, 49, 90-91,

maximization, 136-37, 188

Mill, Harriet Taylor, 83n99

Mill, James, 11, 30, 68, 70, 76, 85, 96, 106, 108, 110, 154, 163, 178; on education, 51-53; on fallacies, 111-12; on happiness, 53-55, 137, 184-85, 189, 207, 209; on method, 50, 53; on names, 189-90; on Plato, 23, 25, 30-31, 34-35, 47-50, 89-90, 94, 97, 99; on Thomas Taylor, 21, 44-47

Mill, John Stuart, 15, 50, 51, 53, 56; on Athens, 69-76; *Autobiography*, 53, 95, 105, 126, 178, 187, 208; on classics, 66-69; *Considerations on Representative Government*, 69, 72, 77, 115; mental crisis, 105-107, 178, 180; on method, 110-17, 159; *On Liberty*, 69, 90, 96, 110, 112, 117, 134, 145, 157, 188, 198; on the Sophists, 11; participation and competence, 71-76; on Plato, 21, 30, 32, 34, 35, 37, 45, 50, 85-91, 94-98, 108-110; *Principles of Political Economy*, 126, 168; *A System of Logic*, 108, 110, 111, 114, 125, 189; *Utilitarianism*, 116, 128, 134, 177, 186, 188, 189, 190, 193, 193, 198

mind, *see* reason

Mitford, William, 90, on Athens, 7-13, 67, 73; on Socrates, 27-29

Montaigne, Michel de, 46, 57n29

morality: and Art of Life, 131-40, 167, 186, 192, 201; and Athens, 7, 10-11, 69, 73-74; in Bentham, 178-79, 180; and character, 157-60, 163, 165-66, 167, 170, 185, 199; Christian, 25, 30;

common, 66-67, 169, 180; and error, 111, 118, 120n69; and education, 68, 141, 142-43, 210; and government, 55, 72, 75, 76; and justice, 116-17; in Plato, 22, 24, 31, 36, 46, 48, 53, 86, 87-88, 94, 96, 97, 107, 129, 131-32; and pleasure, 54, 196, 199; and punishment, 117, 134, 136-37; and Socrates, 28, 29, 91, 93, 109; and Victorians, 154-55; and virtue, 154, 179-80, 169, 193; *see also*, aesthetics; Art of Life; expediency; justice; nobility; virtue

motive, 45, 52, 60n89, 96, 106, 136, 144, 155, 158, 162, 163-64, 165, 168, 172n33, 180, 203n74

names, theory of, 114, 189-91

nationality, 116, 189

nature, 113-16, 117, 120n69, 140, 155, 199; human, 50, 52, 54, 59n52, 66, 70, 77, 88, 91, 107, 126, 137, 141, 143, 153-55, 157-61, 163, 165, 167, 180, 197, 199, 200; *see also*, Art; character; education; ethology

Neoplatonism, 23-25, 27, 44, 47, 57n32, 94

nobility, 55, 111, 129, 136, 167, 185; of character, 134-38, 140, 155, 158, 164, 185, 192, 195-96, 197, 198, 200; and emotion, 87, 98, 131; *see also*, aesthetics; Art of Life; beauty; character; education; ethology; kalon; virtue

obligations, 75, 110, 135-36, 139-40

Owen, Robert, 153-54, 156, 162

Pericles, 7, 70, 74-75, 76

phrenology, 154, 161

Plato: and art, 88-90, 128-30, 145; and Art of Life, 130-33; and Coleridge, 33-37; and government, 76, 78; on happiness, 183, 186-87, 188, 196, 197, 198-99, 200, 201; James Mill's appropriation of, 47-49, 51-55; John Stuart Mill's readings of, and virtue, 85-88, 94-98; and Radicals, 30-33, 44-47, 91-94; and Taylor, 24-27; transcendentalism, 22, 24-25, 33, 37, 38n27; and virtue, 163, 165-66, 167-

68, 180, 192-93; worth of, 108-110, 112-16

pleasure, 7, 26, 27, 87, 106, 134, 147n33, 187, 189, 191; and Art of Life, 144, 150n101, 186-87, 200-201; Bentham on, 178-79, 181-82, 183; competence in judging, 184, 192, 194, 196, 200; and agency, 181-83, 185, 186-87, 197-99; and hedonism, 177, 178; higher vs. lower, 193-94, 196-97; James Mill on, 49, 50, 51, 52, 53-55, 134, 191-92; and virtue, 138, 142, 156-59, 179-80, 192, 195-96; *see also*, ethology; happiness; utility

prudence, *see* expediency

psychology, 142, 154, 159; Benthamite, 106; *see also*, associationism

Radicalism, 6, 7, 8, 66, 86, 159, 207; Philosophic 29, 31, 210; *see also*, Grote, George; Mill James; Mill, John Stuart; Plato

reason, 24, 34, 36-37, 51, 53, 54, 70, 73, 76, 97, 109, 137, 199; and action, 125-30; cultivation of, 4, 5, 140-43, 168; and emotion, 86, 91, 98, 145, 156-58, 163-66; and happiness, 177, 179, 183-88; vs. routine, 66-67, 95-96, 110, 127, 167, 170, 208; *see also*, character; duty; education; ethology; deliberation; happiness

religion, 10, 71, 75, 109; and classics, 14, 30, 32, 90; and education, 4, 142-43, 165; of humanity, 210; and Plato, 22-24, 27, 28, 32, 33, 34-37; and Socrates, 27-30

responsibility, 76, 170

rights, 55, 116, 198

Romanticism, 13, 38n29, 93; and character, 156, 157; and John Stuart Mill's 'mental crisis', 106-107

Rome, 5, 13-14, 16n22, 70

routine, *see* custom

security, 6-9, 13, 48, 185, 198; for good government, 27, 31, 41n101, 49-50, 58n44

self-development, 160, 161-63, 166-69, 198, 199; *see also*, beauty; character; education; ethology; individuality

self-education, *see* education

self-examination, *see* introspection

self-interest, 6, 36, 97, 135, 165, 209; and sacrifice, 36, 97, 137, 179, 209; *see also*, altruism; character; duty; deliberation; education; ethology; expediency

Sidgwick, Henry, 87, 148n50, 172n36, 177, 205n128, 209-210

Socrates, 12, 21, 23, 26, 27-33, 34, 45-46, 50, 53, 54, 86-88, 89, 91-99, 205, 107, 140-42, 163, 165, 167, 170, 210; and Art of Living, 128-29, 131-32, 140, 145-46; on happiness, 181-82, 186, 188, 192, 196, 200-201, 209; and method, 108-110, 112-13, 115; *see also*, Athens; dialectic method

Sophists, 7-8, 10-11, 27-28, 45, 57n16, 86, 88, 94-95, 96; *see also*, Athens

Sparta, 6, 12, 16n32

Stoicism, 71, 125, 128, 130, 144-45, 172n36

supererogation, *see* virtue

sympathy, 87, 97, 137-38, 149n89, 155, 158, 166, 169, 192, 203n74; *see also*, education; emotion; ethology

Taylor, Thomas, 21, 24-27, 32, 34, 35, 44, 46, 90, 91

teleology, *see* Art of Life

theory and practice; 50-53, 55, 95, 106, 126-30, 133, 144

Thirlwall, Connop, 9, 11-13

Tocqueville, Alexis de, 161

toleration, 145, 163; and education, 48; in Athens, 12, 67, 70, 77-78

tradition, *see* custom

truth, 11, 29, 48, 51, 52, 70, 77, 86, 90, 92, 110-11, 115-16, 117-18, 127, 128, 133, 138, 160, 170, 180, 200; and classics, 68; and dialectics, 35, 67, 96, 98, 148; half-truths, 66, 78, 98, 108-110; and Plato, 26, 34, 36, 37, 87, 89, 91, 95, 163-64; and Socrates, 88; *see also*, custom; dialectic method; education; liberty

tyranny: of democracy, 8, 27; social, 120n69, 166

utility, 33, 100n11, 116, 117, 150n101, 166, 167, 171, 175n87, 189, 200,

209-210; and agency, 181-82, 186-87, 193, 197-98, 199; and Art of Life, 131-32, 139-40; and education, 146, 164-65; and expediency, 10, 135-36; and eudaimonia, 106, 170, 178-81, 195; James Mill on, 53-55; in Plato, 87, 89; *see also,* happiness; pleasure; virtue

virtue: in Aristotle, 156-57, 170-71; and Art of Life, 136-37, 138; and classics, 26-27; cultivation of, 52, 77, 90-91, 106, 111, 112, 141, 144, 163-66, 168-70, 190-92, 209; and happiness, 54, 78, 129, 132, 167, 178-79, 184-85, 196, 197-98, 210; in Plato, 45, 87-88, 96-98, 185-86; *see also,* aesthetics; beauty; ethology; individuality; self-development

well-being, *see* happiness
Whewell, William, 5, 16n20, 94, 101n60
wisdom, 5, 11, 40n96, 46, 47, 50, 52, 67, 91, 97, 105, 156, 200; as part of happiness, 78, 181
women, subjection of, 159-60, 170, 173n45